LANGUAGE AND GERMAN DISUNITY

Language
and German Disunity

A Sociolinguistic History of East and West
in Germany, 1945–2000

PATRICK STEVENSON

OXFORD
UNIVERSITY PRESS

OXFORD

UNIVERSITY PRESS

Great Clarendon Street, Oxford OX2 6DP

Oxford University Press is a department of the University of Oxford.
It furthers the University's objective of excellence in research, scholarship,
and education by publishing worldwide in

Oxford New York

Auckland Bangkok Buenos Aires Cape Town Chennai
Dar es Salaam Delhi Hong Kong Istanbul Karachi Kolkata
Kuala Lumpur Madrid Melbourne Mexico City Mumbai Nairobi
São Paulo Shanghai Taipei Tokyo Toronto

Oxford is a registered trade mark of Oxford University Press
in the UK and in certain other countries

Published in the United States
by Oxford University Press Inc., New York

The moral rights of the authors have been asserted

Database right Oxford University Press (maker)

First published 2002

British Library Cataloguing in Publication Data

Data available

Library of Congress Cataloging in Publication Data

Data applied for

ISBN 0–19–829969–9
ISBN 0–19–829970–2 (Pbk.)

1 3 5 7 9 10 8 6 4 2

Typeset by Newgen Imaging Systems (P) Ltd., Chennai, India
Printed in Great Britain
on acid-free paper by
Biddles Ltd., Guildford & King's Lynn

Contents

Preface

Throughout the period from 1949 to 1989, when central Europe was dominated by the two states that had emerged from the ruins of Germany after the Second World War, the relationship between language and national and social identities continually resurfaced as a topic of academic research and public debate both in the GDR and in the Federal Republic. Many then hoped that the political unification of Germany in 1990 would create the conditions for social unity, and it was also widely (but not universally) assumed that the 'language question' would automatically become redundant. However, not only has social unity proved a more elusive goal than the optimists believed, but the issue of 'language in east and west' has continued to be subjected to intense analysis, in both academic and non-academic contexts. The first decade of the unified state was characterized by a tension between continuities and discontinuities: some aspects of life changed or even disappeared virtually overnight, others remained the same or re-emerged in a new light after an initial period of disruption and turbulence. What role, if any, has been played by language in these processes is a question that has excited enormous interest and provoked considerable controversy. This was my principal motivation for writing this book.

I hope that my discussion of the subject will make a contribution to the socio-linguistic study of disunity at a number of levels: it takes a broad historical perspective, incorporating a range of different research orientations, and it is written from the standpoint of the 'engaged outsider', seeking to present a critical but balanced account of the German situation that addresses the specialized interests of German scholars and students while also stimulating research in other speech communities. I discuss my conception of the book as a study of 'language in history' in detail in Chapter 1. However, since a book on this topic could have taken many other forms, I would like to say a few words at the outset about the scope of my study, about my position in relation to the topic, and about the kinds of reader I have had in mind while writing the book.

Earlier studies have typically concentrated on one of a wide range of approaches and methodologies, from textual studies of lexical difference and change to critical interpretations of competing discourses, quantitative analyses of language attitudes, empirical studies of speech behaviours, and interpretations of ethnographic interviews. In one of the most recent contributions to the subject, Auer and Hausendorf (2000b) criticize the fragmented nature of the research on the (socio-) linguistic consequences of unification, and in different ways their anthology (2000a) and the essays in Stevenson and Theobald (2000a) represent first steps towards a more integrated, multi-disciplinary approach. In this book, I have tried to go a stage further by showing how this complex process demands analysis at many different levels and that a better understanding of the situation will not emerge by pressing the claims of one approach at the expense of another. In doing so, I have drawn on a wide range of both spoken and written texts deriving from many different settings and communicative genres. However, while I have tried to cast my net as wide as possible and to reflect the major trends in recent research, it is clearly impossible to offer a comprehensive coverage of all aspects of this history and so a degree of selectivity is inevitable. On the one hand, therefore, I have excluded from my attention material that might be classified as creative or fictional writing (literary texts, film, *Kabarett*, popular music, and so forth: on these topics, see, for example, Baumann 2000, Durrani 2000, and the contributions by Reifarth, Hörschelmann, and McNally in Stevenson and Theobald 2000*a*). On the other hand, I have included in the bibliography publications that have informed my research for this book in various ways in addition to those actually referred to in the text.

The position of the researcher in academic studies has come under increasing scrutiny in recent years (see, for example, Cameron *et al.* 1992), but in most publications on the east–west question the authors are surprisingly silent on their own origins and readers are left to infer this important aspect of the research from the way it is reported (Fiehler 1995, for example, is relatively unusual in explicitly stating the author's 'western' identity and acknowledging the relevance of this for his interpretation of his material). Yet this is particularly important in an area of research that deals with relations between two social groups which are conceived of in opposition to each other; all the more so, when the majority of studies focus on one of the groups—in this case, the easterners. Lothar Fritze (1996: 922) no doubt speaks for many east Germans when he complains of the methodological consequences of this imbalance (referring, presumably, to west German research):

Unterschiede zwischen Ost und West—etwa im Wahlverhalten, Unterschiede im Grad der konfessionellen Gebundenheit, unterschiedliche Vorstellungen von Gerechtigkeit oder von sozialer Sicherheit, habituelle Unterschiede und dergleichen mehr—werden sehr häufig, ja nahezu ausschließlich als *ostdeutsche Abweichungen von der Normalität* gedeutet. Als normal gilt die westdeutsche Art, sich zu verhalten oder sich zu geben; die Standards der Normalität werden durch die westdeutschen Standards definiert. (Italics in original)

Differences between east and west—in voting behaviour, for instance, or differences in the degree of affiliation to particular religious denominations, different conceptions of justice or of social security, differences in everyday behaviour and so on—are very often, indeed almost exclusively interpreted as *east German deviations from normality*. What counts as normal is the west German way of behaving; standards of normality are defined in terms of west German standards.

This is not necessarily the case, of course, and in my judgement it would be unfair to suggest that all studies from one 'side' or the other are tarred with the same brush or to allege an inherent prejudice in individual researchers. Nevertheless, I think it is true to say that much west German research has—often only implicitly—taken western patterns of language use as the norm, and there is clearly a risk that this approach may obscure or exaggerate the significance of differences in sociolinguistic practices. It seems to me important to acknowledge the inevitability that the researcher's perspective will be influenced by their social origins. As an outsider, I naturally lack the advantage of those who, as native Germans, can appeal to their own experiences and intuitions, but I hope that this may be outweighed by what former Chancellor Helmut Kohl might call 'die Gnade der fremden Geburt' (the blessing of being born foreign),[1] and I have certainly tried to approach this emotive subject in a critical but non-partisan way.

A glance at a bibliography on east–west research (see, for example, Hellmann 1999) will show that it has not only been conducted almost exclusively by Germans but also that it has been reported virtually entirely in German. This is perfectly reasonable, of course, but it is a sad fact that publications in German now reach very few readers outside the German-speaking countries. Yet it seems to me that the issue at the heart of this book is not only potentially of interest to a much wider audience, but also could be relevant to other divided speech communities, both in the present and in the past. These might include not only the more obvious parallel cases of politically divided nations such as Vietnam or Korea, but also multilingual contexts as diverse as the Balkan states, Catalonia, Quebec, and Jerusalem, where political struggle is bound up in complex ways with linguistic practices. All such instances serve to remind us that the German experience may have been special and of particular significance in the course of European (even world) history, but it was not unique.

For this reason, I have not only written the book in English and provided English translations of all German words and passages cited in the text, but also tried not to take a detailed knowledge of German history and institutions for granted. Furthermore, I have not assumed that all readers will be trained linguists—I rather hope they may include, amongst others, historians, sociologists, political scientists, and more generally interested readers with no particular academic orientation—and have therefore reproduced samples of spoken material in a simplified form, as opposed to using phonetic script or the transcription conventions of conversation analysis. I hope that those researchers whose work I have cited in this way, and those readers who would prefer to have a technically more precise version at their disposal, will understand the reasons for this decision.

Finally, while this book is the result of many years of my own preoccupation with the subject, by its very nature it relies heavily on the work of many individual researchers and I would like to acknowledge my debt to all of them here. In particular, I would like to express my gratitude to those German scholars—in east and west—who have provided me with material, and have generously found time to discuss their work with me and to help me understand their perspectives on this complex topic: I am thinking here especially of Peter Auer, Gerd Antos,

---

[1] In 1984, Kohl famously distanced himself—and, by implication, his generation in Germany—from the period of National Socialism by referring to the 'blessing' of having been 'born too late' to have been directly involved ('Die Gnade der späten Geburt').

Karin Birkner, Ursula Bredel, Norbert Dittmar, Ulla Fix and her colleagues in Leipzig, Manfred Hellmann, Friederike Kern, Ingrid Kühn, Jörg Palm, Jörg Pätzold, Margita Pätzold, Peter Porsch, Stefan Richter, and Ruth Reiher. They may not approve of everything I have written but I have tried to do justice to their work and to take account of their different opinions.

Alissa Shethar and John Theobald, who share my outsider status on the topic of the book and a long-standing engagement with it, have contributed in many ways to my project, and I would like to thank them for their continued interest, for their encouragement, and above all for their own stimulating research on discourses of identity in Germany.

I am hugely indebted to three people who kindly read the entire manuscript and commented on it in detail: Rodney Ball, Stephen Barbour, and Wolfdietrich Hartung. Their constructive criticism on matters of content and style brought home to me the inadequacies and weaknesses of the first draft and I have done my best to rectify these in the final version. Readers of the book in its published form will no doubt find fault with it, but it would have been a far less satisfactory account without the intervention of these early critics. I naturally take full responsibility for every aspect of the finished product.

Given the intense pressures of contemporary academic life, it would have been simply impossible to write this book without the support and, in some cases, personal sacrifice of immediate colleagues. I therefore owe a special debt to Bill Brooks, who as head of my department was unwavering in his support and encouragement, and especially to Alan Bance and Clare Mar-Molinero, who shouldered substantial extra burdens of teaching and administration during the period of special leave in which the bulk of the work on the book was done. Their kindness and friendship, both recently and over many years, help to make it all worth while and I hope I shall be able to find a way to repay them. I would also like to thank Heidi Armbruster, Alan Bance, Claudia Fellmer, and Julia Siekmann for helping me with a whole string of last-minute translation problems; and Bill Abbey for resolving a particularly problematic bibliographical question.

I would like to record my gratitude to John Davey at OUP for his light touch and constant reassurance, and to several institutions that also provided indispensable support. A period of special leave was made possible by a grant from the Arts and Humanities Research Board, and several research visits to Germany were funded by the British Academy and the German Academic Exchange Service. As always, the Institut für Deutsche Sprache in Mannheim provided relaxed hospitality and excellent resources for research, and I am particularly grateful to Eva Teubert and her colleagues in the library for their cheerful assistance and advice.

Finally, I want to thank Jo once again for her constant support and companionship, and Rosie and Jack for putting up with my grumpiness at times of stress and for being a source of great pleasure and pride.

Abbreviations

ABV	Abschnittsbevollmächtigte(r): community police officer (GDR)
ADN	Allgemeiner Deutscher Nachrichtendienst: state news agency (GDR)
CDU	Christlich-Demokratische Union: Christian Democratic Union, political party (FRG and GDR)
CSU	Christlich-Soziale Union: Christian Social Union, sister party of west German CDU (FRG)
DFD	Demokratischer Frauenbund Deutschlands: Democratic Women's Association (GDR)
EOS	Erweiterte Oberschule: senior high school (GDR)
FDGB	Freier Deutscher Gewerkschaftsbund: Free German Trade Union Organisation (GDR)
FDJ	Freie Deutsche Jugend: Free German Youth (GDR)
FDP	Freie Demokratische Partei: Free Democratic Party, political party (FRG)
HO	Handelsorganisation: state-run organisation for retail, hotel, and catering trades (GDR)
KPD	Kommunistische Partei Deutschlands: Communist Party of Germany, which merged with the SPD in the Soviet occupation zone in 1946 to form the SED
LDPD	Liberal-Demokratische Partei Deutschlands: Liberal-Democratic Party, one of the so-called 'block parties' (GDR)
MDR	Mitteldeutscher Rundfunk: Central German Broadcasting Company, a regional radio and television service founded in 1991
NDPD	Nationaldemokratische Partei Deutschlands: National Democratic Party, one of the so-called 'block parties' (GDR)
NDR	Norddeutscher Rundfunk: North German Broadcasting Company, a regional radio and television service (FRG)
NVA	Nationale Volksarmee: National People's Army (GDR)
ORB	Ostdeutscher Rundfunk Brandenburg, East German Broadcasting Company, a regional radio and television service founded in 1991
PDS	Partei des Demokratischen Sozialismus: Party of Democratic Socialism, the successor party to the SED, founded in December 1989
PGH	Produktionsgenossenschaft des Handwerks: craftsmen's cooperative (GDR)
POS	Polytechnische Oberschule: secondary school (GDR)
SED	Sozialistische Einheitspartei Deutschlands: Socialist Unity Party, the ruling communist party in the GDR
SPD	Sozialdemokratische Partei Deutschlands: Social Democratic Party, political party (FRG)
USV	Upper Saxon Vernacular: a collective term for non-standard speech forms in Upper Saxony
VEB	Volkseigener Betrieb: company/concern in public ownership (GDR)

1

Introduction

'In diesen Tagen besichtigt der Kanzler den fremden Osten der Republik. Er trifft auf eine Gesellschaft, die nach zehn Jahren Einheit neue Distanz zum Westen sucht.' (The Chancellor is currently visiting the alien eastern part of the country. He is encountering a society that after ten years of unity is seeking to distance itself again from the west.) (*Die Zeit*, 24 August 2000) This unremarkable newspaper headline—unremarkable because it is one of many similar statements that could be read in the press at that time, and also because it expresses a sentiment that was anything but new—accompanied an article by east German sociologist Wolfgang Engler, in which he explores a specific dimension of the continued (and allegedly growing) tendency to disunity in the unified German republic. The main headline for the article reads: 'Sie sprechen doch Deutsch. Trotzdem verstehen Ost und West einander nicht' (They both speak German, but east and west still don't understand each other), and the author offers what are billed as 'Anmerkungen zu einem Kulturkampf' (notes on a cultural struggle). This, too, seems unremarkable, as attempts to understand 'the Germans' and their 'culture' have always had to confront the paradox that they have little in common other than the German language but that it is also the language, as much as anything else, that divides them.

However, two points are worth making here. First, while the linguistic landscape of German-speaking Europe has always been highly variegated, with regional and often local contrasts in all directions, the east–west axis has never been salient in this respect: all accounts of naturally occurring geographical variation in German stress latitude over longitude. Secondly, while reports of continuing economic and social imbalance between the old and the new federal states (*Bundesländer*) ten years after unification would not necessarily have seemed an unlikely prospect in 1990, it would surely have been disconcerting to look a decade into the future and learn that east and west Germans were apparently (still) unable to communicate satisfactorily.

So it seems that an explanation of this commonplace notion is needed after all. Why should an entire sheet of newsprint be devoted to the idea of east–west communication problems, when an article dealing with the more evidently substantial issue of north–south contrasts would never even be considered for publication? How can it be that after ten years of unfettered contact this most fundamental of obstacles to the construction of community has not been overcome? And is reference to a 'cultural struggle' not a rather wild piece of journalistic licence?

Now, Engler is a sociologist, not a linguist, and linguistic issues are not the substance but the starting point of his discussion. What ostensibly triggered his deliberations on what he portrays as the cultural struggle between east and west Germans is an anecdote related by a west German television journalist. After filming an interview with an east German forester about the situation of the forests in Brandenburg, she was taken aback when he declared: 'Sie sind bestimmt kein Wessi. Sie sprechen doch deutsch.' (You can't be a westerner—you speak German.) He then explained this cryptic remark by telling her: 'Ich war neulich auf einer Versammlung. Da rief ein Podiumsredner vor seinem Vortrag in den Saal: "Ist hier ein Anwalt unter uns?" Keiner hob die Hand. "Sitzt hier ein Wessi?" Niemand meldete sich. "Na, dann können wir ja deutsch reden." ' (I was at a public meeting recently. Before he began his talk, the speaker on the platform called out: 'Is there a lawyer amongst us?' No one raised their hand. 'Is there a westerner here?' No one responded. 'OK then, we can talk German.')

What this story is intended to illustrate is the difference between the concepts of *Verständigung* (communicating) and *Verstehen* (understanding) (see Schiewe 1998: 259, and Paul 2000*b*). The issue is not in fact whether east and west Germans can communicate with each other: there may well be difficulties in this respect, but they are minor and anyway they had existed long before the hardening of the east–west boundary through the formation of separate states (although these difficulties were undoubtedly exacerbated by the prolonged lack of contact after 1949) (see Barbour and Stevenson 1990/1998: Chapter 1). The newspaper headline is in a sense to be understood rather literally: it suggests that east and west Germans may understand each other's words but they don't understand what each other is saying—or, more plainly, they don't understand each other.

There is an inescapable allusion in this formulation to Deborah Tannen's famously controversial claim that men and women 'just don't understand' each other (Tannen 1991), and this sweeping assertion about east and west Germans is equally contentious. But both of these issues are, in the broadest sense of the term, profoundly political ones and it is the political functions of language (or, more precisely, of texts) that motivate my study. For Engler, the production and reception of written and spoken texts as a means of both identifying and establishing community is no more than a launching pad for an investigation of cultural difference (see Engler 2000*a*). For me, the objective is to explore in detail those issues to do with language that contribute to debates on difference in the context of contemporary Germany. The emphasis will be less on individual linguistic forms—although they have their part to play in the narrative—than on linguistic practices and on ways in which language is dragooned into political and social disputes over 'belonging'. Underlying the linguistic analysis, therefore, is an understanding of language use (or perhaps rather of linguistic activity) as political—adopting both Hans Jürgen Heringer's (1990: 9) dictum that 'politische Tätigkeit [ist] sprachliche Tätigkeit' (political activity is linguistic activity) and its converse.

There have been innumerable studies of aspects of the theme of linguistic and communicative differences between east and west German speech communities (Manfred Hellmann's bibliography lists over 700 in the period 1990–9 alone). However, virtually all of them (an exception is Bauer 1993) fix their gaze either on the period of political division before 1989–90, or on the transitional period of the *Wende*[1] (turning point) in 1989–90, or on the current period of the unified state. What has been lacking—and what I hope to provide here—is a study of sociolinguistic disunity that sets the contemporary situation in a broader historical context and that draws out not only the self-evident discontinuities in this history but also the important continuities. For the phenomena of sociolinguistic difference and communicative dissonance in contemporary Germany, which are the principal focus of Part II of the book, can only be understood against the background of the four decades of division that preceded unification and, more broadly still, in the context of the role that the idea of 'the German language' has played in the construction and contestation of national identities over the last 200 years.

The sociolinguistic history that follows is organized according to two different principles. First, it is divided into two parts on a simple chronological basis: Part I deals with the period up to and including the *Wende*, and Part II is concerned with the first decade after unification, from 1990 to 2000. Secondly, the two chapters within each of these two halves of the book are constructed thematically rather than following a linear progression through time. In this way, I hope to capture both the historicity of the east–west issue and the complex web of questions underlying the central problem: why, and in what ways, is language repeatedly (perceived as) a source of both unity and disunity in the German speech community?

My study is concerned, then, not only with the recent history of the German language but also—more importantly—with the role of language in recent German history, both at the macro level of relations between east and west and at the micro level of the experiences of easterners and westerners. This will certainly entail considering ways in which the German language has changed since 1945, but the particular perspective on linguistic change will be on its relationship with social change. In Chapter 2, I want to outline a way of construing this relationship as one means of understanding the complex issue of national identities in the context of Germany in the second half of the twentieth century. In the title of the chapter—'Germany and the *Questione della Lingua*'—I have borrowed a term that social and linguistic historians (see, for example, Steinberg 1987 and Joseph 1987) use in reference to debates on language and regional or national identities in the equally problematic Italian context, in order to situate the discussion within a broader, European framework (see Barbour and Carmichael 2000 for an authoritative survey of language and nationalism in Europe) and to emphasize the historical

---

[1] Since this term is so widely used in both academic and everyday contexts, I shall use it rather than an English equivalent throughout the book.

dimension of this approach to the 'German question'. Before proceeding any further, I should explain what I mean by the 'historical dimension' of this issue.

My study is intended as a narrative that acknowledges the significance of the sequence of events and the passage of time, but also draws attention to the complex 'layering' of Germans' social experience of and with language. Jan Blommaert (1999*b*: 3–4), drawing on the work of Fernand Braudel (1958*a*), argues for an approach to the study of language in history which is based on 'a concept of time that recognizes both different "objective", chronological speeds and different ways of perceiving time by subjects'. On the one hand, there is 'traditional historical time', which 'is the time people can see, feel and control'. On the other hand, 'there are other times or temporalities: slow processes that are beyond the reach of individuals, the time of social, political and economic systems'. From this point of view, history is 'the study of overlapping, intertwining and conflicting temporalities in the lives of people, . . . [which] are not only objective chronometrical phenomena; they also refer to perceptions and experiences of time by humans, in other words . . . to the social nature of time'. The friction between these different 'temporalities' in the lives of people is fundamental to my understanding of the role of language in the history of Germanness.

One of the effects of these competing patterns of time is that discontinuities in one dimension may mask continuities in another. As Blommaert (1999*c*: 425–6) goes on to argue:

There are crucial moments in history during which languages become targets of political, social and cultural intervention, and there are moments in which very little in the way of drama and crisis seems to happen. . . . [But] every moment of intense struggle and debate is intertextual with and develops against the background of previous developments over a longer span of time.

Although historical 'events' may occur suddenly and abruptly—the assassination of a head of state, the surrender of an army, the opening of a sealed border— changes in social practices, structures, and relationships that give rise to, or result from, such moments typically come about more slowly and less perceptibly. As Blommaert (ibid.) puts it, 'a highly intensive and fast-moving *événement* [is] set against very slow (and very deep) processes'. The same applies to language change, since—apart from exceptional cases when it is ordained 'from above' by an agency with the authority and resources to enforce it—it is a social process and therefore in that sense an aspect of social change. Furthermore, both language change and, more generally, social change are by and large continuous processes (although the pace of change may vary considerably), which means that any study of change in a particular time frame more or less arbitrarily defines a 'period' with a beginning and an end that in fact are points on a continuum.

Admittedly, it is convenient to think of change in terms of chunks of time bounded by 'catastrophic' moments such as the erection and dismantling of the

Berlin Wall, and of course such events may genuinely represent a revolutionary rather than evolutionary movement in the historical process: some moments evidently have a greater impact than others. However, even after such significant occasions, some things change while others do not, and although the use of labels such as 'before' and 'after' the fall of the Wall may be justifiable in as far as it makes dealing with complex processes more manageable, it nevertheless risks creating the illusion that history is segmentable. It could be argued that the *topic* of this book— the disunity of east and west in Germany—exceptionally permits such a categorical approach: the creation of two German states in 1949 and their merger in 1990 do represent an unusually clearly circumscribed development in German political history. However, the *theme* of the book—the place of language in the continuity of social divisions between east and west—is based on the premise that social change is less susceptible, indeed potentially more resistant, to sudden shifts than political change. So while the terminal point of my study (the end of the first decade of unification) is arbitrary, its extent (encompassing both the period of political division before 1990 and the period of unification after 1990) is essential to the argument.

The starting point of my deliberations—the fragmentation of Germany after the Second World War, first into four zones of occupation, then into the two frontier states of the emerging power blocks—at first sight seems to require less explanation. However, while this moment saw the birth of the east–west divide, it is important for the understanding of the meaning of this development to see it in the context of the tension between centrifugal and centripetal forces (regionalization and centralization) that had characterized the history of Germany for at least the preceding 200 years, if not much longer. From this perspective, the east–west division is only the most recent fracturing of the 'German people', and the current nation-state the most recent experiment in unifying it.

It would be well beyond my scope to discuss this complex and tortuous history of disunity at length. However, while focusing on the specific phenomenon of the east–west divide, it is important to acknowledge the historical depth of social and linguistic dislocation in Germany. What I want to pursue in Part I therefore is first the idea that language has always played a crucial role in constructing, challenging, and dismantling social divisions in Germany, and secondly the political embeddedness of Germans' experience of language. To make these points, I shall not take the probably obvious step of moving back one 'stage' in time and discussing the role of language during the Third Reich.[2] Instead, I shall begin by deliberately removing the discussion to a still earlier point in time. My aim in 2.1 will be to establish the historicity of this contentious relationship between language and social and political identities in Germany by taking the debates on language in the first half of the nineteenth century as an illustration of the coincidence of sociopolitical upheavals and linguistic crises, and as a demonstration of

---

[2] For detailed analysis of this, see, for example, Bauer (1988) and Maas (1984). Shorter discussions, in English, can be found in Townson (1992: Chapter 4) and Wells (1985: 407–19).

how values attached to the 'national language' or 'mother tongue' at that time foreshadowed many later developments of relevance to my theme.

Debates on the linguistic and cultural heritage and the relationship between language and national identity from the 1950s to the 1980s need to be seen in the context of these earlier debates. For if one objective of intellectuals in the early nineteenth century was to create an *Öffentlichkeit*, a public domain in which social and political issues could be openly discussed for the first time (see Townson 1992: 53–6), the contributions to the language debates that developed during the Cold War showed how this public domain could be exploited by developing discourses on language to promote competing ideologies. In 2.2, I shall trace the course of these debates, showing how they track the shifting political climate of east–west relations in post-1945 Germany, and examine the links between political and academic agendas.

The final section of Chapter 2 moves the discussion from discursive representations of language to language change and language use. While debates about language failed to establish a basis for claims of distinct languages in the GDR and the Federal Republic (as we shall see in 2.2), the nature, extent, and significance of linguistic and sociolinguistic differences between the two speech communities have often been underplayed in studies that adopt an 'objective', quantitative approach. I shall argue in 2.3 that the alienation experienced by many east Germans, in particular, after 1989 (see 4.1) can only be explained on the basis of important lexical and semantic differences. More specifically, I shall suggest that the ideological force of linguistic practices such as naming (states, towns, political processes, etc.) outweighs the extent of quantitative differences, that the use of key words to construct contexts is more important than the mere existence of distinct lexical sub-sets.

In Chapter 2, then, I shall show how language and (socio)linguistic change were issues that were integral aspects of the emergence and development of the two German states after 1945 and of the fluctuating relationships between them. In Chapter 3, I shall focus attention on public language use in the GDR, but my purpose in doing so will not be to contrast it with language use in the Federal Republic, let alone to represent it as deviating from a 'norm' defined by western practice. Rather, my aim will be to explore the crucial phenomenon of how language was conscripted in the complementary processes of assembling and dismantling a society that was to have been the very model of internal consistency and unity, but which was in fact fatally fractured and whose demise appeared to offer the opportunity to create a new society accommodating both German communication communities.[3] The central question here then will be: how did the very ways in which language was used in the GDR—formally and informally—apparently contribute paradoxically to its downfall?

---

[3] This perspective ignores, of course, the plural nature of this society, as if it were not in fact multilingual and multicultural. This question is beyond my scope here but will be the subject of a subsequent study.

All political cultures—and this applies to the 'old' Federal Republic just as much as to the GDR—develop discursive strategies and techniques that competing interest groups exploit to gain and retain power and, once in power, to maintain a degree of distance between the rulers and the governed (through, for instance, calculated vagueness, imprecision, cliché, and euphemism—see Wodak and Kirsch 1995*b*: 11). However, the fundamental difference between totalitarian and democratic societies in this respect is that the modes and possibilities of 'talk'—of linguistic interaction and exchange—within and between the various social layers are more tightly constrained in the former (which is not to say, of course, that societies which can be considered democratic in terms of their political structures and processes are necessarily characterized by wholly open and transparent communicative practices). What is interesting in our context is how patterns of communication were developed and controlled in the process of building a new society in the GDR—to what extent and in what ways was it 'talked into existence'?—and how the state, through doing this, sowed the seeds of its own destruction—in what sense can we say that it was 'talked out of existence'?

It follows from this that the approach here will focus not on debates about language or on individual linguistic features, but rather on language use in the construction of competing discourses.[4] I shall begin, in 3.1, by examining the official discourse of the Socialist Unity Party (Sozialistische Einheitspartei Deutschlands, hereafter SED) as manifested in public statements of various kinds (for example, announcements of Party policy and speeches at Party congresses). This forms the bedrock of 'public language' in the GDR—not the language of everyday social intercourse, but the discourse of authority and political orthodoxy, which ordinary citizens would inevitably encounter and in which they would develop at least a passive competence. For if the principal aim of the SED was to construct an all-embracing socialist society, in which every member had a role to play, it was clearly essential that the Party's policies, and the beliefs and values on which they were predicated, should be communicated to 'the people', but at the same time it

---

[4] I am using the term 'discourse' here and throughout the book in what has become a more or less conventional usage in critical linguistics (or critical discourse analysis, CDA), associated with linguists such as Norman Fairclough and Ruth Wodak. Drawing primarily on the work of Michel Foucault, critical linguists regard language as a form of social practice and use 'discourse' to refer to 'different ways of structuring areas of knowledge and social practice' (Fairclough 1992: 3). For example, Fairclough argues, 'the discourse of "medical science" is currently the dominant one in the practice of health care, though it contrasts with various wholistic "alternative" discourses (e.g. those of homeopathy and acupuncture) as well as popular "folk" discourses' (ibid.). For my purposes, a particularly pertinent definition is given by Gunther Kress (1985: 6–7, cited in Fowler 1991: 42): 'Discourses are systematically-organized sets of statements which give expression to the meanings and values of an institution. Beyond that, they define, describe and delimit what it is possible to say and not possible to say (and by extension—what it is possible to do or not to do) with respect to the area of concern of that institution, whether marginally or centrally. A discourse provides a set of possible statements about a given area, and organizes and gives structure to the manner in which a particular topic, object, process is to be talked about. In that it provides descriptions, rules, permissions and prohibitions of social and individual actions'. For a concise but wide-ranging introduction to discourse theory, see Mills (1997).

was also necessary to define and restrict the limits of *Öffentlichkeit*, the public domain as a space for open debate. Therefore, constraints on the production and reception of media texts need to be taken into account here too. Finally, since control was a vital feature in the implementation of policy, I shall explore how the obsessive and paranoid world of the state security operation is revealed through the hermetic code of its private lexicon, the *Wörterbuch der politisch-operativen Arbeit* (Dictionary of Political/Operational Work).

The most significant and characteristic aspects of the official discourse can be subsumed in the notion of rituality. As we shall see, the same linguistic features and textual patterns recur with strikingly monotonous regularity in Party texts. This ritual nature of text construction corresponds to the highly ritualized patterns of formal public events such as Party congresses and organized celebrations like the *Tag der Republik* (Republic Day, marking the founding of the GDR). In 3.2, I shall consider the functions and importance of the ritualization of speech events involving, at one time or another, most members of the population (focusing on May Day and the *Jugendweihe*, the secular equivalent of confirmation).

The emphasis on written texts here (including those intended for oral delivery, such as speeches and forms of ceremonial address) may seem to give a distorted and misleading impression of language use in the GDR. I should therefore stress again that my concern is not with everyday speech in informal and semi-formal domains, where there is no evidence to suggest that east German language use was distinguishable from west German language use, other than through the occurrence of regional or local variants (see 2.3). Rather, the focus is precisely on the materiality of the written text and its potential for the reproduction, transmission, and circulation of ideas, beliefs, and values. In order to explore the extent to which this potential was realized for ideological purposes and in the implementation of official policy, I shall also analyse here ways in which official discourse patterns permeated every level of discursive activity within a particular domain: education and the institution of the school.

The monotony of the official discourse and its monopoly of public language in the GDR were finally shattered by an eruption of competing discourses in the autumn of 1989, the *Wende*: on the one hand, the desperate but doomed last-ditch attempts of the SED leadership to cling onto power by changing the discursive habits of a lifetime, on the other hand, the deritualized voices of organized opposition, of intellectuals, and of the man and the woman—literally—in the street. The final section of this chapter (3.3) will therefore explore what Peter von Polenz (1993) calls the *Sprachrevolte* (language revolt) of 1989, showing how the voice of 'the people' was more 'eloquent' (Joseph 1987) than that of the Party, and how the way had been prepared for the spontaneous and multi-faceted outburst of popular dissent by the experience of everyday life in the GDR and the practices that ordinary people had developed for dealing with it.

Part I will therefore conclude with the battle between competing voices in the period of the *Wende* and the ultimate reassertion of the dominant west German discourse. However, was the result in the longer term a harmonious symphony of diverse but complementary and mutually affirming tunes, or a cacophony of discordant sounds? While *Wende* was the preferred metaphor at the time, and seems an appropriate concept for the pivotal point in the structure of my narrative, the alternative term *Umbruch* (radical change) is perhaps more suited to the theme of Part II. We shall be concerned here not with a catastrophic moment of change, the volcanic eruption of Germany's 'hot autumn' of 1989, but rather with its aftermath in the first decade of unification. As the dust began to settle, how did the German speech community—in Peter Pulzer's pithy phrase, 'unified but not united' (Pulzer 1995, chapter title)—emerge from the turmoil? On the one hand, of course, it will be as well to remember that there has always been regional variation in Germany. On the other hand, these traditional differences are now overlaid with myriad new features, and this is as true of language forms and linguistic practices as it is of other social, political, and cultural phenomena. Our task here will therefore be to disentangle these more recent characteristics and to investigate their legacy and their impact on the process of unification.

In Chapter 4, I shall begin this analysis by exploring some of the ways in which the 'communicative environment' (Townson 1992) changed in the period of *Umbruch* in the early 1990s, and ways in which east Germans in particular have adapted to life in a new 'speech ecology' (Mühlhäusler 1996), with its own inventories of linguistic forms and repertoires of speech behaviours. The key question here then is: how has sociolinguistic difference been experienced by Germans, east and west, in this new context, and how have they responded to its challenges? I shall begin in 4.1 with the most evident changes in the form of lexical and textual differences confronting east Germans and with the effects of an awareness of difference in terms of resisting, accepting, and facilitating change.

More subtle than differences in vocabulary and text construction, the linguistic patterns that characterize 'communicative genres' (for example, job interviews and consumer advice sessions) are less susceptible to surface analysis, and any problems they may give rise to cannot be resolved by simple substitution exercises. In 4.2, I shall therefore examine the impact of different experiences of such forms of everyday interaction and consider how far this represents (or represented) an obstacle to the integration of east Germans into the 'new' German speech community.

Following on from these two sections, I shall investigate in 4.3 the more general relationship between social and linguistic mobility in Germany after unification: how far, and in what ways, have east Germans adapted their speech behaviours to changed social circumstances and linguistic environments—and are there any indications that west Germans now living in eastern Germany have accommodated to *their* new surroundings?

Underlying all of these issues is the question of attitudes towards variation and difference in language. Before 1989, each of the two 'communication communities' had its own sets of values in relation to components of its repertoire of speech varieties. The merging of these two communities inevitably led to a reassessment or recalibration of these values—at least amongst east Germans—and, since speech features are amongst the most salient markers of social difference, language attitudes are a potent resource for discrimination and the expression of prejudice. In 4.4, I shall therefore consider research on the changing evaluations of particular linguistic varieties (such as vernacular speech and standard forms in Berlin), on the ideology of standardization, and on ways in which the disparagement of linguistic varieties can function as a tool of social domination.

In Chapter 5, I shall develop the theme of Chapter 4 in a different direction. The focus of attention here will be on ways in which (perceptions of) language use and reflections on language are more directly instrumental in constructing and negotiating different kinds of eastern and western identities: how do people 'reprocess' the past from their present perspective, and how do they project their experience of the past onto their present circumstances? At the heart of this chapter will be the tension between the essentializing of 'eastness' and 'westness' on the one hand, and the desire to personalize or individualize experience on the other—or to put it the other way round, the tension between the rejection of reductive generalizations embodied in the contrast between the vernacular categories *Ossi* and *Wessi* and the tenacity of underlying beliefs in *Ossizität* (eastness) and *Wessizität* (westness).

Taking my cue from Wolfgang Thierse's often quoted remark that Germans in the GDR and the Federal Republic did not have a different language but rather a different relationship to language (Thierse 1993: 116), I shall first discuss in 5.1 personal narratives in which individuals reconstruct their experience of the past and reflect on the role of language in their lives. What does the way they organize their personal biographies reveal about their perspective on the past, and what do their comments on language use and language change suggest about their attitudes to social change?

The conduct of interactions depends to a large extent on the mutual perceptions of the interlocutors. While we shall see in Chapter 4 how social values are associated with linguistic judgements in the German context and how they are consciously deployed in discussions of otherness, I shall explore in 5.2 ways in which internalized images of 'eastern talk' and 'western talk' are activated in interaction through contextualization cues (Gumperz 1982): what linguistic or communicative knowledge do speakers draw on to identify whether they are talking to an easterner or a westerner, and what consequences can this have?

In 5.3 I shall then develop the question of perceptions further by analysing how images of eastness and westness are variably realized in the course of personal interaction (for example, in talk shows, phone-ins, and group discussions) and in public discourses (for instance, in advertising). How are these perceptions used by participants in interaction to situate themselves and others, and what effects does this have on their relationships with each other? The combined effect of public discourses (especially media discourses such as advertising) and face-to-face encounters is often the construction and confirmation of prejudice and stereotypes. While this may apply in equal measure to both east and west Germans, it is only the former who are likely to suffer direct consequences of this. I shall therefore consider finally what kinds of stereotypes of 'eastness' and 'westness' have emerged, and whether it is possible to develop an 'eastern' voice and be heard without being stigmatized.

In Chapter 6, I shall then resume some of the fundamental questions raised in the course of the study and consider ways of interpreting linguistic encounters between east and west in Germany and the broader relevance of this specific issue to the study of sociolinguistic conflict in general.

PART I

1945–1990 Language, Nation, and State

2

Germany and the *Questione della Lingua*

2.1 Political change and linguistic crises

Germany has, at different times, been variously referred to as a 'difficult' nation, a 'belated', 'insecure', 'confused', 'wounded', 'disunited', 'overstretched' nation (Busse 1995: 204). All such labels express the fundamental uncertainty and insecurity of 'Germans' in their sense of nationhood, and both the continued discord between east and west and the growing local and regional, rather than national, loyalties in contemporary Germany seem to indicate that this is as true today as in the past. However, it is not my purpose here to analyse the nature and constitution of national identities in Germany nor to account for the rise and fall of different nationalisms in German history (see, for example, Dann 1992). My aim is more limited and more specific: I want to provide a context for the theme of our subsequent discussion of how 'talk' (socially situated uses of language) contributes to the conflicting processes of developing and contesting social identities. In particular, the argument to be examined in Chapter 3—that the GDR as a social project was both talked into and talked out of existence—may seem less extravagant if we first consider the role of language in earlier periods of German history, and then (in 2.2) explore the ways in which language resurfaced as a critical social issue after the collapse of the 'unified' fascist state in 1945. (For more extensive discussion of linguistic nationalism in Germany, see Barbour 1993, 2000b, Coulmas 1997, Townson 1992.)

The rapid development of economic and cultural globalization in the last quarter of the twentieth century increasingly cast doubt on the long-term integrity of established nation-states in Europe and elsewhere, indeed many observers have come to consider the nation-state as an anachronistic concept in a world dominated by supra-national organizations such as the European Union and the Association of South East Asian Nations, the World Bank and the International Monetary Fund, and by multinational corporations such as Shell and General Motors. There is therefore something ironic about the formation—or better, consolidation—in 1990 of a polity called Germany as a political and territorial location for the 'German nation'.

Yet this display of unity came in the year after both the Federal Republic and the GDR had celebrated their fortieth anniversaries. While the official positions of the two states remained quite distinct, with the GDR vigorously promoting its independence as a socialist state and the Federal Republic maintaining its constitutional stance as a provisional arrangement pending the 'reunification' of the German people, the general tenor of discussion in both states reflected the growing public acceptance of the status quo. In the space of virtually two generations a separate state (if not national) consciousness had developed in east and west, and few voices would have dissented from views such as those expressed by Polenz (1990: 9):

Als langfristige Folge der von der Regierung Brandt/Scheel eingeleiteten Entspannungs- und Normalisierungspolitik wird es heute...immer deutlicher, daß das Nebeneinander und Miteinander mehrerer deutschsprachiger Staaten sich mit gemeinsamen...kultur- nationalen Beziehungen und Bindungen durchaus verträgt.

As a long-term consequence of the policy of détente and normalization introduced by the Brandt/Scheel government it is becoming increasingly clear that the coexistence of several German-speaking states is perfectly consistent with common relations and ties in terms of continuing national cultural identity.

and by Coulmas (1990: 181):

As a result of World War II, the (near) identity of language, state and nation—that is, the somewhat fictitious ideal of linguistic nationalism—has been destroyed in Germany.

Within a matter of weeks, however, the view that a single state uniting the territory and people (although both of these terms remained controversial) of the Federal Republic and the GDR was somehow 'natural' and would give due recognition to the existence of a single German nation had established itself as the quasi-orthodox position. Although widespread misgivings persisted both about unification itself and about the cultural assumptions that were appealed to in order to legitimate it, the long-running dispute over the inheritance of German culture and the right to speak for the German people was apparently swept aside. The German question as it re-emerged after November 1989 might then be seen in terms of reconciling these two conflicting positions: on the one hand, the acceptance of the evolution and maturity of two German states and on the other hand, the almost atavistic belief in some kind of primordial Germanness. The act of unification therefore reopened the debate on the association between language, state, people, and nation that has been conducted under various guises since at least the early nineteenth century.

There are many definitions of nation in the literature on the subject, but the following ones offered by Peter Alter and Anthony D. Smith are not untypical:

a social group (and by this we mean a people or a section of a people) which, because of a variety of historically evolved relations of a linguistic, cultural, religious or political nature, has become conscious of its coherence, political unity and particular interests....A *nation* is constituted by the social group's (the *people's*) consciousness of being a nation, or of wanting to be one, and by their demand for political self-determination. (Alter 1994: 11) (Italics in original)

a named human population sharing an historic territory, common myths and historical memories, a mass, public culture, a common economy and common legal rights and duties for all members. (Smith 1991: 14, cited in Barbour 2000*a*: 4)

At least until the early nineteenth century, virtually none of the shared character-istics listed in these definitions—apart from the common, yet highly diverse, lan-guage—could be appealed to as the basis for a sense of nationhood in Germany, and the long tradition of highly localized loyalties impeded the development of a widespread political consciousness of a German nation in Alter's sense. Indeed, more than any other European nation, the Germans may be best conceived as a *Sprachvolk*, a people defined almost exclusively by language: early forms of the term *deutsch* referred first to varieties of language spoken in central and eastern Europe and only later to speakers of these varieties (Townson 1992: 77–80). In terms of political organization, the German people was dispersed across many principalities and mini-states, and the appendage of the phrase 'deutscher Nation' (of the German nation) to the title of the Holy Roman Empire did no more than create an illusion of unity in what was in reality a fragmented confederation. Moreover, with the stability of the established order and in the absence of a pub-lic domain, there was no serious prospect of the emergence of a national con-sciousness before the demise of the moribund Empire in 1806 and before the French occupation of German territories provoked a reaction amongst intellec-tuals and the rising but powerless bourgeoisie (see Fulbrook 1990: 98–101 and Polenz 1999: 10–13).

The question even then was what could be used to ignite this consciousness of 'wanting to be a nation'. Writing about the turmoil in central and eastern Europe in the early 1990s, Hobsbawm (1991: 16) quotes the Czech historian Miroslav Hroch:

Where an old regime disintegrates, where old social relationships have become unstable, amid the rise of general insecurity, belonging to a common language and culture become the only certainty in society, the only value beyond ambiguity and doubt.

This aphoristic formulation appears to invest the assertion with a general validity, and certainly 'belonging to a common language and culture' is a topos invoked on many occasions—for good or ill—when people seek a safe haven in turbulent times and when loyalties are tested. However, in the moral and political vacuum following the collapse of old certainties in Germany in the early years of the nine-teenth century, it was by no means clear that belonging to a common language and culture could be construed as a 'value beyond ambiguity and doubt'. The pro-tracted process of developing a standardized variety of German and 'fixing' it in a uniform and stable way through the publication of dictionaries and grammars was largely complete by the end of the eighteenth century (see Wells 1985: Chapter 8, Polenz 1994: Chapter 5.6), but this in itself was not a sufficient condition for the promotion of a national consciousness. On the one hand, a standard literary language was not necessarily a 'flag' around which a still predominantly illiterate population would unite. On the other hand, the resolution of the *form* of the language had not automatically enhanced its *status* to the point where it challenged the dominance of French as the language of political administration and Latin as the language of academic study and scholarly debate. The irony of the common language which defined the German people but had no place in the dominant institutions of German society became a political issue only when what Townson (1992: 539 ff.) calls the communicative environment changed—as a result of modernization processes such as urbanization, a higher degree of political organization, increased mobility through new forms of transport, and advances in communication technology—in such a way that the conditions for public debate were met.

Discussions of the relationship between language and national identity in Germany (indeed in Europe generally—see Mar-Molinero 2000: Chapter 1) almost always focus on the seminal ideas of Johann Gottfried Herder and Wilhelm von Humboldt.[1] Herder's conception of language as an essentially changeable social product (see especially Herder 1770) fostered the view that languages were naturally developing organisms that derived their nature from the particularity of the *Volk* with which they were associated. Humboldt, for instance, argued in *Über die Verschiedenheit des menschlichen Sprachbaues und ihren Einfluß auf die geistige Entwicklung des Menschengeschlechts* (1830–5) that 'der Bau der Sprachen im Menschengeschlechte darum und insofern verschieden ist, weil und als es die Geisteseigenthümlichkeit der Nationen selbst ist' (the structure of languages in the human race varies because, and to the extent that, the individual spirit of the nations themselves varies) (Humboldt 1963b: 413), and in the earlier essay *Über die Verschiedenheiten des menschlichen Sprachbaues* (1827–9) the indissoluble link between language and nation is asserted emphatically: 'Die Sprachen [aber] werden nur von Nationen erzeugt, festgehalten und verändert, die Vertheilung des Menschengeschlechts nach Nationen ist nur seine Vertheilung nach Sprachen' (But languages are only produced, retained, and changed by nations, the distribution of the human race in terms of nations is only its distribution in terms of languages) (Humboldt 1963a: 161).

However, it is not the thesis of language as the 'soul' or 'spirit' of the nation in itself that promoted early linguistic nationalism in Germany: there is an important step from the academic exercise of attempting to develop a fundamental principle of human social organization to the political project of attempting to generate a national consciousness and mobilize patriotic fervour. The key task for a history of the language in modern German history is therefore to account for the

---

[1] A recent exception is Gardt (1999), who traces what he calls 'linguistic patriotism' in Germany back before the eighteenth century.

transformation of Herder's and Humboldt's ideas into expressions of nationalist ideologies as articulated, for example, by Ernst Moritz Arndt in his essay *Ueber Volkshaß und über den Gebrauch einer fremden Sprache* (On hatred between nations and on the use of a foreign language) (1813), or a century later by Friedrich Kluge in his diatribe on the experience of the First World War, *Vaterland und Muttersprache* (Fatherland and Mother-tongue), in which he insists: 'Die Muttersprache ist das Wahrzeichen des Vaterlandes. Die Einheit der Sprache ist die Einheit der Heimat.... Pflege der Muttersprache ist Pflege des Deutschtums' (The mother-tongue is the symbol of the fatherland. The unity of the language is the unity of the homeland. Cultivating the mother-tongue means cultivating Germanness.) (Kluge 1918: 284, cited in Ahlzweig 1994: 179.) (For discussions, see, for example, Townson 1992: Chapter 3, Wells 1985: Chapter 10, Polenz 1999: Chapter 6.0–6.3.)

Kluge was writing at a time of massive social and political upheaval in Germany, since the end of the war meant not only national defeat but the collapse of the Empire. Moments such as this are extreme illustrations of what Gramsci (1985: 183) was referring to when he maintained in a familiar passage in his cultural writings that 'every time the question of the language surfaces, in one way or another, it means that a series of other problems are coming to the fore'. The emergence of this *questione della lingua*, the question of the relationship between language and Germanness, over 100 years earlier was motivated by a similarly radical period of social change in the aftermath of the French Revolution, but it appeared at that stage in a different guise. The work of late eighteenth- and early nineteenth-century language purists such as Joachim Heinrich Campe and Carl Gustav Jochmann (see Schiewe 1998: 125–49) was inspired by the rationalist ideals of the Enlightenment and the aspirations to political emancipation underlying the overthrow of the *ancien régime* in France. They understood that increased public participation in political processes depended not only on the development of new political structures and the introduction of civil rights but also, crucially, on the construction of a public domain (*Öffentlichkeit*[2]) for the exercise of these rights and the exchange of ideas—and this in turn required a thorough overhaul of the German language as a democratic vehicle for conducting debates.

It was these very gradual changes in political culture and the project of—as we might now say—modernizing the German language as a suitable medium for public discourse that, together with the expansion of elementary education, constitute the most significant changes in the communicative environment in the first half of the nineteenth century. The creation of a collective public with the (albeit limited) opportunity to engage in debates fulfilled the essential prerequisite for the circulation of ideas. But the status and the form of the language remained fiercely contested issues on the political agenda created by this development throughout the nineteenth century, erupting at critical moments in outbursts of frustration or naked

---

[2] Townson (1992: 54) points out that the term *Oeffentlichkeit* appears in an encyclopaedia for the first time only in the 1819 edition of the Brockhaus.

jingoism (Polenz 1967 argues, much in the same vein as Gramsci, that the most vehement waves of linguistic purism have always accompanied heightened political appeals to nationalist sentiments, from the end of the Thirty Years War in the mid-seventeenth century to the beginning of the fascist period in the 1930s). A particular bone of contention that underlies two quite distinct forms of purism in this period is the influence of 'foreign' (especially French, later also English) vocabulary. While for Campe and Jochmann, for example, the elimination of French terms from the German lexicon represented the removal of an impediment to the free and efficient exchange of ideas and was therefore advocated as an internally liberating enterprise, their successors pursued a similar goal but with a radically different purpose: to assert the superiority of German over other languages and to defend it against 'contamination' by other, 'inferior' languages (Kirkness 1975; see also Busse 1995: 213, Schiewe 1998: 155 ff.).

Linguistic purism in the early part of this period was therefore about promoting social inclusion and maximizing access to public intercourse, while the later purism (associated most concretely with the Allgemeiner Deutscher Sprachverein, founded in 1885) was about fostering national exclusiveness, using a purified language as a symbolic representation of a 'fortress Germany' to which access was strictly limited. Both of these forms of 'language management' are manifestations of what Deborah Cameron (1995) calls 'verbal hygiene', a collective term for a wide range of social practices that have in common a refusal to 'leave language alone' and an insistence on the importance of intervening in the life of a language in order to 'regulate [it], control it, make it "better"' (9)—an idea that I shall return to at various points in this book.

The dominance of the chauvinist discourse of purity over the emancipatory discourse of purity is explicable only in terms of changes in the political climate and condition of Germany from the early years of the nineteenth century. What many felt as the exhilaration and liberating energy of the French Revolution was vitiated for others by the effects of the subsequent French occupation of German states. The idea of the German language as the repository or embodiment of the German *Volksgeist* (the soul or spirit of the nation) did not at this stage have sufficiently wide currency to represent a 'value beyond ambiguity and doubt' (see above), but since the publication in 1770 of Herder's *Abhandlung über den Ursprung der Sprache* it had been in the public domain and available to be seized upon by political polemicists and pressed into service as a cultural conceit and as the foundation on which a nationalist ideology could be constructed. The ideological mobilization of the German language as the *national* language—the mother-tongue of the fatherland—was theoretically driven but reinforced by practical campaigns advocating action. Friedrich Ludwig Jahn, for example, declares in general terms (but in the context of an essay on German): 'In seiner Muttersprache ehrt sich jedes Volk, in der Sprache Schatz ist die Urkunde seiner Bildungsgeschichte niedergelegt, hier waltet wie im Einzelnen das Sinnliche, Geistige, Sittliche' (Every people honours itself in its mother-tongue, the charter of its cultural history is set down in the treasure of its language, here as in each individual the material, the spiritual, and the moral prevail), and he goes on to warn of the dire consequences of neglecting this mother-tongue: 'Ein Volk, das seine eigene Sprache verlernt, giebt sein Stimmrecht in der Menschheit auf' (A people that forgets its own language forfeits its place in humanity) (Jahn 1806: XII, cited in Schiewe 1998: 155). In the year in which Napoleon created the Confederation of the Rhine, incorporating sixteen German states, and the Holy Roman Empire was formally abolished, the political message could not be clearer.

At the same time, Ahlzweig (1994: 132 ff.) shows how the use of German was promoted as a necessary patriotic act. In 1814, for example, Bernhard Joseph Docen called on all Germans to throw off the yoke of foreign (i.e. French) domination and grant the German language the veneration and sovereignty it should command—and to use it:

Mögen also die Teutschen Fürsten, der Adel und die ganze vornehmere Welt die Selbständigkeit und die naturgemäßen Rechte der heimischen Sprache endlich einmal völlig anerkennen, vorzüglich dadurch, daß es eine der ersten, gern erfüllten Pflichten Aller werde, in der früheren Erziehung schon der Jugend das zu gewähren, daß sie in der eigenen Sprache sich schön und edel auszudrücken wisse, damit sie eben durch die Bildung des Geistes und Herzens, die ihnen durch die liebevollste Lehrerin, die heimische Sprache geworden, all jene Achtung und Neigung gegen die empfinden, die auf dem bisherigen Wege Französischer Erzieher und Erzieherinnen frühzeitig unterdrückt wurde. (Docen 1814: 301)

So the German princes, the nobility and the whole of polite society should at long last grant full recognition to the autonomy and natural rights of the native language, especially by making it one of everyone's first and most willingly performed duties to enable young people in the earliest stage of their upbringing to know how to express themselves in a fine and noble manner in their own language, so that through the spiritual and emotional education that has become available to them through that most affectionate teacher their native language they experience all that respect and affection towards the language which until now has been suppressed very early by French teachers.

In the same year, Johann Christoph August Heyse published a German grammar, in which he declared that 'die blutig erkämpfte Befreyung Deutschlands' (the bloodily won liberation of Germany) justified the expectation that 'our language' should also regain its liberty and be used 'in der Kirche wie in der Schule, in den Gesellschaftskreisen wie in den Gerichts- und Geschäftsstuben etc.' (in church and in school, in social intercourse and in the law courts and places of business etc.). Beyond this impersonal expression of aspirations for the language, Heyse calls directly on his fellow Germans to contribute to the 'renaissance of their Germanness' by giving priority to their mother-tongue, since it is 'mit der Nation aufs innigste verschmolzen' (most profoundly fused with the nation):

Wohl uns, wenn wir alle, wenigstens jetzt in der ewig denkwürdigen Zeit der Wiedergeburt unserer Deutschheit anfangen, als ächte Deutsche unsere Muttersprache, als das schätzbarste Vermächtniß unserer Voreltern, zu achten, als das einzige unter allen politischen

Stürmen, die unser Vaterland schreckten, unauflöslich gebliebene Band, als den sichersten Hoffnungsgrund einer desto festern Wiedervereinigung und Genesung unserer durch das Schwerdt eines Barbaren blutig zerrissenen Völkerschaften, kurz, wenn wir sie als unseren Triumph betrachten, sie vor allen andern Sprachen ehren und immer gründlicher zu erlernen suchen! (Heyse 1814: 30–3)

As true Germans, we would all do well, in this eternally memorable time of the rebirth of our Germanness, to begin to respect our mother-tongue as the most valuable legacy of our forebears, as the only bond to have remained intact through all the political storms that have shaken our fatherland, as the most secure cause for hope of an all the more solid reunification and recovery of our peoples, who have been bloodily torn apart by a barbarian's sword; in short, to look upon it as our triumph, to honour it above all other languages, and to seek to learn it more and more thoroughly!

And Karl Wilhelm Kolbe (1804: XVIII) provides a bluntly dogmatic statement of the alternative: 'Wer die Muttersprache verschmäht, der verschmäht die geistigen Formen seiner Nation und kan keiner wahren Vaterlandsliebe empfänglich sein' (Whoever spurns his mother-tongue, spurns the spiritual forms of his nation and cannot be receptive to a true love of his country).

So what had been an instrument of personal and collective emancipation became in a relatively short space of time a putative symbol of national unity, the medium became the message: the German language, the mother-tongue, was the foundation on which the edifice of an 'actually existing' German nation had to be built. This ambitious mission was easier to proclaim than to accomplish, however, and the rhetoric of frustrated unity continued through the decades after the 'wars of liberation' (1813–15) in a kind of 'complaint tradition' (to borrow a term used by Milroy and Milroy 1999: 24 ff. in a rather different context). For example, in the second edition of his work *Über den Wortreichthum der deutschen und der französischen Sprache*, published in 1818, Kolbe reiterated the refrain that the mother-tongue was the voice of the nation's soul, and that language and literature were 'das einzige Band..., so die auseinander strebenden Gemüter noch zusammenhält, der einzige feste Punkt, an den Gemeinsin und Vaterlandsliebe sich noch anknüpfen lassen' (the only bond that still holds all the divergent spirits together, the only fixed point to which public spirit and patriotism can still be attached), but then complains:

Das scheinen weder unsere Staatsmänner, denen jedes Mittel die schlummernde Kraft der Nation zu wekken willkommen sein müste, noch unsere gelehrten, die Ausbreitung veredelnder geistesbildung bezwekken, zu wissen oder wissen zu wollen. (Kolbe 1818, cited in Dieckmann 1989*b*: 35–6)

Neither our statesmen, who should welcome every means of arousing the slumbering strength of the nation, nor our scholars, who aim to spread the ennobling education of the mind, seem to know this or to want to know it.

Yet thirty years later, on the threshold of the 1848 revolution, another writer was still bemoaning the lack of a 'Gesammtsprache der Gebildeten' (common language of educated people), which was 'ein Loch in unserer Sprachnationalität, dessen wir uns zu schämen haben; eine Lücke in unserer Nationalität überhaupt' (a gap in our national linguistic identity, that we should be ashamed of; a gap in our national identity full stop) (J.F. 1846, cited in Dieckmann 1989b: 214).

Nevertheless, this same period saw the development of an academic engagement with the language, which focused on its historical reconstruction and its aesthetic representation in the form of a national literature (Townson 1992: 91). The foundation at this time of the academic discipline of *Germanistik* (German Studies)—associated most frequently, but by no means exclusively, with the work of Wilhelm and especially Jacob Grimm—was a thoroughly political enterprise, aimed at giving substance to the concept of the Germans as a nation united by cultural traditions if not yet by citizenship in a unified state. In a speech to the conference of Germanists in Frankfurt in 1846, Jacob Grimm declared unequivocally:

Lassen Sie mich mit der einfachen frage anheben: Was ist ein volk? Und ebenso einfach antworten: ein volk ist der inbegriff von menschen, welche dieselbe sprache reden. Das ist für uns Deutsche die unschuldigste und zugleich stolzeste erklärung. (Grimm 1847: 11)

Let me begin with a simple question: what is a nation? And answer just as simply: a nation is the embodiment of people who speak the same language. For us Germans that is the most innocent and at the same time the proudest declaration.

For Grimm therefore the *questione della lingua* could not be more fundamental, and elsewhere in his writings he makes it clear that the identity of 'language' and 'people' is rooted not only in (current) practices but in the historicity of language itself: 'unsere sprache *ist* unsere geschichte' (our language *is* our history) (Grimm 1864: 285).

This conception of a nation's history being inscribed in its language was one of the most significant and far-reaching outcomes of the increasingly intertwined and interdependent debates on the German language and on the German nation in the first half of the nineteenth century. A sense of 'belonging to a common language and culture' first had to be generated before it could be exploited as an anchor for a people tossed in the social and political storms of the modern era, but the idea of the language as a legacy offered the prospect of roots in—a route to—a national past. The national language was therefore much more than a shared means of communication, an instrument of unification on a par with a common currency, a common system of weights and measures, or a common railway gauge. It was both a symbol of unity and a means of accessing and accumulating a body of myths from the past in order to sustain the invention, or imagination (Anderson 1991), of the nation. The cultural tradition, in this sense of the stories that we tell our children about our/their past, is literally '*tradiert*', handed down, through the principal collaborative achievement of the national language.

However, there is a further consequence of this view, which is particularly significant in the current context, and that is that the language is not only a conduit for the transmission of national stories across time but also the means by which our contemporary history is written. In other words, we make our own history in the present through the texts—written and spoken—that we produce. These two aspects of the role of (ideas about) language in German history—the diachronic and the synchronic—are crucial to an understanding of the contribution of debates on language to the ideological contestation of the right to speak for the 'German people' in the years following the Second World War, which is the subject of the next section.

2.2   Language, society, and politics

8 May 1945 is represented in German historiography and in the collective memory of Germans in many different ways—as a humiliating defeat, as the collapse of a régime, as liberation from tyranny. From the broader historical perspective we are adopting here, and from the position of the outsider, it can also be seen as the confirmation that another experiment at unifying 'the German people' had failed, leaving once again a political and cultural vacuum that was rapidly filled by external forces. The German Question, as it re-emerged at this time, had many facets, the most obvious of which for the occupying powers were of course political and security issues: how do you establish effective democratic structures and institutions in a country where democratic procedures and processes of participation had been systematically eliminated, how do you ensure that any potential for renewed aggression is reliably suppressed, how do you re-educate a population imbued with the destructive values of authoritarianism and national chauvinism so that it can play its part in the creation of a stable and peaceful international community, above all perhaps, how do you impose your ideology in order to establish and sustain this geopolitically crucial territory as a bulwark against your rivals for global influence?

For the Germans, this was—however else it was interpreted—another catastrophic moment of the kind Hroch refers to in his remark quoted in the previous section, and while for them too the reconstruction of the physical infrastructure and the establishment of new political, economic, and industrial systems were paramount, it should not be surprising that cultural questions also became increasingly drawn into the debates on the future of Germany. Cultural reconstruction in this context has both concrete manifestations—for example, the development of new media institutions, especially print media and radio (see Badenoch forthcoming), to create a new *Öffentlichkeit*—and intellectual and aesthetic ramifications—what should be the role and the proper concerns of German writers and dramatists, artists and film-makers?

Underlying all of these issues was the challenge of how to create something new and forward-looking while at the same time reconnecting with the highly problematic traditions of the national past. It should therefore also not be surprising that the *questione della lingua* resurfaced too, again in a different guise: the question now was not 'is there a common language around which we can unite?', but 'who owns the common language with which we may salvage our identity as a nation?'. In time, as we shall see, this question in turn gave way to different issues, and my aim in this section is to explore the relationship between the language question, as it evolved between 1945 and 1989, and changes in the political climate and in academic agendas.

This will entail examining how several interlocking sets of issues create the crucial question for the present context: *how*, and *to what extent*, do changes in the political climate *within* and *between* the two German states condition changes in the study of language in society and in the nature of the debates on east–west sociolinguistic disunity? The main focus will naturally be on the last issue—the consequences of changes in political relations between the GDR and the Federal Republic—but it cannot be isolated from the others, since however much some linguists may wish to conceive of language as a distinct phenomenon, the position I am representing here is that both language and society are inextricably rooted in the historical conditions in which they are produced or conducted. Understanding the significance of the language debates in this period therefore in turn involves taking account of the following issues:

- Despite its now iconic status in popular discourse, the 1989–90 *Wende* was not the only major turning point in east–west relations in Germany after 1945: other crucial moments include at least the formalization of the 'temporary' division through the establishment of the two states in 1949, the confirmation and consolidation of the division following the building of the Berlin Wall in 1961, and—above all—the partial normalization of relations between the Federal Republic and the GDR culminating in the signing of the Basic Treaty in 1973.
- At the same time, major changes were taking place within each state, especially in the late 1960s and early 1970s, as the post-war generation came of age in the Federal Republic, and the revitalization of the socialist project and the Honecker era began in the GDR.
- As the academic disciplines of linguistics and *Germanistik* sought to re-establish themselves in the two states, their purpose and rationale were contested in different ways, and even within the field of 'language in society' there were other topics beside 'language and nation' vying for attention. Here, too, the late 1960s and early 1970s represented a major turning point.

I shall concentrate here on the last of these issues, but the others will inevitably be drawn into the discussion.

For the first two decades after the war, the study of language in society was dominated in the Federal Republic by the venerable discipline of dialectology, but although language in this tradition had always been seen as a social artefact, the product of 'real speakers in the world' (the term *soziallinguistisch* was first used in 1903 by Ferdinand Wrede, one of the leading figures in early dialectology), the concepts of language and society were essentially discrete entities: society was conceptualized vaguely as the setting or milieu in which language occurred and as an assemblage of categories, only some of which could reliably be taken as sources of the real language of a particular geographical location (later to be immortalized by Chambers and Trudgill 1980/1998 as NORM—non-mobile, older, rural, male).

To this extent, while dialectology was an empirical[3] and descriptive discipline, dialectologists none the less shared the sense of purpose of seventeenth- and eighteenth-century prescriptive grammarians, to catalogue and thereby fix the forms of the language (in this case, always with reference to place). Where difference was identified, it was perceived not as variation within the linguistic repertoire of a stable community but as turbulence on the margins of the community (see Barbour and Stevenson 1990/1998: Chapter 3). While the internal linguistic homogeneity of even small, rural communities may always have been more an assumption than an empirical fact, this approach was clearly ill-suited to the analysis of a complex and dynamic social world in which lack of variation would be positively dysfunctional. The beginnings of a methodologically and analytically more sophisticated approach can be discerned in a number of studies conducted in the early to mid-1960s (see Barbour and Stevenson 1990/1998: Chapter 4), but this new urban dialectology—for all its greater openness to other disciplines such as sociology, social geography, and social psychology—did not develop as extensively as elsewhere (especially in the US and in the UK), not least because the social upheaval in the late 1960s created conditions in which a different, more radical kind of social linguistics forced itself onto the academic agenda and even into the public domain.

The crisis of democracy in the Federal Republic in the 1960s revolved around the contested legitimacy first of the 'new', consensus-oriented political establishment, fatally compromised in the eyes especially of the younger generation by its support (*inter alia*) for US imperialism in Vietnam and for the repressive dictatorial regime of the Shah of Iran, and secondly of the ossified structures and elitist traditions of higher education. At the same time, the electoral victory of the Social Democrats under Willy Brandt in 1969 came as a shock to the complacent conservatism of the Christian Democrats, who had to accept that they were no longer the 'natural party of government' and realized too late that their left-of-centre opponents had stolen a march on them in recognizing the power of discourse in the new media age (see Townson 1992: 192–204 for an excellent, concise analysis of the ensuing 'semantic battles' between political parties in the 1970s). In the midst of these highly charged debates on the direction of political change and the nature of social justice, a new language question emerged as a focus of both academic and public controversy in the Federal Republic: the question of language and social discrimination.

With the discipline of *Germanistik* in search of a new self-image (Schlieben-Lange 1991: 56), a student population frustrated and alienated from its studies, and

---

[3] Albeit only in the sense of being based on data collected from real speakers: most of this data was intuitive and gathered in the form of questionnaire responses rather than from observations of actual language use.

a society divided over educational principles, the ground was well prepared for the reception of a controversial theory that appeared to show how class-based differences in socialization led to different degrees of access to the dominant linguistic codes in the classroom and thus to different life chances. The British sociologist Basil Bernstein's theory of linguistic codes (1971a), characterized by different degrees of syntactic complexity and different patterns of discourse organization, was transformed in the German context into a debate on the disadvantaging of traditional dialect speakers in an educational system in which success was dependent on competence in standard German (for a critical analysis of the academic reception of Bernstein's theories in Germany, see Barbour and Stevenson 1990/1998: Chapter 6 and Barbour 2000c). From our perspective, the important point about this work was not its treatment of Bernstein's ideas so much as the fact that the code theory provided a concrete focus for the various aspects of the conflict in west German society: academic, social, and educational. In particular, it appeared to offer students a radical alternative to the conventional canon of 'philological studies' and a sense of purpose. Linguists were divided between those who continued to adhere to traditional areas of philology, and those who turned to (American) structuralism and either persevered with it or rejected its abstraction and its silence on questions of language behaviour in favour of a linguistics of everyday life.

Ultimately the euphoria and intense enthusiasm surrounding these debates gave way to renewed disillusion, when they failed to usher in a brave new world and the years of expansion in higher education were succeeded in the second half of the 1970s by a chillier climate of retrenchment and stagnation. Nevertheless, at the time many believed that new approaches to the study of language could spearhead a radical change in west German society. It was not merely a different way of looking at language, nor even simply one that offered a more adequate account of actual language use: early west German sociolinguistic studies were imbued with a sense of almost missionary zeal. Dieter Wunderlich, for example, argued:

Wenn man nach wissenschaftspraktischen Möglichkeiten der Soziolinguistik fragt, so liegen diese m.E. tatsächlich im Bereich der Sozialisation und der Bewußtmachung ihrer Voraussetzungen in Familie, Schule, usw., dann in der Klärung von Kommunikationskonflikten, Medieneinflüssen, Aktivierungen gesellschaftlicher Erfahrung, usw. Es soll sich hier nicht um Chancengleichheit handeln im Sinne einer bewußtseinslosen Anpassung, sondern im Gegenteil um einen Prozeß der öffentlichen Bewußtwerdung, Einschränkung der Manipulation und Diskrimination, Hinterfragung von Voraussetzungen, Vermeidung von Stereotypen, deutlichen Austragung von Konflikten. (Wunderlich 1971: 317–18)

As far as the practical possibilities of sociolinguistics as a discipline are concerned, in my opinion these lie in the area of socialization and in drawing attention to its preconditions in the family, the school etc., and then in clarifying communicative conflicts, media influences, the activation of social experience etc. It should not be a question of equality of opportunity in the sense of unthinking conformity, but rather on the contrary it should be about a process of awakening public consciousness, of restricting manipulation and dis-crimination, questioning assumptions, avoiding stereotypes, openly conducting conflicts.

In the same vein, in addition to commonly expressed hopes that sociolinguistics could offer both a socially valuable activity for linguists and concrete social benefits especially in the emancipation of the proletariat, Ulrich Ammon and Gerd Simon (1975: 10–15) also sought the development of a critical social aware-ness among the participants in the educational process: students, teachers, and schoolchildren.

In retrospect, the sweeping claims for the possibilities of sociolinguistics may seem over-optimistic, but these statements of purpose nevertheless have an importance in the longer term in that they represent an attempt at radicalizing the study of language in society in the west German context, introducing a decisive break with the past (Dittmar 1983: 22). Above all, the new emphasis on conflict was crucial in directing attention towards linguistic practices that construct and sustain social barriers—whether they be between standard and non-standard speakers, or native and non-native speakers, or men and women.

The major preoccupations in the study of language in society in the Federal Republic in the 1970s and 1980s were therefore predominantly internal concerns: in terms of motivation, the focus was on pragmatic questions (what can linguistics contribute to the analysis and understanding of contemporary social and political issues?), and in terms of methodology, on social interaction (with new theoretical emphases and the stress on empirical foundations, what methods can be devised to gather 'good data' on language use in concrete social settings and to analyse it in a productive way?).

The study of language in society in the GDR followed an independent path from that in the Federal Republic, although there were some similarities, and here too the late 1960s saw significant developments, occasioned, rather than directly determined, by changes in the political climate (see also Barbour 2000*b*). On the one hand, a number of major studies in social dialectology were published in the 1960s and early 1970s (for example, Rosenkranz and Spangenberg 1963, Schönfeld 1974*a*), re-establishing the link with the 'acceptable' tradition of studying social aspects of language use that pre-dated the fascist period. On the other hand, increasing emphasis was laid on the special role of constructing a progressive dis-cipline that would contribute to the development of a harmonious and integrated socialist society.

Various moments in GDR social and political history in the late 1960s and early 1970s have been identified as key events in relation to academic developments, but it is probably more realistic to think in terms of trends being given added impe-tus at particular times. Certainly, the restructuring of major research institutions around 1968 was associated with the articulation of research agendas—albeit in general terms—by the Politburo of the SED. Fix (2000*b*: 102) sees this as a deci-sive step in the 'ideologization of linguistics' in the GDR, citing programmatic statements such as Werner Neumann's declaration[4] that the task of linguistics was to convey 'die Überzeugung vom unaufhaltsamen Sieg des Sozialismus und vom unaufhaltsamen Untergang des Imperialismus' (the conviction of the unstoppable victory of socialism and the unstoppable demise of imperialism) (1973: 276; for a very different view on the impact of such statements, see for example Hartung 1991*b*). Whether these directives actually determined the conduct of linguistic research is debatable: it is certainly difficult to discern the impact of this on socio-linguistic studies. By contrast, the more anodyne formulation of the Politburo, that linguistics was to answer 'die Grundfragen der gesellschaftlichen Wirksamkeit der Sprache' (the fundamental questions of the social effectiveness of language) (see Fix 2000*b*: 102), suggests a very flexible framework, and the main thrust of theoretical and, admittedly to a lesser extent, empirical work in sociolinguistics in the 1970s and 1980s could be seen as a response to this general challenge. The principal strands of this work were the developing of stronger theoretical foundations to account for the role of language as a constituent of society, building a more solid empirical base for the description of sociolinguistic variation, and seeking means for the practical transfer of knowledge to serve the interests of the developing socialist society.

While west German linguists were influenced by work conducted in other western countries, sociolinguists in the GDR drew much of their inspiration and theoretical apparatus from the work of colleagues in the Soviet Union and other socialist states, especially Czechoslovakia. First, for example, sociolinguistic variation was described in terms of the Soviet model referred to in German as the *Gefüge der Existenzformen* (literally, 'structure, or framework, of varieties'), which embraced not only the *Literatursprache* (standard variety), *Umgangssprache* (colloquial speech forms), and *Dialekt*, but also 'social varieties' such as technical registers and other group-specific forms. This *Gefüge* was seen as a dynamic system that was in constant flux responding to changing social and political structures and communicative needs (Schönfeld 1985: 209–10). Secondly, the concept of *Tätigkeit* (activity) was adopted and developed as part of the theoretical basis for studying language use. The first task in this respect was to identify the means through which links between complex social processes and language were mediated, and this was possible only 'wenn die sprachliche Kommunikation als eine gesellschaftliche Tätigkeit verstanden wird, die in ein System übergeordneter Tätigkeiten eingeordnet ist' (if linguistic communication is understood as a social activity, which is embedded in a system of superordinate activities) (Schönfeld 1983: 214). It was on the basis of these concepts that one of the central notions of GDR sociolinguistics was developed: the *soziolinguistisches Differential*, which is an analytical framework based on the four key factors of code, speaker, interlocutor, and communicative situation, and which also incorporates regional,

---

[4] Neumann was a linguistic theorist at the Zentralinstitut für Sprachwissenschaft der Akademie der Wissenschaften in Berlin (GDR).

social, and functional variability (see Große and Neubert 1974*a*: 13–16 and Schönfeld 1983: 215).

Fundamental to this approach is the theoretical concept of the *Gesellschaftlichkeit der Sprache* (literally the 'socialness of language') (Hartung 1981*b*), according to which 'the linguistic' and 'the social' are not independent categories, nor do they merely co-vary in some kind of mechanical fashion, but rather they exist in a dialectical relationship. *Gesellschaftlichkeit der Sprache* is a property of language, which derives from the communicative activity of social subjects and therefore emphasizes the concrete historical conditions in which communication takes place (see also Fleischer 1987: 16–19, 27–9). The emphasis on communication derives directly from the ultimate purpose of GDR sociolinguistics, to identify speakers' 'communicative knowledge' in order to promote efficient social interaction, and one of the significant outcomes of this was a series of painstaking empirical studies of language use in the workplace (see, for example, Donath 1974, Donath *et al.* 1981, Herrmann-Winter 1977, 1979, Schönfeld 1974*a,b*, 1977, Schönfeld and Donath 1978).

In the course of the 1970s, this overriding objective was pursued under the programmatic label *Sprachkultur*. This concept had first been developed by the Prague School of linguists in the 1920s and 1930s, but was adopted in the GDR only at the time when cultural policy in the form of developing 'socialist personalities' (Hartung 1981*c*: 293, Fleischer 1987: 21) was given a higher profile. In the first half of the GDR's history, 'language cultivation' took the form first of eradicating 'fascist elements' in language use and then of promoting the *Literatursprache* (standard variety) as a universal means of communication that would ensure equal access to all important social processes. This represented a sharp volte-face in official attitudes towards the standard variety, which in the early years had been seen as a powerful weapon in maintaining the dominant social position of elites in bourgeois societies (Hartung 1981*c*: 298). However, it also entailed a rather simplistic and heavy-handed approach to the status and function of non-standard varieties. The development of concepts such as the *soziolinguistisches Differential* made it possible to conceive a more refined approach, that Große and Neubert (1974*a*: 16) for example refer to as a 'gesunde (healthy) Sprachkultur', taking a middle road between prescriptivism and linguistic laissez-faire.

In different ways and for different reasons, then, the study of language in society changed direction in both German states at around the same time, shifting away from preoccupations with formal and descriptive issues of regional variation in non-standard speech to functional and theoretical questions to do with the role of language in determining social relations. In the Federal Republic, this academic change was precipitated by internal tensions and conflicts both within west German society and in academic disciplines; in the GDR, it was motivated at least in part by an intensified political focus on harnessing intellectual endeavour more directly to the objective of achieving a socialist society. The east–west question therefore did not dominate the academic agenda in either state to the exclusion of all else, but at the same time it was the one significant question that was debated throughout the period from 1949 to 1989. How, then, did this language question develop over time, and how did its development relate to changes in the political climate and in approaches to the study of language? (For good overviews of this question, see Hellmann 1989*a* and Hess-Lüttich 1990; a very detailed account is given in Bauer 1993.)

During the most intense period of the Cold War, i.e. the 1950s and early 1960s, political positions were firmly staked out: neither German state recognized (the sovereignty of) the other, both officially propagated conflicting conceptions of the unity of the German people and laid claim to the cultural inheritance of the pre-fascist period. The emblematic function of the language was exercised even before then, however, and as early as October 1948 the prospect of a divided language was raised in the western press:

Sprechen wir in vier Zonen aufgeteilten Deutschen noch ein und dieselbe Sprache? Die Bewohner der Westzonen werden, was sie selbst angeht, diese Frage bejahen. Aber in der Sowjetzone sind heute Wörter und Redensarten im Gange, die wir in Westdeutschland nicht kennen und kaum verstehen. Um so mehr sind sie bezeichnend für den gegenwärtigen Lebensstil der Menschen im russisch besetzten Deutschland. (*Rheinische Post*, 27 October 1948, cited in Hahn 1995: 340)

Do we Germans, divided as we are into four zones, still speak the same language? The inhabitants of the western zones will answer this question in the affirmative, as far as they themselves are concerned. But in the Soviet zone words and expressions are being used that we in west Germany do not know and barely understand. They are all the more indicative of the present lifestyle of people in that part of Germany under Russian occupation.

In early eastern publications, such dire prognoses were typically rebutted as attempts to orchestrate permanent political division. Consider, for example, the preface to the fourteenth edition of the Duden orthographical dictionary published in Leipzig in 1951 (cited in Glück 1995: 191):

Die Feinde unseres Volkes aber, die seine Spaltung und damit seine Vernichtung erstreben, mögen wissen, daß keine Interessenpolitik der Imperialisten das feste Band zerreißen kann, das die Gemeinschaft unserer Sprache um die deutschen Menschen schlingt, die ihr Vaterland lieben.

But the enemies of our nation, who seek to divide and thereby destroy it, should take note that no imperialist policies can tear apart the strong bonds with which the community of our language holds together the German people who love their fatherland.

But once such a graphic conceit as a divided language—or two separate languages—is in circulation, it can readily be appropriated to serve different interests. From the early 1950s, academic writers and other commentators in both states (but especially in the Federal Republic) engaged in polemical tirades on the theme of language and national unity, with mutual allegations that the public language of the other state was infected by the discourse of fascism (see Stötzel 1995: 369–73) and being used to destabilize and threaten the unity of the nation. The violence of the rhetoric in many of these early contributions to the debate is strongly reminiscent of the nineteenth-century complaint tradition discussed in 2.1. August Köhler, for example, accused the SED of imposing a linguistic dictatorship and of violating east German citizens' linguistic human rights through enforced 'abuse' of their mother tongue:

Wir fordern für unsere deutsche Sprache Freigabe aus der politischen Zwangsjacke und für unsere deutschen Brüder und Schwestern das Recht, ihre Muttersprache so zu gebrauchen, wie es deren Wesen entspricht. Mehr verlangen wir nicht. Das aber müssen wir fordern, denn der freie, unverfälschte und mit der Wahrhaftigkeit vereinbarte Gebrauch der Muttersprache ist eines der ersten Naturrechte der menschlichen Seele. (Köhler 1954: 14)

We demand that our German language be released from its political straitjacket and that our German brothers and sisters have the right to use their mother-tongue in accordance with its nature. That is all we ask. But we must demand this, because the free, unadulterated, and truthful use of one's mother-tongue is one of the primary natural rights of the human soul.

Using a common military metaphor, he claims a deliberate campaign of linguistic corruption in the GDR and warns of an impending threat to the language:

Die deutsche Sprache in der Sowjetzone wird bewußt, planmäßig und zielsicher als politische Waffe angewandt und mißbraucht. Das ist eine Angelegenheit, die alle Menschen angeht, denen die Sprache ein hohes und edles Gut ist, das nicht verdorben, gefälscht und vergewaltigt werden darf. Das, was wir schon heute feststellen, beweisen und belegen können, ist zu ernst. Wahrscheinlich hat der deutschen Sprache noch nie eine größere Gefahr gedroht als gegenwärtig. (Köhler 1954: 5)

In the Soviet zone, the German language is being deliberately, systematically, and purposefully used and abused as a political weapon. This is a matter that concerns everyone for whom language is a great and noble possession, which must not be corrupted, falsified, and violated. What we can already see and demonstrate is too serious. The German language has probably never been threatened by a greater danger than it is today.

At the same time, a prominent language critic in the GDR, Viktor Klemperer, made a similar, if less intemperate, warning, explicitly linking the risk to national unity with what he calls 'linguistic dissonance':

Da nun die Einheit der deutschen Nation aufs schwerste gefährdet ist und da alles darauf ankommt, dass ihr geistiger Zusammenhang, ihr einander Verstehen unbedingt gewahrt bleibt, so bedeutet schon die leiseste sprachliche Dissonanz eine schwere Gefahr. (Klemperer 1954: 16)

Since the unity of the German nation is now in great jeopardy and since it is absolutely essential to safeguard its spiritual cohesion and its inner understanding, the slightest linguistic dissonance is a serious danger.

These expressions of anxiety about the threatened integrity of the German nation and 'its' language are relatively diffuse and unspecific, but not much later than this other west German writers explicitly articulated the claim that the SED was expressly pursuing a policy of linguistic division and alienation. For example:

Die sogenannte DDR erhebt den Anspruch, ein selbständiger deutscher Staat zu sein. Sie sondert sich immer stärker von der Bundesrepublik ab. Als letztes Band bleibt schließlich nur noch die Sprache. Da stehen wir vor einem sehr ernsten Problem: Gibt es noch eine gemeinsame Sprache, in der sich die Menschen diesseits und jenseits der zur Staatsgrenze gewordenen Zonengrenze verständigen können? Genauer formuliert: Welche Sonderentwicklung ist in der auf den sowjetischen Kommunismus ausgerichteten SED-Sprache im Gange? Welche sprachlich-geistige Entfremdung und Spaltung vollzieht sich auf deutschem Boden durch das östliche Machtstreben? (Gaudig 1958–9: 1008)

The so-called GDR claims to be an autonomous German state. It is separating itself more and more strongly from the Federal Republic. Language is all that is left as the one remaining tie. But we are faced with a very serious problem: is there still a common language which people on either side of the zone boundary, that has now become a state border, can use to communicate with each other? To be more precise: what separate development is the SED language undergoing, directed as it is towards Soviet communism? What linguistic-spiritual alienation and division is being carried out on German soil through the drive for power in the east?

However, Gaudig goes beyond the assertion of the perceived threat, identifying what he sees as the political responsibility of (west German) linguistics to combat it:

Das Problem hat eine politische und eine sprachwissenschaftliche Seite. Die Sprachwissenschaft hat ein eigenes Interesse an ihm, sie leistet mit ihrer Analyse aber zugleich einen sehr wichtigen Beitrag zum geistig-politischen Abwehrkampf. (Ibid.)

The problem has a political and a linguistic aspect. Linguistics has a specific interest in it, but with its analysis it also makes a very important contribution to spiritual and political defence.

Although not in direct response to Gaudig's call to arms, much of the west German work on the east–west language question, throughout the later Adenauer period (up to 1963) and until the publication of Walther Dieckmann's (1967) swingeing critique of this research, was conducted on the premise that what remained only vaguely specified as 'the German language' was becoming increasingly divided and that the western 'model' constituted the (traditional) norm, from which the eastern 'model' was diverging. The most influential representation of this approach was probably the collection of papers known as *Das Aueler Protokoll* (after the conference venue at which the papers were presented in 1962), which, according to the volume's editor Hugo Moser, were motivated by linguistic concerns. Yet in his introduction, Moser declares:

Wie die Sprache des Dritten Reichs, so sind auch die sprachlichen Veränderungen im Osten Deutschlands von der Ideologie her bestimmt. Wenn man nicht in extremer Weise die Sprachinhalte, *meaning*, von vornherein und grundsätzlich von der Sprache trennen und von der sprachwissenschaftlichen Betrachtung ausschließen will, muß man also auch von dieser Ideologie und damit dem politischen Charakter der sprachlichen Neuerungen reden. (Moser 1964: 12, cited in Bauer 1993: 54; italics in original)

As with the language of the Third Reich, the linguistic changes in the east of Germany are also ideologically determined. Unless one adopts the extreme position of strictly separating language content, meaning, from language and excluding it from linguistic analysis, one must then talk about this ideology and therefore about the political nature of the linguistic innovations.

As Dieckmann (1967: 139) points out, the argument pursued in the *Aueler Protokoll* (and in many other publications both earlier and later), that the supposed linguistic division of the German people was reinforcing the political division of the two states, conflicted with the official position of the government of the Federal Republic, which continued to stress the fundamental unity of the nation. However, the building of the Berlin Wall in 1961 and the subsequent consolidation of discrete political and economic systems in the two states made this official policy position seem increasingly unrealistic. For those west Germans who were ideologically opposed to the establishment of a socialist state in the east and committed to the principle of the indivisible bond of language and nation, therefore, the analysis of the German language in the GDR as deviant and corrupt was plausible and convenient, even though the evidence adduced in support of this thesis was highly questionable. By contrast, those east Germans for whom this period represented a confirmation of the status quo and a time of stabilization typically took a more dispassionate view, emphasizing the continued underlying unity of the language while acknowledging linguistic innovations in both states as inevitable, and specifically in the GDR as progressive signs of positive social change (Bauer 1993: 60–2, Hellmann 1989a: 305, Welke 1992: 4).

In his detailed critique of the *Sprachspaltung* (language division) thesis, Dieckmann (1967) systematically dismantles the methodologies and evidence used to support it. He identifies ten points of agreement amongst west German linguists and other commentators, then subjects them to close scrutiny and finds all of them wanting at least to some degree. His two most fundamental criticisms concern the ideological determination of key words in political vocabulary, and the relationship between words and their referents. First, then, the discovery that words such as *Freiheit* (freedom), *Demokratie* (democracy), or *Gleichheit* (equality) had acquired a particular meaning in the public discourse of the SED was taken by many western observers as evidence that the German language was being perverted in the GDR. Dieckmann argues that not only are such words necessarily ideologically determined (157), that they have no 'basic' meaning that is susceptible to 'distortion', but also it is illusory to suppose that they have a unitary meaning within any given society or speech community: *Freiheit* is as open to conflicting interpretations within the Federal Republic or the GDR as it is between the two communities.

Secondly, the introduction of new terminology to designate new social realities is not taken by the critics as an inevitable aspect of social change but as an attempt to subvert the language. Dieckmann (while not using these terms) rejects this analysis as a confusion between language and discourse. For example, he argues, you may oppose the collectivization of agriculture, but

die bloße Tatsache..., daß das herrschende Regime die deutsche Sprache benutzt, um die Organisationsformen dieser kollektivierten Landwirtschaft nun auch zu bezeichnen, hat nichts mit dem Polizeistaat zu tun....In dem Akt der Benennung selbst steckt...kein Polizeistaat und kein Totalitarismus, und die deutsche Sprache wird auch nicht kränker dadurch, daß sie jetzt einen kommunistischen Feinplan, einen Kooperationsbetrieb, eine Neubauernstelle u.a. bezeichnen muß. (152–3)

the mere fact that the ruling regime uses the German language to designate the organizational structures of this collectivized agriculture has nothing to do with the police state.... The act of naming does not in itself entail a police state or totalitarianism, and the German language is not becoming any more sick as a result of having to designate new concepts such as 'kommunistischer Feinplan' (detailed communist plan), 'Kooperationsbetrieb' (co-operative concern), 'Neubauernstelle' (redistributed land), and so on.

Furthermore, any impediment to understanding arises not as a result of linguistic change per se, but through ignorance of the social reality of which it is a part. This, too, applies just as much within one society as between the two, for the repertoire of any speech community includes specialized registers that are accessible only to a qualified minority of speakers. Many west Germans would probably find a memorandum from the Federal Ministry of Defence, for instance, as difficult to understand as official texts produced in the GDR, and 'vermutlich weiß ein Arzt in Leipzig mit *Arbeitsvorbereiter, Ingenieur-Ökonom, Bauperspektivplan* usw. genauso wenig anzufangen wie sein Kollege in Köln' (a doctor in Leipzig probably has no more idea what terms like *Arbeitsvorbereiter* [person responsible for setting work norms], *Ingenieur-Ökonom* [economist with additional technical training], *Bauperspektivplan* [strategic building plan] mean than his counterpart in Cologne) (162).

Dieckmann's withering attacks on the lack of rigour in earlier research made it impossible to sustain the position represented in it. However, the publication of his article came at a time when major political and social changes were taking place in the Federal Republic, which—as we have seen—had a radical impact on the whole agenda of linguistic research. With the collapse of political consensus in the late 1960s and the increasingly violent rejection of parliamentary politics by sections of the west German population, for many of whom the existence of two German states represented not an aberration but the normal condition of the German people, the focus of political tension shifted—as Townson (1992: 180) puts it—from external *Abgrenzung* (separation) of the two states to internal *Ausgrenzung* (exclusion) of particular elements of west German society (see above, and also Wengeler 1995). From the western perspective, this phase in the development of east–west relations is generally characterized by a move towards rapprochement, initiated during the Grand Coalition (1966–9) and then accelerated by the Social Democrat-dominated government under Willy Brandt.

Although this brought a greater intensity to German–German dialogue and resulted in a degree of mutual recognition and reduced tension between the two states, it fell short of an acknowledgement of the sovereignty of either state. On the one hand, the west German government continued to stress the unity of the German nation, on the other hand, the SED increasingly distanced itself from common ethnicity as a defining criterion of nationhood in favour of an ideological conception. Thus, while Brandt asserts in his state of the nation (*sic*) address in 1970:

25 Jahre nach der bedingungslosen Kapitulation des Hitler-Reiches bildet der Begriff der Nation das Band um das gespaltene Deutschland. Im Begriff der Nation sind geschichtliche Wirklichkeit und politischer Wille vereint. Nation umfaßt und bedeutet mehr als gemeinsame Sprache und Kultur, als Staat und Gesellschaftsordnung. Die Nation gründet sich auf das fortdauernde Zusammengehörigkeitsgefühl der Menschen eines Volkes. Niemand kann leugnen, daß es in diesem Sinne eine deutsche Nation gibt und geben wird, so weit wir vorauszudenken vermögen. Im übrigen: auch oder, wenn man so will, selbst die DDR bekennt sich in ihrer Verfassung als Teil dieser deutschen Nation.

Twenty-five years after the unconditional capitulation of the Hitler-Reich the concept of the nation forms a bond around the divided Germany. The concept of the nation unites historical reality and political will. Nation includes and means more than a common language and culture, more than state and social system. The nation is based on the continued sense of belonging felt by the members of a people. No one can deny that in this sense there is a German nation and that there will be one for as long as we can imagine. Furthermore: the GDR also—or, one might say, even the GDR—declares itself in its constitution to be a part of the German nation.

SED General Secretary Walter Ulbricht declares in the same year:

Die DDR ist der sozialistische deutsche Nationalstaat, in ihr vollzieht sich der Prozeß der Herausbildung einer sozialistischen Nation. Dafür sind bereits unwiderrufliche Tatsachen entstanden. Die BRD ist ein imperialistischer Staat der NATO und verkörpert den verbliebenen Teil der alten bürgerlichen deutschen Nation unter den Bedingungen des staatsmonopolistischen Herrschaftssystems. (Both passages cited in Bauer 1993: 73–4)

The GDR is the socialist German nation-state, in the GDR the process of constructing a socialist nation is being carried out. To this end irrevocable facts have already come about. The FRG is an imperialist NATO state and embodies the remnants of the old bourgeois German nation under the conditions of the system of state monopoly rule.

In his speech, Brandt concedes that 'Die Deutschen in ihrer Gesamtheit [sind] in unseren Jahren keine Staatsnation' (the Germans in their entirety are not at this time united within a single state) but insists on the political objective of 'die Bewahrung der Nation' (preserving the nation). In the GDR, 'the Germans in their entirety' were not ignored but they were marginalized in favour of the broader international community of socialist states.

   To reinforce this ideological move, the conceptual distinction was introduced in political discourse in the GDR between *Nationalität* (for common historical

markers of ethnicity, such as language, culture, and customs) and *Nation* (for polit-
ical and economic systems, conditions of production, and so forth) (Bauer 1993: 76,
Hellmann 1989: 311). In a speech at the thirteenth congress of the central commit-
tee of the SED in 1974, Ulbricht's successor Erich Honecker makes this distinction
clear: 'Unser sozialistischer Staat heißt Deutsche Demokratische Republik, weil ihre
Staatsbürger der Nationalität nach Deutsche sind.... Staatsbürgerschaft—DDR,
Nationalität—deutsch. So liegen die Dinge.' (Our socialist state is called the
German Democratic Republic because its citizens are Germans in terms of nation-
ality.... Citizenship—GDR, nationality—German. That's the way it is.) (*Neues
Deutschland*, 13 December 1974, cited in Schlosser 1990*a*/1999: 52)

The official west German position was therefore that there was one German
nation divided between two states, but the official east German position was that
there were two neighbouring nations (i.e. states) whose citizens shared a common
nationality (i.e. ethnicity). This policy of withdrawal from the historic mission of
reconstructing the German nation in favour of constructing a socialist nation is
enshrined in changes to the GDR constitution at this time (see Schlosser 1990*a*/
1999: 51). In the original version in 1949, Article 1, Paragraph 1 read: 'Deutschland ist
eine unteilbare demokratische Republik' (Germany is an indivisible democratic
republic). The first revision in 1968 changed this to: 'Die Deutsche Demokratische
Republik ist ein sozialistischer Staat deutscher Nation' (The German Democratic
Republic is a socialist state of the German nation; see Brandt's reference above), but
in 1974 the reference to the German nation is removed altogether: 'Die Deutsche
Demokratische Republik ist ein sozialistischer Staat der Arbeiter und Bauern' (The
German Democratic Republic is a socialist state of workers and peasants).

So while Dieckmann's assault on the inadequacy of previous research undoubtedly marked a watershed in the study of the east–west language question in the
Federal Republic, the shifting political conditions (both within the Federal
Republic and between the two states) also contributed to a changed context for
academic research and public debate. As a linguistic topos, *Sprachspaltung* had
been discredited, and politically it was either difficult or undesirable to sustain as
an expression or instrument of partition: difficult, since the increasing popular
perception of the established existence of the two states[5] did not appear to conflict
with public confidence in the fundamental unity of the language; undesirable,
since this might seem to provide support for the 'separatist' position of the SED.[6]

More pressing linguistic issues arising from domestic political tensions and the
normalization of relations between two maturing states therefore combined in

---

[5] To the extent that *deutsch* and *Deutschland* were frequently used in popular discourse with
specific reference to the Federal Republic; see Hellmann (1989*a*: 315), Polenz (1988: 204).

[6] Perhaps the most important recognition here is Dieckmann's argument (1967: 161–2, 1969: 69) that
any problems of understanding between east and west Germans were not in any sense a language
problem (nor a peculiarly east–west issue) but rather the result of inadequate knowledge of the respective social realities—an argument to be echoed and amplified, especially by east German linguists, in
the debates on sociolinguistic difference after the *Wende* over twenty years later (see, for example,
Lerchner 1992*b*: 314–15, and Part II of this book).

complex ways to draw the sting of the east–west language question in the Federal Republic, and much of the research in the 1970s and 1980s consists of more sober and more detailed descriptive analysis of lexical developments in corpora of written material.

East German linguists disagree on the extent to which the new agenda of sociolinguistic research in the GDR from the late 1960s was dictated 'from above', but internal issues relating to the new political focus on the development of the socialist nation clearly dominate from that time. However, since this new political direction involved disengaging from the debates on the representation of 'the German people', the language question of the 1950s and 1960s lost its relevance and therefore effectively became redundant. Much has been made of the histrionic rhetoric of Ulbricht's declaration in 1970 that

die einstige Gemeinsamkeit der Sprache ist in Auflösung begriffen. Zwischen der traditionellen deutschen Sprache Goethes, Schillers, Lessings, Marx' und Engels', die vom Humanismus erfüllt ist, und der vom Imperialismus verseuchten und von den kapitalistischen Monopolverlagen manipulierten Sprache in manchen Kreisen der westdeutschen Bundesrepublik besteht eine große Differenz. Sogar gleiche Worte haben oftmals nicht mehr die gleiche Bedeutung. (Ulbricht 1970, cited in Bauer 1993: 73)

the once common language is disintegrating. There is a great difference between the traditional German language of Goethe, Schiller, Lessing, Marx and Engels, which is imbued with humanism, and the language in some circles in the west German Federal Republic which is poisoned by imperialism and manipulated by the capitalist monopoly publishers. Even the same words often no longer have the same meaning.

But these remarks need to be seen in the context of the generally hostile public discourse of the SED in and around 1970, designed to mark the sharpest possible contrast between the two states during their negotiations over 'good neighbourly relations', rather than as the formulation of an 'isolationist language policy' (Polenz 1999: 428). More significant in terms of the relationship between political positions and research directions are Honecker's statements at the nineth congress of the central committee of the SED in 1973, arguing plainly that language alone can neither divide nor unite a nation:

Nicht Sprache und Kultur haben die Grenze zwischen der DDR und der BRD gezogen, sondern die unterschiedliche, ja gegensätzliche soziale Struktur der DDR und der BRD.... Gemeinsamkeiten in der Sprache können diese Realität nicht hinwegzaubern. (*Neues Deutschland*, 29 May 1973, cited in Fleischer 1987: 14; see also Dieckmann 1989*a*: 170–4)

The boundary between the GDR and the FRG has not been drawn by language and culture but by the different, indeed opposing social structures of the GDR and the FRG.... Common features in the language cannot dispel this reality.

Nevertheless, since exploring the relationship between the two constructs 'language' and 'society' had been identified as one of the key objectives of linguistic research (see above), it is only to be expected that the question of 'language and the nation' should be included in the programme. But that is not to say that an official policy on this issue was ever articulated, let alone promoted, as has sometimes been argued (see, for example, Hellmann 1989*b*, Dahl-Blumenberg 1987). The conduct of debates on this question within the GDR and the reception of them in the Federal Republic (where they were barely registered until the 1980s) are complex and fraught with contradictions and misconceptions. Most subsequent attention from outside the GDR (especially in the Federal Republic, but also among commentators in other eastern-bloc states) focused on the thesis proposed by Gotthard Lerchner (1974, 1976) and generally referred to as the *Vier-Varianten-These* (for detailed critical analyses see Bauer 1993: 75–93, Dieckmann 1989, Stevenson 1993). However, since this idea was not widely accepted by other east German linguists (see, for example, Hartung 1990: 452 and Fleischer 1983), who generally concentrated on developing ideas more consonant with the overall emphasis on the internal concerns of GDR society, the prominence achieved by Lerchner's thesis outside the GDR can be explained only in terms of its potential political impact.

This potential arises from the stark conclusion of Lerchner's argument: 'Wir haben es nunmehr mit vier nationalsprachlichen Varianten zu tun: dem Deutschen in der DDR, der BRD, in Österreich und in der Schweiz' (we now have four national language varieties: German in the GDR, in the FRG, in Austria, and in Switzerland) (Lerchner 1976: 11), and the characterization of these varieties as 'vier gleichberechtigte nationalsprachliche Varianten im Geltungsbereich von vier selbständigen Nationen' (four equally valid national language varieties in the areas governed by four autonomous nations) (Lerchner 1974: 265). Here, and in statements such as 'Die Wirklichkeit des sprachlichen Gebrauchs ist hier wie dort [i.e. in the GDR as in the Federal Republic] von der Realität gegensätzlicher Gesellschaftsordnungen bestimmt' (the reality of language use is determined in both countries by the reality of opposing social structures) (1976: 11), there appear to be clear echoes of Honecker's remarks quoted above. However, as Lerchner himself recognized when reflecting on this period after the *Wende*, the interpretation of his argument depended heavily on understandings of controversial and ambiguous concepts such as *Nation, Nationalsprache,* and *nationalsprachliche Variante* (Lerchner 1992*b*: 302–3; see also Bauer 1993: 82). The essence of the confusion that this gave rise to is whether the argument concerned formal differences in the standard variety of German in each state or differences in the use of, and relationships between, all the varieties within a 'diasystem' encompassing all linguistic forms that could be subsumed in the abstract concept 'the German language' (see Dieckmann 1989*a*: 167–9, Stevenson 1993: 344–5). In other words, is the thesis primarily a linguistic or a sociolinguistic one? Lerchner (1992*b*: 300) seeks to clarify this retrospectively, asserting explicitly that he had intended the latter, although he had more often been understood as proposing the former.[7] The explosive potential of an argument appearing to claim the existence of standard

---

[7] See also Lerchner (2000), where he revisits the issue once again.

varieties of German that were discrete, equally valid, and associated with separate and independent nations (or states!), lay for conservative west German linguists especially in the explicit challenge to the 'unifying bond' of the language,[8] to the hegemonic dominance of 'German German' (of which the Federal Republic remained 'the true guardian'), and of course to the unity of the nation itself.

Many east German linguists were never comfortable with the mechanical determinism implied by this reading of the situation (see, for example, Hartung 1990: 453), and argued that the whole issue was a distraction in the context of studying the development of the German language in the GDR in terms of the social and communicative needs of its users (*Sprachliche Kommunikation und Gesellschaft* 1976, Fleischer 1987: 19, 29 ff.). For them, the salient distinction was not the confrontation of east and west, but the relationship between *Sprachgemeinschaft* (language or speech community) and *Kommunikationsgemeinschaft* (communication community), with the emphasis on the latter. These concepts were, of course, not peculiar to the GDR tradition of sociolinguistics (see Hudson 1996: 24–30), but the particular conceptions developed in the 1970s and 1980s were central to the main enterprise of exploring 'die deutsche Sprache in der DDR' (the German language in the GDR). The following definition of *Sprachgemeinschaft* clearly derives from a long tradition which takes monolingualism as the norm and would therefore (as the author concedes) be limited in its applications: its members are people 'die eine Sprache (in der Regel) als Muttersprache sprechen und die sich (in der Regel) der ethnischen und/oder kulturellen bzw. historischen Zusammengehörigkeit, die in dieser muttersprachlichen Gebundenheit liegt, bewußt sind' (who as a rule speak one language as their mother-tongue and who as a rule are conscious of the sense of ethnic and/or cultural or historical belonging associated with this attachment to a mother-tongue) (Hartung 1981*a*: 14). However, the important point in the present context is that the definition rests not only on knowledge and habitual use of a shared language, but also on the consciousness of belonging to a historical tradition associated with the language. But in the context of the *Gesellschaftlichkeit der Sprache*, with its focus on communicative activity (see above), the emphasis on the language itself makes the *Sprachgemeinschaft* of secondary importance to the *Kommunikationsgemeinschaft*:

Der entscheidende Faktor ist die gesellschaftliche Praxis: Sie ist an kommunikative Beziehungen gebunden, deren Inhalte und Strukturen, deren Motive, Zielstellungen und Verlaufsweisen durch das gesellschaftliche Zusammenwirken und seine Konflikte bestimmt sind. (Fleischer 1987: 30)

The decisive factor is social practice: it is bound to communicative relations, whose contents and structures, motives and aims, and the ways in which they are conducted, are determined by social interaction and its conflicts.

[8] Lerchner (1974: 265) insists that his argument leaves no room 'für auch noch so geschickt manipulierende Versuche, ein angeblich immer noch "einigendes Band der deutschen Sprache" im Sinne des "Fortbestandes der deutschen Kulturnation" ... anzuführen' (for manipulative attempts, however skilfully done, to cite a supposedly still 'unifying bond of the German language' in the sense of the 'continued existence of the German cultural nation').

Kommunikationsgemeinschaften, 'soziale Gruppen mit geregelter und stabiler Kommunikation' (social groups with regulated and stable communication) (ibid.), therefore occupy the central place in this scheme of things as the social locations of communicative practices. Individuals typically belong to several such communities, which may be as small as the family or the school class and as large as the state. Furthermore, the emphasis on participation in specific communicative practices relating to common social conditions, rather than on knowledge of particular languages, provides a theoretical basis for postulating closer communicative relationships between speakers of different languages in the GDR and neighbouring socialist states than between east Germans and other members of the German *Sprachgemeinschaft*. The importance of this theoretical perspective for the analysis of actual social relations will play a significant role in Part II of this book.

If there was a dominant view in the GDR after 1970 on the relationship between German in the east and German in the west it was not the *Vier-Varianten-These*, but rather this:

Die Frage nach der deutschen Sprache in der DDR ist ... nicht prinzipiell einzuengen auf die drei, vier Jahrzehnte, die seit der offiziellen Gründung unserer Republik vergangen sind. Die Entwicklung der deutschen Sprache ist ein Element des Geschichtsprozesses, der schließlich zur Gründung des ersten sozialistischen deutschen Staates geführt hat.... Es gibt kein besonderes 'DDR-Deutsch', wie von manchen—vor allem von Gegnern unserer gesellschaftlichen Entwicklung—behauptet wird.... Allerdings existiert die deutsche Sprache in der DDR auch nicht unberührt von den spezifischen Verhältnissen und vor allem von den damit verbundenen Benennungs- und Kommunikationsbedürfnissen sowie den spezifischen Bedingungen sprachlich-kommunikativer Tätigkeit. (Fleischer 1987: 15, 29)

The question of the German language in the GDR cannot in principle be restricted to the three or four decades since the official founding of our republic. The development of the German language is an element of the historical process which ultimately led to the founding of the first socialist German state.... There is no special 'GDR-German', as some would claim—particularly opponents of our social development.... It is true though that the German language in the GDR has also not been unaffected by the specific circumstances and above all by the naming and communicative requirements associated with them and the specific conditions of linguistic-communicative activity.

Moreover, at least by the 1980s, most west German linguists shared this view of the parallel development of German in the two German states (see, for example, Hellmann 1989). It is therefore quite consistent with the converging perspectives of sociolinguists in both states that a consensus was reached at the latest by the mid-1980s on the basis of a 'plurizentrische Sprachkultur' (pluricentric language culture). The idea of German as a pluricentric language had been mooted by Heinz Kloss (1978), but its acceptance amongst west German linguists owed more to the outside influence of Michael Clyne (1995). The concept of pluricentricity, as it was then developed especially by Peter von Polenz (1987, 1988, 1990), removed the hierarchical emphasis of previous west German work (for example, Moser 1985) by adopting a more neutral and more abstract conception of 'variety' with no

implication that any variety had the status of a norm. The emphasis on the fundamental integrity of the language ('die deutsche Sprache als Kultureinheit' (the
German language as a cultural entity)—Polenz 1987: 64), coupled with the acceptance of independent variation arising from different historical conditions in different *Kulturgemeinschaften* (cultural communities) accords quite closely with the
perspective of Fleischer, Hartung, and others in the GDR. So, while not considering such a concept as necessary, Hartung (1990: 462–3) was able to say:

Man könnte also die in den vier Staaten verwendeten Arten des Deutschen durchaus als
Varietäten oder Varianten bezeichnen.... Nur sind diese Sprachformen sehr unterschiedlich entstanden, haben ein unterschiedliches Erscheinungsbild und werden unterschiedlich beurteilt. Eine begrifflich gleiche Behandlung könnte die Aufmerksamkeit davon
weg- und auf eine Parallelität hinlenken, die gar nicht existiert.... Das Plurizentrismus-
Konzept beinhaltet, daß von mehreren (staatlichen, kulturellen) Zentren Einflüsse auf die
in den jeweiligen Kommunikationsgemeinschaften verwendete deutsche Sprache ausgin-
gen und ausgehen, die aber gleichzeitig Beiträge zur Entwicklung und Ausprägung der einheitlichen deutschen Sprache sein konnten und sein können und die jedenfalls nicht als
Sonderungen oder Abweichungen von einer Norm zu begreifen sind, die durch eine der
staatlichen Kommunikationsgemeinschaften gesetzt wurde.

The forms of German used in the four states could therefore certainly be characterized as
varieties or variants.... But these language forms came about in very different ways, they
have a different appearance, and they are evaluated differently. Treating them conceptually
in the same way could distract attention away from this and suggest a parallelism that
does not actually exist.... The concept of pluricentricity means that the German language
used in the respective communication communities was and continues to be influenced by
several (state and cultural) centres, but at the same time these influences were and still are
able to contribute to the development and shaping of the unified German language, and
at any rate are not to be understood as deviations from a norm established by one of the
state-based communication communities.

In this section, I have tried to show the continuous—but continually shifting—
nature of the debates on language in the German context during the period from
1945 to 1989. In particular, I wanted to situate these various preoccupations with
language in the process of political and academic development within and
between the two German states. I shall conclude this chapter by moving in the
next section from debates about language to a discussion of the substance of linguistic and sociolinguistic difference between German in the GDR and German in
the Federal Republic.

2.3   Linguistic and sociolinguistic difference

The common conception of language as a reflection of an essentially non-linguistic
reality, and therefore of language change as contingent on social change, brings
with it the temptation to anticipate sudden and sweeping consequences for a language in the event of social upheaval. Taken to its extreme, this view encourages

an approach to linguistic historiography that is based on the segmentation of a language's history into discrete epochs and gives rise to apocalyptic pronouncements such as the 'death of the language of Goethe and Schiller' in 1933 or the myth of Germans' '*Sprachlosigkeit*'[9] after 1945. Stripped of their rhetorical flourish, such arguments are easily shown to have little substance and to be deployable only in the kinds of polemic discussed in the previous section. To a large extent, this is because they rest on a confusion between language form and language use, and between the totality of a language and one element of it (usually an area of its vocabulary).

So to seek an abrupt change in the language as a direct consequence of the end of the fascist period would be to assume the identity of an ideology and the language through which it is articulated. Furthermore, this would overlook the distinction between the 'technical register' (*Fachsprache*) of National Socialism—the elaborate but nevertheless restricted terminology required to name the structures and procedures of the state apparatus—and the less specific political and philosophical vocabulary which may be the source of fascist texts but is not their exclusive preserve, let alone the general lexicon of the *Alltagssprache* (language of everyday life) (see Townson 1992: Chapter 4). As Walther Dieckmann (1983: 90) observes drily, not only did the political caesura of 1945 not result in radical linguistic change, but 'die kranke, vergiftete, zersetzte, ja tote Sprache erwies sich als überraschend lebensfähig, die Sprachtrümmer als weiterhin handhabbar' (the sick, poisoned, decomposed language, the dead language even, turned out to be surprisingly capable of surviving, the linguistic debris was evidently still usable).

The search for a meaningful connection between social and linguistic change across watershed moments in political history therefore has to start from a less mechanical and more differentiated conception. It should be evident, for example, that the disappearance from texts after 1945 of words such as *Winterhilfswerk, Blockleiter,* and *Jungmädel*[10] is not evidence that 'the Germans' suddenly became anti-fascists, any more than the appearance of new words in itself heralded the emergence of a more humane society (Dieckmann 1983: 96): language should not be invested with properties—whether wickedness or humanity—that can be attributed only to its users. What is necessary here is an understanding of the relationship between language and social change that takes linguistic change not only as a symptom, but also as an integral element, of social change. Furthermore, such an approach should not postulate a direct connection between linguistic and social change but rather emphasize the mediating effect of changes in ways of interpreting, explaining, and evaluating the conditions in which language users as social subjects operate. The implications of such a view are that even following

[9] The German word *sprachlos* is ambiguous, meaning both 'speechless' and 'being without language': see Jackman (2000).

[10] *Winterhilfswerk* refers to an aid organization set up in 1933 by the Nationalsozialistische Volkswohlfahrt (National Socialist People's Welfare Association) to help the needy; a *Blockleiter* was a leader of a regional unit of the Nazi Party; and *Jungmädel* were 10–14 year-old girls in the Hitler Youth.

periods of social crisis linguistic change will be partial rather than systematic (some things will change while others will not), gradual rather than immediate (it will take time for new patterns of language use to become established), and it will affect some areas of communication and linguistic expression more than others (domains of use, such as politics or economics, sport reporting or class-room interaction), and therefore some groups of users more than others.

It follows from this that the parallel development of two societies after 1949 inevitably entailed linguistic change, but also that while some aspects of change were predictable (especially, for example, in domains relating to structures and processes of political organization), others were not. Furthermore, over time the respective linguistic inventories and repertoires of the two societies would show signs of change and lack of change in relation to their common origin, in other words, signs of discontinuity and of continuity. We therefore need to take account not only of difference but also of lack of difference.

On the one hand, then, the massive changes in patterns of social organization within the two German states between 1949 and 1989 were not matched by the extent of the changes in the language. Even after forty years, the standard varieties of German as used in the Federal Republic and the GDR remained virtually ident-ical at the levels of syntax, morphology, orthography, and phonology, and some-thing like 95 per cent of the lexicon remained common too. At the same time, since the communicative barrier between the two societies was far more perme-able than is often supposed, some linguistic trends were convergent rather than divergent: Bauer (1993: 137–9), for example, identifies common trends such as the increased preference for a nominal style in written and formal spoken texts (for instance, *etwas zur Durchführung bringen* versus *etwas durchführen* 'to carry some-thing out'), the construction of longer compound forms, the extensive use of abbreviations, changes in the use of the subjunctive, and the influence of English (admittedly stronger in the Federal Republic, but always more pervasive in the GDR than east German dictionaries would suggest).

On the other hand, where difference did emerge it was attributable to various causes. For instance, while there were obviously many linguistic innovations that were peculiar to one state or the other (if anything, probably more in the Federal Republic than in the GDR: see Polenz 1993: 142, Schlosser 1990a/1999: 196, and 4.1 below), the converse also applied: certain older forms were selected for retention within one speech community but not in the other—*Referendar* (not yet fully quali-fied civil servants, such as trainee teachers) in the Federal Republic, for example, or *Reichsbahn* (State Railways) in the GDR (see also Hess-Lüttich 1990: 119, Schlosser 1990a/1999: 35–7, 201). Furthermore, while many innovations resulted from the introduction and elaboration of separate and distinct social, political, and eco-nomic systems, the origins of these respective systems in the pre-war period and earlier are evident in the continued use of 'older' vocabulary, such as the termino-logy of capitalist economics in the west and of socialist ideology—largely deriving from the workers' movement in the nineteenth century—in the east.

The extent and the significance of linguistic difference in the context of the two German states between 1949 and 1989 are therefore difficult to assess. This problem is exacerbated by the fact that virtually all lexicological and lexicographic work published in this area focused on the specificities of German vocabulary in the GDR or on a contrastive approach that takes west German usage as the norm. Fleischer's *Wortschatz der deutschen Sprache in der DDR* (Vocabulary of the German Language in the GDR) (1987), for example, explicitly avoids a comparative approach, and while there are a number of dictionaries of language in the GDR (such as Kinne and Strube-Edelmann 1980, Ahrends 1986, 1989, Schröder and Fix 1997, Wolf 2000), they follow different principles of selection. Wolf (2000), for example, includes both 'official' and 'alternative' terms, but only those that were either peculiar to the GDR (such as *endversorgt*, 'provided with adequate accommodation') or used with a specific reference (such as *Freundschaft*, 'friendship', used in the GDR in the additional sense of a formal greeting between members of the FDJ, the youth wing of the SED). Schröder and Fix (1997), by contrast, attempt to characterize the general vocabulary of the average GDR citizen (including both GDR-typical words and words common to all German-speaking communities) and arrange them according to domain (work, education, travel, and so forth) and denotative properties (such as person, object, action, institution). Moreover, while the east German *Wörterbuch der deutschen Gegenwartssprache* (Dictionary of the Contemporary German Language) (1961–77) identifies over 1,000 words as 'west German innovations' (*Neuprägung BRD*), no west German dictionaries followed this practice and there were no dictionaries of vocabulary specific to the Federal Republic.[11]

Most of the comparative research that was conducted during the period up to 1989 followed quantitative and taxonomic approaches (see, for example Hellmann 1984), that have the advantage of providing some sense of the scope of lexical and semantic difference and its classification in terms of processes of innovation and change, but are not unproblematic. Various models of classification have been proposed, but lexical and semantic differences in the vocabulary of everyday public language can broadly be subsumed in three principal types: new words for new things; old words with different meanings; and different words with the same (or similar) meaning.[12] The most predictable linguistic development under conditions of structural social and political change is the introduction of new terms to designate new concepts, processes, and institutions. In some instances, the new terms may have more or less equivalent referents in each state (such as *Ministerrat*

---

[11] A new dictionary currently being prepared by Ulrich Ammon, Birte Kellermeier, and Michael Schloßmacher will for the first time identify words and usages that are specific to (regions of) Germany as well as those that are peculiar to Austria and German-speaking Switzerland (see *Sprachreport*, 2/2001: 13–17).

[12] Most of the examples here are taken from the following sources: Clyne (1995: 67–73), Glück (1995: 195–9), Bauer (1993: 139–142), Schlosser (1990a/1999: 13–16), Hess-Lüttich (1990: 118–21). See also Hellmann (2000).

and *Bundesregierung* for 'government' in the GDR and the Federal Republic respectively), but more often, as in the following relatively random list, both word and referent are specific to one speech community or the other:

GDR term	Federal Republic term
Erweiterte Oberschule	*Gesamtschule*
secondary school	comprehensive school
Elternaktiv	*Arbeitsmarkt*
parents' work group	job market
Kinderkombination	*Wirtschaftsgutachten*
combined crèche and nursery school	economic report
Kombinat	*Konzern*
combine	business, firm
Arbeiterveteran	*Azubi*
retired senior Party official	trainee, apprentice
Reisekader	*Alternativbewegung*
member of the (political, sporting, academic) elite permitted to travel abroad	alternative movement
Solibasar	*Instandbesetzung*
stall (in schools etc) raising money for humanitarian aid or in support of 'liberation movements' etc.	squatting (in an empty house)
Delikatladen	*Prolo*
shop selling expensive luxury goods, including western imports	prole, pleb

This category would also include consumer product and brand names, as well as fixed expressions relating to particular aspects of social organization, such as:

GDR term	Federal Republic term
Ökonomische Hauptaufgabe	*sozialer Wohnungsbau*
main economic task	social housing
vorfristige Planerfüllung	*konzertierte Aktion*
fulfilling work plan ahead of schedule	concerted action
friedliebende Völkergemeinschaft	*Wohlstandsgesellschaft*
peace-loving community of nations	affluent society

A second broad category contains words of older origin that continued to be used in both speech communities but with shifts in meaning:

GDR meaning	Shared term	Federal Republic meaning
	Brigade	
small group of people working together in a socialist enterprise		unit in the army

Aktivist

honorary title awarded for   member of citizens' action group
    good service

Neuerer

member of workforce responsible   innovator
    for proposing improvements to
    working methods etc

The third category is the converse of the second, with different words being used with the same or similar meaning:

GDR term	referent	Federal Republic term
Feierabendheim	retirement home	*Seniorenheim*
Kaufhalle	supermarket	*Supermarkt*
Kollektiv	(work) team	*Team*
Rekonstruktion	renovation	*Renovierung*
Feinfrostgemüse	frozen vegetables	*Tiefkühlgemüse*
Territorium	area, region	*Gebiet, Region*

However, there are a number of serious limitations to this quantitative approach. First, counting vocabulary is not as straightforward as the compilation of lists like those above might suggest. For example, should we count types or tokens (that is, the number of individual words or the number of times they occur)? We may identify 1,000 distinctive items but the significance of this discovery will surely depend on the frequency with which they are used, as well as on how far their usage is restricted to particular domains and groups of speakers. Secondly, it fails to take account of the fact that the sociolinguistic 'burden' of some words is substantially greater than that of others. The word pairs listed under the third category above, for instance, are more or less genuine synonyms and are neutral with respect to evaluative or affective content. However, word pairs such as those below that are often included under this heading may share the same denotative meaning, but they carry quite distinctive connotations and their use in texts therefore often imparts more secondary information than simply the origin of the speaker or writer.

GDR term	referent	Federal Republic term
Kaderakte	personnel file	*Personalakte*
Werktätige(r)	worker	*Arbeitnehmer*
Staatsgrenze West	Berlin Wall	*Mauer*
Menschenhandel	helping people to leave the GDR	*Fluchthilfe*
Republikflüchtige(r)	person leaving the GDR illegally	*Flüchtling*

For example, a *Kaderakte* might contain a considerable range of personal details that it would be inappropriate or even illegal to keep in a *Personalakte*, and while *Arbeitnehmer* would generally have been considered a neutral term for 'employee' in the Federal Republic, it was conceived in official GDR usage at least as an expression of the exploitation of workers under capitalist conditions (since the so-called 'employer', rather than the 'employee', was really the 'taker of labour'— the literal meaning of *Arbeitnehmer*, see Scherzberg 1972: 196–7). Moreover, the preferred term *Werktätige(r)* had a more comprehensive scope: 'Die DDR-Gesellschaft verstand sich weit mehr als die der Bundesrepublik durch Arbeit und Leistung definiert.... Insofern erfaßte der Begriff Werktätige(r) in der DDR auch faktisch fast die ganze Bevölkerung.' (GDR society defined itself far more than that of the Federal Republic in terms of work and achievement.... The concept of the *Werktätige(r)* in the GDR therefore encompassed virtually the entire population.) (Schlosser 1990*a*/1999: 70)

Thirdly, it attaches more weight to isolated words than to the texts in which they occur and the speech events they help to construct. On the one hand, by concentrating on a particular domain (such as 'looking for accommodation': see Hellmann 1991), it is possible to reveal the often considerable density of vocabulary specific to one speech community, which at least potentially constituted an impediment to mutual understanding between east and west Germans, especially in terms of processing written texts. On the other hand, the quantity of lexical differences within a given inventory is not necessarily the most significant predictor of communicative success or failure, since speakers with a common language have other resources at their disposal to 'manage' communication (see 4.2). Furthermore, the frequent use of words with different connotations in each speech community is significant only to the extent that these connotations are available to the recipients of the texts in which they are used. For example, a fundamental contrast between the dominant ideologies in the two societies was the focus on individualism in the Federal Republic and on collectivism in the GDR, and these contradictory values generated the negative connotations of words such as *individualistisch* (individualistic), *spontan* (spontaneous), or *subjektiv* (subjective) in east German texts intended for public consumption. Similarly, the emphasis on personal responsibility in the Federal Republic created a different perspective on social issues: Hopfer (1996), for instance, argues that reducing unemployment, resolving military conflicts, or preventing environmental disasters would typically be conceptualized in west German contexts as a *Herausforderung* (challenge) rather than—as in east German contexts—a *Pflicht* (duty) or *Aufgabe* (task).

The quantitative, descriptive approach to lexical developments therefore does contribute to an understanding of language change as a constituent of social change, but even the most detailed and refined taxonomy of linguistic difference is not sufficient for the purpose of understanding the function of language in constructing social difference and the experience of social change through changes in language use. Individual words can play a part in such processes, but (as we shall see especially in Chapter 3) only to the extent that they are embedded in particular discursive contexts. The difference between *Kaufhalle* and *Supermarkt*, for instance, is ultimately no more than a regional contrast, comparable to north–south distinctions such as *Schlachter* versus *Metzger* (butcher). But even words with potential sociolinguistic impact, such as *fortschrittlich* (progressive) or *schöpferisch* (creative), depend on their use in specific contexts for the realization of this potential: there is nothing inherently different about such words in the east German and west German lexicons.

In the discursive context that we are concerned with here—the debates on unity and disunity in Germany after 1945—one of the most potent linguistic devices in the arsenal of political and ideological opponents was the symbolism of naming practices. The thoroughness with which east German streets, schools, and other public institutions, even towns and cities, were renamed after 1990 demonstrates the perception that names designated by the GDR authorities were invested with an ideological force which had to be expunged in order to eradicate any lingering vestige of an undesirable past (see Schreiber 1994, Sommerfeldt 1992*a,b*, 1994, Kühn 1993, 1996, 1999). Naming is therefore an act of power, a means of asserting and exercising control, as Tony Crowley (1996: 196) argues, referring to Brian Friel's play *Translations*, in which a British Army officer, charged with implementing the systematic translation of Irish topographical names into English in the 1830s, declares: 'It is not the literal past, the *facts* of history, that shapes us, but the images of the past embodied in language'.

The names of the two German states, and the various ways in which they were referred to in official contexts and in the media, show more clearly than any other feature of the vocabulary how 'images of the past' were 'embodied in the language', and how respective practices of naming self and other helped to shape relations between east and west.[13] Of the two main proposals for the name of the state that was to unify the western *Länder, Bundesrepublik Deutschland* had finally been preferred to *Bund deutscher Länder*, since the explicit reference to *Deutschland* was a declaration of commitment to the unity of the German nation. When it was formally brought into being five months after the Federal Republic, in October 1949, the GDR proclaimed its credentials as the legitimate representation of the German people—indeed, of Germany—in Article 1 of its constitution: 'Deutschland ist eine unteilbare, demokratische Republik' (Germany is an indivisible democratic republic). Since there had never been (and there still has never been) a state with the official title 'Germany', this claim was clearly an attempt to wrest back from the fledgling Federal Republic the right to the German heritage. The battle over 'Germany' was therefore ignited by the word *Deutschland,* as the vehement opposition of (amongst others) a KPD member of the Parliamentary Council in Bonn makes clear in a speech anticipating in its phrasing the founding of the GDR:

Ich bin der Auffassung, daß der Parlamentarische Rat kein Recht hat, dieses Westdeutschland oder Restdeutschland schlechthin als Deutschland zu bezeichnen. Ich möchte mich an dieser

---

[13] For detailed discussion and documentary illustrations of the complex question of naming Germany, see Berschin (1979), Glück (1992), Hermanns (1995, 1996), Heß and Ramge (1991), Latsch (1994), Röding-Lange (1997).

Stelle nicht weiter über die rechtlichen und politischen Hintergründe auslassen, die den Parlamentarischen Rat in Funktion gebracht haben, sondern nur zum Ausdruck bringen, daß mit dieser Bildung des westdeutschen Staates zerschlagen wird, was jeder wirklich deutsch fühlende Mensch verlangen muß: daß Deutschland als eine unteilbare und demokratische Republik in seiner Gänze erhalten bleibt. (Cited in Falkenberg 1989: 20)

In my opinion, the Parliamentary Council has no right to designate this west Germany or 'residual Germany' as simply Germany. I don't want to go on any further here about the legal and political background to the setting up of the Parliamentary Council; I want to make the point that establishing this west German state will destroy what everyone who really feels himself to be German must demand: that Germany should remain in its entirety an indivisible and democratic republic.

In the GDR, until the policy shift of the late 1960s (see 2.2) which led to the marginalizing of the Germanness issue there, the Federal Republic was referred to in public texts variously as *Westdeutschland, westdeutsche Bundesrepublik,* or (later) *BRD.* The official position of the government of the Federal Republic, however, remained (and still does today) that the only acceptable names for the Federal Republic were either the full constitutional title *Bundesrepublik Deutschland* or, if the context made the full title 'unnecessary' (a not uncontentious specification— see 2.2), simply *Deutschland*: according to guidelines laid down in 1965, neither the abbreviation *BRD* nor the short form *Bundesrepublik* on its own should be used. The Federal Republic's policy on the representation of the German people was formulated unambiguously by its first Chancellor, Konrad Adenauer, in October 1949 in response to the founding of the GDR: 'Die Bundesrepublik Deutschland ist ... bis zur Erreichung der deutschen Einheit insgesamt die alleinige legitimierte staatliche Organisation des deutschen Volkes' (Until complete German unity has been achieved, the Federal Republic of Germany is the only legitimate state organization of the German people) (cited in Hahn 1995: 297).

This declaration of the Federal Republic's 'Alleinvertretungsrecht' (sole right of representation; rejected by the GDR government as 'Alleinvertretungsanmaßung'— presumption of sole right of representation) was the basis for the foreign policy since known as the Hallstein doctrine,[14] according to which not only was the GDR not recognized as a sovereign state but diplomatic relations would be severed with any other state (apart from the Soviet Union) which did recognize the GDR. The popular linguistic expression of this doctrine was a plethora of alternative names: *Ostzone* (eastern zone), *Sowjetzone* (Soviet zone), *sowjetische Besatzungszone* (Soviet zone of occupation), *Mitteldeutschland* (central Germany), *Ostdeutschland* (East Germany), '*DDR*' ('GDR'), *sogenannte DDR* (so-called GDR). Not all of these were officially sanctioned, however, since the implications of certain terms were held to conflict with the government policy on the 'recovery' of the territories to the east of the Oder and Neiße rivers, which had formed the western

---

[14] After Walter Hallstein, Minister of State in the Ministry of Foreign Affairs in the 1950s (see Parkes 1997: 127–8).

border of Poland since 1945.[15] The 1958 edition of the handbook of the west German Ministry for all-German Affairs *SBZ von A bis Z* (Soviet Occupation Zone from A to Z), for example, disapproved of the common term *Ostzone*:

Die viel gebrauchte Bezeichnung 'Ostzone' für die SBZ ist irreführend. Die SBZ hat als 'Mittelzone' zu gelten, da sie mitten zwischen der Bundesrepublik und den zur Zeit von Polen und der SU verwalteten deutschen Ostgebieten liegt. (Cited in Hahn 1995: 293)

The frequently used term 'eastern zone' for the Soviet Occupation Zone is misleading. The Soviet Occupation Zone is to be considered as the 'central/middle zone', since it lies between the Federal Republic and the German eastern territories, which are currently administered by Poland and the Soviet Union.

and as late as 1965 official guidelines stipulated:

Das 1945 von der Sowjetunion besetzte Gebiet Deutschlands westlich der Oder-Neiße-Linie mit Ausnahme Berlins wird im politischen Sprachgebrauch als *Sowjetische Besatzungszone Deutschlands*, abgekürzt als *SBZ*, in Kurzform auch als *Sowjetzone* bezeichnet. Es ist nichts dagegen einzuwenden, daß auch die Bezeichnung *Mitteldeutschland* verwendet wird. (From *Gemeinsames Ministerialblatt* 1965: 227, cited in Townson 1992: 191, 208)

The area of Germany that was occupied by the Soviet Union in 1945 and which lies to the west of the Oder-Neiße line, with the exception of Berlin, is referred to in political usage as the Soviet Occupation Zone of Germany (abbreviated in German as SBZ), or with the shorter form Soviet Zone. There is no objection to the use of the alternative form Central Germany.

Despite the gradual easing of tensions in the mid- to late 1960s, conservative west German politicians continued to have difficulty in finding a comfortable way of referring to the GDR without compromising their opposition in principle to its existence. On taking office in 1966 Chancellor Kurt Georg Kiesinger, for example, declared the Grand Coalition government's policy of rapprochement with the GDR but without using its name:

Wir wollen entkrampfen und nicht verhärten, Gräben überwinden und nicht vertiefen. Deshalb wollen wir die menschlichen, wirtschaftlichen und geistigen Beziehungen mit unseren Landsleuten im anderen Teil Deutschlands mit allen Kräften fördern. (Inaugural speech 1 December 1966, cited in Hahn 1995: 303)

We want to relax conditions, not harden them, to overcome the gulf between us, not deepen it. We therefore want to do everything in our power to promote human, economic, and spiritual relations with our compatriots in the other part of Germany.

In another speech a year later he again avoided naming the state but conceded:

daß sich da drüben etwas gebildet hat, ein Phänomen, mit dessen Vertretern ich in einen Briefwechsel eingetreten bin, ein Phänomen, mit dem wir bereit sind,... Kontakte aufzunehmen, Vereinbarungen zu treffen. (ibid: 304)

---

[15] The disputed status of this border, which was a major stumbling block in negotiations on German unification in 1990, was also articulated in competing names: for east German and Polish politicians it was the *Oder–Neiße-Grenze* (border), but many west German politicians and newspapers acknowledged it only as the (temporary) *Oder–Neiße-Linie* (line) (see Hahn 1995: 288–90, Stötzel 1991: 3–4).

that something has emerged over there, a phenomenon with whose representatives I have entered into correspondence, a phenomenon with which we are willing to establish contact, to make agreements.

The partial recognition of the GDR accorded by the signing of the Basic Treaty between the two states in 1972 made the use of the abbreviated form *DDR* more generally acceptable, although the newspapers published by the right-wing Springer concern continued to concede it no more than a virtual reality by consistently printing the name in scare quotes ('*DDR*'), ironically electing to drop them only in August 1989, just weeks before the onset of the *Wende*:

Geschichte bewegt sich so langsam, daß wir es kaum bemerken. Zur Zeit bewegt sich Geschichte aber so rasant, daß manchem der Atem stockt.... Zu den Wandlungen der Zeit gehört auch, daß die Supermächte, wenn auch langsam, aufeinander zugehen. Angesichts dieser Veränderungen hat sich die Redaktion in Übereinstimmung mit Aufsichtsrat und Vorstand der AXEL SPRINGER VERLAG AG entschlossen, DDR ohne Anführungszeichen zu schreiben.... Wir ändern unsere Schreibweise. Wir ändern nicht unsere Überzeugung. (*Bild-Zeitung*, 2 August 1989, cited in Glück 1992: 144)

History moves so slowly that we scarcely notice it. At the moment, however, history is moving breathtakingly fast.... One of the changes going on is that the superpowers are getting closer to each other, albeit slowly. In the light of these changes, the editorial staff—in agreement with the supervisory board and the board of directors of Axel Springer Publishers—has decided to write DDR without quotation marks.... We are changing the way we write. We are not changing our beliefs.

However, while west German use of *DDR* expressed a degree of normality in western relations towards the GDR in the early 1970s, the increased use of *BRD* for the Federal Republic by official east German bodies around the same time created a renewed source of friction with conservative sections of the west German population (see Hellmann 1997c). Before the 1965 guidelines were issued (see above), the abbreviated form *BRD* had been quite commonly used even by official sources in the Federal Republic and did not appear to be controversial until it became identified with official GDR discourse. So although the name *BRD* had been coined in the west, and had not been used in the GDR until about 1969, it came to be perceived by the right in the Federal Republic as a subversive instrument of the SED's policy of denial in relation to German unity. It was argued first that the parallel use of the two abbreviated forms *DDR* and *BRD* invested the two entities with a spurious equivalence as two equally legitimate states, and secondly that the invisibility of *Deutschland* detracted from and undermined the unifying national character of the west German state. Following considerable public debate, new guidelines were agreed at national and regional level in the Federal Republic, reiterating the requirement to use the full title in all official contexts, and the use of *BRD* was prohibited in schoolbooks. It nevertheless proved difficult to suppress and the controversy continued throughout the 1970s. The state government of

Lower Saxony, for example, felt compelled to issue a further banning order in 1978 because the abbreviation

die geschichtliche Identität der Deutschen nicht mehr erkennbar werden läßt mit der Folge, daß die Wörter 'Deutschland' und 'deutsch' zunehmend aus dem politischen Bewußtsein unserer Schüler und Jugendlichen sowie des In- und Auslands verdrängt werden. Diese abträgliche Abkürzung schadet dem deutschen Anliegen. (Cited in Glück and Sauer 1997: 16–17)

conceals the historical identity of the Germans, with the result that the words 'Germany' and 'German' are increasingly being pushed out of the consciousness of our schoolchildren and young people and more generally both here and abroad. This harmful abbreviation is damaging German interests.

'Images of the past' were embodied not only in the naming of the two states but also in terms used to refer to the potential unification of 'the German people' and to the processes through which this might be achieved. Since the official position in each state during the height of the Cold War was that the other state was responsible for dividing the German nation, the objective on both sides was to achieve (on their own terms, of course) the 'reunification' (*Wiedervereinigung*) of the German people. However, while this remained the position in the Federal Republic until 1990, the concept became problematic and then unacceptable in the GDR. Reunification implied the return to a previous condition, but this was a contentious proposition because it was not clear what condition was to be restored. The German nation could scarcely have been considered to be 'unified' between 1945 and 1949, so the alternative could only be the condition that had obtained until the annexation of Austria in 1938. However, this would have included precisely the populations of those territories in the east that since 1945 had belonged to Poland and the Soviet Union. The implication of revanchism meant that the prefix re- (*Wieder-*) became a shibboleth in the discourses of the German question: *Vereinigung* became the preferred term in the GDR until the objective, and therefore any designation for it, was abandoned in the late 1960s. This also explains the extreme sensitivity towards the terms during the *Wende* in 1989–90. While Chancellor Helmut Kohl insisted from the outset, in November 1989, on the aim of achieving *Wiedervereinigung*, his opposite number in the GDR, Prime Minister Hans Modrow, declared in December:

Unsere Verbündeten sagen ebenso wie meine Regierung, daß eine Vereinigung der beiden deutschen Staaten zu einem Staat nicht auf der Tagesordnung steht. Und von einer Wiedervereinigung sollte man richtigerweise überhaupt nicht reden, weil das Wort wieder [*sic*] ein Anachronismus ist und berechtigte Bedenken, ja Ängste vor großdeutschem Chauvinismus weckt. (From *Neues Deutschland*, 9/10 December 1989, cited in Teichmann-Nadiraschwili 1993: 60)

Both our allies and my government say that a unification of the two German states in a single state is not on the agenda. And strictly speaking there should be no talk of a reunification, because the word 're-' is an anachronism and arouses concerns and fears of chauvinistic German expansionism.

However, within weeks this position had to be abandoned under pressure from Soviet leader Mikhail Gorbachev, and as the east German resistance to unification gave way, *Wiedervereinigung* was gradually displaced in west German rhetoric by more emollient terms such as *Zusammenwachsen* (growing together) and *neue Gemeinsamkeit* (new community of interest) (ibid.: 68).

At the same time, different designations for the formal procedure by which unification was to be achieved continued to articulate the profound tensions in the population. The constitutional position in the Federal Republic had been set out in the 1949 Basic Law. According to Article 23, the Law was to apply 'for the time being' (*zunächst*) in those *Länder* which made up the Federal Republic, but this was a provisional arrangement that left open the possibility of extending the validity of the Law to 'other parts of Germany': 'In anderen Teilen Deutschlands ist es nach deren Beitritt in Kraft zu setzen' (In other parts of Germany it [i.e. the Basic Law] shall be put into force on their accession—official translation). However, while this provided a neat and simple mechanism for bringing unification about, it ascribed the status of supplicant to the GDR population, since it entailed not the launching of a new state but the enlargement of an existing one, once the constituent elements of the GDR had expressed their willingness to join the Federal Republic. Opposition to this procedure therefore found expression in alternative terms to *Beitritt* (accession), such as *Einverleibung, Vereinnahmung,* and even *Anschluß*, drawing an analogy with the enforced annexation of Austria in 1938 (for a linguistic analysis of the relationship between these terms, see Herberg 1997). Moreover, the fact of unification was not sufficient either to allay these fears or to achieve a sense of unity, and competing discourses of German–German relations continued after 1990 to be marked by different ways of referring to the 'older' and the 'newer' parts of the Federal Republic (see Hahn 1995: 333–8, Glück and Sauer 1997: 10–11).

The distinction I have tried to establish in this section between linguistic and sociolinguistic difference—between simple lexical contrasts and discursive oppositions—is fundamental to an understanding of the significance of the language question in the developing relationship between the two German states and their respective 'communication communities' (see 2.2). Throughout this chapter, I have focused on the competing interests of the two states in relation to the problematic ideas of 'the German people' and 'the German nation' and on the inextricable links between these political issues and the uses of language. In the next chapter, I want to explore the implications of this particular kind of relationship between language and politics—between 'doing language' and 'doing politics'—for answering the questions of how the GDR was built and how it was demolished, ostensibly creating the conditions for the formation of a 'unified' speech community in Germany.

Building and Unbuilding the GDR

3.1 The Byzantine architecture of official discourse

While state power can be exercised through force—as in the suppression of the workers' uprising in the GDR in June 1953 or of the demonstrations in the Federal Republic against the Vietnam war in 1967—even most totalitarian regimes recognize that it is more effective in the long run to secure and sustain control through engineering the compliance of the population rather than through coercion. The knowledge that the state has the potential to resort to violent means is of course an important factor in achieving this aim—the iron fist in the velvet glove—and no one in the GDR, for example, would have been left in any doubt about the intended implications of the SED's declaration of support for the Chinese communist party in its brutal crushing of the 'counter-revolutionary revolt' in Tiananmen Square in Beijing in June 1989 (Pätzold 1992: 105–6). However, by then the guarantee of military support for the SED from the Soviet Union had been withdrawn and the increasingly dissatisfied and disenchanted population of the GDR was beginning to articulate the conflicting views that had been successfully marginalized and contained for the previous forty years. Until then, the Party had largely succeeded, as Ralph Jessen (1997) puts it, in sustaining power and control as a 'communicative practice'.

The success of this approach to the exercise of authority through the achievement of hegemony—the way in which people collude in their own oppression—depended on a number of connected processes. First, a highly codified register was developed for the formulation and expression of Party policy, a form of language that was quite distinct from the conventional political *Fachsprache* (technical terminology or jargon). Secondly, this means of articulating political ideas and objectives was disseminated—together with the ideas and objectives—through other domains outside the narrow sphere of government, such as education, the media, and the workplace (see 3.3). Thirdly, its use in official and semi-official texts within these domains became virtually obligatory: 'Mehr oder weniger streng wurden die kommunikativen Normen...einer zwar nicht dekretierten, aber praktizierten offiziellen Sprache der DDR befolgt oder nachgeahmt' (The communicative norms of what was *de facto*, if not *de jure*, an official language of the GDR were more or less strictly observed or imitated) (Schmidt 2000: 2023). Finally, as a complementary measure to these steps, all possible alternative forms of expression relating to political issues were suppressed or contained within the specified confines of a particular domain, such as the Church; the only real exceptions were cultural events and publications—such as carnival (Marr 1998), the political satire of *Kabarett* (McNally 2000) or *Eulenspiegel* magazine, or television programmes such as *Prisma*, dealing with criticisms of social conditions and consumer complaints (see 3.3)—which were tolerated in small doses as a means of 'inoculating' audiences against more general 'infection' through subversive influences. These measures together ensured that participation in any kind of public communicative activity was regulated by the constraints of the official discourse (see again Kress's definition of discourse in Chapter 1); the furtive publication of *samizdat* journals such as *Grenzfall* (see Theobald 2000) testifies to the exclusion of alternative discourses from the public sphere. *Öffentlichkeit* in the GDR was therefore not an open space for debates on issues of public concern, but stage-managed and constructed within the discursive frame designed by the Party.

The language in which the official discourse was couched was not new in the sense of consisting of new vocabulary or grammar. It was fashioned to a large extent out of the existing resources of the standard language, so that it was not the components that were distinctive but the particular ways in which they were used in the construction of texts. The product of this process is often referred to as *langue de bois*, a term used by French discourse analysts and more widely in the French media since the early 1970s in relation not only to the SED in the GDR but to communist parties generally and the 'Banalisierung ihrer Diskurse' (trivialization of their discourses) (Teichmann 1991: 253). The 'woodenness' of this language lies in the rigidity and clumsiness of its form and in the drily unemotional, pedantic, solemn, and humourless nature of its tone.[1] The following extract from a speech by Erich Honecker at the seventh Congress of the Central Committee of the SED in 1988 should illustrate this general characterization:

Die Entfaltung der sozialistischen Demokratie ist eng verbunden mit der planmäßigen Ausgestaltung unseres sozialistischen Rechtsstaates. Das kommt auch in den seit dem VIII. Parteitag neu erlassenen, veränderten oder ergänzten 82 bedeutenden Gesetzen und Verordnungen zum Ausdruck. Sie wurden in breiter Öffentlichkeit vorbereitet und werden in gemeinsamer Verantwortung verwirklicht. Auf der Grundlage des beschlossenen Gesetzgebungsplanes setzen wir diesen bewährten Weg konsequent fort.

Unsere Partei ist stets dafür eingetreten und hat es in der Praxis durchgesetzt, daß die verfassungsmäßigen Grundrechte und Grundfreiheiten der Bürger im Einklang mit den Pflichten geschützt und ausgebaut werden. Die Vervollkommnung der sozialistischen Demokratie ist undenkbar ohne Festigung der Rechtsordnung, wie umgekehrt die durchdachte

---

[1] Gärtner (1992: 221) points out how comic effects did occasionally occur unintentionally, for example through the juxtaposition of text and physical location: 'Alle heraus zum 1. Mai' (Everyone out on the first of May; slogan on a cemetery wall); or through ambiguous formulations: '10 Jahre DDR—10 Jahre staatseigener Zirkus' (10 years of the GDR—10 years of the state-run circus; the intended reference being to the tenth anniversary of the founding of the GDR State Circus).

Erweiterung der Rechte und Pflichten die demokratische Mitwirkung der Bürger fördert. (Cited in Gansel and Gansel 1993: 147)

The development of socialist democracy is closely bound up with the planned organization of our law-governed socialist state. This is also explicit in the 82 important laws and decrees that have been enacted, changed, or amended since the 8th Party Congress. They have been prepared in a broad public forum and are being implemented in a spirit of common responsibility. On the basis of the agreed legislative plan we are consistently continuing down this well-established route.

Our Party has always committed itself to the principle, and has always achieved this in practice, of protecting and extending fundamental constitutional rights and freedoms of our citizens in accordance with their duties. The full realization of socialist democracy is unthinkable without securing the rule of law, just as, conversely, the properly thought-out extension of rights and duties requires the democratic participation of the citizens.

Much earlier in his period of office, Honecker himself had severely criticized the didactic and often incomprehensible style of much public speaking in the GDR, complaining of the 'langweilige Doziererei und schulmeisterliche Belehrung,... pseudowissenschaftlichen Pomp, die übertriebene und formelhafte Behandlung mancher Fragen, die schwerverständliche Sprache.... Vieles wirkt nüchtern, blutleer und trocken' (tedious pontificating and schoolmasterish lecturing,... pseudo-scientific pomposity, the exaggerated and clichéd treatment of many issues, the barely comprehensible language.... Much of it seems dull, bloodless, and dry) (speech at the eighth Party Congress of the SED in 1971, cited in Geier 1997: 347). That this had little or no effect is clear from most subsequent political writings.[2] However, if the lifeless prose of such texts was not intentional, the underlying purpose of representing an unswerving commitment to the straight and narrow path leading to the realization of socialism meant that they were often devoid of contentious or controversial content, highly repetitive, and marked by extreme redundancy.

The complacency of such texts is in marked contrast to the militancy and strident tone of other texts, especially in the earlier part of GDR history, which bristle with aggressive energy, extravagant linguistic gestures, and quasi-religious fervour—with expressions like '*heroischer Sieg*' (heroic victory), '*Bollwerk des Sozialismus*' (bastion of socialism), '*unser heiliges Recht auf Frieden*' (our sacred right to freedom), '*unerschütterlicher Glaube an die historische Mission der Arbeiterklasse*' (unshakeable belief in the historic mission of the working class) (see, for instance, Schlosser 1990*a*/1999: 37 ff.). Consider, for example, the following passage taken from a long speech by Walter Ulbricht, which was broadcast on

---

[2] Discussing an even earlier period, Kronenberg (1993: 51–2) shows that the SED leadership was sensitive to the need to address the public in a clear, comprehensible, and undogmatic style following the workers' protests in June 1953, but that the new tone was short-lived.

GDR television on 18 August 1961, five days after the sealing of the boundary between the sector of Berlin under Soviet control and the rest of the city.

Die Arbeiter und mit ihnen alle ehrlichen Werktätigen der Deutschen Demokratischen Republik atmen erleichtert auf. Das Treiben der Westberliner und Bonner Menschenhändler und Revanchepolitiker hatten alle satt. Mit wachsendem Zorn hatten sie zugesehen, wie sie von dem militaristischen Gesindel für dumm gehalten und bestohlen wurden. Unsere Geduld wurde von den Bonner Militaristen für Schwäche angesehen. Ein politischer Irrtum, wie sich inzwischen erwiesen hat. (From Schafarschik 1973: 100–15)

The workers, and with them all honest working people in the German Democratic Republic, breathe a sigh of relief. All of them were sick of the machinations of the traffickers in human beings and the revanchist politicians in West Berlin and Bonn. With growing anger, they had looked on while the militaristic rabble treated them like fools and robbed them. The militarists in Bonn regarded our patience as weakness. A political mistake, as it has since turned out.

Cold War rhetoric was not uniquely articulated in GDR texts, of course, but there is a distinctively raw edge to the tone here in the crude imagery of '*Menschenhändler*' (traffickers in human beings) and '*militaristische[s] Gesindel*' (militaristic rabble) embedded in a vernacular diction (*satt haben*, to be sick of; *jdn. für dumm halten* to treat someone like a fool).

The bombastic aspect of the official discourse is crystallized in the metaphor of struggle (*Kampf*), which had a long tradition in the history of German political discourse, from the workers' movement in the nineteenth century through the fascist period. In the first years of the GDR, it was possible to appropriate and rehabilitate the concept in the context of the historic 'class struggle' and of the 'struggle against fascism' in the guise of the 'illegitimate' state of the Federal Republic (see Good 1995: 266, 270–1), and these metaphors continued to feature prominently in the ideological projection of the SED's programme. However, in the context of the principal aim of GDR domestic policy and international relations with 'friendly states'—the *Aufbau des Sozialismus* (construction of socialism)—the struggle metaphor had to be reconstrued and adapted to fit the experience of everyday life in the post-revolutionary, advanced industrial period. Now the site of struggle was not in the streets or on the barricades but in the factories and in the fields: 'der kämpfende Werktätige' (the battling worker) was the prototype of the ideal citizen, committed to the realization of the socialist project and fighting for peace through his (sic) dedication to work— 'mein Arbeitsplatz, mein Kampfplatz für den Frieden' (my workplace, my battlefield for peace) (see Reiher 1995a: 180–220 for a wide range of original texts relating to this theme). However, here as in other manifestations of official discourse, the energy and vitality of early texts, with their vigorous exhortations to commit to the cause, were dissipated long before its final collapse, and the discourse of struggle became increasingly ossified and lacking in credibility (Störel 1997: 98; and see also 3.2 and 4.2).

The official discourse can be characterized in terms of recurring linguistic features—many of which appear in the first Honecker passage quoted above (see examples below)—and textual structures. The formulaic and repetitive manners of expression serve various purposes but above all they articulate—or rather, are intended to articulate—control, order, rationality, consistency, and conviction. The strictly hierarchical structure of the society, for instance, was constantly reasserted in formal written contexts by the virtually obligatory identification of public figures by their full titles (Good 1995: 264): contrast, for example, 'President Bush' or 'Bundeskanzler Schröder' (Federal Chancellor Schröder), with 'Der Generalsekretär des Zentralkomitees der Sozialistischen Einheitspartei Deutschlands und Vorsitzende des Staatsrates der Deutschen Demokratischen Republik Genosse Erich Honecker' (The General Secretary of the Central Committee of the Socialist Unity Party of Germany and Chairman of the State Council of the German Democratic Republic Comrade Erich Honecker). However, although communication between Party, or government, and people was essentially an asymmetrical, 'top down' process, the key conceit of the Party as the voice of the people had to be sustained, and this was achieved by frequent allusions to collective identities through the use of inclusive *wir* (we) and *unser* (our) ('*unsere Partei*', our party; '*unser sozialistischer Rechtsstaat*', our law-governed socialist state; '*unsere Menschen*', our people) and by emphasizing the supposedly collaborative nature of making and carrying out decisions ('*in breiter Öffentlichkeit vorbereitet*', prepared in a broad public forum; '*in gemeinsamer Verantwortung verwirklicht*', implemented in a spirit of common responsibility).[3]

Many of the salient features of the *langue de bois* are common to bureaucratic styles of all modern German-speaking societies: for example, the preference for nominal forms over verbs (*Entfaltung*, development; *Ausgestaltung*, organization, formation; *Vervollkommnung*, full realization; *Festigung*, strengthening, consolidation; *Erweiterung*, extension) and the heavy reliance on passives and related impersonal constructions ('*sie wurden ... vorbereitet und werden ... verwirklicht*', they have been prepared and are being realized; '*das kommt ... zum Ausdruck*', this is expressed); the Party itself ('*Unsere Partei ist stets dafür eingetreten*', our Party has always committed itself to ...) is one of the few exceptions to the general invisibility of agents, so that the emphasis is constantly placed on the accomplishment of processes rather than on the participation of individuals or social groups (see also Schäffner and Porsch 1998: 165). Even what was probably the most striking aspect of the expression of official SED discourse, what Hellmann (1989*b*) calls 'permanenter Optimismus', was and still is also a standard feature of western governments' rhetorical repertoire. The crucial difference in the GDR was that underlying problems were never openly identified as such and that official optimism could not be challenged publicly by oppositional discourses. Since texts in the public domain were, at least theoretically, available not only to an east German

---

[3] The idea of the collective engagement in the common enterprise was also promoted by the practice, especially among Party members, of using the informal/familiar *Du*-form of address in contexts where the more formal/distancing *Sie*-form would be normal in other German-speaking communities (see Kretzenbacher 1991).

readership but also to an 'antagonistic' west German audience, it was clearly important to paint the best possible picture of life in the GDR. This entailed on the one hand the emphatic use of positive, assertive vocabulary (*vollständig*, completely; *allumfassend*, all-embracing; *unverbrüchlich*, steadfast; *stets*, constantly; *konsequent*, consistently; *heute und in Zukunft*, now and in the future) and the exclusion of any relativizing modality (*vielleicht*, perhaps; *wahrscheinlich*, probably; *teilweise*, partly). The desired sense of robust confidence was further reinforced by the frequent use of (near-)synonymous or complementary doublets (*Grundrechte und Grundfreiheiten*, fundamental rights and fundamental freedoms; *Rechte und Pflichten*, rights and duties; *Achtung und Anerkennung*, respect and recognition; *geschützt und ausgebaut*, protected and extended; *sind und bleiben*, are and remain) (see also Fix 1994*b*). On the other hand, less than satisfactory conditions were routinely cast in a (relatively) positive light as 'good but not yet good enough': in addition to the preferred, congratulatory reading of expressions like 'die noch bessere Versorgung der Bevölkerung' (the even better supply of goods for the population) and 'die Vorzüge des Sozialismus noch besser zur Entfaltung bringen' (to develop the advantages of socialism even better), the domestic audience would automatically discern an underlying critical and often threatening reading (Fix 1992*a*, Bergmann 1992: 219). The euphemistic function of the construction '*noch* (even) + comparative adjective or adverb' and analogous patterns played a significant part in the 'spin-doctoring' of progress—Fix (1992*a*: 16–19), for example, identified no fewer than sixty-six instances in a single speech by Education Minister Margot Honecker.

Of course, all political parties and all governments develop 'mission statements', in which their core objectives and values are enshrined and to which they make constant reference in order to reinforce their message to their electorate and construct an impression of consistent, principled, and coordinated thinking. In most cases, these statements of intent change over time as political realities and economic conditions change and provoke a recasting of priorities and a redirection of public discourses. In the GDR, however, as in other 'developing socialist societies', adherence to Marxist-Leninist theory precluded acknowledging the possibility of changing political direction (irrespective of actual shifts in policy) and therefore required an unchanging political discourse. So official texts from all periods of GDR history are replete with fixed collocations (*allseitige Stärkung*, comprehensive strengthening; *von weltgeschichtlicher Bedeutung*, of great importance in world history; *Errungenschaften der wissenschaftlich-technischen Revolution*, achievements of the scientific-technological revolution; *die Hauptaufgabe in ihrer Einheit von Wirtschafts- und Sozialpolitik*, the main task in its unity of economic and social policy), which especially in the later years acquired the status of 'canonical terms' (Schlosser 1990*a*/1999: 111–13), constantly reiterated in precisely the same form. This practice, together with the use of words like *planmäßig* (according to plan) and *verfassungsmäßig* (in accordance with the constitution) and expressions such as *diesen bewährten Weg konsequent fortsetzen* (continue down this well-established route) (see again the Honecker speech quoted above), projected a sense of confidence and of being in control, even when this was demonstrably no longer the case.[4]

However, this need to present a positive image, both to the GDR population and to the (potential) west German audience, of undeviating progress towards the attainment of a fully fledged socialist society (*die Vervollkommnung der sozialistischen Demokratie*, the full realization of socialist democracy) created problems for the management of discourse. In particular, the introduction of new economic strategies in the 1960s and early 1970s and the shift of emphasis from social to economic issues under Honecker (Geier 1998: 351) posed a challenge for incorporating these policy changes into what was theoretically a stable political discourse. For example, the recognition that efficiency gains and productivity improvements were necessary in the 'new economic system' but that they could only be achieved by motivating the workforce through incentives of various kinds brought concepts such as 'competition' and 'profit' into the discourse of economic policy. However, these terms had been associated exclusively with capitalism and therefore could not be adopted without reconfiguring the way they were used and understood.

In the case of these two key concepts, semantic intervention was possible by exploiting the existence of (previously) synonymous word pairs: by assigning different meanings to *Konkurrenz* and *Wettbewerb* and to *Profit* and *Gewinn*, it was possible to distinguish between competition and profit in capitalism on the one hand and in socialism on the other. In each of these word pairs, the first term was reserved for reference to the exploitation of the working class in capitalist societies, while the second was ascribed a positive connotation exclusively within the context of socialist societies. So while the purpose of *Konkurrenz* was to increase the market share of one company by reducing that of another and thereby threatening workers' conditions or even their livelihood—'Du sollst begehren deines Nächsten Marktanteil' (Thou shalt covet thy neighbour's market share) (one of the commandments of capitalism used in an advertising text in *Wirtschaftswoche* magazine; see Störel 1997: 109)—*sozialistischer Wettbewerb* was introduced to encourage competition between working groups (*Brigaden*) within a commercial concern for the benefit of all: 'Aus jeder Mark, jeder Stunde Arbeitszeit, jedem Gramm Material einen größeren Nutzeffekt!' (Greater effectiveness from every mark, from every hour's work, every gram of material!) (from a promotional poster from 1975, reproduced in Reiher 1995a: 186–7). The object of the exercise was therefore general *Gewinn*, not individual *Profit*:

Der Gewinn im Sozialismus unterscheidet sich grundlegend vom kapitalistischen Profit.... Im Kapitalismus ist das Streben nach Profit und damit nach höchstem privaten Gewinn [*sic*] erstes Bedürfnis des Kapitalisten und Ziel aller Produktion. Im Sozialismus dient der Gewinn der ständigen Erweiterung der sozialistischen Reproduktion und ist wichtigste

---

[4] Of course, western governments also invest considerable discursive and rhetorical efforts in presenting a public image of consistency and coherence in policy—the dogmatic slogan of the first Thatcher government in the UK (1979–83), 'There is No Alternative', is a classic example—but again the crucial distinction is that while alternatives to prevailing policies did exist both in the GDR and in the west, they could only be publicly articulated in the latter.

Quelle für die systematische Verbesserung der Arbeits- und Lebensbedingungen der Bevölkerung. (From *Kleines Politisches Wörterbuch* 1967: 250–1, cited in Scherzberg 1972: 198).

Profit in socialism is fundamentally different from capitalist profit.... In capitalism, striving for profit and thus for the highest personal gain is the first requirement of the capitalist and the aim of all production. In socialism, profit serves the constant expansion of socialist reproduction and it is the most important source of the systematic improvement of the working and living conditions of the population.

By the late 1980s, as economic and political problems were mounting, there were signs that the need to temper this spirit of collectivism with a degree of individualism was finally being acknowledged, the need for a citizen 'der initiativreich und risikobereit ist, aber auch Plandisziplin hält; der politisch selbständig denkt und selbstbewußt entscheidet und zugleich sich einzuordnen versteht' (who is full of initiative and willing to take risks, but also sticks to the plan; who is politically an independent thinker and has the confidence to make decisions, while at the same time knowing their place) (Kirchhöfer 1988: 81, cited in Bergmann 1992: 109). But as we shall see in 3.3, this was not reflected in fundamental changes in the official discourse, which ultimately proved too inflexible to respond effectively to changes in the communicative environment.[5]

The extreme manifestation of the objective of achieving order and control in the development of GDR society was the operation of the Ministerium für Staatssicherheit (Ministry for State Security, colloquially referred to as the *Stasi*). This massive organization eventually employed 90,000 permanent personnel within the Ministry and over 100,000 'unofficial collaborators' (*Inoffizielle Mitarbeiter/IM*) in all walks of life, providing intelligence reports on individuals and groups at all levels. This activity generated vast quantities of documentation in the form of files on those under observation and internal communication, all of which was of course 'strictly confidential'. Nevertheless, considerable attention was paid to the language used to formulate reports, instructions, and policy documents (for a detailed analysis, see Bergmann 1996, 1999, Lüdtke 1997), and in 1969/1970 a specialized lexicon—the *Wörterbuch der politisch-operativen Arbeit*, Dictionary of Political-Operational Work—containing 747 items was produced by the Law College (Juristische Hochschule) in Potsdam as an authoritative source of reference within the Ministry. The second and final edition, published in 1985, was expanded to 915 entries and represents the most detailed and comprehensive account available of the thinking behind the practice of state security in the GDR.[6] The preface to the second edition sets out the aims of the dictionary:

Das 'Wörterbuch der politisch-operativen Arbeit' soll helfen,
—sich über die Grundorientierungen des Ministers zur Realisierung des dem MfS durch den X. Parteitag der SED übertragenen Kampfauftrages schnell zu informieren;

---

[5] For a detailed study of language in relation to the development of economic policy in the GDR, see Kronenberg (1993).

[6] This second edition has since been made generally available by the government department set up in 1992 to process the *Stasi* documents (see Suckut 1996).

—sich an den neuen Kriterien und höheren Maßstäben der politisch-operativen Arbeit der achtziger Jahre zu orientieren;
—tschekistische[7] Erfahrungen und Arbeitsweisen in verallgemeinerter und konzentrierter Weise für die ständige Qualifizierung der politisch-operativen Arbeit zugänglich zu machen;
—die weitere Durchsetzung der einheitlichen operativen Fachsprache als einer wichtigen Voraussetzung für die präzise Verwirklichung der Befehle und Weisungen, der analytischen Arbeit sowie der Abstimmung und Koordinierung in den Diensteinheiten des Ministeriums zu unterstützen.

The Dictionary of Political-Operational Work is to:
—help readers to inform themselves quickly about the Minister's basic intentions for the realization of the task assigned to the Ministry by the 10th Party Congress of the SED;
—help readers to orientate themselves to the new criteria and higher standards of political-operational work of the 1980s;
—make the experiences and working methods of *Tschekisten*[7] available in a more generalized and concentrated way for continuous training in political-operational work;
—support the further establishment of the unified operational register as an important precondition for the precise implementation of the commands and directives, the analytical work, and agreement and coordination in the departments of the Ministry.

Bernward Baule (1995: 865) interprets these aims as being designed to fulfil three purposes: the dictionary was to act as an instrument of ideological training, to harmonize internal language use through specifying and regulating the understanding and use of key concepts, and to represent and comment on the practices of the Ministry. In terms of developing the staff's political consciousness—the first of these aims—Baule identifies three levels of instruction: ideological (through concepts such as *Subversion*; *tschekistisches Feindbild*, 'tschekist' concept of the enemy), moral (*Haß*, hatred; *Treue*, loyalty; *Verräter*, traitor), and operational (*Operativer Vorgang*, operational process or file, dossier; *Differenzierung*, differentiation). Although it is unlikely that it was actually used as systematically as this might suggest, since its distribution amongst staff was limited, the writing of this specialized glossary is significant in our context because unlike more general, and more widely available, dictionaries (such as the Leipzig *Duden*) it was intended as a manual to be consulted routinely in the everyday production of texts by its in-house readership (see also Fix 1995). In stylistic terms, these texts frequently share many of the grammatical features characteristic of bureaucratic writing and of official (Party) discourse (see above)—complex sentences, passive constructions, nominalization, doublets, phrasal verbs, cumulative genitive phrases, and so on:

Operative Vorgänge sind anzulegen, wenn der Verdacht der Begehung von Verbrechen gemäß erstem oder zweitem Kapitel des StGB—Besonderer Teil—oder einer Straftat der

---

[7] *Stasi* personnel referred to themselves as *Tschekisten*, a loan term from Russian, based on the short form *Tscheka* for *Tschreswytschajnaja Kommissija* (Extraordinary Commission), which was set up in 1917 to combat the counter-revolution in Russia (see Henne 1995: 214).

allgemeinen Kriminalität, die einen hohen Grad an Gesellschaftsgefährlichkeit hat und in enger Beziehung zu den Staatsverbrechen steht bzw. für deren Bearbeitung entsprechend seinen dienstlichen Bestimmungen und Weisungen das MfS zuständig ist, durch eine oder mehrere bekannte oder unbekannte Personen vorliegt. (*Richtlinie Nr. 1/76 zur Entwicklung und Bearbeitung Operativer Vorgänge*, cited in Bergmann 1999: 88)

Operational files are to be started when there is a suspicion that one or more known or unknown persons have committed crimes in the terms of the first or second chapter of the Criminal Code—Special Section—or a common criminal offence which carries a high degree of danger to society and is closely related to crimes against the state and/or which the Ministry is responsible for handling in accordance with its regulations and directives.

The dry style and indigestible structure of such texts also make them indistinguishable at the surface level from public texts on topics from economic policy to higher education, so the importance of the dictionary in this regard is that it reveals the real source of the particularity of *Stasi* discourse as lying in its vocabulary.[8] More precisely, it is the semantic specification of the lexical items in the dictionary that invests the texts in which they are used with their special character. As ordinary a concept as *Haß* (hatred), for example, is constructed here as 'ein wesentlich bestimmender Bestandteil der tschekistischen Gefühle, eine der entscheidenden Grundlagen für den leidenschaftlichen und unversöhnlichen Kampf gegen den Feind' (a fundamental component of *Tschekist* feelings, one of the decisive bases for the passionate and irreconcilable struggle against the enemy) (Suckut 1996: 168). And whereas the simple verb *bearbeiten* (to handle, deal with, process) is normally collocated solely with inanimate objects (usually documents of various kinds—files, application forms), it is used in *Stasi* texts with reference to both people and things. The definition of 'operative Bearbeitung' (operational processing)—'Bezeichnung für alle Aktivitäten und Maßnahmen zur politisch-operativen Arbeit an einer Person bzw. zur Klärung eines bestimmten Sachverhalts, wenn Hinweise auf feindlich-negative Handlungen vorliegen' (designation for all activities and measures to do with the political-operational work on a person or with investigating a particular matter when there are indications of hostile-negative actions)—thus permits the generation of sentences such as:

X unterhält persönliche und briefliche Verbindungen zu einer Person nach Leipzig, die bereits in einem OV [Operativen Vorgang] der BV [Bezirksverwaltung] Leipzig...bearbeitet wird (Bergmann 1999: 17)

X maintains connections in person and by correspondence with a person in Leipzig, who is already being processed in an operational file of the Leipzig district administration.

[8] I think Hans Jürgen Heringer (1994: 171–2) is right to argue that *Stasi* discourse might not seem quite so exotic to us if we knew what the secret service language of the Federal Republic (either pre- or post-1990) was like, and it may well be that many of the concepts in the dictionary derive from an international 'lingua securitatis' (Suckut 1996: 18). Bergmann (1999: 106–7) also concedes that *Stasi* language is probably not unique but justifies his study of it as a contribution to what he calls 'eine Kultur der Erinnerung' (a culture of remembering), part of the process of dealing with the past (see also 5.1 below). It is on the basis of what it might reveal about the importance of language in the historical process of making GDR society what it was that I would justify its inclusion in the present discussion.

The banality of the texts in which such sentences occur derives from the sober, matter-of-fact use of words and expressions that has the effect of reducing people to the status of a file. Such textual practices are part of a larger discursive process, in which the exercise of power is concealed behind bureaucratic proceduralism or what Jessen (1997: 71) calls 'technokratische Scheinwissenschaftlichkeit' (a technocratic pseudo-scientific approach or operation).[9]

However, far-reaching though the workings of the *Stasi* may have been, the discursive impact of its operation was, by its nature, confined to its internal organization and membership. In more public contexts, continuity and control could be achieved—superficially at least—not only through determining and constantly reproducing fixed expressions of Party ideology and policy, but also through 'conventionalizing' the structure of texts and the meticulous management of speech events and communicative processes. This is apparent even in routine communication within institutions (and by no means only in hermetically sealed units like the *Stasi*: see Jessen 1997: 64, and 3.2 below), but it is most visible in the production of texts for public consumption (such as political speeches and media texts).

Since the purpose of official discourse was the formulation, proclamation, and affirmation of Party policy and ideology, the texts that constitute it are not only largely invariant in form and content but also generally linear in structure. As Wedel (1990, cited in Geier 1998: 360) puts it: 'Die Linie ist die geometrische Figur der monopolisierten Rede.... In der Verlängerung der Linie lag die Verheißung des gelobten Landes. Fortschritt entstand kumulativ.' (A straight line is the geometric shape of the monopolized speech.... Extending the line led to the Promised Land. Progress came about cumulatively.) This applies not only to the architecture of individual texts but also to the way in which whole speech (or, more exactly, discursive) events such as Party congresses were orchestrated. Ostensibly an opportunity for the ordinary members and the leadership to debate future policy, congresses were in fact highly ritualized events, the purpose of which was to stress the continuity of the Party's programme of social and economic development, and in so doing to reaffirm the continuity of the discourse (Geier 1998: 338). For this reason, both the content and the textual pattern of the various contributions were largely predictable.

As Schäffner and Porsch (1998: 150–1) show, these communicative encounters between leadership and rank-and-file members (*Basis*)—replicated at all levels in the hierarchy—were predicated on the rule of consensus and were directed towards a predetermined outcome (cf. also the prescribed procedures for annual election meetings of the FDJ in Fricke 1990: 144). First, the leadership gave an 'account', in which they asserted that decisions made at the previous congress had been shown to be justified but that 'unforeseen problems' had arisen, thus

---

[9] A particularly bizarre example of this is the concept of *Geruchsdifferenzierung* (smell detection), according to which the unique smell of individuals can be used to trace and identify the subjects of investigative operations. Their smells can be 'gathered' with swabs from, say, furniture with which they have been in contact, these can then be 'stored' in glass phials and used by specially trained dogs (*Differenzierungshunde*) to match against other evidence material.

necessitating the current congress. Secondly, representatives of the *Basis* had the opportunity in the misleadingly named 'debate' to report on their implementation of previous decisions and to raise any problems they had encountered. Finally, the pre-formulated 'directive' was issued, providing instructions on future action.[10]

The conventionalization of media texts, by contrast, had less to do with their structure than with the ways in which information was controlled and communicated. Following Lenin's principles of media management, the media in the GDR— as the 'collective propagandist, organizer, and agitator' of the Party (see Good 1995: 265, Fix 1993: 33–6)—had two primary tasks: first, to carry out *Überzeugungsarbeit*, that is, to persuade and convince its audience of the 'correctness' of the Party's policies, and secondly, to promote the active commitment of the audience in implementing them. It was therefore the responsibility of 'socialist journalists' to 'die Werktätigen mit der Wirtschaftspolitik der Partei der Arbeiterklasse und des sozialistischen Staates... vertraut machen und sie für ihre Verwirklichung aktivieren' (familiarize working people with the economic policy of the Party of the working class and of the socialist state and engage them in the process of implementing it) (from the *Wörterbuch der sozialistischen Journalistik*, cited in Barz 1992: 145). Ultimate control of the achievement of these aims could obviously be secured through rigorous censorship, ensuring the exclusion of 'inappropriate' topics (such as pollution or food shortages), ideas, or language, in accordance with the official interpretation of the Constitution. Freedom of the press, radio, and television was guaranteed by Article 27, but the official commentary set out clearly how this freedom was to be understood:

Die Freiheit der Presse, des Rundfunks und des Fernsehens zu sichern heißt [deshalb] vor allem, keinerlei Mißbrauch der Massenmedien für die Verbreitung bürgerlicher Ideologien zu dulden und ihre Tätigkeit bei der Verbreitung der marxistisch-leninistischen Ideologie als Foren des schöpferischen Meinungsaustausches der Werktätigen bei der Organisierung des gemeinsamen Handelns der Bürger für die gemeinsamen sozialistischen Ziele voll zu entfalten. (from Riemann *et al.* 1969, cited in Schlosser 1990a/1999: 104)

Guaranteeing the freedom of the press, radio, and television therefore means above all not tolerating any kind of misuse of the mass media for disseminating bourgeois ideologies and fully developing their activity in the dissemination of Marxist-Leninist ideology as forums for creative exchange of opinion amongst working people in the process of organizing the citizens' joint action for the common socialist goals.

The most palpable impact of this media policy on the language of media texts was again the constant litany of ritual formulas and fixed expressions, producing an almost incantatory, didactic effect, designed to 'drill' the audience's consciousness and to achieve the 'naturalization' of the official discourse (Fairclough 1989: 91–2).[11]

[10] See also Burkhardt (1992) on the lack of real debates in the Volkskammer, the GDR parliament.
[11] And as Fix (1993) shows, this pedagogical principle of repetition and reinforcement was applied, as it were, synchronically as well as diachronically: official policy was not only articulated consistently across time in successive editions of newspapers, for example, but also across different text-types within a single edition, from reports through leading articles to readers' letters.

However, the linguistic construction of media texts was also conditioned by the need to control the flow of information and the kind of information that was to be communicated to the public. On the one hand, attention was deflected from the lack of hard information by the punctilious reporting of often spurious details (especially statistical data, such as the exact number of electrical appliances manufactured by a particular factory: see Geier 1998: 352). On the other hand, this apparently virtually 'unmediated' communication between state and citizen-reader contrasts with the highly mediated, indirect communication of more sensitive issues. Since most east Germans had access to west German broadcast media, the state's ability to regulate the flow of information was limited, other than in relation to matters such as domestic economic performance, where it could reveal or conceal as much or as little as it chose. On problematic issues that would come to the public's attention through other routes, attempts to suppress the story would therefore have been ineffective and other techniques of containment were preferred.

For example, the catastrophic accident at the nuclear reactor in Chernobyl, Ukraine, in April 1986 was handled in various ways by western news media, and since some western European countries—notably France, the Federal Republic, and the UK—had invested heavily (both financially and politically) in nuclear power, it was clearly in their interests to play down the significance of the accident and to seek to focus attention on the ageing technology and low safety standards in the Soviet Union (see Heringer 1990: 120 f.). However, news editors could not have failed to recognize this disaster as a sensational story and it duly became one of the major media, as well as political, events of the year in the west. Yet when it finally had to be acknowledged publicly in the GDR, it was confined to a short, deceptively sober paragraph (taken directly from the Soviet news agency TASS) on page 5 of *Neues Deutschland*:

Havarie in ukrainischem Kernkraftwerk
Moskau (TASS). Im Kernkraftwerk Tschernobyl in der Ukraine hat sich eine Havarie ereignet. Einer der Kernreaktoren wurde beschädigt. Es werden Maßnahmen zur Beseitigung der Folgen ergriffen. Den Betroffenen wird Hilfe erwiesen. Es wurde eine Regierungskommission eingesetzt. (Reproduced in Schlosser 1990a/1999: 118)

Accident in nuclear power plant in Ukraine
Moscow (TASS) An accident has occurred in the Chernobyl nuclear power plant in Ukraine. One of the nuclear reactors has been damaged. Measures are being taken to deal with the effects. Help is being given to those affected. A government commission has been set up.

Most east German readers would by then have had the opportunity to follow the breaking story at great length on west German television, so the state-run news media in the GDR opted for the tactic of minimizing and marginalizing the story, rather than denying it.

In the context of the GDR media market, both journalist and reader operated within the constraints of a tightly regulated communicative space. While this imposed strict limits on what could be *said*, it did not necessarily have such a restrictive effect on what could be *read*: practised readers (with the added resource of western television) knew how to interpret the spare prose of news reports such as the Chernobyl story, for example. So although the composition of media texts was constrained by the requirement to conform to specific norms of expression, writer and reader both inhabited a communicative environment in which a combination of 'intertextual knowledge' and knowledge of textual conventions permitted a high degree of indirect communication. For example, the shared intertextual knowledge that journalist (or news agency) and reader would have brought to the following story (see Pätzold 1992: 99–101) would have included the reports on west German television two days earlier about successful 'escapes' across the Baltic by GDR citizens.

DDR-Grenzschiff nahm Personen an Bord
Berlin (ADN). In der Nacht zum Montag wurden durch ein Grenzschiff der DDR auf der Ostsee mehrere Personen aufgebracht und an Bord genommen. Sie hatten sich mit ihrem Boot unberechtigt in den Territorialgwässern der DDR bewegt. Nach einer ersten medizinischen Versorgung an Bord wurden sie an Land gebracht. Nur durch das umsichtige Verhalten der Schiffsbesatzung konnten die Betroffenen aus der gefährlichen Situation geborgen werden, in die sie sich vorsätzlich gebracht hatten. Andere Personen kostete es in ähnlichen Fällen das Leben. Der Vorfall wird durch die zuständigen Organe untersucht. (*Neues Deutschland*, 19 October 1988)

GDR border patrol boat takes people on board
Berlin (ADN). On Sunday night a number of people were picked up and taken on board by a GDR patrol boat in the Baltic Sea. They had been travelling without authorization in their boat in the territorial waters of the GDR. Following medical checks on board they were taken ashore. Only the prudent behaviour of the ship's crew made it possible to rescue those concerned from the dangerous situation in which they had deliberately put themselves. Other people have lost their lives in similar situations. The incident is being investigated by the relevant authorities.

Together with the reader's knowledge of textual conventions, this would have enabled them to retrieve through inference some crucial but unstated points about the story: for instance, if the people arrested had been foreigners, they would have been identified as such; but if they were GDR citizens, travelling 'without authorization' in the territorial waters of their own country can only mean that they were attempting to enter the territorial waters of a neighbouring country, and this in turn would only create a 'dangerous situation' if the neighbouring country were the Federal Republic (or Denmark). On this basis, Pätzold (ibid: 101) derives the 'intended' reading: 'DDR-Bürger wollten Montag nacht...mit ihrem Boot...über die Ostsee in die BRD (oder nach Dänemark?). Dabei wurden sie erwischt und festgenommen.' (On Sunday night GDR citizens tried to go by boat over the Baltic Sea to the FRG (or perhaps Denmark). In doing so, they were caught and arrested.) This reading, finally, reveals the illocutionary force of the text as 'warning' and 'threat': 'We are keeping a close watch on border waters. Anyone who nevertheless tries to escape may drown, or be arrested or shot'.

In this section, I have outlined some of the main distinctive linguistic and textual features that characterized the official discourse of state and Party in the GDR. The material on which the discussion here was based derives from a range of formal and, for the most part, public sources. One of the most conspicuous characteristics that is common to all manifestations of official discourse considered here is the highly ritualized nature of the linguistic forms and textual patterns: the constant repetition of formulaic expressions, the emphasis on the collective historic mission, the recycling of apodictic statements asserting the rationality of official doctrine, the legitimization of Party policy. In the next section, I shall explore the nature and importance of rituality in the discursive construction of GDR society more closely and examine the extent to which the ritualized forms and structures of official discourse penetrated beyond formal, official contexts into the less formal, semi-public domains of everyday life. At the same time, it will be important to expose to critical scrutiny the widespread assumption among western observers that east Germans developed a quasi-diglossic linguistic repertoire, with a clear disjunction between public and private language use.

3.2   Rituality in the discourses of everyday life

Ritual behaviours are typically associated with the performance of events that are invested with symbolic significance in the lives of individuals or communities—for example, conferring powers and obligations, as in the inauguration of a head of state or the opening of a new parliamentary session; marking transitions from one phase or cycle of life to another, as in baptism, harvest festivals, or carnival; or admitting new recruits to membership of a closed group or order, as in the initiation ceremonies of scout troops or freemasons. The ritual event itself usually comprises a prescribed series of ritual acts, both verbal and non-verbal: repeating wedding vows and placing a ring on the spouse's finger, or pledging allegiance to the constitution and saluting the national flag. Moreover, since the substance of ritual events is virtually or entirely predictable, content is dominated by form (Jessen 1997: 66)—what matters is that all participants conform to a standard procedure, and since for the most part what is said and done is always the same, the 'texts' (verbal and non-verbal actions and sequences) fulfil an expressive or demonstrative rather than an informative function: when witnesses are sworn in during a trial, we know that they will undertake to 'tell the truth, the whole truth, and nothing but the truth', but they must be seen and heard to declare this oath in open court and to do so in a particular way.

  Some speech events are rituals by their very nature: their rituality is essential for their function and for their recognition as performances of social rites—solemn ceremonies such as weddings and funerals, celebratory occasions like award- and prize-giving, religious acts such as communion and confession. Each enactment of these event-types is identifiable as such by many non-linguistic features—dress, music, decoration, choreography, the sequence of individual actions, the rights and duties of individual participants—as well as by linguistic and textual characteristics: greetings, opening and closing formulas, fixed expressions, repeated patterns of utterance and response, conventional rather than original text formulation.

Other speech events are not inherently ritualistic (although they may be associated with certain routines[12]), but they may be capable of *ritualization*. A school lesson or a staff meeting, for example, will normally have certain predictable characteristics but the absence of these features would not necessarily put their validity as 'a lesson' or 'a meeting' in doubt (although it might make them less effective). Conversely, if the language and textual structure of lessons or meetings become highly conventionalized, they may still fulfil their primary function quite adequately, but they will also acquire a secondary, and possibly unrelated, function. The question for us here, therefore, is: what role did language play in the instrumentalization both of new rituals and of ritualized speech events in the discursive construction of GDR society?

The existence of ritual practices is almost certainly a universal feature of human societies. It is their absence rather than their presence that would require explanation. What is therefore of interest in any given society or community is the form that particular rituals take, their function in creating and reproducing roles and relationships within the society, and the extent to which social and communicative interaction is ritualized. On the level of political communication before 1989 (speeches, public statements, contributions to parliamentary debates, manifestos), west German texts were, of course, imbued with ritual features: for example, the constant reiteration of governments' 'achievements' or deprecation of their 'failures', the appropriation and repetition of core values, the use of slogans and declarations in place of rational argument. All of these discursive rituals contributed to the development of political culture in the Federal Republic. However, the plural nature of west German political structures meant that the political culture openly accommodated competing discourses (such as the CDU/CSU focus on the 'social market economy' versus the SPD's emphasis on 'social justice') and consequently that it was subject to reorientations at different moments in its history. Rituality in west German politics therefore served the purpose of promoting the interests of political parties in competition with those of their opponents within the Federal Republic, but in the political monoculture of the GDR rituality was deployed to sustain the (officially) uncontested aims of Party-and-state, overtly against the external threats from the antagonistic western neighbour, but also against potential internal deviations from the goal. In the GDR, unlike in the Federal Republic, the interests of Party and state were synonymous, and so the

---

[12] See Marquardt (1998: 3–4) for the distinction between these two concepts, and *passim* for a detailed theoretical and historical discussion of rituals and rituality in the German context.

particular ritual effects of political communication (that we have seen in 3.1) could be developed cumulatively over the forty years of the state's existence.

To achieve this global aim, the rituality of public discourse in the GDR needed to fulfil three principal functions (Jessen 1997: 66–7; see also Fix 1992*b*, 1993, 1994*b*). The first function was to create and maintain order: the fixed, invariant forms of ritual communicative practices (from the use of full titles through greetings and structural patterns of formal gatherings to the catalogue of standard expressions) themselves symbolized order and authority. Secondly, the constant repetition of core ideological values, without the 'turbulence' that the intervention of alternative discourses or even critical analysis might have introduced, was to confirm and legitimize these values and thereby have a stabilizing effect on the audience. And thirdly, socializing the population into a common code or form of language was to have a 'bonding' effect, promoting social integration through participation in shared linguistic practices. Whether, or to what extent, these functions were actually fulfilled is another matter, but if the consistency of efforts to achieve these effects was, as Jessen (1997: 75) puts it, intended to reinforce the fiction 'daß offizielles Weltbild und Welt identisch sind' (the official image of the world and the real world are identical), this was ultimately counter-productive (see 3.3). As we shall see, rituality lost any power it might have had to bind the people because the symbolic link between ritual and social reality was broken— rituals became free-floating, detached from their referent, and constant exposure to, and habitual usage of, ritual(ized) patterns (Jessen 1997: 68–9) gave people the raw material for the private practice of parody and ridicule.

However, if the Party strategists were unaware that they were sowing the seeds of their own destruction by allowing the ritual practices of official discourse to stiffen and lose any positive symbolic resonance they might have had in the early years, there is clear evidence that they recognized the need to extend the scope of official discourse beyond the limited sphere of direct political communication— not least because this form of direct contact between the governors and the governed could be disconnected by an inattentive or uncommitted audience and rendered ineffective unless it was reinforced and consolidated through other means. The strategy therefore had to be not merely to proclaim and defend the aims of the Party-and-State, but to secure the active participation of the whole population in realizing these aims. The construction of the socialist society of the GDR depended on the hegemonic effect of the official discourse, which in turn depended on the discursive saturation of institutional aspects of everyday life and on exploiting the persuasive power of ritual.

To explore the implementation of this strategy, we need to look beyond the rarefied domain of government to forms of action and interaction that were less detached (and less detachable) from the everyday experience of life of ordinary people. The highly 'organized' nature of the contexts in which people lived their lives outside the home, whether in the workplace or in the school—Party organizations, unions, collectives—created strong social networks marked by a high degree of density and multiplexity.[13] The powerful internal dynamics of strong networks typically act as 'norm enforcement mechanisms' (Milroy 1987: 136, 179), as a means of stabilizing linguistic (and other) behaviours amongst participants in the network through mutually exerted pressure to conform to practices from which they derive a common identity. Where there is an overt awareness of additional external pressure to conform to prescribed norms, the cohesive effect of this mechanism is likely to be even stronger.[14] Furthermore, where social networks are to a fairly high degree externally regulated—where individuals are allocated membership rather than actively contracting into it—this permits access to the networks by non-participating members of the outside authority.

This might help to explain the heavy reliance on ritual in the GDR, the extreme significance apparently attached to rituality there in comparison to other developed societies (Fix 1998: xiii). The fixed, invariant form of ritual practices is in itself a means of exercising control over the performance of social actions (see above), but in addition to this, the frequent enactment of rituals (and ritualized behaviours) is a means of constantly reinforcing the cohesion of social units, such as the work collective or the family, and through them of society as a whole. Furthermore, this challenges the social dichotomy of the public and the private, because in a society in which priority is given to social roles rather than to individual biographies many aspects of personal life are drawn into a more public zone than would be the case in less collectively organized societies. At the latest since Politburo member Kurt Hager's proclamation at the seventh Party Congress of the SED in 1971, for example, the purpose of education in the GDR was to make the archetypal 'allseitig entwickelte sozialistische Schülerpersönlichkeit' (all-round socialist school student) a reality, and, as Colin Good (1995: 264) points out, all forms of work activity were included within the production process and the concept of labour: not only 'workers' and 'peasants' but also, for instance, intellectuals and artists (officially referred to as *Kulturschaffende*) were subsumed in the concept *Werktätige(r)* (see 2.3). Where everyone and (virtually) everything is defined in terms of a public context, 'unpolitical private spaces' (Hoffmann 1998: 53) may be marginalized, and the personal and individual become drawn into a complex web of ties.[15]

---

[13] In social network theory, density is a measure of the internal integration of a network (how many members know and interact with other members?), and multiplexity is a measure of the strength of the ties between members (how many kinds of social relationship exist between them—for example, workmate only, or also neighbour, relative, and fellow member of local football team?). See Milroy 1987 and also 4.3 below.

[14] At the same time, it is important to stress that these effects are not automatic. The operation of social networks, even within the more constrained context of a society like the GDR, should not be interpreted in too mechanical a fashion: it conditions, rather than determines, actual behaviour.

[15] This should not be taken to mean that there were no 'unpolitical private spaces' in the GDR. On the contrary, all the evidence suggests that constraints on the public life of individuals endowed private spaces with even greater significance than they have in other, less regulated, societies. The point here is rather the way individuals were conceived within the official discourse: the obverse of that isolation and displacement of individuals outside social networks that is characteristic of western societies—and which, indeed, found its ultimate expression in former British Prime Minister Margaret Thatcher's declaration that there was 'no such thing as society'.

The central position allocated to the concept of work in the official self-image of the GDR was ceremonially underpinned and confirmed by the celebration of May Day, one of the most important political rituals in the GDR (Fix 1998: xvi).

The carefully orchestrated and highly choreographed demonstrations on 1 May were significant as a very public manifestation of the state's 'historic mission' (the ongoing struggle for peace and against imperialism, the strengthening of socialism within the GDR, solidarity with the community of socialist nations), but the ritual construction of May Day as a *Kampf- und Feiertag* (a day for struggle and celebration, as it was even in 1989), in which participation was often required rather than merely encouraged, indicates a further function. If rituals are a repository of collective memory, and political rituals store memories of decisive moments in the national past, then the enactment of the ritual should serve to activate these memories. However, to serve the interests of the state memories must be activated for a purpose other than evoking a reverential reflection on the past. Through its rituality, the event transcends the moment of its performance (Hoffmann 2000: 239) and therefore—in theory at least—looks to the future as well as to the past. In so doing, it should motivate participants to renew their commitment to the values and beliefs associated with them (Jessen's stabilizing and integrating functions: see above).

The importance of this purpose is emphasized by the constant references to past, present, and future in texts relating to 1 May, and in the conceptualization of the day as an occasion for celebration but also for continued struggle. However, as Hoffmann (2000) shows in his analysis of May Day texts from 1946 to 1989, this was not unproblematic. On the one hand, the references to the history and traditions of the workers' movement provided a sense of continuity with the struggle for workers' rights and legitimized the leading role of the SED (ibid.: 241). On the other hand, since the 'traditional' conflicts of interest between labour and capital, between unions and employers, were by definition irrelevant within the GDR, the metaphor of struggle could only be retained in this context if it was reassigned to other objectives (see 3.1). This becomes clear as early as 1946, in an article in *Neues Deutschland* (ibid.: 249), which begins by establishing the historical link: 'Es [der 1. Mai] ist und bleibt zuerst und vor allem der Tag der deutschen Arbeiter, der alte Kampf- und Ehrentag der Arbeiterbewegung' (The 1 May is and remains first and foremost the day of the German workers, the age-old day for celebrating the struggle of the workers' movement). But the modality of this sentence (*zuerst und vor allem*, first and foremost) foreshadows the expansion of the focus of the celebrations, proclaimed in the rest of the article, to encompass peace, freedom, and national unity (*Friede, Freiheit, das ganze deutsche Volk*). Two years later, these key concepts remain central to the May Day message of the SED (ibid.: 252) but democracy and socialism are added to the list, a series of concrete objectives is declared—demands for land reform, educational reform, expropriation of property belonging to 'war criminals' and 'capitalists', and the right to workers' participation—and the purpose of struggle is identified as being to achieve political unity for German workers and unity of representation.

Following the founding of the GDR, the same themes reappear but with an increasingly international emphasis and (especially in the 1950s) repeated hostile contrasts with the Federal Republic. But in salvaging a crucial concept and refocusing the discourse of struggle, the SED had committed itself to what in the longer term would be a counter-productive strategy. For the vitality and vigour of the early texts, which were able to appeal both to the proud traditions of the workers' movement and to memories of recent catastrophe, eventually gave way to the bathos of limp rallying cries: 'Nehmt teil an der Kampfdemonstration am 1. Mai! Wir demonstrieren für das Wohl des Volkes, für die Sicherung des Friedens—für die Verwirklichung der Beschlüsse des XI. Parteitages!' (Take part in the demonstration for the struggle on 1 May! We shall demonstrate for the welfare of the people, for the safeguarding of peace—for the implementation of the resolutions of the eleventh Party Congress!; from *Neues Deutschland* 22 April 1987, cited in Hoffmann 2000: 260).

The redevelopment of the May Day ritual was therefore conceived as a means of securing the loyalty, commitment, and cohesion of the people, of enlisting their active participation in the project of building the socialist nation. Regardless of whether or not the state was successful in this enterprise, the staging of mass demonstrations is a form of ritual that emphasizes the sublimation of the individual not simply in a social group but in the amorphous and remote collectivity of 'the people'. To reach into everyday life, rituality has to touch individuals on a more local basis.

In the secular society of the GDR, the intricate network of contacts between the individual and the supra-local authority of the Church was tolerated but obviously subject to constraints. The non-religious counterpart to the Church as an agent of socialization and organization for the dissemination of values and beliefs was, of course, the Party and its affiliated bodies—the trades union organization FDGB, for example, and the youth movements the Pioniere and the FDJ. Membership of these organizations, as of the Church, involved participation in many kinds of ritual, some of which—such as the *Zehn Gebote der sozialistischen Moral* (Ten Commandments of Socialist Morality; first promoted in the late 1950s and abandoned in the mid-1970s—see below)—were derived from religious models (other examples include *Die Gebote der Jungpioniere* and *Die Gesetze der Thälmannpioniere*, the Commandments of the Young Pioneers and the Laws of the Thälmann Pioneers: see Fix 1992*b*: 94–9).

1 Du sollst Dich stets für die internationale Solidarität der Arbeiterklasse und aller Werktätigen sowie für die unverbrüchliche Verbundenheit aller sozialistischen Länder einsetzen.

2 Du sollst Dein Vaterland lieben und stets bereit sein, Deine ganze Kraft und Fähigkeit für die Verteidigung der Arbeiter-und-Bauern-Macht einzusetzen.

3 Du sollst helfen, die Ausbeutung des Menschen durch den Menschen zu beseitigen.

4 Du sollst gute Taten für den Sozialismus vollbringen, denn der Sozialismus führt zu einem besseren Leben für alle Werktätigen.

5 Du sollst beim Aufbau des Sozialismus im Geiste der gegenseitigen Zusammenarbeit handeln, das Kollektiv achten und seine Kritik beherzigen.
6 Du sollst das Volkseigentum schützen und mehren.
7 Du sollst stets nach Verbesserungen Deiner Leistungen streben, sparsam sein und die sozialistische Arbeitsdisziplin festigen.
8 Du sollst Deine Kinder im Geiste des Friedens und des Sozialismus zu allseitig gebildeten, charakterfesten und körperlich gestählten Menschen erziehen.
9 Du sollst sauber und anständig leben und Deine Familie achten.
10 Du sollst Solidarität mit den um ihre nationale Befreiung kämpfenden und den ihre nationale Unabhängigkeit verteidigenden Völkern üben.

1 You shall constantly commit yourself to the international solidarity of the working class and of all working people and to the steadfast solidarity of all socialist countries.
2 You shall love your fatherland and always be ready to commit all your strength and abilities to the defence of the Workers' and Peasants' power.
3 You shall help to do away with people's exploitation of others.
4 You shall do good deeds for socialism, for socialism leads to a better life for all working people.
5 You shall work for the construction of socialism in the spirit of mutual cooperation, respect the collective, and heed its criticisms.
6 You shall protect and increase the property of the people.
7 You shall always strive to improve your performance, be economical, and strengthen socialist work discipline.
8 You shall bring up your children in the spirit of peace and socialism to be people with an all-round education, firm in character and physically toughened.
9 You shall lead a clean and respectable life and respect your family.
10 You shall practise solidarity with those nations who are fighting for national liberation and national independence.

However, the most important secular ritual, in terms of participation rates (90 per cent of the year group by 1960, according to Kauke 1998: 117) and the significance attached to it in the lives of individuals and families, was the *Jugendweihe*, the secular equivalent of confirmation and the ceremony through which 14 year-olds were introduced to the rights and obligations of adulthood.

Like 1 May, the *Jugendweihe* had a long tradition reaching back to the eighteenth century (see Kauke 1998), and it too had to be reinvented to justify its place in the socialist society of the GDR. Unlike 1 May, however, the *Jugendweihe* was not a mass public celebration open to the gaze of both internal (national) and external (international/foreign) audiences, but a local, semi-public event restricted to participants, their families and teachers, and officials.[16] Furthermore, although this

---

[16] Although the young people's *Patenbrigaden* (sponsoring, or mentoring, group) were also present to provide a link with the world of work (see Kauke 1998: 133).

traditional ritual was conscripted into the service of the Party, it retained an underlying personal and social function in addition to its overtly political purpose (Kauke
1997: 369–72).[17] Both of these functions—marking the transition to adulthood and
stressing the responsibilities of socialist citizens—were addressed in the ceremonial
texts, but the centrepiece of the whole speech event was the highly ritualized
Gelöbnis (solemn vow), which was dedicated exclusively to the political/ideological
level (see Kauke 1997: 370–1, 1998: 144–59, 2000: 282–4).

Unlike other texts in the ceremony, such as the *Festrede* and the *Dankesrede der
Jugendlichen* (celebratory speech and the young people's speech of thanks; for
examples, see Reiher 1995a: 54–60), the text of the *Gelöbnis* was prescribed at
national level and left no room for adaptation to personal or local circumstances.
It was a scripted dialogue, in the form of a litany, between the Party-and-State and
its young people.

LIEBE JUNGE FREUNDE!

Seid ihr bereit, als junge Bürger unserer Deutschen Demokratischen Republik mit uns
gemeinsam, getreu der Verfassung, für die große und edle Sache des Sozialismus zu arbeiten
und zu kämpfen und das revolutionäre Erbe des Volkes in Ehren zu halten, so antwortet:

JA, DAS GELOBEN WIR!

Seid ihr bereit, als treue Söhne und Töchter unseres Arbeiter-und-Bauern-Staates nach
hoher Bildung und Kultur zu streben, Meister eures Fachs zu werden, unentwegt zu lernen
und all euer Wissen und Können für die Verwirklichung unserer humanistischen Ideale
einzusetzen, so antwortet:

JA, DAS GELOBEN WIR!

Seid ihr bereit, als würdige Mitglieder der sozialistischen Gemeinschaft stets in kamerad-
schaftlicher Zusammenarbeit, gegenseitiger Achtung und Hilfe zu handeln und euern Weg
zum persönlichen Glück immer mit dem Kampf für das Glück des Volkes zu vereinen, so
antwortet:

JA, DAS GELOBEN WIR!

Seid ihr bereit, als wahre Patrioten die feste Freundschaft mit der Sowjetunion weiter zu
vertiefen, den Bruderbund mit den sozialistischen Ländern zu stärken, im Geiste des pro-
letarischen Internationalismus gegen jeden imperialistischen Angriff zu verteidigen, so
antwortet:

JA, DAS GELOBEN WIR!

Wir haben euer Gelöbnis vernommen. Ihr habt euch ein hohes und edles Ziel gesetzt.
Feierlich nehmen wir euch auf in die große Gemeinschaft des werktätigen Volkes, das unter
der Führung der Arbeiterklasse und ihrer revolutionären Partei, einig im Willen und

---

[17] The fact that the *Jugendweihe* actually had a broad social appeal and met a widely felt need is reinforced by its continued popularity after unification. Kauke (2000: 272), for example, gives the following figures: in 1998, 100,000 young people in the east took part in the *Jugendweihe*, while only 31,000
were confirmed. It should therefore not be seen solely as a mechanism of state control.

Handeln, die entwickelte sozialistische Gesellschaft in der Deutschen Demokratischen Republik errichtet. Wir übertragen euch hohe Verantwortung. Jederzeit werden wir euch mit Rat und Tat helfen, die sozialistische Zukunft schöpferisch zu gestalten.

DEAR YOUNG FRIENDS!

If you are willing, as young citizens of the German Democratic Republic, to work and fight together with us, true to the Constitution, for the great and noble cause of socialism, and to honour the revolutionary legacy of the people, then answer:

YES, WE DO SO SOLEMNLY VOW!

If you are willing, as loyal sons and daughters of our Workers' and Peasants' state, to strive for a high standard of education and culture, to become masters of your subject, to learn tirelessly, and to commit all your knowledge and ability to the implementation of our humanist ideals, then answer:

YES, WE DO SO SOLEMNLY VOW!

If you are willing, as worthy members of the socialist community, to act constantly in comradely cooperation, with mutual respect and assistance, and always to unite your path to personal happiness with the struggle for the happiness of the people, then answer:

YES, WE DO SO SOLEMNLY VOW!

If you are willing, as true patriots, to continue deepening the firm friendship with the Soviet Union, to strengthen the fraternal bond with all socialist countries, to defend against all imperialist assaults in the spirit of proletarian internationalism, then answer:

YES, WE DO SO SOLEMNLY VOW!

We have heard your vow. You have set yourselves a high and noble goal. We formally accept you into the great community of working people, which is building the developed socialist society in the German Democratic Republic under the leadership of the working class and its revolutionary party, united in will and action. We confer great responsibility on you. We will at all times help you in word and deed to shape the socialist future creatively.

The version reproduced here was the final one, introduced in 1968, which had been preceded by two earlier versions in 1955 and 1963. Although the basic pattern remained the same, there were significant shifts of emphasis in the content and in the style, and the general thrust mirrored closely the trends in the political discourse of the SED. For example, the second 'verse' of the 1955 text read: 'Seid ihr bereit, alle eure Kräfte für ein einheitliches, friedliebendes, demokratisches und unabhängiges Deutschland einzusetzen?' (Are you willing to commit all your strength to build a unified, peace-loving, democratic, and independent Germany?). This was replaced in 1963 with the following: 'Seid ihr bereit, mit uns gemeinsam eure ganze Kraft für die große und edle Sache des Sozialismus einzusetzen, so antwortet mir: ...' (If you are willing to commit all your strength, together with us, for the great and noble cause of socialism, then answer: ...). As we have seen earlier (see 2.2), the prospect of achieving a united Germany diminished from the perspective of the SED from the early 1960s, and while the 1963 version of the *Gelöbnis* refers to the more ambivalent 'German people' ('*für ein glückliches Leben des gesamten deutschen Volkes'*, for a happy life for the whole German people), it juxtaposes this with the (implictly distinct) 'treue Söhne und Töchter unseres Arbeiter- und Bauernstaates' (loyal sons and daughters of our Workers' and Peasants' state). The 1968 version makes a more radical move even than the revised constitution of the same year (again, see 2.2) and anticipates the 1974 constitution, deleting all references to Germanness apart from the name of the state itself.

The style becomes correspondingly more assertive: the (apparently) open questions of the original (Are you willing...?) are replaced by implicit commands (If you are willing,... then:...),[18] and the tone becomes more militant, with a greater emphasis—here too—on struggle (*'für die große und edle Sache des Sozialismus zu arbeiten und zu kämpfen'*, to work and struggle for the great and noble cause of socialism; *'Kampf für das Glück des Volkes'*, struggle for the happiness of the people). But the language of the text as a whole places the *Gelöbnis* unmistakably within the official discourse of Party-and-State. This text, recited to every cohort of *Jugendweihlinge* and reproduced on their personal *Jugendweihe* certificates, is formulated in accordance with the linguistic and textual features we have identified as characteristic of formal, official texts (see 3.1):

- Positive, emotive, but vague abstract terms: *'Ideale'* (ideals), *'Glück'* (happiness), *'Frieden'* (peace); *'treu'* (loyal), *'würdig'* (worthy).
- Absolute modifiers/intensifiers: *'jederzeit'* (at all times), *'stets'* (constantly), *'unentwegt'* (tirelessly).
- Nominal forms preferred to verbs: *'die Verwirklichung unserer humanistischen Ideale'* (the implementation of our humanist ideals), *'in gegenseitiger Achtung und Hilfe'* (in mutual respect and assistance).
- Doublets: *'zu arbeiten und zu kämpfen'* (to work and to struggle), *'Wissen und Können'* (knowledge and ability).
- Fixed expressions: *'die entwickelte sozialistische Gesellschaft'* (developed socialist society), *'die feste Freundschaft mit der Sowjetunion'* (the firm friendship with the Soviet Union), *'die sozialistische Zukunft schöpferisch gestalten'* (to shape the socialist future creatively).

However, although the *Jugendweihe* was more closely identified with 'ordinary life' than national, public events like May Day, it remained a special occasion, isolated to some degree from the steady flow of daily life precisely by its overt rituality. For the majority of the former *Jugendweihlinge* interviewed by Wilma Kauke (see, for example, Kauke 2000: 286–91), it was the ceremony as a whole that formed a lasting impression, not the individual components and not the specific commitments undertaken. Yet this does not necessarily indicate that this ritual encounter with official discourse patterns made no impact: it is just as likely that they were not consciously registered because of their extreme familiarity. Ritual

---

[18] This change appears more subtle in German, as the same syntactic pattern—*Seid ihr bereit*—is used in both cases, while the ambiguity is removed by the context of the whole sentence.

events such as May Day and *Jugendweihe* are the tips of an iceberg, and what remains generally invisible—paradoxically because of its ubiquity—is the ritualization of the mundane, the penetration of official discourse into the unexceptional texts of everyday life.

If work was the cornerstone of the socialist ethic in the GDR, education for work was the principal purpose of the socialist institution of the school. This is established explicitly in the *Gesetz über das einheitliche sozialistische Bildungssystem* (Law on the Unified Socialist Education System, 1965): 'Eine lebensnahe, sozialistische Erziehung, in deren Zentrum die Erziehung zur Arbeit steht, ist zu gewährleisten' (a socialist education that is closely related to life and focuses on education for work is to be guaranteed; cited from Schlosser 1990a/1999: 90), and although the two terms *Bildung* and *Erziehung* are often used interchangeably and in apparently synonymous doublets ('die Bildung und Erziehung allseitig und harmonisch entwickelter sozialistischer Persönlichkeiten', the education and formation of all-round, harmoniously developed socialist personalities: ibid.), they are also used to distinguish between general 'humanist' education (*Bildung*) and the preparation for playing a role in the construction of the socialist society (*Erziehung*). Parents were reminded of these aims in an introductory letter ('Unser Kind kommt zur Schule', Our Child Starts School) when their children started school:

Vom ersten Schultag an werden die Kinder mit den vielfältigsten Fragen des Lebens vertraut gemacht. In unserer Schule erhalten die Kinder eine hohe Bildung und eine gute sozialistische Erziehung. Dazu gehört auch die Vorbereitung auf die Arbeit, die Erziehung zur Liebe der Arbeit und zu den arbeitenden Menschen. Bis Ihr Kind zum ersten Mal zum Unterricht in die sozialistische Produktion gehen wird, vergehen noch einige Jahre. Aber die Erziehung zur Arbeit erfolgt bereits in der ersten Klasse. Es werden den Schülern zum Beispiel Grundfertigkeiten und Grundkenntnisse im Werkunterricht und im Schulgartenunterricht vermittelt. Sie verrichten auch schon kleine gesellschaftlich nützliche Tätigkeiten. (From Reiher 1995a: 35)

From their first day at school, the children are familiarized with all the diverse aspects of life. In our school the children receive a high standard of education and a good socialist upbringing. This also includes preparing them for work, and instilling in them the love of work and of working people. It will be some years before your child goes to have lessons in the socialist workplace for the first time. But education for work begins straight away in the first year. For example, children are taught basic skills and knowledge in craft and school garden lessons. They also already carry out small, socially useful activities.

The school was therefore both a *Lerngemeinschaft* (learning community) and a *Lebensgemeinschaft* (community for life/living) (Schmidt 1991), a wide-ranging social project in which students, teachers, and parents were constantly involved—not only in the process of learning and teaching, but in various forms of collective commitment, from *Pionier* and FDJ groups to *Elternaktive* (parents' work groups) and *Patenbrigaden* (groups of workers within an organization, designated as mentors for individual school students) (for an overview, see Schlosser 1990a/1999: 102–3; for a discussion of the relationship between family and school, see Helwig 1991). Apart from a relatively small number of specialist schools, there was only one school type (the POS—*Polytechnische Oberschule*), which provided a uniform organizational structure, and this in turn facilitated the transmission and distribution of communications from the Party at national level throughout the system. In terms of hierarchical structure, roles and relationships of individuals and groups, and patterns of communication, therefore, the school was a microcosm of the state.

As an institution, the school constructs itself through the texts it generates, processes, and consumes. The most obvious category of school text consists of the written and spoken materials used in the classroom, and in a centrally organized education system this is clearly the most direct route through which ideas, values, and beliefs can be communicated from the central authority to the students. In the curriculum of GDR schools, the core ideas were not only represented in the transparent form of *Staatsbürgerkunde* (civics) but also smuggled into unlikely texts such as mathematics exercises:

(i) Vor der Sowjetmacht gab es in dieser Stadt 6 Schulen. Jetzt gibt es in dieser Stadt 32 Schulen. Wieviel Schulen wurden durch die Sowjetmacht gebaut? (*Lehrbuch für die zweite Klasse*, cited in Reiher 1995*a*: 38)

(ii) Trotz der gewaltigen Ausmaße war die Bauzeit des Palastes der Republik sehr kurz:

Beginn der Ausschachtungsarbeiten	13.8.1973
Grundsteinlegung durch Erich Honecker	2.11.1973
Richtfest	18.11.1974
Fertigstellung	23.4.1976

(a) Wieviel Monate lagen jeweils zwischen den Terminen?
(b) Wieviel Monate betrug die Bauzeit insgesamt?
   (*Lehrbuch für Klasse 4*, cited in Fix 1992*b*: 54)

(i) Before the Soviet power there were 6 schools in this town. Now there are 32 schools in this town. How many schools have been built by the Soviet power?

(ii) In spite of its massive proportions, the Palace of the Republic was built in a very short time:

Start of excavation work:	13.8.1973
Laying of foundation stone by Erich Honecker:	2.11.1973
Topping-out ceremony:	18.11.1974
Completion:	23.4.1976

(a) How many months were there between each stage?
(b) How many months did the entire construction process take?

However, many other kinds of text contribute to the discourse of education: students' progress reports, announcements, correspondence between teachers and parents, project proposals, syllabus outlines, work plans, and so on. These texts vary in terms of source (internal and external), status (official and unofficial), intended audience (general and specific), and formality. The examples I have selected for analysis here illustrate this diversity, but at the same time they demonstrate how in various forms official discourse patterns percolated down from one level to another to permeate the entire discursive field.[19]

Text 1 Konzeption zum 35. Jahrestag der DDR
In der Vorbereitung des 35. Jahrestages der DDR geht es vor allem darum, das Wissen der Schüler über die 35jährige Entwicklung ihres Heimatlandes zu erweitern und zu vertiefen, sowie Stolz auf die Errungenschaften der Werktätigen zu wecken. Sie sollen erkennen, daß die erreichten Erfolge das Ergebnis großer Anstrengungen und Leistungen der von der SED geführten Werktätigen sind und daß auch in Zukunft der Kurs der Hauptaufgabe in ihrer Einheit von Wirtschafts- und Sozialpolitik konsequent fortgesetzt wird.

gez. XXX (Parteisekretär)   YYY (Direktor)

Arrangements for the 35th anniversary of the GDR
Preparations for the 35th anniversary of the founding of the GDR should concentrate on extending and deepening the students' knowledge about the 35-year development of their native country, and on creating a sense of pride in the achievements of the working people. They are to understand that past successes are the result of great efforts and achievements of the working people under the leadership of the SED and that the course of the main objective in its unity of economic and social policy will be resolutely maintained in the future.

signed XXX (Party Secretary)   YYY (Head Teacher)

This text is an extract from a set of guidelines (that is, instructions) for teachers, indicating how the 35th anniversary of the founding of the GDR was to be celebrated in the school. The guidelines were determined centrally and transmitted to the staff in this document from the local Party secretary, countersigned by the head teacher. Originating from the highest level of the hierarchy, it clearly has official status and is intended for the widest circulation amongst all staff. It is therefore predictable that even a short extract will bear the hallmarks, in content and style, of the official discourse: rhetorical doublets (*'das Wissen der Schüler... zu erweitern und zu vertiefen'*, extending and deepening the students' knowledge), phrases from the standard corpus of expressions (*'die Errungenschaften der Werktätigen'*, the achievements of the working people; *'Hauptaufgabe in ihrer Einheit von Wirtschafts- und Sozialpolitik'*, main objective in its unity of economic and social policy), the leading role of the Party (*'Leistungen der von der SED geführten Werktätigen'*, achievements of the working people under the leadership of the SED), the emphasis on continuity (*'der Kurs... [wird] konsequent fortgesetzt'*, the course... will be resolutely maintained in the future). The body of the text could therefore have appeared without alteration in a ministerial speech or leading article in *Neues Deutschland*, the main organ of the SED: it occupies the most official, formal, and public end of the spectrum of school texts in

---

[19] Unless otherwise indicated, the texts are taken from the archives of a school in Cottbus, Brandenburg. An earlier version of the discussion of these texts appeared in Stevenson (1995).

the archive. The remaining texts differ from this in various ways in terms of authorship, function, and intended readership, but they contain linguistic and textual features that locate them within the same discursive process.

Text 2 Arbeitsplan des Fachzirkels Deutsch—Schuljahr 1983/84
I Zielstellung Mit der Einführung neuer Lehrpläne im Fach Deutsche Sprache und Literatur erhöhen sich die Anforderungen, die an jede Unterrichtsstunde gestellt werden. Es gilt, die Qualität des Literaturunterrichts zu verbessern und — wie Margot Honecker auf der zentralen Direktorenkonferenz formulierte — 'die dem literarischen Kunstwerk innewohnenden Möglichkeiten für die Persönlichkeitsentwicklung' zu nutzen. Der Literaturunterricht soll stärker als bisher einen wirkungsvollen Beitrag zur kommunistischen Erziehung leisten. Daher sind im Rahmen der Arbeit des Fachzirkels Deutsch alle Möglichkeiten auszuschöpfen, die einen erziehungswirksamen und bildungseffektiven Unterricht fördern.... Dabei stehen sich alle Kollegen mit Rat und Tat zur Seite.

Plan of Work for the German Section—School Year 1983/84
I Objectives With the introduction of the new syllabuses for German language and literature, increased demands will be made of each lesson. It will be necessary to improve the quality of literature teaching and—as Margot Honecker put it at the central conference of head teachers—to make use of 'the opportunities for personal development that are inherent in literary works of art'. Literature teaching is to make a more effective contribution than in the past to the communist education of the students. Therefore, in the context of the work of the German Section full use is to be made of all possible ways of promoting educationally effective teaching.... All colleagues will give each other their full support in achieving this.

This text is taken from a paper written by the head of the German section, outlining the aims and objectives of the coming year's work. Its immediate target audience is therefore the small group of teachers working in this section, but any text committed to paper and circulated even within such a small group would automatically become available to higher levels of the hierarchy, both inside and outside the school. The double status of such texts imposes certain constraints on their authors, and the extract reproduced here shows clearly how practical pedagogical business needed to be conducted not only within the formal context of institutional norms but also within the frame of the official discourse.

The thrust of the section head's message to her colleagues is that they must consider how to implement the new syllabuses that have just been introduced, and the bulk of the plan (not reproduced here) sets out her proposals in formal but entirely concrete terms. However, the opening passage of the document is couched in quite different terms: it is largely redundant for the practical purposes of the plan, and no obvious connection is made between this opening statement and the actual proposals, but it constructs a necessary filter that situates the plan within the appropriate ideological framework. It begins with the apodictic assertion that the introduction of new syllabuses (inevitably) increases the demands made of every school class. No justification is offered for this statement and no alternative is envisaged: impersonal formulations ('*es gilt*', it will be necessary to) and imperative modal constructions (*'soll stärker als bisher einen wirkungsvollen Beitrag leisten'*, is to make a more effective contribution; *'alle Möglichkeiten sind auszuschöpfen'*, full use is to be made of all possible ways) preclude discussion, and the 'ritual intertextuality' (Geier 1998: 338) of what in the context of a supposedly internal planning paper appears to be a gratuitous reference to the speech of Education Minister Margot Honecker seals the necessity of the assertion that further improvements are needed. What is meant by 'improving the quality of literature teaching' becomes clear when the text asserts that it must 'make a more effective contribution than in the past to the communist education of the students', and the logical connector *daher* (therefore) introducing the following sentence suggests that 'educationally effective teaching' must be understood in this very specific sense. Finally, this passage concludes with the ritual formula 'dabei stehen sich alle Kollegen mit Rat und Tat zur Seite' (compare, for example, the final sentence in the 'solemn vow' in the *Jugendweihe* ceremony, above), that simultaneously declares solidarity and mutual support on the one hand, and collective responsibility and commitment on the other.

Text 3 Rechenschaftsbericht der Klasse 10b

Im vergangenen Schuljahr erfüllten wir unseren Arbeitsplan nur teilweise. Wir veranstalteten zwar einen Kuchenbasar, dessen Erlös wir für die Solidarität spendeten, und eine Weihnachtsfeier, welche wohl bei allen Begeisterung fand, aber es kamen z.B. ein gemeinsamer Kinobesuch sowie eine Radtour zu kurz, auch mit einer Einladung eines Arbeiterveterans klappte es nicht ganz.... Man darf natürlich auch die politischen Gespräche, welche unser Agitator B. S. leitete, nicht vergessen. Den Lehrgang für Zivilverteidigung schlossen wir mit guten Ergebnissen ab. Einige Schüler erhielten wegen ihrer Einsatzbereitschaft eine Auszeichnung.... In der 10. Klasse muß noch mehr darauf geachtet werden, daß es nicht dazu kommt, daß ständig dieselben FDJ-ler an freiwilligen Einsätzen teilnehmen. Der Arbeitsplan der 10. Klasse müßte also noch konkreter die Arbeit der einzelnen Schüler kennzeichnen.

Annual Report of Class 10b

In the past school year we only partially fulfilled our plan of work. We did organize a cake sale, the proceeds from which we donated to the solidarity fund, and a Christmas party, which was enthusiastically received by all, but, e.g., a group visit to the cinema and a bicycle trip didn't really come off, and the invitation of a veteran of work didn't quite work out. ... The political discussions, which our political instructor B. S. led, should of course not be forgotten. We successfully completed the course in civil defence. A number of students received a commendation for their readiness for action.... In the 10th class even more attention must be paid to ensuring that it is not always the same FDJ members who take part in voluntary activities. The work plan of the 10th class should therefore specify even more concretely the work of individual students.

It was the job of each class to produce an annual report on its activities, written by the students themselves but obviously under the guidance and supervision of the class teacher (see also Straßner 1985). These texts are therefore also in the public domain and subject to similar constraints to the texts produced by teachers, but with a greater degree of tolerance in terms of stylistic consistency. The general formality of Text 3, for example, is disrupted in places by a more colloquial style: contrast 'wir erfüllten unseren Arbeitsplan nur teilweise' (we only partially fulfilled our plan of work) with 'mit einer Einladung eines Arbeiterveterans klappte es nicht ganz' (the invitation of a veteran of work didn't quite work out). Several GDR-specific terms are used, which would not necessarily be understood by German-speakers outside the GDR, but these are standard concepts within east German society rather than features of the official discourse as such.[20] However, the focus on political activities and the euphemistic expression of criticism of insufficient commitment on behalf of some students ('...*muß noch mehr darauf geachtet werden*', even more attention must be paid to; '...*müßte also noch konkreter die Arbeit der einzelnen Schüler kennzeichnen*', should therefore specify even more concretely the work of individual students) are clear indicators of discursive conformity.

Text 4 Zeugnis
Auch in diesem Schuljahr wies Sabine gute Leistungen auf. Als 1. Sekretär der GOL [Grundorganisationsleitung] leistet Sabine an unserer Schule eine vorbildliche gesellschaftliche Arbeit. Auch im Klassenkollektiv nimmt Sabine eine führende Rolle ein. In Auseinandersetzungen und Diskussionen mit Klassenkameraden und Schülern unserer Schule bezieht sie einen festen Klassenstandpunkt. Im Ensemble unserer Schule arbeitet sie aktiv mit.

Report
Sabine's performance has again been of a high standard this year. As First Secretary of the organizing committee of our school she performs exemplary social work. Sabine also takes a leading role in her class collective. In debates and discussions with classmates and students of our school she adopts a firm class position. She participates actively in the general life of our school.

Text 5 Brief an Eltern
Liebe Frau Neuhoff, lieber Herr Neuhoff!
Sehr herzlich möchte ich Ihnen nach dreijähriger Tätigkeit als Klassenleiter dafür danken, daß Sie durch Ihre Erziehung im Elternhaus dazu beitrugen, Ihren Sohn Gerd zu einem vorbildlichen Pionierfunktionär und Schüler heranwachsen zu lassen. Als Freundschaftsratsvorsitzender trägt er entscheidend zur Entwicklung des Klassen- und Schulkollektivs bei. Seine hervorragenden Fähigkeiten unterstützen den Lernprozeß in der Klasse und sein politisches Wissen half bei der Standpunktbildung der anderen Schüler. Diesen Dank darf ich im Namen unserer Schulleitung aussprechen. Wir wünschen Ihnen und Ihrer Familie Gesundheit und Erfolg im persönlichen Leben und in der Arbeit und hoffen auf weitere gute Zusammenarbeit!
Mit sozialistischem Gruß!

gez. Richter (Direktor)   Wilfried Zaratowski (Klassenleiter)   (From Reiher 1995a:73)

---

[20] For example: *Solidarität* (funds collected to support the 'struggle' of socialists in other countries), *Arbeiterveteran* (a retired worker who had received a commendation for their contribution to the development of the socialist society), and *Agitator* (political instructor).

Letter to parents

Dear Mrs and Mr Neuhoff,

As class teacher for the last three years, I would like to thank you very much indeed for helping your son Gerd to develop into an exemplary Pioneer official and student by the way that you have brought him up at home. As Chair of his Pioneer group's committee he makes a decisive contribution to the development of the class and school collectives. His outstanding abilities support the learning process in the class and his political knowledge has helped the other students form their point of view. I am expressing these thanks on behalf of our school leadership. We wish you and your family health and success in your personal lives and in your work, and look forward to continuing good cooperation!

With socialist greetings!

Signed: Richter (head teacher)   Wilfried Zaratowski (class teacher)

The standard school report included factual information on the students' academic performance in terms of grades, but the commentary supplied by the class teacher or head was concerned almost exclusively with their contributions to the 'social life' of the school, in the sense of their commitment to the school as a social collective and their political correctness. The extract in Text 4 begins by reporting that 'Sabine's performance had again been of a high standard', and although this could refer to her studies, the lack of a syntactic link (such as 'furthermore') between this and the following sentence strongly suggests that it refers to her leading role in the FDJ within the school. Similarly, the class teacher's letter (Text 5) gives priority in its praise to Gerd's prowess as a *Pionier* over his success as a student, and the context seems to imply that the 'learning process' which Gerd's 'outstanding abilities' support is political rather than academic. The emphasis in both of these texts is on the importance of reinforcing and reproducing the collective identity of the institution, rather than on the personal development of the individual student.

Text 6 Mit Pioniertreffen-Schwung ins neue Schuljahr

... Natürlich ist für alle Schüler eine fleißige und gewissenhafte Lernhaltung das ganze Jahr über das Wichtigste. Im Unterricht und in der Pionier- und FDJ-Arbeit wollen wir uns mit den neuesten Erkenntnissen von Wissenschaft und Technik vertraut machen, denn wir sind die Erbauer und Gestalter der Zukunft.

AG 'Junge Reporter', 24. POS

Liftoff into the new school year at the Pioneer gathering

... Of course, the most important thing for all students is a hard-working and conscientious attitude to studying. In lessons and in our Pioneer and Free German Youth work we shall familiarize ourselves with the latest developments in science and technology, for we are the builders of our future.

'Young reporters' working group, 24th Polytechnic School

Text 7 Lehrvertrag

Das Lehrziel ist die Erziehung und Bildung eines Facharbeiters, der sich bewußt für den Sieg des Sozialismus einsetzt, den die Fähigkeit zu hoher Qualitätsarbeit sowie die Entwicklung solcher Eigenschaften wie Liebe zur Arbeit, Fleiß, Gewissenhaftigkeit, Exaktheit, Pünktlichkeit und Disziplin, Ordnungssinn, beharrliches Eintreten für das Neue, Unduldsamkeit gegenüber Mängeln in der eigenen Arbeit und in der Arbeit anderer auszeichnet.

Training contract
The aim of the training is to educate and train a skilled worker, who consciously commits himself[21] to the victory of socialism, and who distinguishes himself by the ability to do high quality work and by the development of such qualities as love of work, diligence, conscientiousness, precision, punctuality and discipline, tidiness, constant commitment to new ideas, and refusal to tolerate deficiencies in his own work and that of others.

Text 8 Verpflichtungserklärung
Mein Studium ist eine Auszeichnung durch unseren Arbeiter-und-Bauern-Staat. Dieser Auszeichnung werde ich mich stets würdig erweisen. Im Bewußtsein meiner hohen Verantwortung gegenüber unserer sozialistischen Gesellschaft verpflichte ich mich, während meines Studiums meine ganze Kraft einzusetzen für die allseitige Stärkung unseres Arbeiter-und-Bauern-Staates, der Deutschen Demokratischen Republik, bewußt und kämpferisch an der Gestaltung unseres sozialistischen Lebens mitzuwirken, um ausgezeichnete Studienleistungen zu ringen und zur Stärkung der Verteidigungsbereitschaft unserer Republik durch aktive Teilnahme an der militärischen oder an der Ausbildung in Zivilverteidigung beizutragen. Ich verpflichte mich, nach erfolgreicher Beendigung meines Studiums meine Arbeit dort aufzunehmen, wo es unser sozialistischer Staat für notwendig und zweckmäßig erachtet. (from Reiher 1995a: 89)

Declaration of Commitment
My university place is a mark of distinction awarded by our Workers' and Peasants' state. I shall always show myself to be worthy of this distinction. Conscious of my great responsibility towards our socialist society, I commit myself to devote all my strength during my studies to the all-round reinforcement of our Workers' and Peasants' state, the German Democratic Republic, to play my part consciously and with determination in shaping our socialist way of life, to struggle to achieve excellent results, and to contribute to the strengthening of the defensive capability of our country by actively taking part in military or civil defence training. On the successful completion of my studies, I undertake to work wherever our socialist state considers necessary and appropriate.

Text 6 is an extract from an article written by a team of 'young reporters' at the school and published in the regional newspaper *Lausitzer Rundschau* (28 September 1988) to mark the beginning of the school year. Its tone is pious and earnestly enthusiastic, its content is wholly affirmative of the official educational ethic, and it draws heavily on the stock of core concepts ('*die neuesten Erkenntnisse von Wissenschaft und Technik*', the latest developments in science and technology; '*die Erbauer und Gestalter unserer Zukunft*', the builders of our future). Although ostensibly an 'original' piece of writing, this passage is strikingly similar in both

---

[21] I have used the 'generic masculine' form here, as it remained normal practice in the GDR—unlike in the Federal Republic since at least the 1980s—not to use gender-neutral language in such contexts. See Diehl (1992), Fleischer (1987: 331–8).

content and expression to Texts 7 and 8, which are both official documents. Text 7 is taken from the standard contract of employment for trainees (school students doing compulsory training in industry) and spells out the objectives of the training. Both technical skill in a specific sphere of work (in this case, it is a girl training as a bricklayer) and personal development within the larger enterprise of securing 'the victory of socialism' are equally stressed: 'high quality work' must be complemented by total dedication to the success of the collective enterprise. Text 8 is also a form of 'contract', in which university students acknowledge their privileged position and declare their commitment to devote their energies as students to the struggle to construct and defend their country and the socialist way of life.

I have dwelt on the analysis of these texts from the educational domain at some length in order to give some impression of the extent of the politicization of everyday life in the GDR. Although the texts were selected more or less at random from a substantial corpus of materials, I am confident from many discussions with east Germans who studied and taught in GDR schools (and universities) that they are not unrepresentative of the kinds of text that students, parents, and teachers—in other words, the entire population at some time or another—would inevitably and frequently encounter. The impact of the constant exposure to such texts can only be judged by those concerned: the object of the present discussion is to explore the strategy of what I have been calling the 'discursive penetration' of official discourse, rather than its effects. However, even if this account of the pervasiveness of the official discourse within one sphere of everyday life is persuasive, it leaves open the question of how much of the everyday experience of language in public and semi-public contexts in the GDR can be characterized in this way. Many western commentators (see, for example, Schlosser 1990*b*, Jackman 2000: 7–8) seem convinced that east Germans in the GDR operated in a communicative environment that imposed such severe constraints on language use that they were obliged to 'commute' between two 'worlds of discourse': the private world of family and friends and the public world of work and study. Many east Germans, however, do not recognize this image as the environment in which they lived (see Reiher 1995*c*: 235, Hartung 1990: 459–60, Fleischer 1992: 17–18).

Hartmut Schmidt (2000: 2023), for example, concedes that there were countless contexts—from the workplace to stamp collecting clubs—in which ordinary citizens would expect to encounter and produce texts that, to varying degrees, bore the stamp of the official discourse. Virtually no aspect of everyday life appears to have been exempt from this influence—even mundane texts like traffic regulations were composed within an ideological template:

Bei der weiteren Gestaltung der entwickelten sozialistischen Gesellschaft und den damit zu schaffenden grundlegenden Voraussetzungen für den Übergang zum Kommunismus in der Deutschen Demokratischen Republik ist das Wohl, die Sicherheit und Geborgenheit der Bürger vornehmstes Anliegen. Das erfordert auch eine hohe Ordnung, Sicherheit und Flüssigkeit im Straßenverkehr. Unter den Bedingungen der ständig zunehmenden Verkehrsdichte gilt es, jederzeit das Leben und die Gesundheit der Bürger sowie das sozialistische und persönliche Eigentum zu schützen und die Erfüllung der wachsenden volkswirtschaftlichen Aufgaben im Straßenverkehr zu sichern. (*Straßenverkehrs-Ordnung* 1977, cited in Schmidt 2000: 2027)

In the context of the continued construction of the developed socialist society and the fundamental prerequisites that this is to create for the transition to communism in the German Democratic Republic, the welfare, safety, and security of citizens is the foremost concern. It is therefore also necessary that road traffic is orderly and safe, and flows smoothly. Under conditions of constantly increasing traffic density, it is necessary at all times to protect the lives and health of citizens, as well as socialist and personal property, and to ensure that the growing economic tasks in relation to road traffic are carried out.

Omnipresent slogans on banners, posters, and hoardings (billboards), exhorting citizens to play their part in the national enterprise (see 3.3), were part of the life-long didactic process of tutoring the population, and features of official language use in texts marking significant stages in life—birth, marriage, retirement, death—testify that the official discourse accompanied ordinary people quite literally from the cradle to the grave (see again Reiher 1995a for many examples; also Kühn 2000).

However, to derive from this evidence the view that east Germans were somehow trapped inside a linguistic cage whenever they departed from the safe environment of hearth and home would require an assumption that the GDR population as a whole was chronically insecure and docile. Furthermore, this view overlooks a wealth of counter-evidence. Personal observation and discussions with 'ordinary' east Germans indicate that spoken communication in the GDR spanned as broad a range of styles and genres as in other German-speaking communities, but there is relatively little authentic data still available for analysis. Yet even if we continue to restrict our discussion to written texts, it can be shown that textual practices were by no means uniform, even within institutional settings. I shall consider just two examples here.

One of the most fascinating and revealing sources of information about the experience of everyday life in the GDR and about perceptions of normality is the vast body of correspondence (*Eingaben*) generated by ordinary people complaining to various state authorities about personal problems and shortcomings in the workings of institutions. One of the consequences of a paternalistic state is that the state will be held responsible for everything that goes wrong, and if people are required to 'refuse to tolerate deficiencies in their own work and that of others' (see Text 7, above) this positively encourages the development of an *Eingabenkultur* (culture of complaint: see Merkel and Mühlberg 1998: 11). There are benefits for both parties in this exercise: the public have the opportunity to raise issues of personal and social concern directly with the responsible authority, and the state acquires extensive insights into the 'mood of the nation'. However, even if the opportunity to voice dissatisfaction was no more than tolerated as a means of releasing the pressure of frustration in the population, for ordinary people it represented a form of compensation for the lack of *Öffentlichkeit*, of a forum for public debate (ibid.: 13). Furthermore, the language of these letters is not that of a cowed and submissive populace—they are often frank and forthright, sometimes quite unrestrained in their criticism, and composed in varying degrees of formality. Consider, for example, the following two extracts from letters about shortages of consumer goods, sent to the popular investigative television programme PRISMA (taken from Merkel 1998: 143, 109–10)

Text 9 Obst und Gemüse

...Unsere Kleingärtner haben im Herbst viel Obst angeliefert. Was davon aber in den Kaufhallen angeboten wurde, war vielfach nicht des Kaufens wert. Wo sind die Boscop, Hasenköppe, Grafenssteiner? Wo sind die Birnen Gute Louise, und die William Christ? Warum gibt es kein Backobst? Backobst spielte vor dem Kriege für die Ernährung eine große Rolle. ... Jetzt komme ich zu den Kartoffeln, was da mitunter angeliefert wird ist der reine Hohn. Im Fernsehen sieht man, wie die Frauen sortieren. Wenn man den Beutel aufmacht sind mindestens 3 faule dazwischen. Von der Größe gar nicht zu sprechen.... Ich will es heute dabei bewenden lassen. Als gelernter Lebensmittel engros Kaufmann vor dem Kriege hätte ich noch vieles zu schreiben.

Mit freundlichem Gruß!

Richard Bammel, Berlin, den 17. Februar 1983

Fruit and vegetables

...Our allotment gardeners supplied a lot of fruit in the autumn. But what was then put on sale in the supermarkets was often not worth buying. Where are the *Boscop, Hasenköppe, Grafenssteiner*? Where are the *Gute Louise* and *William Christ* pears? Why is there no dried fruit? Before the war, dried fruit was a very important source of nourishment.... Now I'm coming to potatoes: what is on sale sometimes is just a mockery. On television, you can see women sorting. When you open the bag, there are at least three rotten ones amongst them. Not to mention the size.... I shall leave it at that for now. As a qualified wholesale food merchant before the war, there's a lot more I could write.

Yours sincerely!

Richard Bammel, Berlin, 17 February 1983

The author of this letter makes few concessions to the genre of the formal letter and no attempt to adopt features of official discourse (not even in the closing formula). The text reads more like the transcript of an extemporized spoken diatribe (the series of rhetorical questions, the predominantly paratactic sentence structure, the partially random sequence) than a deliberately composed letter. His criticism of the current market situation could hardly be more blunt, and he has no qualms about making unflattering comparisons with the situation 'before the war'.

Text 10 Zigarren

Werte Genossen!

Seit Jahren verfolge ich mit Interesse Ihre Sendung 'Prisma'. Zeigt sie doch kritisch auf, daß in den verschiedensten Bereichen der Volkswirtschaft noch Mißstände bestehen, die es abzuschaffen gilt. Aus gegebenem Anlaß sehe ich mich gezwungen, auch auf einen Mißstand hinzuweisen.

Ich bin Zigarrenraucher (Weiße Elster elegant). Eine Zigarrensorte, die in Qualität und Preis mit keiner anderen vergleichbar ist. Seit Monaten ist die Zigarrenversorgung im

Bezirk Halle, genauer Kreis Merseburg, sehr schlecht; speziell vorgenannter Marke. Da diese Marke in den letzten Wochen in keinem Geschäft der näheren Umgebung mehr zu bekommen war, habe ich mir Auskünfte eingeholt.

Der Großhandel gab die Auskunft, daß diese Zigarren schon lange nicht mehr geliefert wurden und verwies mich an den Hersteller. Vom VEB Zigarrenfabrik Dingelstädt erhielt ich die Auskunft, daß diese Zigarren nicht mehr hergestellt werden, da der Bedarf zu gering ist.

Mit dieser Auskunft kann ich (und viele andere) mich nicht einverstanden erklären.

In jedem Geschäft, das diese Zigarre führte, mußte man immer wieder feststellen, daß die Nachfrage größer war, als das Aufkommen. Diese Angelegenheit steht doch im Widerspruch zu der von Dingelstädt gemachten Aussage und außerdem zu den Beschlüssen der letzten Parteitage in bezug auf immer bessere Befriedigung der Bedürfnisse der Bevölkerung.

Im Namen aller Zigarrenraucher bitte ich Sie hiermit um Überprüfung und sehe einer baldigen Antwort mit Interesse entgegen.

Mit sozialistischem Gruß

Helfried Schreiter, Merseburg, den 8. Januar 1985

Cigars

Comrades!

I have been following your programme 'Prisma' with interest for years. It reveals critically the fact that there are still deficiencies in all sorts of areas of the economy, which we must get rid of. In the light of recent circumstances, I too feel obliged to draw attention to a deficiency.

I am a cigar smoker (*Weiße Elster elegant*). A brand of cigar that cannot be compared with any other in quality and price. For months, the cigar supply in the Halle district, more precisely in Merseburg, has been very bad, especially of the aforementioned brand. Since this brand has not been available in any shops in this area in recent weeks, I made enquiries.

The wholesaler informed me that these cigars had not been supplied for a long time and referred me to the manufacturer. The VEB Cigar Factory in Dingelstädt told me that these cigars are no longer produced because the demand is too small.

I (and many others) cannot accept this information.

In every shop that stocked this cigar, it was the case over and over again that the demand was greater than the supply. This situation surely contradicts the statement from Dingelstädt and, what's more, the decisions made at the last Party Congresses as regards ever greater improvements in meeting the needs of the population.

In the name of all cigar smokers I hereby ask you to look into this matter and look forward with interest to hearing from you soon.

With socialist greetings

Helfried Schreiter, Merseburg, 8 January 1985

By contrast with Text 9, this letter is composed for the most part in a consciously formal style, it develops a carefully structured argument, and adopts the standard opening and closing formulas of official correspondence ('*Werte Genossen!*', Comrades!; '*Mit sozialistischem Gruß*', with socialist greetings). Nevertheless, while conforming to something more like the official model, the author makes a direct and uncompromising criticism of the manufacturer, and reinforces his complaint with the apparently unanswerable contention that the inadequate supply situation is a flagrant breach of 'the decisions made at the last Party Congresses as regards ever greater improvements in meeting the needs of the population'. In their different ways, therefore, these two letters both take an unashamedly critical stance towards state institutions and either resist official discourse patterns or adapt them for their own purposes (for example, Helfried Schreiter establishes his credentials as a 'loyal citizen' by using the standard opening and closing formulas and showing his awareness of Party Congress decisions, with the effect that his criticisms cannot be dismissed as mere 'whingeing' of the disaffected).[22]

Considerable stylistic diversity is also evident in internal correspondence within those state institutions in which—unlike education, for example—mutual appraisal of members' ability and willingness to conform to a prescribed mode of expression was not an issue. For example, the discussion amongst officials and members of the Central Committee and Politburo over ways of dealing with the dissident songwriter Wolf Biermann in the mid-1960s (see Eberle 1998: 226–9) is conducted in a sober, direct, and business-like manner with no ritual flourishes.[23] In the following short note, for instance, Kurt Hager passes on to Erich Honecker (at that time responsible for security and legal issues in the Politburo) a suggestion from a junior colleague that Biermann should be expelled from Berlin. The opening and closing mark the formal status of the communication, but the body of the message is relatively informal:

Text 11

Werter Genosse Honecker!

Von der Abt. Kultur erhalte ich beiliegenden Vorschlag betr. Biermann. Was ist Deine Meinung? Meines Wissens wäre dies auch ein ungewöhnlicher, bisher nicht praktizierter Schritt, der zu einer neuen Kampagne im Westen und zu Diskussionen unter der Intelligenz bei uns führen würde. Wäre es nicht besser, die Abteilung Arbeit einzuschalten und ihm eine Arbeitsstelle zu vermitteln?

Mit sozialistischem Gruß

K. Hager

Comrade Honecker!

I have received the enclosed proposal re Biermann from the Culture Dept. What do you think? To my knowledge, this would be an unusual, in fact unprecedented step, which would lead to a new campaign in the west and discussions amongst the intelligentsia here. Wouldn't it be better to bring in the Work Dept. and get him a job?

With socialist greetings

K. Hager

---

[22] It is also worth noting that the response to Herr Schreiter's letter from an official source is couched in the style of conventional bureaucratic / commercial correspondence and is therefore indistinguishable, apart from the opening and closing, from equivalent west German business letters.

[23] Contrast these with the highly conformist readers' letters on the Biermann case published in newspapers such as the *Leipziger Volkszeitung* (see Fix 1993, and 4.2 below).

The most plausible representation of actual linguistic variation in spoken and written German in the GDR speech community seems to me to be Schmidt's balanced account:

Die Beherrschung mehrerer Sprachregister stellte kaum eine Besonderheit dar, sie dürfte zu den Sprachfertigkeiten der Teilhaber aller Sprachgemeinschaften zählen. In gewisser Weise charakteristisch für das DDR-System war aber wohl die Intensität und Unausweichlichkeit, mit der Kommunikationsformen der Zwischenzone (Ausübung offizieller Sprachformen durch Sprecher der Alltagssprache in Gegenwart und unter Beteiligung der Vertreter der Macht) in der DDR praktiziert wurden. (Schmidt 2000: 2022–3)

Competence in several registers was scarcely anything unusual—it must belong to the linguistic skills of members of all speech communities. What probably was in a certain way characteristic of the GDR system though was the intensity and inevitability with which forms of communication belonging to an intermediate domain were used in the GDR (i.e. the use of official linguistic forms by speakers of everyday language in the presence of, and talking to, representatives of authority).

This greater intensity of linguistic practices arguably fostered a greater sensitivity towards sociolinguistic variation and difference amongst east Germans than amongst west Germans. As we have seen in the earlier part of this section, the contexts of language use in the public and semi-public domains were imbued with a consciousness of the political status of texts produced within those domains and therefore of the potential consequences and sanctions associated with non-conformity. However, as texts 9–11 show, this does not mean that east Germans were socialized as code-switching automata with a linguistic repertoire restricted to a public and a private code. Such a view is not only misleadingly reductive, it also both overlooks the particular nature of switching in GDR settings and probably exaggerates the quantity and frequency of it in relation to other speech communities.

For example, we have seen that the fundamental characteristic of public discourse in the GDR was its consensus orientation (see 3.1 above, and Schäffner and Porsch 1998). Switching between public and semi-public or private contexts therefore has to be analysed not (only) on the strictly linguistic level but in terms of changes from a consensual discourse to at least potentially resistant, conflictual discourses. Furthermore, on the level of interpersonal behaviour, many would argue that switching was less characteristic under certain circumstances in the GDR than in western speech communities. For example, while there would typically be no change in speech behaviour between the situations 'outside a meeting' and 'inside a meeting' within an east German setting, west Germans would typically switch from casual/colloquial speech to self-consciously abstract/technical/academic speech styles: in other words, the change in context would be marked metaphorically only (or more often) by the west Germans, and it is therefore the *absence* of switching that is striking in the east German setting.[24]

---

[24] Again, this argument is based on personal observation and extensive discussions with both east and west Germans over many years rather than on empirical investigations. There may, of course, be

My purpose in this section was to explore the extent of ordinary people's exposure to the ritual and ritualized language use associated with official discourse in the GDR. There seems to be little doubt that the pervasiveness of ritual(ized) texts made members of this speech community experts in reading and, to varying degrees, in reproducing this form of language use. However, this competence in the language of Party and state was a two-edged sword. The strategic aim was to educate and 'form' loyal citizens, fluent in the discursive patterns of state socialism and therefore equipped to carry the message forward, but the extreme familiarity with these patterns also provided people with the resources ultimately to subvert the message by enabling them to appropriate ritual practices (especially the *Losungen* or political slogans) for critical purposes: *de*ritualization became an essential means of voicing political dissent during the *Wende*. Indeed, long before the *Wende*, the alienation induced by overexposure to the *langue de bois* provoked the private rehearsal of alternative modes of articulation (Teichmann 1991: 256), of ironic 'language games' (Pätzold 1992: 94–5) in which the language of official texts was manipulated to humorous and subversive effect. The elaborate attempts to secure the formation of the 'socialist nation' of the GDR at least in part through linguistic and discursive measures therefore provided the basis for challenging and eventually rejecting the model developed over forty years by the SED. This will be the subject of the final section in this chapter.

3.3   The polyphony of *Wende* discourses

The German autumn of 1989 has been characterized in many ways—as *Aufbruch* (departure, fresh start), *Umbruch* (radical change), even *(sanfte) Revolution* (gentle revolution)—but the term that eventually occupied a fixed place in post-unification German vocabulary is, in retrospect perhaps surprisingly, the *Wende* (change of direction, turning point). This may seem surprising for two reasons. First, of the various alternatives for designating this astonishing and dramatic period the anodyne *Wende* is the least emotive, and secondly—paradoxically—it had been one of the most contentious concepts in circulation during the period itself. Furthermore, it has not been applied exclusively to this period: in the GDR, for example, the introduction of new economic policies that led to the workers' uprising in June 1953 (the so-called *Neuer Kurs*, new course/direction) had been portrayed as a positive *Wende* by the SED (Schlosser 1990a/1999: 185), while in the Federal Republic the term had previously denoted the 'conservative turn' in west German politics when Helmut Kohl's coalition government of CDU/CSU and FDP replaced Helmut Schmidt's SPD/FDP government in 1982.[25]

various explanations for this apparent contrast, but it seems likely that the greater status-orientation in the western setting invests interaction in the more formal arena with a dual function: the overt function is, say, to discuss an important issue, while the covert function is intra-group competition or 'personal profiling'. I shall return to this issue in 5.1, considering it from the perspective of insiders' reflections on their experience of language and language use in the GDR.

[25] This sea-change in west German political culture has also been identified as a linguistic—or more precisely, a discursive—phenomenon (see Uske 1986).

However, in the collective political vernacular of contemporary Germany, the unqualified use of the term *Wende* can only refer to the period roughly from the first protest marches in Leipzig in September 1989 to the first truly democratic parliamentary elections in the GDR in March 1990, or more narrowly to the weeks before and after the opening of the Berlin Wall (and the border between GDR and Federal Republic) on 9 November 1989. In popular usage, it has become the standard secular point of reference in the timeline of post-1945 German history: the *Wende* is now less important in itself than as a means of personal and social orientation in relation to the recent past, which in everyday discourse is bisected into time before and time after the *Wende* (*vor der Wende* versus *nach der Wende*). In the present context, however, I shall focus precisely on the crucial period between 'before' and 'after'.

Locating the beginning of this period is a rather arbitrary process but the trigger for the 'autumn of discontent' is generally taken to be the waves of GDR citizens first seeking refuge in the west German embassies in Warsaw, Prague, and Budapest in July and August 1989, and then taking advantage of the opening of the border between Hungary and Austria to go the Federal Republic. The ensuing chain of events developed very rapidly, involving not just a few hundred disaffected citizens looking for 'a better life' in the west, but hundreds of thousands of protesters initially determined not to leave ('*Wir bleiben hier!*'—'We're staying here!') but demanding improvements in living conditions and in the political process in the GDR. In September, *Neues Forum* (New Forum), the first openly constituted reform group, was launched and others (such as *Demokratischer Aufbruch*, Democratic Awakening, and *Demokratie jetzt*, Democracy Now) followed shortly afterwards. At the end of September, the first of what was to become a series of regular Monday demonstrations was held in Leipzig despite the forcible intervention of the police. Two days after the triumphal official celebrations of the fortieth anniversary of the founding of the GDR on 7 October, a large demonstration in Leipzig delivered a blunt challenge to the SED—'*Wir sind das Volk!*', '*We* are the people!'—but passed off peacefully. On 18 October, as the drama lurched into a crisis for the government, Erich Honecker was deposed as head of government and Party leader and replaced by Egon Krenz.

By now, the protests had developed considerable momentum and the new Party leadership failed to placate the demonstrators with offers of dialogue and reform, so that on 4 November a massive demonstration was held in and around the Alexanderplatz in east Berlin with addresses from prominent intellectuals as well as leading members of the SED. Then, in rapid succession, the government (*Ministerrat*) and the Politburo of the SED resigned en masse, and the borders with the Federal Republic and the Berlin Wall were opened (9 November). A new government was formed, still dominated by the SED, but on 1 December the Party's constitutional claim to leadership was abolished and within days the core of the Party apparatus—the Central Committee and the Politburo—was dissolved and Egon Krenz resigned his position as *Staatsratsvorsitzender* (head of state).

Meanwhile, the demonstrations continued in Leipzig and elsewhere: although the initial modest demands for freedom to travel and political reform had been met (at least to an extent), the call for internal changes had been superseded by the call for unification—'*Wir sind* ein *Volk!*' (We are *one* people!). As John Sandford (2000: 31) puts it, the dominant mood had turned 'from the assertion of the rights of the "Volk" as "demos" to those of the "Volk" as "ethnos"'. By the end of the year, the new Prime Minister, Hans Modrow (SED), had engaged in negotiations with Helmut Kohl on ways of establishing a new relationship between the two states. But when all political parties—both newly formed and re-formed—declared their support for German unification in advance of the parliamentary elections in March 1990, the *Wende* was effectively complete.

This brief chronology of key moments in the development of the *Wende* should be sufficient to indicate the enormity of the changes that took place in GDR society within the space of a few months. The question we now need to address is how the dominant discourse in the GDR changed within this short time from the discourse of unwavering commitment to socialism and the sovereignty of the GDR to the discourse of German unity. What happened to the communicative environment in the GDR between Erich Honecker's insistence on 7 October 1989 , the fortieth anniversary of the founding of the GDR, that 'wir werden unsere Republik in der Gemeinschaft sozialistischer Länder durch unsere Politik der Kontinuität und Erneuerung auch künftig in den Farben der DDR verändern' (we shall continue in the future to change our republic in the community of socialist countries through our policy of continuity and renewal in the colours of the GDR) and Hans Modrow's assertion on 1 February 1990 that 'Deutschland soll wieder einig Vaterland aller Bürger deutscher Nation werden' (Germany is once again to become the united fatherland of all citizens of the German nation)?

It is a widely held view that language played a crucial part in the acting out of the political processes of the *Wende*. Jackman (2000: 9), for example, argues that 'the *Wende* was in some respects above all a linguistic event', and Polenz (1993: 128) even characterizes it as a 'Sprachrevolte' (language revolt). East German linguist Reinhard Hopfer (1992*a*: 112) attributes a dual role to language in this period: 'Die Beseitigung der deformierten Verhältnisse des öffentlichen Sprechens war ein selbständiges Revolutionsziel und zugleich ein Indikator für den gesamten revolutionären Prozeß' (the removal of the deformed conditions of public speaking was in itself a goal of the revolution and at the same time indicative of the entire revolutionary process), echoing west German Georg Stötzel (1991: 9), who sees language 'als Symptom und wirkender Faktor der Revolution selbst' (as a symptom and contributory factor of the revolution itself). Such judgements gain support from the fact that memories of the *Wende*, shared by participants and outside observers, always give a prominent position to linguistic actions of one kind or another: the banners and chants of the demonstrators, the powerful, ringing speeches at demonstrations in Leipzig and Berlin, the complacent assurances of SED leaders at the height of the crisis, the confused and stumbling announcements by Politburo spokesman Günter Schabowski at the hastily convened press conference declaring the Berlin Wall open—even the very absence of speech, the speechlessness of the border guards as the crowds streamed through the Wall, was eloquent in its own way.

However, the thesis that the GDR was 'talked out of existence'—or perhaps rather, to emphasize that this was an active process carried out internally within the GDR, that it 'talked itself out of existence'—needs to be justified, since the outcome was not automatic or predictable, even if, with the benefit of hindsight, that may seem to have been the case. The *Wende* cannot be reduced to the simple displacement of one discourse by another. On the one hand, just as there was no single 'language *of* the GDR' but rather a complex linguistic constellation that we may call 'language *in* the GDR' (see 2.2), so there was no single 'language of the *Wende*' (*Sprache der Wende*) but rather a polyphony of *Wende* discourses. On the other hand, while a powerful state apparatus can impose an official discourse over time through the complementary processes of censorship, ritualization, and the saturation of public and semi-public contexts (see 3.2), alternative discourses have no such mechanisms for ensuring successful resistance. What, then, were the competing discourses of the *Wende*, how did they relate to each other, and how did alternative discourses ultimately supplant the apparently secure discourse of the SED?

Out of the overall complex of discourses that constituted the *Wende* we can identify four loose clusters, although with the possible exception of the first it would be a mistake to consider them as discrete and homogeneous entities (see also Fraas and Steyer 1992: 174): the discourse of the SED and its media; of reform groups and opposition parties; of influential opinion-formers, especially artists and intellectuals; and of ordinary people, literally in the street. For the purposes of discussion, I shall consider each of these in turn, but it is important to emphasize that none of them was operating in a vacuum and that each fed into, and fed from, the others. The principal focus of my discussion will be on the re-emergence of a (new kind or quality of) *Öffentlichkeit* in GDR society.

Despite growing signs of unrest amongst the general population, especially in relation to the conduct of supposedly democratic processes (there were already public protests over the manipulation of local election results in May 1989, for example), the SED appeared to remain confident of its position until it was on the verge of collapse. The annual ritual of publishing official slogans (*Losungen*: see 3.2) for use on May Day and other public celebrations was observed, and the slogans conformed to the now characteristic patterns in both content and expression, with their references to the international fellowship of socialist nations, their exhortations to participate in implementing Party policy, their appeals to (sometimes unspecified) collectivities, and their stereotypical lexical and syntactic constructions. For example:

Solidarische Kampfesgrüße den kommunistischen und Arbeiterparteien in aller Welt!
Mit dem Blick auf den XII. Parteitag der SED lösen wir die Aufgaben der Gegenwart!

So wie wir heute arbeiten, so werden wir morgen leben!
Weiter voran auf dem bewährten Kurs der Einheit von Wirtschafts- und Sozialpolitik![26]

Greetings in solidarity and struggle to the communist and workers' parties all over the world!
With our eyes on the 12th Party Congress of the SED we will solve today's tasks!
As we work today, so we shall live tomorrow!
Onwards on the tried and tested course of the unity of economic and social policy!

However, the growing number of east Germans trying to leave the country, either through west German embassies in Prague and elsewhere or by crossing the Hungarian–Austrian border, presented a challenge. On the one hand, this could not be completely ignored, as it was widely reported on west German television, to which most people had access. On the other hand, it could not be acknowledged as a crisis, since this would suggest that the government was not in control of matters. The Party's strategy was to remain firmly within its standard discursive framework and go on the offensive. The first tactic was to displace the source of conflict from an internal issue within the GDR to the external antagonism between the GDR and the Federal Republic.

Wie aus Budapest verlautete, wurde den sich in der UVR aufhaltenden DDR-Bürgern illegal und unter Verletzung völkerrechtlicher Verträge und Vereinbarungen in einer Nacht- und Nebelaktion über die Grenze zu Österreich die Ausreise in die BRD ermöglicht. Dabei handelt es sich um eine direkte Einmischung in die inneren Angelegenheiten der Deutschen Demokratischen Republik. Unter dem Vorwand humanitärer Erwägungen wird organisierter Menschenhandel betrieben. Mit Bedauern muß festgestellt werden, daß sich Vertreter der Ungarischen Volksrepublik dazu verleiten ließen, unter Verletzung von Abkommen und Vereinbarungen diese von der BRD von langer Hand vorbereitete Aktion zu unterstützen. (*Neues Deutschland*, 11 September 1989, cited in Bresgen 1993: 53)

According to reports from Budapest, the GDR citizens who had been staying in the People's Republic of Hungary have been enabled to leave the country via the border with Austria and travel to the FRG. This cloak-and-dagger operation was illegal and in breach of international agreements. It constitutes direct interference in the internal affairs of the German Democratic Republic. Under the pretext of humanitarian considerations organized trafficking in human beings is being perpetrated. Regrettably, it must be noted that representatives of the Hungarian People's Republic, breaching treaties and agreements, have misguidedly allowed themselves to be led into supporting this action that had been carefully orchestrated by the FRG.

In this short article from the official news agency ADN, the individuals concerned are characterized as virtually passive participants in an 'illegal operation' planned by the Federal Republic and supported by 'misguided' representatives of the Hungarian government. Passive and impersonal grammatical constructions focus attention on the actions and events—'*die Ausreise wurde ermöglicht*' ([they] have been enabled to leave the country), '*es handelt sich um eine direkte Einmischung*'

---

[26] For the full list, see Fix (1994*b*: 144–5).

(it constitutes direct interference), '*Menschenhandel wird betrieben*' (human trafficking is being perpetrated)—but the perpetrator, implicit in the first three sentences, is finally named: '*diese von der BRD von langer Hand vorbereitete Aktion*'
(this action that had been carefully orchestrated by the FRG). To reinforce this
construction of events, concepts and images are used that are strongly reminiscent
of texts from the height of the Cold War: '*Nacht- und Nebelaktion*' (cloak-and-
dagger operation), '*Einmischung in innere Angelegenheiten*' (interference in internal affairs), '*organisierter Menschenhandel*' (organized trafficking in human
beings), '*unter Verletzung von Abkommen und Vereinbarungen*' (in breach of
treaties and agreements), '*von langer Hand vorbereitet*' (carefully orchestrated).

However, this approach could only work in the short term, if at all, and when
the number of 'leavers' continued to rise a second tactic was deployed. By early
October, those leaving were no longer portrayed merely as victims of the Federal
Republic's machinations but as guilty of moral and political betrayal: 'Sie alle
haben durch ihr Verhalten die moralischen Werte mit Füßen getreten und sich
selbst aus der Gesellschaft ausgegrenzt. Man sollte ihnen deshalb keine Tränen
nachweinen.' (Through their behaviour, they have all trampled on moral values
and excluded themselves from society. So no tears should be wasted on them.)
(*Neues Deutschland*, 2 October 1989, cited in Hopfer 1991: 118)

The characterization of the leavers' actions as betrayal and self-exclusion
from GDR society was an important attempt—albeit by that time far too late—
to protect one of the cornerstones of SED discourse: 'das unerschütterliche
Vertrauensverhältnis zwischen Partei und Volk' (the unshakeable relationship of
trust between Party and people). To contemplate their actual motives for wanting
to leave would have entailed an acknowledgement that this supposedly solid bond
had broken down. At the same time, the Party leadership clearly recognized the
need to (be seen to) 'restore' the relationship of trust with those who remained. In
the context of its self-image as the voice of the people, the Party's new 'policy of
dialogue', launched in early October, should have been a sign that it acknowledged
the need to reconnect with the people and engage in an open exchange of views.
However, it was immediately clear that only a particular kind of dialogue was on
offer. What had been one of the central demands of the various reform groups was
appropriated by the SED leadership as part of a broader strategy of neutralizing
the opposition and regaining the initiative.

Colin Good (1991: 52) cites Kurt Hager's brazen claim, in a television interview
on 12 October, that 'wir [i.e. the Politburo] sind doch diejenigen, die den Dialog
erfunden haben' (after all, we [i.e. the Politburo] were the ones who invented dialogue), and accordingly the concept was embedded into the unchanged discourse
of Party dominance: 'über den Dialog verwirklicht die Partei ihre führende Rolle
in der Gesellschaft' (through dialogue the Party realizes its leading role in society)
(Günter Schabowski in *Neues Deutschland*, 21 October 1989, cited in Fraas and
Steyer 1992: 181). In the official media and in statements by Party leaders, *Dialog*

was most frequently collocated with the verb *führen* (to lead, conduct), which reinforced the perception of an asymmetrical process (for further examples, see Hellmann 1993: 204–5, Läzer 1993: 100, Schäffner and Porsch 1998: 153–4), and newspaper headlines such as 'Was bei unserem Dialog unterm Strich stehen muß' ('What must come out of our dialogue', in *Junge Welt*, 21 October 1989, cited in Läzer 1993: 93) demonstrate the intention to control and constrain the dialogue with the people. The prescription 'Dialog ja, aber nicht auf der Straße' (dialogue yes, but not on the street) meant not only that the street was an inappropriate venue for serious dialogue but that the street was now the people's territory, a place where the Party could no longer exercise its authority. As a banner proclaimed on one demonstration: 'Die Straße ist die Tribüne des Volkes!' ('The street is the people's platform!') (see Reiher 1992: 50).

In this sense, it was probably true to say that the Party had 'invented' dialogue, and this discursive genre was a logical extension of the *Aussprache* or *Diskussion* practised in schools as an exercise in the reproduction of orthodox arguments rather than an open debate (Schlosser 1990*a*/1999: 94). This is clear, for example, in Krenz's inaugural speech as General Secretary of the SED on 18 October (see Teichmann 1991: 259):

Für den Dialog, den wir mit aller Entschiedenheit erstreben, sind also zwei Voraussetzungen hervorzuheben. Erstens: Alles, worüber wir uns einig sind und worüber wir uns streiten, muß eindeutig in seinem Ziel sein: den Sozialismus in der DDR weiter auszubauen, die sozialistischen Ideale hochzuhalten und keine unserer gemeinsamen Errungenschaften preiszugeben. Wer das in Zweifel zieht, stellt das Lebenswerk von Generationen in Frage.

Two preconditions must therefore be emphasized for the dialogue that we are resolutely determined to bring about. First, everything on which we agree and disagree must be clear in its aim of continuing to consolidate socialism in the GDR, of upholding socialist ideals, and of refusing to betray what we have achieved together. Anyone who calls that into question jeopardizes the life's work of generations.

The SED's *Dialogpolitik* was a crucial part of what Fraas and Steyer (1992: 178) call the phase of 'Übergang ohne Wandel' (transition without change) in October and November, in which the Party resorted to a strategy of semantic and discursive manoeuvres designed to outflank the protesters by giving the impression that it not only shared their objectives but indeed was (and always had been) leading the way to achieving them. Since actually embracing and implementing the protesters' demands would have undermined, if not demolished, the Party's authority, the strategy had to operate on two levels: it had to incorporate key concepts such as dialogue and reform into the dominant discourse to demonstrate 'flexibility' and 'responsiveness', but in such a way that the fundamental principles and values remained intact and the correctness and consistency of the Party's analysis and its policies were not put in doubt.

So even as Erich Honecker was being deposed at the ninth Congress of the Party's Central Committee on 18 October, in order to signal decisive leadership and an intention to introduce changes,[27] official statements emphasized that the Party was not breaking with its past and that it was, on the contrary, maintaining its tradition of continuous change and reform: 'Der Aufbau des Sozialismus in der DDR war von Anbeginn ein Prozeß tiefgreifender Wandlungen und Reformen in allen Bereichen' (From the outset, building socialism in the GDR was a process of profound changes and reforms in all areas) (from an editorial in *Neues Deutschland*, 18 October 1989, cited in Good 1991: 48; see also further extracts from Krenz's speech on 18 October in Teichmann 1991: 260). The absorption of the key concepts of *Dialog*, *Wende*, and *Reform* (or, as here, the preferred notion of *Erneuerung*, renewal) into the official discourse is most concisely captured in this extract from Krenz's television address on 3 November (i.e. on the eve of the mass demonstration in Berlin that was to be the decisive turning point in the overall process):

Mit vollem Recht können wir davon reden, daß mit der 9. Tagung des Zentralkomitees der SED eine neue Etappe in der Entwicklung unseres sozialistischen Vaterlandes begonnen hat. Die politische Wende, die wir eingeleitet haben, erfaßt inzwischen alle Bereiche unserer Gesellschaft. Vor allem sind davon Millionen Menschen berührt und bewegt. Es geht ihnen— es geht uns allen—um die Erneuerung des gesellschaftlichen Lebens mit dem Ziel, den Sozialismus für jeden Bürger unseres Landes lebenswerter zu gestalten. Der Neubeginn, der Aufbruch des Volkes ist von vielen Gesprächen, Diskussionen, Auseinandersetzungen, Demonstrationen und anderen Willensäußerungen begleitet. Für alle diese Formen steht der Begriff des Dialogs. (From Schäffner 1992: 139)

We are fully justified in saying that with the 9th Congress of the Central Committee of the SED a new era has begun in the development of our socialist fatherland. The change in political direction that we have introduced now encompasses all areas of our society. Above all, it has touched and affected millions of people. What they want—what we all want—is the renewal of social life with the aim of making socialism more worth living for every citizen of our country. The fresh start, the new departure of our people is accompanied by many conversations, discussions, debates, demonstrations, and other expressions of intent. All of these forms are covered by the concept of dialogue.

What Krenz presents here as a 'new stage' in the development of the GDR— political change 'introduced by the Party' and 'accompanied' by public debates— closely resembles the policies of *glasnost* (openness) and *perestroika* (reform, restructuring) that Mikhail Gorbachev had been promoting in the Soviet Union. However, these concepts had been resisted by the SED, most famously by Politburo member Kurt Hager in an interview with the west German magazine *Stern* in April 1987. When pressed to respond to the question whether *perestroika* would be introduced in the GDR, Hager replied: 'Würden Sie, nebenbei gesagt, wenn Ihr Nachbar seine Wohnung neu tapeziert, sich verpflichtet fühlen, Ihre

---

[27] The new General Secretary, Egon Krenz, declared immediately: 'Mit der heutigen Tagung werden wir eine Wende einleiten, werden wir vor allem die politische und ideologische Offensive wiedererlangen' (With today's conference we shall introduce a change of direction, we shall above all get back onto the political and ideological offensive) (see Teichmann 1991: 259).

Wohnung ebenfalls neu zu tapezieren?' (By the way, would you feel obliged to repaper your home just because your neighbour repapers his?) (*Stern*, 9 April 1987). This casual dismissal of a policy central to political developments in the 'Bruderland' Soviet Union would later resound through the discourse of defiance during the *Wende* (see below), but the official discourse was consistently framed in terms of the 'Politik der Kontinuität und Erneuerung' (policy of continuity and renewal) with which the Party sought to square the circle of remaining resolutely on course while appearing to envisage and promote change. However, the insistence on 'continuity that has always included change' was interpreted by the Party's opponents as a sign of its unwillingness, or perhaps even inability, to contemplate real change.

The rigour with which the official discourse had been maintained and consolidated over many years meant that the Party leadership had unwittingly sown the seeds of its own downfall. It had ultimately been less successful in securing the integrity and solidarity of the people (at least, not in the way it had intended) than in trapping itself inside a rigid discursive framework, and in the radically reconfigured communicative environment of late 1989 the old discourse appeared anachronistic and manifestly divorced from the social and political realities of daily life in the GDR. Real signs of change appeared only after the discursive strategy of the short-lived Krenz regime had failed to turn the tide of popular opinion, and although the new government under Hans Modrow was still dominated by the SED it was clear that the Party was not only losing its grip on political power but had already lost its hold on public discourse. For example, while Modrow acknowledged the crisis situation, he continued at first to talk in terms of renewal within existing structures (*'Erneuerungsprozeß der sozialistischen Gesellschaft'*, process of renewal of socialist society; *'Erneuerung des Sozialismus in unserem Lande'*, renewal of socialism in our country—see Schäffner and Porsch 1998: 160). Although this was precisely what most reform groups had been demanding, it was no longer sufficient to satisfy the people on the street, who by early December were calling for 'German unity'. The open pluralization of both politics and the media, following the formation of new political parties and groupings and the abolition of censorship, meant that the SED had lost its monopoly of the public domain. By early 1990, the challenge from competing discourses both within the GDR and from the Federal Republic, together with political pressure from the Soviet Union, finally made the pressure to abandon the objective of a reformed socialist society irresistible.

However, while the conservative grouping *Allianz für Deutschland* (Alliance for Germany), that was to attract an overall majority of the votes in the election to the final Volkskammer in March 1990, openly campaigned with the uncompromising slogan 'Nie wieder Sozialismus!' (Socialism—never again!), it too had travelled a long way in a short space of time. Even conceiving of themselves as an 'opposition' was highly problematic both for political parties such as the eastern CDU and for the various citizens' action groups within the reform movement (see Sandford 2000). Until their decisive break with the past in early 1990 (and not all of these groupings did this even then), the common denominator amongst these 'alternative' voices was not (explicit) opposition to the SED (with the implication of opposition to the socialist mission and the identity of the GDR) but the call for internal reforms. This meant that they had to conduct their own discursive struggle to disengage from the dogmatic prescriptions of the official discourse and develop a new discourse without threatening the integrity and independence of their state and capitulating to the discursive model of west German politics. The various groupings did this in different ways but the overall process was part of the deritualization of political activity during the *Wende*, although as Manfred Hellmann (1997*a*: 136–7) points out, this was itself a transitional phase between the dominance of one form of ritualized expression in politics and another: politics in the Federal Republic, before and after unification, was (and is) characterized by its own abstruse diction, which is no more reader-friendly than the SED's *langue de bois*.[28]

Between September and December 1989, the political party that would eventually be the principal player in the short-lived government from March to October 1990, the eastern CDU, transformed itself from one of the *Blockparteien*[29] sharing the supposed consensus of pre-*Wende* GDR politics but representing a particular constituency in the east German electorate (practising Christians) into a more broadly based party rejecting socialism and positioning itself in the 'middle ground' of the new political landscape. Reinhard Hopfer (1994) shows how the CDU progressively relocated itself by loosening its ties to the conventional discourse of 'partnership' with the SED and other parties. In early September, for example, the then chair of the party, Gerald Götting, asserts 'die Zusammenarbeit von Marxisten und Christen in unserer Republik' (the cooperation of Marxists and Christians in our country) as a fundamental element of social and political development in the GDR and a month later he emphasizes the CDU's principle of seeking harmony within the 'Democratic Block'—'das Gemeinsame über das Trennende zu stellen' (to place what unites us above what divides us)—and reaffirms the party's self-image: 'So sammelt die CDU als gleichberechtigter Partner im Bündnis erneut ihre Kräfte als Partei des Friedens, der Demokratie und des Sozialismus' (In this way, the CDU as an equal partner in the alliance is regathering its strength as a party of peace, democracy, and socialism) (Hopfer 1994: 134–5). By mid-November,

---

[28] Hellmann quotes in this context Erhard Eppler's grotesque parody of west German political style: 'Ich gehe davon aus, daß die Entwicklung der Lage die Lösung der Probleme erleichtert, aber auch eine Herausforderung darstellt, denn die unverzichtbare (unabdingbare) Voraussetzung für die Akzeptanz unserer Politik ist es, daß wir den Bürgern nicht in die Tasche greifen, sondern uns durch gezielte Maßnahmen als Partei des Aufschwungs profilieren' (I am working on the assumption that the development of the situation will facilitate the solution of the problems but that it also represents a challenge, for the indispensable prerequisite for the acceptance of our policy is that we should not hit people in their pockets but rather take targeted measures to create a distinctive image for ourselves as the party of economic upturn). (Eppler 1992: 179–80).

[29] The SED was not the only political party in the GDR, but it dominated the 'Democratic Block', which was the umbrella term for all officially sanctioned mass organizations (such as the trade union organization FDGB) and other political parties (such as the eastern CDU) which were eligible for election to parliament (see Wolf 2000: 41–2, Schlosser 1990*a*/1999: 40–1).

however, following the opening of the Wall, the communicative environment has changed sufficiently for a CDU member of the Volkskammer, Christine Wienyk, to declare in a parliamentary debate:

Keine Partei sollte sich über andere Mandatsträger die Möglichkeit einer Überrepräsentation schaffen. Die bestehende Verfassung ist vor allem... im Sinne der Gleichberechtigung und Eigenständigkeit der Parteien zu überarbeiten.... Wir erwarten eine angemessene Beteiligung an der Regierungsverantwortung.... Eine administrativ ausgeübte Führungsrolle hat unser Vertrauen in das Bündnis tief verletzt. Wir haben in der Vergangenheit zu viel auf Gemeinsamkeit gesetzt und zu wenig eigenständig gehandelt, wo wir öffentlich hätten widersprechen sollen. (Cited in Hopfer 1994: 137)

No party should create for itself the possibility of over-representation above other mandate holders. The current constitution must be revised above all in terms of the equality and autonomy of the parties.... We expect to take an appropriate share in the responsibility of government.... An administrative leadership role [of one party] seriously damaged our trust in the alliance. In the past, we put too much emphasis on common ground and did not act sufficiently independently, when we should have publicly voiced our disagreement.

Even here, the tone is as much self-critical as critical of the SED, and further texts in the following weeks make it clear that the CDU needed to confront and acknowledge its own past failings before it could move forward. New party leader (and later Prime Minister) Lothar de Maizière, for example, declared to the special party conference in mid-December:

Er, der demokratische Zentralismus, war der genetische Defekt der DDR und des in ihr betriebenen Pseudosozialismus.... Unser Grundübel war die Einbindung der CDU in ein politisches System ohne Bewegungsfreiheit, ohne eigenständige Wirkung.... Die CDU trägt durch den politischen Sündenfall der geduldeten Gleichschaltung Mitschuld am moralischen Verfall der ganzen Gesellschaft. (Ibid.: 138–9)

Democratic centralism was the genetic defect of the GDR and of the pseudo-socialism practised in it.... Our fundamental problem was that the CDU was tied too closely into a political system without freedom to manoeuvre, without the ability to function independently.... By tolerating *Gleichschaltung* [enforced conformity], the CDU fell from grace politically and must therefore bear its share of guilt for the moral decline of the whole society.

The reference at that point to 'pseudo-socialism' is an indicator of the CDU's ultimate inability to sustain its commitment to the socialist project. In common with other parties and reform groups, the CDU wrestled with this fundamental but problematic concept (see, for example, Sandford 2000, Stötzel 1991: 12–13, Schlosser 1993: 224, 227), seeking first to construct a contrast between 'true' social-ism and its 'distorted' realization in the GDR in order to argue for its 'renewal':

Wir sind der Überzeugung: nicht der Sozialismus ist am Ende, wohl aber seine adminis-trative, diktatorische Verzerrung. Wenn Sozialismus zukunftsträchtig ist, dann nur als grundlegend erneuerter, demokratischer Sozialismus. Denn echter Sozialismus bedeutet nicht weniger, sondern mehr Demokratie. (From a CDU statement on 18 November 1989, cited in Hopfer 1994: 140–1)

We are convinced that it is not socialism that is at an end but rather its administrative, dictatorial distortion. If socialism is to have a future, then it can only be as a fundamentally renewed, democratic socialism. For true socialism means not less, but more, democracy.

Then, however, it finally abandoned it when it no longer appeared salvageable in the discursive context of mid-December: 'Nach meiner Überzeugung ist dieses Wort eine leere Hülse geworden und daher nicht mehr verwendbar' (It is my conviction that this word has become an empty shell and is therefore no longer useable) (ibid., from a speech by Lothar de Maizière).

Three months after declaring itself (still) a 'party of socialism', the CDU entered an election alliance with other parties of the 'centre', proclaiming 'Der Sozialismus muß weg' (socialism must go). In spite of their radically changed style, though, the CDU's public texts continued to rely both explicitly and implicitly on their readers' textual knowledge of the 'old' discourse.[30] For example:

Für einen freiheitlichen demokratischen Rechtsstaat, durch Teilung der Macht zwischen Regierung, Parlament und Rechtssprechung und deren Kontrolle!

- Freie Wahlen mit gleichen Chancen für alle Parteien
- Beseitigung der SED-Medienvorherrschaft
- Keine Parteiorganisationen in Betrieben und Institutionen
- Bildung, die vom Elternrecht und von der Individualität des Kindes ausgeht
- Gewaltfreies Lösen von Konflikten zwischen Personen, Gruppen und Staaten

Für soziale Marktwirtschaft—gegen sozialistische Experimente!

- Leistung soll sich endlich entfalten können und auszahlen
- Leistung ist die Voraussetzung für echte Sozialpolitik
- Wohlstand in einer gesunden Umwelt
- Soziale Gerechtigkeit statt kommunistischer Gleichmacherei
- Solide Altersversorgung statt magerer Rentengroschen
- Solidargemeinschaft von Alten, sozial Schwachen, Behinderten in der großen Familie aller Bürger
- Überwindung des Pflegenotstandes und Aufbau eines leistungsfähigen Gesundheitswesens
- Erhalt und Wiederaufbau unserer zerfallenen Städte und Dörfer

Für die deutsche Einheit in Freiheit und Selbstbestimmung!

(From a CDU election campaign document, cited in Teichmann 1991: 261)

For a free and democratic state based on the rule of law, by sharing power between government, parliament, and the administration of justice, and keeping these under scrutiny!

- Free elections with equal opportunities for all parties
- Removal of the SED's domination of the media

---

[30] Ironically, even traces of the old textual patterns persist in texts denouncing the old system. The opening sentence of a campaign text for the *Allianz für Deutschland*, for example, curiously juxtaposes an expression redolent of countless SED texts with a demand for true democracy: 'Mit vereinten Kräften wollen wir dafür kämpfen, daß endlich Schluß ist mit der Entmündigung unserer Bürger' (We shall combine forces in the fight to ensure that our citizens at last have the right to make their own decisions) (see Teichmann 1991: 260).

- No party organizations in businesses and institutions
- Education that is based on parents' rights and the individuality of the child
- Solving conflicts between individuals, groups, and the state without violence

For the social market economy—against socialist experiments!

- Hard work and achievement must finally be allowed to develop and be rewarded
- Hard work and achievement are the prerequisite for genuine social policy
- Prosperity in a healthy environment
- Social justice instead of communist levelling down
- Proper provision for the elderly instead of a pittance of a pension
- Supportive community of the elderly, the socially disadvantaged, and the disabled in the big family of all citizens
- Overcoming the shortage of nursing staff and building an efficient health service
- Maintaining and rebuilding our crumbling towns and villages

For German unity in freedom and self-determination!

Although the SED is mentioned only once in this campaign document, the significance for the electorate of some of the programme points is fully comprehensible only if the text as a whole is read as part of a counter-discourse to that of the old regime and an assault on those responsible for the prevailing shortcomings in social conditions. This is explicit in the contrastive pattern of demands such as 'soziale Gerechtigkeit statt kommunistischer Gleichmacherei' (social justice instead of communist levelling down), and the implication of 'endlich' (finally) in 'Leistung soll sich endlich entfalten können und auszahlen' (hard work and achievement must finally be allowed to develop and be rewarded) is clear. Other references, however, are less transparent. The goal of education 'die vom Elternrecht und von der Individualität des Kindes ausgeht' (based on parents' rights and the individuality of the child) has to be set against the SED's policy of forming 'allseitig entwickelte sozialistische Schülerpersönlichkeiten' (fully developed socialist student personalities; see 3.2), and the reference to a 'healthy environment' has greater impact in the knowledge that this had previously been a taboo topic in public discourse. At the same time, there are signs of attempts to develop a new discourse that is more than a reaction to the past or a slavish adoption of western norms. The support for 'einen freiheitlichen demokratischen Rechtsstaat' (free and democratic state based on the rule of law) and 'soziale Marktwirtschaft' (social market economy) and the intertextuality of the slogan 'gegen sozialistische Experimente!' (against socialist experiments, an unmistakable echo of Konrad Adenauer's 1950s appeal 'Keine Experimente!', No experiments!) are clear expressions of allegiance to the western model, but the concepts of individuality and prosperity, which are central to this model, are relativized by concern for the environment and 'solidarity' with vulnerable members of society, which would have had a particular resonance for those socialized in the GDR.

Like the CDU, some of the reform groups—such as *Demokratischer Aufbruch* and *Demokratie jetzt*—initially sought to rehabilitate the tarnished concept of socialism and to identify ways of revitalizing the existing system. However, by remaining at least to some extent within the old discursive framework, they imposed constraints on their own capacity to innovate, which resulted in rather vague calls for 'democratic restructuring' ('*demokratische Umgestaltung*', the officially preferred equivalent to *perestroika*) and apparently paradoxical formulations like 'die Einheit von Wirtschafts- und Sozialpolitik auf neue Grundlagen stellen' (to put the unity of economic and social policy on a new footing) and 'das Zusammenspiel von Plan und Markt' (the interaction of plan and market) (see. Schlosser 1993: 224–5, 227). By contrast, *Neues Forum*, the most influential group in the early part of the *Wende*, adopted from the outset an independent discursive strategy, deliberately bypassing established modes of political and ideological expression—avoiding the discursive patterns typical of public language in the GDR, but not adopting the model of west German political discourse. The opening sentence of the text with which they launched their campaign on 10 September diagnoses a fundamental disruption in communication between state (i.e. Party) and society: 'In unserem Lande ist die Kommunikation zwischen Staat und Gesellschaft offensichtlich gestört' (In our country communication between state and society has clearly broken down) (see Schüddekopf 1990: 29). In this and subsequent texts they seek to repair this damage by cultivating what Volmert (1992: 68) calls the 'Sprache des unpolitischen Alltags' (language of everyday unpolitical life). Their texts have none of the linguistic or textual features characteristic of official discourse, but rather than developing an alternative conceptual framework they concentrate on presenting a concise analysis of social and political problems and putting forward concrete proposals and demands for action. For example:

Wir wollen Spielraum für wirtschaftliche Initiative, aber keine Entartung in eine Ellenbogengesellschaft. Auf der einen Seite wünschen wir uns eine Erweiterung des Warenangebots und bessere Versorgung, andererseits sehen wir deren soziale und ökologische Kosten und plädieren für die Abkehr von ungehemmtem Wachstum. (Schüddekopf 1990: 29; see also Hellmann 1997*a*: 135–8 and Teichmann 1991: 256–8).

We want room for manoeuvre for economic initiatives, but we do not want to degenerate into a dog-eat-dog society. On the one hand, we would like to see a broader range of goods available and an improvement in the supply situation, but on the other hand we are aware of the social and ecological costs associated with this and advocate the rejection of unrestricted growth.

The central demand in *Neues Forum*'s launch text *Aufbruch 89*—according to Bresgen (1995: 279) 'one of the few classic texts of the GDR revolution', signed by 200,000 people within two months—was for a 'democratic dialogue on the tasks of the state, the economy, and culture'. The text insists that this must be an inclusive process: 'Über diese Fragen müssen wir in aller Öffentlichkeit, gemeinsam und im ganzen Land, nachdenken und miteinander sprechen' (We must reflect on and discuss these questions publicly, collectively, and in the whole country). However, the subsequent absorption of the concept of dialogue into the SED's discourse (see above) provoked a sceptical response from *Neues Forum*; their definition of 'genuine dialogue' in the following text presupposes a competing and 'unacceptable' conception:

Wenn das Politbüro der SED jetzt einen echten Dialog mit der Bevölkerung, mit den unterschiedlichsten Kräften und Strömungen innerhalb der Gesellschaft sucht, besteht die Gefahr, daß auch dieser Ansatz wieder durch die vorhandenen Strukturen erstickt wird. Deshalb muß ein echter Dialog institutionalisiert werden!

... Echter Dialog bedeutet:

1 Zulassung des Neuen Forum und aller anderen Basisgruppen, Parteien und Bürgerinitiativen, die sich für die Demokratisierung der Gesellschaft einsetzen,
2 Zugang zu den Massenmedien,
3 Pressefreiheit und Abschaffung der Zensur,
4 Versammlungs- und Demonstrationsfreiheit.

Dieser echte gesellschaftliche Dialog hat auf allen Ebenen gewaltfrei zu erfolgen, bei Anerkennung der Eigenstaatlichkeit der DDR, bei strikter Abweisung aller rechtsradikaler und faschistischer Haltungen, auf dem Boden der Verfassung. (From a statement published by *Neues Forum* on 12 October 1989, cited in Teichmann 1991: 256–7)

If the Politburo of the SED is now seeking a genuine dialogue with the population, with all the various forces and currents within society, there is a danger that this attempt will again be stifled by the present structures. Therefore a genuine dialogue must be institutionalized! Genuine dialogue means:

1 authorization of Neues Forum and all other grass-roots organizations, parties, and citizens' action groups which are committed to the democratization of society,
2 access to the mass media,
3 freedom of the press and abolition of censorship,
4 freedom of assembly and freedom to demonstrate.

This genuine social dialogue must take place, without force, on all levels, in recognition of the sovereignty of the GDR, categorically rejecting all far-right and fascist attitudes, and in accordance with the constitution.

The rejection of a process controlled by the SED and the appeal to all social groups committed to the democratization of GDR society to engage in the restoration of *Öffentlichkeit* stimulated public responses not only from political parties, reform groups, and other interest groups (for example, anti-fascist and peace organizations, trade unions) but also from a wide range of groups representing artists and intellectuals. Taking their lead from *Aufbruch 89*, writers, actors, *Kabarett* performers, and musicians published their own declarations of support for 'democratic dialogue', couched in what Hellmann (1997a: 136) calls the 'Vokabular der Gefühle und der menschlichen Moral' (vocabulary of feelings and human morality). On 18 September, for example, a group of rock musicians distributed a statement expressing their 'concern about the current state of the country' and declaring:

Wir wollen in diesem Lande leben, und es macht uns krank, tatenlos mitansehen zu müssen, wie Versuche einer Demokratisierung, Versuche der gesellschaftlichen Analyse kriminalisiert bzw. ignoriert werden. Wir fordern jetzt und hier sofort den öffentlichen Dialog mit allen Kräften. (From Schüddekopf 1990: 39–40)

We want to live in this country and it makes us sick to have to stand idly by and watch while attempts at democratization and attempts at social analysis are criminalized or ignored. We demand here and now immediate public dialogue with all forces.

And at the end of October, young activists within *Demokratischer Aufbruch* published a list of eight demands for change, preceded by the following gesture of verbal defiance:

Null Bock auf FDJ!? Wir wollen keine Generation von Mitläufern mehr sein! Wir haben die Schnauze voll von Bevormundung und Gängelung und wollen nicht mehr Kampfreserve und Handlanger einer Partei sein, deren Politik viele unserer Freunde fortgetrieben hat. Auf wie viele sollen wir noch verzichten müssen? (Ibid.: 175).

Pissed off with the FDJ!? We're not going to go on being a generation of fellow travellers any more. We're fed up with being treated like children and having our minds made up for us. We're not willing to go on being the reserve troops and dogsbodies of a party whose policies have driven many of our friends away. How many more must we say goodbye to?

Once texts such as these came into circulation, in a way that had never previously been possible, they simultaneously called for and contributed to the construction of *Öffentlichkeit*. They responded to each other and interacted with other public texts—government statements, speeches at public gatherings, demonstration slogans—in a continuous process of what Hopfer (1992*a*) calls intra- and interdiscursivity.[31] And while dialogue between the state and the people ultimately proved unattainable, dialogue between different constituents of the people—'ordinary citizens', prominent public figures, representatives of occupational and other interest groups—evolved in complex ways through the production and reception of myriad written and spoken text types (Polenz 1993: 134). All this was part of the deritualization process, in which a new communicative environment was developed: even before censorship was abolished and freedom of assembly was granted, the people had begun to experience, and take advantage of, a new kind of political community, above all on the streets (see Volmert 1992: 62).

In reclaiming the right to speak on their own behalf[32] (the illocutionary force of the slogan '*Wir* sind das Volk!') the people were transferring into the public arena the subversive linguistic behaviour that had been practised for many years in more private contexts:

Gemeinsprache und Wahrheit blieben ein Reservat der mündlichen Rede, des 'Buschfunks', der Familie am Wochenende, in der Arbeiterschaft, auch des kollegialen Gesprächs am

---

[31] By intradiscursivity, he means ways in which texts within a discourse (here: the discourse of protest) draw on and give rise to others, and interdiscursivity refers to ways in which texts from different discourses relate to each other.

[32] The writer Christoph Hein addressed the crowd on the Alexanderplatz in Berlin on 4 November as 'Liebe mündig gewordene Mitbürger!' (Dear fellow-citizens, who have now come of age [politically]!).

Arbeitsplatz. Das war die Rednerschule der Revolution. (Niethammer 1990: 262; see also Pätzold 1992: 94–5)

Ordinary language and truth remained confined to spoken discourse, the 'bush telegraph', the family at weekends, in the work force, and to conversations amongst colleagues at work. This was where public speaking skills were learned for the revolution.

The explosion of linguistic creativity that characterized the mass demonstrations in the autumn of 1989 was therefore a public continuation of a private tradition. But whereas in the past the addressee of jokes, puns, and other 'language games' (Schiewe 1997) was an individual interlocutor, a small group of friends, or at most a *Kabarett* audience, the public utterances of so-called *Demo-Sprüche* (demo slogans) and chants at demonstrations were directed at (or at any rate available to) multiple addressees: the SED leadership, of course, but also fellow demonstrators, the broader GDR population, and foreign audiences (especially in the Federal Republic). The interpretation of explicitly critical slogans such as 'Pluralismus— weg mit der Feudalherrschaft einer Partei!' (Pluralism—down with the feudal rule of one party!) (Lang 1990: 56) required no more than the contextual knowledge of their reference to the GDR as (effectively) a one-party state, but the force of other, more esoteric texts relied on intertextual knowledge to which only east Germans were likely to have access.

For example, a number of apparently arcane variations on the theme of wallpaper—'Wir brauchen Architekten statt Tapezierer!' (We need architects, not decorators!), 'Hager am Tapetenende. Sag, wie hoch ist deine Rente?' (Hager's at the end of his roll [of wallpaper]. Hey, how big's your pension?) (Lang 1990: 67–8)—would register only with those members of the audience who were aware of Kurt Hager's rejection of *perestroika* in his interview with *Stern* magazine (see above). Others operated on several levels, with different degrees of textual richness depending on the reader's cultural and contextual knowledge. For instance, on the surface level, the slogan 'Egon, wir haben einen Plan' (Egon, we've got a plan) is simply a facetiously familiar but unspecific proposal addressed to Egon Krenz. However, virtually anyone socialized in the GDR would also make the connection[33] with the highly popular television series (imported from Denmark) *Die Olsenbande*, revolving around the disastrous exploits of a criminal gang, whose leader, Egon Olsen, routinely announces to his accomplices each time he emerges from prison: 'Ich habe einen Plan' (I've got a plan) (see Reiher 1992: 54–6). At an intermediate level, therefore, Krenz is implicitly ridiculed by association with the failed petty criminal who refuses to learn from his mistakes. But a closer reading opens up further layers of meaning that place the slogan within the web of references linking different (strands of) *Wende* discourses. First, the reference to the particular television source invests the utterance with a ritual character, which together with the collective subject 'we' and the mention of a 'plan' evokes the style and content of official *Losungen* (see above). Secondly, however, the 'original' saying has

---

[33] I am grateful to Claudia Fellmer for confirming this from personal experience.

been turned on its head, so that now it is the 'gang', not the 'leader', that is taking the initiative. This transformation, finally, relates the slogan intradiscursively to the underlying 'master slogan' of the democracy campaign: 'We are the people, and *we* have a plan'.

These *Demo-Sprüche* were therefore a potent means of developing new forms of public communication in the absence of opportunities for expressing and exchanging opinions in an unregulated and plural media market. Their power derived not only from their terseness, their pugnacity and wit, but crucially also from their relationship with the official *Losungen* which they displaced on placards and billboards. The traditional *Losungen* were a distillation of the themes and patterns of the official discourse, the most distinctive expression of rituality in public life in the GDR. The successful appropriation of this important tool of the SED's *Überzeugungsarbeit* (persuasion programme) depended not simply on subverting it by substituting alternative messages but on deritualizing it by transforming it into a new genre. Some *Demo-Sprüche* were straightforward parodies of existing *Losungen*, for example: 'So wie wir heute demonstrieren [instead of: arbeiten], werden wir morgen leben' (As we demonstrate [instead of: work] today, we shall live tomorrow). But the vast majority adopted a more original approach, changing both rhetorical function and textual form. Traditional *Losungen* were affirmative, earnest, and optimistic, and consisted largely of exhortations (typically in the form of imperatives) to continued commitment to the cause (see examples above). *Demo-Sprüche*, by contrast, were critical, often humorous, acerbic, and irreverent in their references to leading figures in Party and government, and ranged in content from concise analyses of social and political failings of the current regime to blunt, concrete demands for change. Moreover, the liberating pleasure of composing original material lay as much in breaking away from the limited formal templates of the old *Losungen* as in expressing dissent: Fix (1990), for example, shows how a range of genres were used and adapted—fairy tales, proverbs, aphorisms, advertising slogans, nursery rhymes, poems, letters, quotations from literary and biblical sources (see also Fix 1994, Lang 1990, Schiewe 1997: 137–9, and Reiher 1992).

In her celebrated speech at the mass demonstration in Berlin on 4 November, the writer Christa Wolf brought out the tension between individual creativity and the collective voice of protest that was inherent in the way in which these pithy sayings were composed and 'published'. Quoting some of the most vivid *Sprüche*, she helps to give them a wider distribution than they could enjoy through chance observation, but at the same time classifies them as random examples of what she calls 'literarisches Volksvermögen' (the national literary wealth) (for the full text of the speech, see Schüddekopf 1990: 213–15, or Wolf 1990). Language is the central theme of her speech, which in the space of a few lines encompasses both interdiscursive references to the problematic concepts of *Wende* and *Dialog* and intradiscursive connections with the discourses of street protest and organized reform. The speech is therefore both a complex comment on 'liberated language' and in itself an example of the exercise of liberated language (for a detailed analysis, see Hopfer 1992*a*). On the one hand, she makes frequent references to the (at that stage) still tentative practice of open communication ('Soviel wie in diesen Wochen ist in unserem Lande noch nie geredet worden', people have never talked so much in our country as they have in recent weeks), reflects critically on official language use ('Mit dem Wort Wende habe ich meine Schwierigkeiten', I have problems with the word *Wende*), and comments with approval on how the language of oppression has been disarmed ('Wir drehen alte Losungen um, die uns gedrückt und verletzt haben, und geben sie postwendend zurück', we manipulate old slogans that have oppressed and hurt us, and send them back 'by return' [a pun on *Wende*]). On the other hand, the theme of liberated language serves as a bridge to other themes, to issues that had previously been impossible to articulate: '[Wir] fragen uns: Was tun? und hören als Echo die Antwort: Was tun! Das fängt jetzt an, wenn aus den Forderungen Rechte, also Pflichten werden: Untersuchungskommission, Verfassungsgericht, Verwaltungsreform.' (We ask ourselves: What should we do? And hear the answer echoing back to us: Do something! It's starting now, when demands become rights and therefore duties: investigating commission, constitutional court, administrative reform.) In each case, however, language is associated with action: 'Jede revolutionäre Bewegung befreit auch die Sprache' (every revolutionary movement also liberates language), but this liberated language is then both the instigator and the vehicle of social and political change.

In this section, I have tried to show how an understanding of the role of language in the historical processes of the *Wende* requires an analysis of the interdependence of different, competing discourses. The official discourse of Party and state, intended as an integrating and unifying force, ultimately inhibited the SED leadership's ability to react adequately to rapidly changing political conditions and at the same time provided a focus and a resource for alternative and oppositional discourses. The *Wende* as a linguistic event was therefore dominated not by one discourse but by the interaction between several.

In this final phase of the sociolinguistic history of Germany as a politically divided nation, both language as topos and language as social practice continued to figure prominently, as had been the case throughout the earlier periods in which sociolinguistic difference had supported and sustained political disunity. Part I of this study has explored the complex contribution of language first to the fracturing of the German nation after 1945 and then to the conception and finally to the collapse of the GDR as a social and political project. Part II will examine the extent to which the sociolinguistic fault line separating east from west continued to divide the two speech communities in the first decade of the politically unified Germany after 1990.

PART II

1990–2000 Relocating 'East' and 'West'

4

Conflicting Patterns in the Use and Evaluation of Language

4.1 The linguistic challenge of unification

As we have already seen in 2.3, the development of two discrete social and political systems engendered two communication communities, each developing specific lexical sub-sets for areas of life as diverse as political institutions and consumer products. The collision between these two previously segregated communities in 1989–90 had a number of immediate consequences: some 'old' (characteristically eastern) words became redundant or obsolete; some 'old' (western) words—including many anglicisms—had to be absorbed, at least passively, into the inventories of east German speakers; some words that predated the existence of the two states and had acquired archaic status in the GDR were reactivated for east German speakers (Kühn 1995a)—an unusual example of the older generation being at an advantage in the new context; some complementary word pairs were 'desynonymized'; some words and topics that had been taboo returned to public discourse; some new words were coined; and in terms of everyday interactions, lexically marked patterns of address and personal reference were changed. Some of these processes were more or less automatic, but others were more problematic and subject to variation and negotiation. Common to all of them, however, was the one-sided pressure to adapt imposed on east Germans, although the consciousness of linguistic differences contributed significantly to what were frequently referred to as the 'Befindlichkeiten' (sensitivities) of Germans, both east and west (Eroms 1997).

Consigning words that were either specific to, or typical of, the GDR to a wastebin category was a straightforward and predictable process up to a point. For example, words associated with features of everyday life that ceased to exist, at least in the form familiar in the GDR—*Solibasar* (see 2.3); *Elternaktiv* (parents' collective)—were unlikely to survive except in retrospective or ironic contexts, and terms referring to institutions and structures of the state—*Erweiterte Oberschule (EOS)* (high school, sixth form); *Volkseigener Betrieb (VEB)* (company in public ownership); *Ministerrat* (Council of Ministers)—were supplanted by terms relevant to the western setting. Moreover, the sheer volume of the vocabulary 'turnover' should not be underestimated: Schröder's (1992) lists from the field of education, for example, show how significant the task of 'relearning' was in certain domains. However, even though some GDR 'signifieds' disappeared virtually overnight, some of their 'signifiers' lived on, for a variety of reasons (habit, resistance), and for varying lengths of time—some even made a comeback after appearing to die out in the early 1990s and, perhaps even more remarkably, a few (very few) bucked the general trend and migrated westwards and entered the common German vocabulary. It would be impossible, and beyond the purpose of my investigations, to pursue all these avenues of research in detail here.[1] What I shall try to do instead is to identify and briefly illustrate the most significant aspects of this complex process of ecological change, in order to see what contribution lexicology and lexicography can make to the broader study of sociolinguistic difference and social change.

In a series of publications through the 1990s, the closest observer of east–west lexical contrasts both before and after unification, Manfred Hellmann, charted in minute detail and with great sensitivity the twists and turns of lexical and semantic change (see, for example, Hellmann 1990, 1994*a*, 1997*a, b, d*, 1998). Perhaps the most striking thing about public language use in the immediate post-*Wende* period is the presence of absences: gone in no time were the fixed expressions of official discourses, the routine references to *die Einheit von Wirtschafts- und Sozialpolitik* (the unity of economic and social policy), to *Sozialismus in den Farben der DDR* (socialism in the colours of the GDR), to *unsere Menschen* (our people: see 2.3 and 3.1); the many institutions that constituted the infrastructure of the GDR were rapidly dismantled and their names, where they appeared at all, were no longer collocated with the present tense (*PGH—Produktionsgenossenschaft des Handwerks*, craft cooperative; *HO—Handelsorganisation*, state-owned commercial concern; *Junge Pioniere*, Young Pioneers; *NVA—Nationale Volksarmee*, National People's Army); those terms that derived from, and in themselves expressed, disunification—*Ausreiseantrag* (application for an exit visa), *Reisekader* (see 2.3), and legal terms such as *humanitäre Maßnahmen* (humanitarian measures) and the western counterpart of this phrase, *besondere Bemühungen* (special efforts), both of them euphemisms for the buying out of political prisoners from the GDR by the Federal Republic—instantly lost their currency; administrative terms relating to countless aspects of everyday life no longer had any foundation in the reality of everyday life (*abkindern*: to offset the number of your children against outstanding loans; *nichterfaßter Wohnraum*: accommodation available for rent on a private basis, i.e. not allocated by the official housing authority; see Wolf 2000); and most conspicuously of all, the familiar names of thousands of household products (such as *Sana* margarine, *Perlodont* toothpaste, and *Tip-Fix* insect spray) disappeared from the supermarket shelves as the products themselves were replaced with western goods—and to a large extent the retail outlets which had stocked them suffered the same fate (*Konsum*, co-op store; *Exquisitladen*, shop selling

---

[1] For a detailed analysis of lexical developments based on a large corpus of material from the *Wende* period, see Herberg *et al.* 1997.

foreign luxury goods; *Getränkestützpunkt,* drinks shop) (for detailed discussions, see Hellmann 1994*a*, 1997*b*, Fraas 1990).

But not everything disappeared overnight, and some words characteristic of the GDR survived the clear-out of the *Umbruch* years (and some of these in fact had an even longer pedigree: for example, as Fleischer 1992 points out, the standard GDR collective term for creative artists, *Kulturschaffende,* had been much used by Goebbels). Surveys of newspapers and magazines published in eastern Germany in the early post-*Wende* period show a patchy process of fluctuating lexical fortunes rather than wholesale change. For example, Eroms (1997) found frequent occurrences of GDR remnants in newspapers published in the east (*Leipziger Volkszeitung, Neues Deutschland,* and *Wochenpost*), such as: *Rekonstruktion* (for *Erneuerung* or *Sanierung,* renovation), *vorfristig* (for *vorzeitig,* premature), and *Territorium* (for *Gebiet, Region,* area, region), and there were signs of continuing attachment to terms with an emblematic quality so long as they were not ideologically tainted—*Trabi* (diminutive form for *Trabant,* the popular car) is the classic example, but other words too seemed to confer a sense of familiarity and security: *Kaufhalle* (supermarket), for instance, and the names of certain popular consumer products such as *Club Cola* and *F6* cigarettes (see 5.3 on the importance of consumer power for the revival and remodelling of 'old' eastern products). Even the most marked of GDR-specific terms could survive in certain contexts: for example, while *Kollektiv* might have too strong a flavour to be used on its own, it appeared to be acceptable to many speakers in compound forms such as *Autorenkollektiv, Ärztekollektiv,* or *Klassenkollektiv* (authors', doctors', or class collective) (Reiher 1995*c*: 239, Reiher 1996).

Taking stock of the immediate post-*Wende* situation, Hellmann (1990) listed many words that survived the initial shock of change, but within a few years he had to revise this list down to about a dozen that would not go away (Hellmann 1997*b*: 75–7). Some of these remain within their eastern habitat (*geschuldet sein,* meaning *etwas ist einer Sache zu verdanken,* to be due to; *in Größenordnungen,* meaning *in großem Umfang,* extensively, in large numbers; *jemanden orientieren auf etwas,* meaning *jemandem eine Richtlinie geben für etwas,* to give someone guidance on something, to direct)[2] and now form part of the general vocabulary that may be characterized as 'regional'. But others have been successfully transplanted onto western soil and now seem to be firmly part of the common lexicon: *abnicken* (to approve a plan or proposal, 'to give it the nod'), *andenken* (to give some thought to), and the older term *Lehrling* (trainee, apprentice), which was never fully supplanted in the west by the modern term *Auszubildende/r* (abbreviated to *Azubi*), seems to be returning to favour with the impulse from the east (Müller 1994: 126). They may be few in number, but the common factor to such

---

[2] This also applies to a number of idioms, for instance: *ein Auge ausfahren,* meaning *sehr erstaunt sein* (to be amazed), or *sich einen Kopf machen,* meaning *angestrengt nachdenken* (to rack your brains) (see Fleischer 1992).

survivors seems to be their adaptability to contemporary economic or political contexts: words with an unmistakable aura or whiff of official GDR contexts had no chance of survival anywhere, and even more 'neutral' words marked as GDR-specific had little prospect of acceptance in the west (*rekonstruieren*, to modernize businesses, buildings etc.; *Zielstellung* for *Zielsetzung*, objective: see 4.3), but words associated with economically viable concepts could be more resilient and assert themselves in the new linguistic marketplace: for example, the GDR's state-run waste-recycling operation *SERO—VEB Kombinat Sekundärrohstoffe*—re-emerged as a limited company, *SERO GmbH.*

The overwhelming change, however, was undeniably the irresistible surge of western vocabulary that accompanied and reinforced the social, political, and economic incorporation of the eastern population into the Federal Republic. East Germans were confronted with hundreds, perhaps thousands, of unfamiliar terms and concepts in many different domains (see Hellmann 1997*b*: 68–70 for a representative selection), and while historians of the language may play down the significance of this, west German linguist Horst Dieter Schlosser is surely right to insist on acknowledging the psychological burden it imposed on his eastern compatriots:

Die Konfrontation der neuen Bundesbürger mit einer Fülle an neuen Sachverhalten und Bezeichnungen, die ihnen fremd sein mußten, zwingt zu Anpassungsleistungen, die mehr Kraft erfordern, als sich ein Altbundesbürger überhaupt vorstellen kann. (Schlosser 1993: 150)

Confronted with a plethora of new objects and designations which must have been unfamiliar to them, east Germans are obliged to adapt to an extent that requires more effort than a west German can possibly imagine.

And Wolfgang Schubert's rewriting of the Ode to Joy in the east German satirical magazine *Eulenspiegel* captures the link between new words and new realities succinctly—and untranslatably:

Neuer Audi, Spanien-Reise,
Telefunken, Rewe-Markt,
Mon chéri und Henckell trocken,
Eurocheque und Müller-Quark.
Abgewickelt, Warteschleife,
Kurzarbeit und Arbeitsamt.
Krippenschließung, Mieterhöhung
und vielleicht bald obdachlos.
Wahlversprechen und Reales:
Auch die Niete ist ein Los!
(From: *Eulenspiegel* 21, 1994: 4, cited in Müller 1994: 130, footnote 29)

West Germans were not entirely spared the exposure to this experience of lexical (and in some instances semantic) innovation. Fraas (1990: 596–8) and Hellmann (1997*b*: 66–7) catalogue some of the hundreds of, for the most part, relatively short-lived words and expressions thrown up during the *Wende* (such as *Dableiber, chinesische Lösung, Mauerspecht,* and *Blockflöte*),[3] which were as unfamiliar to west as to east Germans. Political and economic measures and institutions that were introduced in order to deal with the consequences of unification (*Aufschwung Ost, Treuhandanstalt, Gauck-Behörde*)[4] were also new to east and west alike. But it is not the novelty of the words themselves that matters here, of course, so much as the impact of what they represent on the lives of those affected by them. The principal task of the *Treuhandanstalt,* for example, was to 'rationalize' the east German economy by privatizing state-run businesses, and an inevitable consequence of restructuring the economy in line with western market principles was a massive 'release' of 'surplus' labour: English has as abundant a stock of euphemisms for such processes as German. One of the key words associated with the activity of the *Treuhandanstalt,* however, does not have an exact equivalent in English, nor was it in itself new: *abwickeln* is a common enough word, which before 1990/1991 would have meant to most Germans something like 'to deal with, handle (a task)', but a second, technical meaning (to close down a business—and then, by extension, to fire individual workers) rapidly gained notoriety. The west German tax payer was, no doubt, not uninterested in this procedure, but it was east German workers in all walks of life whose existence was directly affected by it. The bitterness of this experience is concisely encapsulated in the cynical notice spotted by Manfred Hellmann (1994: 128) at a news kiosk in Friedrichstraße station in east Berlin shortly after the first chief executive of the *Treuhandanstalt,* Detlev Rohwedder, had been murdered in 1991: 'Treuhandchef abgewickelt' (Treuhand boss dealt with) (for a detailed discussion of *Treuhand* as a key word of the *Wende,* see Herberg et al. 1997: Chapter 11; and for close analysis of *abwickeln,* see Siehr 1993, 1994, Teubert 1993).

'New' is a relative term in this context in other ways too. A word with a long history may be perceived as new if it has been out of use for a long period of time: for example, while *Gesamtschule* (comprehensive school) and *Gastarbeiter* (guest worker) are clearly western neologisms of the post-1949 period, *Aktiengesellschaft* (joint-stock company), *Immobilienberater* (property or real-estate adviser), and *Realschule* (a type of secondary school) were all part of the general German vocabulary before 1949 which had become 'archaic', frozen in suspended animation, in the GDR, until they were resuscitated after unification (Kühn 1995a). Other pseudo-neologisms were words that had been current in the context of an

---

[3] *Dableiber* were those who 'chose to stay' in the GDR; *chinesische Lösung* (Chinese solution) is an allusion to the brutal repression of political dissent in China; *Mauerspecht* (literally 'wall-pecker': *Specht* means woodpecker) was coined to refer to people chipping out bits of the Wall; and *Blockflöte* (literally 'recorder') was a contemptuous expression for members of the Democratic Block, seen as 'singing the same tune' as the SED.

[4] *Aufschwung Ost* (Revitalizing the East) refers to measures introduced to boost the eastern economy; the *Treuhandanstalt* was the government agency charged with privatizing eastern companies; and the *Gauck-Behörde*—named after its head, Joachim Gauck—was the popular name for the organization set up in 1991 to deal with the *Stasi* archives.

earlier *Umbruch*, the period of national reckoning after 1945: then, as in the fall-out from 1989, there was talk of *Mitläufer* (fellow travellers), of *(Un)belastete* (people with(out) a guilty past), of *Lastenausgleich* (financial compensation), and of *Persilscheine* (certificate of blamelessness) (Hellmann 1997b: 67). 'New' too, at least in public discourse, were many words and expressions to do with topics that had been taboo in the GDR media, such as ecological problems: *Waldsterben* (dying of the forests), *Giftmüll* (toxic waste), *Treibhausgase* (greenhouse gases). And although words that were perceived as foreign, especially anglicisms, had actually been in more widespread use in the GDR than was often assumed in the west, their use in all public contexts, from newspaper headlines to shop names, as well as in everyday speech, suddenly became unfettered and they swept across all domains with a speed and vehemence that shocked many older east Germans (Blei 1993, Müller 1994: 128).

So the bulk of the unfamiliar vocabulary encountered by east Germans after the *Wende* had already existed as a normal part of the west German lexicon. On the one hand, there were words and expressions denoting concepts and phenomena peculiar to the social, political, and economic environment of the Federal Republic and which therefore had to be assimilated at the same time as their labels: *Auslandsamt* (office for foreign students' affairs), *Unternehmensberatung* (management consultancy), *Arbeitslosengeld* (unemployment benefit). This was challenging enough for someone socialized in a completely different system, but was at least fairly transparent as an exercise in learning: new concepts—new words. On the other hand, there were many concepts and words that appeared to have equivalents in the 'other' system, and the normal processes of language change would predict a number of possible outcomes in the event of lexical contact: in the case of 'genuine' synonyms, either one of the forms would be displaced by the other, or one (or both) would acquire additional 'meaning components' in order to enable the words to be distinguished from each other and therefore justify their existence in a common system, or again one (or both) would be defined more narrowly in some other way, typically in terms of geographical specificity ('regional').

Since 1990, at least some of these processes seem to have occurred for large numbers of lexical items in German. Almost without exception,[5] west German terms have driven out east German synonyms: *Getränkestützpunkt* (drinks shop) has given way to *Getränkeshop* or *-markt*, *Kaufhalle* (supermarket) by and large to *Supermarkt*, *Abschnittsbevollmächtigte(r)* *(ABV)* (community police officer) to *Streifenpolizist* (Hellmann 1994a: 125). Those east German terms that have withstood the tide of change generally have the status of regional variants, that is to say, they are no longer necessarily associated with the political state GDR but with the geographical region 'eastern Germany': *Dreiraumwohnung* (for *Dreizimmerwohnung,* three-room apartment), *Plastetüte* (for *Plastiktüte*, plastic bag) (Reiher 1995c).

---

[5] One of the few is *Physiotherapeut/in*, which—unlike *Stomatologe* for *Zahnarzt* (dentist)—has become preferred to the older west German term *Krankengymnast/in*.

However, many apparently synonymous words actually contained connotations that distinguished them from each other and tied them, at least for some speakers, to one social context or the other: for example, *Werktätige(r)* applied to a wider range of working people than the supposedly synonymous *Arbeitnehmer* (employee), and furthermore both words carry a specific political/ideological load for speakers who grew up in either state before 1989; and a *Kaderakte* (personal file) contained personal details that would not be allowed to be held in a *Personalakte* (Hellmann 1997*b*: 65; see also 2.3).[6] Where such connotations are part of speakers' shared knowledge, the variant carrying GDR baggage has generally been abandoned, as Reiher (1995*c*) has shown in her empirical analysis of 'desynonymization' (for example, *Kaderabteilung* for *Personalabteilung*, personnel department).

It is also worth noting here that linguistic 'rationalization' took place in relation to polysemy too: individual words with different meanings within each communication community were disambiguated through semantic reduction—Hellmann (1997*b*: 71) shows, amongst other examples, how *Bilanz* has necessarily lost its GDR sense of an exercise in accounting to show whether a business has met its production targets: the only possible meaning now is the western concept of showing the assets and liabilities and therefore the profitability of a company. The potential for misunderstanding here is clearly considerable, and the consequences more significant than with non-technical vocabulary. It is not surprising therefore that what Colin Good calls a kind of 'öffentliche Lexikographie' (public lexicography) (Good 1993: 254) emerged to guide east and west Germans alike through this communicative minefield in the transitional period, for even once western economic and legal models had established themselves as the norm, it was bound to take longer for ways of thinking to change.

This public lexicography took various forms. Columns appeared in regional newspapers:

Teamwork ist Gruppenarbeit—früher vor allem in den USA praktiziert—wird bei uns immer wichtiger. Es wird zwar durchaus auf die Bedürfnisse des einzelnen Rücksicht genommen, aber die Fähigkeit, sich in einer Gruppe einzugliedern, hat Vorrang. (From the magazine *Super*, published and distributed in eastern Germany, 16 June 1991; cited in Good 1993: 254)

'Team work' means group work—previously practised especially in the US, now becoming increasingly important here. Individuals' needs are very much taken into account, but priority is given to the ability to fit into a group.

The Deutsche Bank hastily published a glossary of 200 selected business terms from east and west to assist communication between new business partners across the divide (Kahle *et al.* 1990), and *Sprachberatungsstellen* (language advisory services) sprang up to meet the rapidly growing demand for advice on 'correct usage'

---

[6] Fraas (1990: 595) lists other word pairs that could be classed as 'similar but not identical': e.g. *Kindergarten* and *Kindertagesstätte (Kita)* (nursery school), *Öffentlichkeitsarbeit* and *Public Relations (PR)*, *Feierabendheim* and *Seniorenheim* (retirement home)—and see also Kühn (1995*d*).

(Kühn 1994, Kühn and Almstädt 1997*a,b*). The desire to use language 'correctly' was, of course, not confined to east Germans—many westerners sought advice on spelling, punctuation, stylistic questions and so forth—but, as with so many other aspects of the new speech ecology, easterners encountered a double burden: dealing with common linguistic issues that affect everyone, but also coming to terms with a whole range of linguistic differences within German, which many clearly saw as a source of potential embarrassment or even humiliation. In this situation, well-intended advice is helpful, but some evidently experienced this as a manifestation of the patronizing discourse of 'expert aid' and social discrimination:

'Die Sprache, die wir von unseren Eltern übernommen haben, ist wohl nicht mehr gut genug?'
'Man traut uns wohl nicht zu, daß wir selbständig umlernen können. Das ist wieder so eine Art Bevormundung.'
'Nachdem mein Berufsabschluß nicht anerkannt wurde, soll mir nun auch meine sprachliche Qualifikation aberkannt werden?'
(Kühn and Almstädt 1997*b*: 198)

'So the language that we learned from our parents isn't good enough any more?'
'They don't think we are capable of learning to think differently by ourselves. We're being told what to think again.'
'First they wouldn't recognize my training qualification, now they won't accept my linguistic competence?'

While these complaints may represent only a minority of the callers to this helpline at the University of Halle, they are clearly articulating a deep sense of grievance: feeling their competence as native speakers of German challenged, these speakers see themselves as victims of verbal hygiene practices (see 2.1) designed to reinforce their inferior status in the new society. It is not surprising, therefore, that a common early response to the exposure to new language was a wounded defiance, albeit more in the form of indignant attempts to preserve self-esteem than of strategic resistance. As an east Berlin woman wrote in a letter to the *Berliner Zeitung* on 25 February 1991:

Mein Enkel, stolz darauf dem Krippenalter entwachsen zu sein, weigert sich störrisch, in die Kita zu gehen. Bei dem Wort Kindergarten strahlende Augen, bei Kita Protest und Widerwillen. Ich will alles dafür tun, daß dem kleinen die schöne altdeutsche Bezeichnung Kindergarten nicht abhanden kommt. (Schönfeld and Schlobinski 1997: 130)

My grandson, proud of having outgrown the creche, refuses point blank to go to the *Kita* (day nursery). At the mention of the *Kindergarten* he's all smiles, but say *Kita* and he protests. I intend to do everything I can to ensure that the little fellow doesn't lose the fine old German word *Kindergarten*.

It is easy to ridicule the pathos in such statements, and to dismiss as trivial and inconsequential individual acts of ironic defiance such as the often quoted declaration on an east Berlin fast-food stall 'Hier dürfen Sie noch Broiler sagen' (i.e. you can still use the archetypal east German word for 'roast chicken' here). However, as Schönfeld (1993) argues from an insider perspective, what for the dispassionate linguist may seem like a superficial and readily interchangeable component of an individual's linguistic inventory may for those affected be an integral element of their self-understanding that is truly appreciated only when it is taken away. Many east Germans at that time attested to the feeling of being bereft at the 'loss' (or 'confiscation') of words that had been part of their common currency and that had literally represented those things that were the cornerstones of their everyday lives. The association between language (loss) and social injustice was palpable for some:

Es ist also verdächtig oder sogar 'out', hier im Osten weiter von der 'Kaufhalle', von 'viertel acht'[7] oder vom 'Kollektiv' zu reden. Ich möchte statt der im MZ-Beitrag angeführten Belanglosigkeiten dieses in meinen Augen Sprachterrors einmal ein paar wesentliche neue Vokabeln nennen, die hier hereingebrandet sind: Massenarbeitslosigkeit, Ministergeldskandale, abwickeln, feuern, Obdachlose, Aussteiger, Reps, Rauschgiftszene, Kinderfeindlichkeit, gegauckt werden. (Reader's letter in *Mitteldeutsche Zeitung*, 26 February 1994; cited in Kühn 1995*b*: 331)

So it's suspicious or even 'out' here in the east to go on talking of the *Kaufhalle* or the *Kollektiv* or saying *viertel acht* (for 'a quarter past seven'). Instead of the trivial examples of what I consider to be linguistic intimidation that were listed in the MZ article, I would like to name a few significant new words that have come flooding in here: mass unemployment, ministerial financial scandal, liquidate, sack, homeless people, drop-outs, *Reps* (members of the far-right Republican party), drug scene, hostility towards children, being 'Gaucked'.[8]

This also explains the force of the opposition frequently expressed towards the wave of anglicisms that swept into the east German speech community with the market economy, as in another reader's letter from the same source:

Wenn ich die Fernsehzeitung aufschlage und das Programm lese, breche ich mir manchmal bald die Zunge: fast nur noch englische Worte. Muß denn das sein? Gibt es in unserer deutschen Sprache dafür keine passende Übersetzung? Für ältere Leute und für solche, die nie Englischunterricht hatten, ist das Lesen des Fernsehprogramms eine Zumutung. (Reader's letter in *Mitteldeutsche Zeitung*, 28 May 1994; cited in Kühn 1995*d*: 412)

Sometimes when I look in the TV magazine and read what's on, I can't get my tongue round the words: virtually nothing but English. Is that really necessary? Is there no suitable translation for them in our German language? For older people or those who never learned English, reading the TV schedule is almost impossible.

[7] In fact, as Stephen Barbour has reminded me (pers. comm.), this expression was not actually confined to the GDR, although it was evidently perceived as such by some people.

[8] A colloquial expression derived from the name of the first head of the government agency set up in 1991 to take charge of the *Stasi* archives, Joachim Gauck (see note 4 above). It refers to the process by which, for example, employers could check the files of their employees to see whether they contained any indication of their having worked for the *Stasi*.

As Good (1993: 252) points out, this complaint will have had a very familiar ring to *west* German ears, and he goes on to argue that many of the linguistic changes experienced by east Germans at that time were a kind of 'Reprise der neueren (west)deutschen Sprachgeschichte im Zeitraffer' (speeded up rerun of the recent history of the (west) German language), but what this overlooks is the perception amongst east Germans of an inextricable link between language change and social discrimination (see also Fink *et al.* 1997 and Hampel 1998 on the reception of anglicisms in the east after unification).

The problem for many east Germans in this context was that they found themselves confronted by a social and linguistic dilemma: on the one hand, there was the anxiety and uncertainty that was bound up with the demands of the market economy and expressed in the requirement to be 'flexible and dynamic';[9] on the other hand people wanted to avoid the many shibboleths that anchored texts in the socialist discourse of old. This especially applied to adjectives, such as *fortschrittlich* (progressive), *friedliebend* (peace-loving), and *schöpferisch* (creative). Hellmann (1994*a*: 133) shows the sensitivity towards the use of even more neutral terms in public contexts, citing an internal memorandum circulated by the management of a company in Dresden early in 1991, in which all staff were instructed to avoid *Kader* (specialist, expert), *Brigade* (work team), *Kollektiv* (collective), *Ökonomie* (economy), *Werktätige(r)* (working person), *Territorium* (region), and other concepts 'from the past' because

Diese Begriffe sind für ein westliches Ohr stark vorbelastet und führen zu negativen Assoziationen. Wir machen uns im Umgang mit den westlichen Firmen das Leben unnötig schwer.

To a western ear, these concepts are strongly tainted and lead to negative associations. We (would) make life unnecessarily difficult for ourselves in our dealings with western companies.

The awareness of the need for sensitivity was not entirely lost on west Germans, especially when it was a case of protecting interests such as trade-union membership. West German unions seeking to expand their membership in the east were advised to avoid many of what for them were standard terms like *Solidarität (der Arbeitnehmer)* (workers' solidarity), *Friedenspflicht* (obligation to avoid industrial action during wage negotiations), *Geschlossenheit* (unity), *Funktionär* (functionary, official), *Aufklärung* (political instruction), *Bewußtsein* (consciousness), *Einheit* (unity), *Fortschritt* (progress), *Masse/Massenorganisation* (mass/ mass organization) (Good 1993: 256, Hellmann 1997*b*: 74). Indeed, whole metaphorical fields that were the stuff of trade-union rhetoric in the west became problematic, in particular the central notion of struggle. As Störel (1997: 94) points out, the concept of the *Arbeiter als Kämpfer* (worker as fighter) that grew out of the workers' movement of the nineteenth century followed a bifurcated route after 1949: in the west, the

[9] With the implication that these were qualities that west Germans possessed but east Germans lacked: see 5.2 and 5.3.

struggle was a *Kampf um den Arbeitsplatz* (struggle for jobs), in the east a *Kampf am Arbeitsplatz* (struggle at the workplace)—and if east Germans were happy to leave the latter behind them after unification, they were confronted with a vengeance by the former as they were forced to face up to mass unemployment. In unions in the east today, therefore, 'man zieht nicht in den Kampf, sondern *nimmt aktiv teil, fordert ein* oder *begleitet die Diskussion*' (you don't go to battle, you 'actively participate', 'demand', or 'follow the discussion') (ibid.: 101; see also 3.1 and 3.2).

The social turbulence of the *Umbruch* period in the early 1990s inevitably destabilized individual members of the eastern community, since the familiar markers of their normality had been so abruptly removed. Yet the difficulty, in terms of registering the parameters of the new normality, was precisely that they had been transplanted not into a totally alien environment but into one that in many respects was remarkably similar to the old one. Despite the sensitivity to clearly contaminated words, other features that had been characteristic of language use in the GDR, but which might not have risen above the level of conscious awareness, continued to appear in everyday usage, often in the form of strikingly contrasting collocations: an article in the *Leipziger Volkszeitung* (15 April 1993), for example, describes the establishment of new adult education centres, apparently without irony, as 'eine Errungenschaft der Wende' (an achievement of the *Wende*)—as Eroms (1994: 34) puts it, 'eine hochgradig paradoxe Formulierung, wird hier doch ein sozialistisches Kernwort mit dem Schibboleth seiner Ablösung verbunden' (an extremely paradoxical formulation, linking a keyword of socialism with the shibboleth of its removal).[10] Even some of the generally stigmatized terms persisted for a surprisingly long time—Kühn (1994: 140) cites a job advertisement in the *Mitteldeutsche Zeitung* of 23 August 1993: 'Wir suchen für die Betreuung eines Forschungsprojektes ab September 1993 einen geeigneten *Kader* mit Wohnsitz in Leuna, der auf Stundenbasis die analytische Überwachung des Projektes vor Ort übernimmt' (italics added) (We are looking for a suitable specialist [the characteristic GDR term *Kader*] living in Leuna to take on the analytical supervision of a research project on an hourly-paid basis). While this usage could not fail to strike the western eye, other expressions that would seem perfectly natural in a western context might appear disconcerting to an eastern observer: 'der rauhe Wind des Wettbewerbs' (the harsh wind of competition) is a commonplace, virtually a cliché, of life in a capitalist economy but at least in the early post-*Wende* days could have read like a paradox to someone socialized in the GDR, since 'sozialistischer Wettbewerb' (socialist competition) was the essence of the collective enterprise in GDR industry (see 3.1). Similarly, the notice 'im Angebot' in a store would have evoked strongly diverging responses: for a west German, the implication is that this product is 'on special offer, i.e. reduced in

---

[10] *Errungenschaft*, with its connotations of 'achievement through effort for the common good', was preferred in official GDR contexts to the more characteristically western term *Leistung*, with its implication of 'individual success at the expense of others'. See also 3.1.

price', while an east German would have understood it to mean that the product was (unusually) 'available', 'in stock' (see Schröder 1997*b*: 153, 159).

Simple misunderstandings such as this are trivial in isolation and easily repaired. However, there was potential for conflict on both individual and social levels in the tension between eastern and western readings of particular linguistic usages. Again, just one or two words might have been enough in a given context to trigger conflicting associations and potentially communicative failure. For example, housing was obviously a critical social issue in both states, but housing and building policies differed drastically, as did the values attached to specific kinds of accommodation. These fundamental differences lurking beneath apparently innocuous vocabulary were, especially in the early years after unification, a potent source of misunderstanding and conflict. Hellmann (1994*a*: 132) recounts a disastrous encounter between two west German estate agents and a young couple just arrived from the east:

Relativ schüchtern, 'fast als Bittsteller', nehmen sie die Angebote des Maklers zur Kenntnis, erschrecken über die Mietpreise. Dann bietet ihnen der Makler eine deutlich preisgünstigere Altbauwohnung an, 'ziemlich interessantes Angebot', wie der Makler betont. Darauf pikierte, schließlich verärgerte Abwehr: Keine Altbauwohnung, nicht mit ihnen, das ließen sie 'nicht mehr mit sich machen!'. Das Maklerehepaar ist ratlos, schließlich verärgert; es hält dies Ehepaar für 'anspruchsvoll', 'unbegreiflich', 'undankbar', 'es sind halt doch andere Menschen'.

Quite shyly, 'almost as if making a humble request' [the story is related from the agents' point of view], they register the estate agent's offers and are shocked by the rents. Then the agent offers them a significantly cheaper flat in an old building, 'a pretty interesting offer', the agent stresses. They are put out and then annoyed, and reject the offer: no flat in an old building, not for them, they wouldn't 'be treated like that any more!' The agents are confused and then annoyed; they consider the couple to be 'hard to please', 'incomprehensible', 'ungrateful', 'they're just a different sort of people'.

The root of the problem lies in the different conception of what an *Altbauwohnung* is: in the GDR, this would have been a run-down flat with no modern facilities and in desperate need of renovation; in the Federal Republic, it was (is) an old flat that had been modernized while retaining its original character. The cause of the communicative failure then is that each party imputes inappropriate behaviour to the other: the western agents consider the eastern couple ungrateful for turning down a good opportunity, the eastern couple for their part interpret the agents' proposal as a blatant act of social discrimination.

The communicative difficulties that arise from linguistic and sociolinguistic difference and their roots in different social experience clearly need to be addressed more systematically, and a large part of the problem lies in a lack of shared knowledge—on both sides. The activities of *Sprachberatungsstellen*, discussed earlier, are essentially a kind of trouble-shooting exercise, coping with change in an ad hoc fashion and responding to random specific demands. By contrast, it is the job of professional lexicographers to track, classify, and record lexical change, and so the processes I have been discussing in this section represented a massive challenge for them. People do not generally rely heavily on dictionaries in their everyday production of texts, written or spoken, but these reference works occupy an important and influential position within speech communities, acting as repositories of authoritative statements on linguistic forms and meanings. Yet at the same time there is a paradox here: dictionaries present themselves as definitive accounts of the 'state' of a language and are by their nature static representations of something that is in constant flux. There is also an element of deception in their self-image as objective records, in which most of us, consciously or not, collude. Writing dictionaries, like writing histories, is an interpretative exercise, which entails making judgements. Which words should be selected and according to which criteria? How are the selected words to be categorized and related to each other? On what basis are their meanings to be determined? What kinds of guidance is it appropriate to give on the usage of words?

East German linguist Marianne Schröder acknowledges the peculiarly delicate nature of this task in the German context in her account of her protracted efforts to construct a thesaurus of east German vocabulary, an 'Allgemeinwortschatz der DDR-Bürger' (general vocabulary of GDR citizens) (Schröder 1997*a*; see also Schröder 1992, Hopfer 1996). Originally intended as a practical guide to normal usage in the GDR, with key words organized according to subject groups (such as education, media, art, sport) with cross-cutting categories such as ACTION, OBJECT, and PROPERTY, her dictionary initially fell victim to historical circumstance: largely completed in 1989, it found itself without a valid publication contract and without a market (Schröder and Fix 1997: 5). When it was eventually published, it was as a historical document, and critical commentaries accompanied the word lists in the form of what she refers to as 'erzählende Lexikographie' (narrative lexicography) (Schröder 1997*a*: 167, borrowing a term from Kilian 1994). Her aim had been to compile a corpus of words that constituted 'die am Grundwortschatz orientierte Schnittmenge von Wörtern, den [*sic*] die in der DDR lebenden Deutschen in nicht ausschließlich fach- oder gruppenbezogener Kommunikation vor allem benutzten' (the set of words drawn from the basic vocabulary that were used in particular by Germans living in the GDR in contexts that were not exclusively related to specific subjects or groups) (ibid.: 154), but in the context in which it was ultimately published it was necessary to distinguish further categories in addition to those originally intended. She estimated that about 94 per cent of her 10,000 words were actually part of the general German vocabulary, but the remaining 6 per cent constituted a not insignificant stock of words that she classified as 'DDR-gebunden' (associated with the GDR; further sub-classified into 'DDR-spezifisch' and 'DDR-geprägt', specific to and characteristic of the GDR) (ibid.: 164–5), and the relationships amongst these words and between them and west German words with similar reference required analysis and discussion.

Earlier estimates of the extent of GDR-specific vocabulary tended to be higher: the small dictionaries published by Kinne and Strube-Edelmann (1981) and

Ahrends (1989) contain 800–900 headwords, the six-volume *Wörterbuch der deutschen Gegenwartssprache* or WDG (Dictionary of Contemporary German, published between 1964 and 1976) identified 1,330 words as GDR-specific terms, and other studies suggest the real figure could be between 2,000 and 3,000 (Hellmann 1994*a*: 129–30).[11] However, the WDG also classified 1,271 words as specific to the Federal Republic, a practice not adopted by dictionaries published in the west, either before or after unification, and as Peter von Polenz (1993: 141–2) argues, the failure of west German lexicographers to record the almost certainly far greater number of such innovations fed the long-standing but ill-founded prejudice that language in the GDR had departed more significantly from the pre-1949 'real German' than was the case in the Federal Republic (see also Schaeder 1997: 70–1).

How elusive the objective of achieving a definitive (even an accurate) account of the east–west distribution of German vocabulary was, became clear in early attempts to end the decades of divided lexicography by bringing the 'unified German language' within the covers of a single dictionary. Inevitably, the most scrutinized of these publications was the so-called 'Einheitsduden' (Unity Duden), the twentieth edition of the *Duden. Rechtschreibung der deutschen Sprache* (1991). The first edition of this most revered of German dictionaries was published in 1880 by the Bibliographisches Institut in Leipzig, and twelve more were produced between then and 1949. For the next forty years, however, separate editions of the Duden were published in Leipzig (GDR) and in Mannheim (Federal Republic), and although both enjoyed sovereign status in their respective states they differed radically from each other in their representation of the language (for a detailed history of the Duden as a 'Volkswörterbuch', see Sauer 1988). The 'unified' Duden (unified, like most other things, according to the western model—the previous Leipzig edition had been numbered 18, the previous Mannheim edition 19) was rushed onto the market even earlier than had been announced, no doubt to steal a march on the competition but above all to renew its claim to be *the* German dictionary, the final arbiter in case of doubt ('maßgebend in allen Zweifelsfällen').

As critics were quick to point out, however, unifying the language lexicographically was as fraught with (albeit, of course, less significant) difficulties as political, economic, or social unification. Judging it against its own claim—'Es wurden [aber] nicht nur Neuwörter erfaßt, sondern auch Wörter bewahrt, die in der DDR gebräuchlich waren und die für das Verständnis der jüngeren Vergangenheit von Bedeutung sind' (Not only new words have been included; words that were in common use in the GDR and that are important for understanding the recent past have also been retained)—Schaeder (1994) and Ludwig (1996, 1997) dissected the new edition and found it wanting. In claiming to have recorded words that had been in common use in the GDR and were important for understanding the recent past, the editors were clearly offering a hostage to fortune and a gift to eagle-eyed academic reviewers. Ludwig (1996: 131) asks, for example, why *Arbeiter-und-Bauern-Fakultät*

---

[11] The most recent dictionary, Wolf (2000), has 1,900 head words.

(Workers' and Peasants' Faculty), *Nationalpreis* (National Prize—highest state award for scientific or artistic achievements), *Erntebrigade* (harvesting team), *Objekt* (public or official building), *LDPD*, *SED*, and *FDJ* find their way into the dictionary, while *Betriebsakademie* (further education centre attached to state-run organizations), *Karl-Marx-Orden* (Karl Marx Medal), *Jugendbrigade* (youth work team), *Kaufhalle* (supermarket), *NDPD*, and *DFD* are omitted. Why, challenges Schaeder (1994: 83), is *Kaderleiter* (personnel officer) listed but not *Kaderabteilung* (personnel department) or *Kaderakte* (personal file), *Parteiaktiv* (Party work team) but not *Blockpartei* (Block party), *Staatssicherheitsdienst* (state security service) but not *Ministerium für Staatssicherheit* (Ministry for State Security)?

However, this problem was not confined to the Duden. In a later analysis of several post-1990 dictionaries, Schaeder (1997) reveals a wide range of discrepancies and inconsistencies. One of the most slippery issues was one of the most basic: how to label GDR-specific words and referents—simply 'DDR', or 'in der DDR' (in the GDR), 'in der ehemaligen DDR' (in the former GDR), 'ehemals in der DDR' (formerly in the GDR)? Or should they be identified in other ways—as 'regional', 'selten' (rare), 'veraltend' (becoming obsolete)? A good example of how easy it could be to give the wrong impression through the inappropriate use of such terms is the entry for *Republikflucht* in the twentieth edition of the Duden, which gives the definition 'Flucht aus der ehemaligen DDR' (flight/escape from the former GDR); the interpretation that it is possible to flee from something that no longer exists was then removed in the twenty-first edition (1996) by rephrasing the definition as 'ehemals Flucht aus der DDR' (formerly flight/escape from the GDR) (Schaeder 1997: 63).

What does the mass of evidence accumulated by lexicologists and recorded by lexicographers add up to, and what does it reveal about the development of social relations in Germany since unification? Even though I have no more than scratched the surface in this section, we can surely be in no doubt that the social *Umbruch* of the 1990s was characterized linguistically by very considerable lexical change and that the processes contributing to this change were extremely complex. But there are significant limitations to the value of this work. First, much of the data on language use was collected randomly and although there is good reason to believe that many of the findings were not unrepresentative of wide-scale changes, in the absence of systematic methodologies it is difficult to draw any strong conclusions about the extent of these changes.[12] Secondly, despite the substantial amount of material that has been gathered from a wide range of sources (mostly, in fact, written but some spoken too) we cannot necessarily say that we have learned a great deal from this about how people's actual linguistic behaviour has changed in this time. This calls for a different kind of approach, which will be explored in the next section.

---

[12] Manfred Hellmann's meticulous work is an important exception.

4.2   Communicative dissonance

Individual words may be the most tangible signs of (socio)linguistic change, but we rarely encounter them in isolation, and it is only when we meet them embedded in texts that they acquire salience. Furthermore, when we shift our analysis to this level we often find that it is not necessarily individual words that carry significance, so much as the patterns of text construction and the textual strategies that are used to create contexts. The patterns are what locate specific texts within the larger category of text-types or genres, and the strategies are what reveal texts as elements of the social process of discourse. In other words, individual texts belonging to a particular genre (such as 'conference speech' or 'newspaper editorial') may be identified as such by their sharing common structural features (such as addressing the audience, analysing a specific social or economic issue, proposing a solution, relating the solution to a broader policy or agenda, and so forth), but the ways in which the patterns are realized may differ because the texts have a different purpose within the social context in which they are produced.

A crucial aspect of a changing language ecology is the way that the supplanting of one set of social structures and institutions (with all its values, assumptions, beliefs, and practices) by another is accompanied, or even realized, by a reconfiguration of textual repertoires or more precisely the inventory of communicative genres. Just as some genres disappear because they have no place in the new reality (in our context, for example, characteristic GDR genres like *Kampfprogramm* or *Arbeitsplan*, annual work plan or programme), so other genres that collectively constitute the substance of the new reality appear (such as *Steuererklärung*, tax return, or *Projektantrag*, project proposal). For our purposes, however, the most revealing genres are those that were in some sense common to both societies and have therefore (from the perspective of east Germans) been retained, because a comparative analysis of texts produced before and after the *Wende* may give some measure of the degree of communicative dissonance that was inherent in the newly unified speech community. If east and west Germans bring with them into this communicative environment only partially overlapping knowledge—both in the sense of the substance of specific social phenomena and in terms of their patterns of textual realization—it is at least possible that this mismatch may be a source of communicative conflict. What happens, then, to the production and reception of texts belonging to such genres under changed social conditions?

Kühn (1995*b*) analyses two types of evaluative text (see also 3.2), identifying significant areas of similarity and difference in texts produced in the GDR and by east German writers after unification (see also Fix 1994*b*). She collected thirty-five *Arbeitszeugnisse* (references) written between 1990 and 1995 by east Germans in eastern Germany and compared them with *Beurteilungen* (assessments) written in the GDR. Such texts are clearly a potential source of major contrasts, since they deal with interpersonal relations and with assessments of individuals in terms of prevailing value systems. In analysing the textual material, however, it is important to bear in mind that the texts do not simply derive from differently constituted social systems: the production of such texts was and is an essential element in the reproduction of the social systems themselves.

While the genre *Arbeitszeugnis* is established as part of an employee's rights under civil law in the Federal Republic, the GDR genre *Beurteilung* was placed within the discourse of 'developing socialism' as an essential element of the process of monitoring the contribution of individuals to social objectives (see Fix 1995): 'Bei Beurteilungen haben wir die Aufgabe, einen Kollegen nach den Forderungen, die wir an eine sozialistische Persönlichkeit stellen, einzuschätzen.... Wir gehen deshalb bei der Beurteilung eines Kollegen von seiner Beziehung zur sozialistischen Gesellschaft aus.' (In writing assessments, our task is to judge a colleague in terms of the demands that we place on a socialist personality.... We therefore base our assessment of a colleague on his relationship to socialist society.) (Liebsch 1976: 437, cited here in Kühn 1995*b*: 337) So east Germans practised in the writing of *Beurteilungen* brought with them both a different conception of the purpose of evaluative reports and a different stock of available textual patterns. Converting to the production of *Arbeitszeugnisse*—as with virtually all such situations, the retention of something like the GDR model as a 'regional' variant does not seem to have been an option—was therefore a more complex task than following a different format: the overall structure was in many ways very similar, but the conventional formulations were not.

The gradual process of adapting to this new model not surprisingly produced mixed results. For example, 'old' forms of personal address were often retained (*Kollege/Kollegin*, colleague) and women were frequently still referred to with masculine 'generic' terms ('*sie war Lehrer im Hochschuldienst*', she was a teacher in higher education). Under the unfamiliar heading 'Führung und Sozialverhalten' (leadership and social behaviour), possibly interpreted as equivalent to the old 'Einstellung zur Gesellschaft' (attitude towards society), fixed expressions with instantly recognizable GDR character recurred: '*arbeitete zum Wohle unseres Betriebes*' (worked for the good of our business), '*fügte sich in das Lehrerkollektiv gut ein*' (fitted in well in the teachers' collective). While self-evidently inappropriate terms like *Parteilichkeit* (adherence to the party line) and *Beitrag zur Stärkung der DDR* (contribution to the strengthening of the GDR) no longer appear, other familiar terms stand alongside new ones (for instance, *Betrieb* together with *Firma* or *Unternehmen* (company, concern), *Kollektiv* with *Team*). But expressions belonging to the set of commonplace terms in western *Arbeitszeugnisse* were often avoided, especially if they had negative connotations from the past: *erfolgsorientiert* (achievement-oriented), *Kreativität* (creativity), *Karriere* (career) are words that would be considered perfectly normal in a western report but had been disparaged to such an extent in the GDR that they may well have retained an unacceptable aura for many easterners. An alternative strategy to using either 'old' and inappropriate or 'new' but unacceptable expressions was to abandon conventional formulations of any kind in favour of more individual ones: '*seine Erwägungen waren treffsicher*' (his considerations were sound), '*seine Sensibilität bei der Tätigkeit ist hervorzuheben*' (his sensitive approach to this activity should be emphasized).

The important point here, though, is that a quantitative or taxonomic exercise focusing on the surface layer of linguistic or even textual structures risks mistaking the symptoms of a problem for the problem itself. The material produced in the course of research such as this is valuable, but it has to be read in terms of the social conflict resulting from the absorption of a population into a radically different and in many ways incompatible social system. What it reveals, when analysed as the input to, and the product of, discursive processes of social formation, is the challenge to the validity of east Germans' past experience and practices.

The trend to individualization in the construction of normally highly conventionalized texts, which Kühn refers to as one, relatively minor, aspect of east Germans' responses to the demands of the new discourse of employment in a capitalist economy, is a feature of change in other communicative genres too.[13] However, it is something of a two-edged sword. On the one hand, it can represent an opportunity to release yourself from the constraints of conforming to rigid patterns or templates and to express yourself more freely, but on the other hand it conceals another kind of convention, that imposes its own constraints and pressures on text writers. This, again, is perhaps most evident in genres that existed in some form in both societies but which were subject to quite different conditions of production and reception.

As we have already seen in 3.2, letters to newspapers or investigative television programmes can function as a means of permitting individuals to contribute to public debates, but they can also—as was generally the case in the state-controlled media in the GDR—be a form of stage-managed public communication as much as Party conference speeches or slogans on banners at official demonstrations. Letters published before the *Wende* in the *Leipziger Volkszeitung* or the *Sächsische Zeitung*, for example, were frequently written from a representative perspective with the clear purpose of affirming or justifying official policy and actions, and therefore as a means of reinforcing social integration on the basis of apparent consensus around common values. The following letter[14] is one of many published in 1976 just after the expulsion from the GDR of the singer–songwriter Wolf Biermann for his repeated outspoken criticism of the SED-regime:

Text 1 Leserbrief 1
Es gehört zu den elementaren Kenntnissen und Erfahrungen eines Kommunisten und Künstlers, daß sich unter den Bedingungen der friedlichen Koexistenz der Kampf der sich antagonistisch gegenüberstehenden Klassen vor allem auf ideologischem Gebiet verschärft. Für das Verhalten im Klassenkampf war, ist und bleibt die zentrale Frage: 'Wem nützt es?'

---

[13] It is worth noting here that Hoffmann (1994) analyses what he sees as a trend towards individualization in certain genres in the late years of the GDR.

[14] The three letters discussed here originally appeared in the *Leipziger Volkszeitung*, a major regional paper published by the SED, and are reproduced here from Fix (1993).

Biermann hat spätestens mit seinem Auftreten in der BRD eine unzweideutige persönliche Haltung bezogen. Es war—ganz im Sinne der zentralen Frage—an uns, eine ebenso eindeutige Antwort zu geben. Die Regierung unseres Staates hat damit nicht gezögert und ihm die Staatsbürgerschaft der DDR aberkannt. Ihre Entscheidung ist meine Entscheidung.
Peter Förster, Dozent, Theaterhochschule (Originally published in *Leipziger Volkszeitung* 23 November 1976)

It is part of the elementary knowledge and experience of a communist and artist that under the conditions of peaceful coexistence the struggle between antagonistic classes intensifies especially in the area of ideology. The central question as regards behaviour in the class struggle was, is, and remains: 'For whose benefit is it?' At the latest by the time of his performance in the FRG Biermann adopted an unambiguous personal attitude. It was up to us—in the sense of the central question—to give an equally clear response. The government of our state acted promptly and stripped him of his citizenship of the GDR. Its decision is my decision.
Peter Förster, Lecturer, drama college

The commitment to the state, the doctrinaire expression of political views, the unquestioning support for government action, the identification of self and state, the implicit message of 'zero tolerance' of dissent all situate this text firmly in the official discourse. Text 2 is completely different in tone and structure but serves the same fundamental purpose of supporting the programme of the Party:

Text 2 Leserbrief 2
In den Ferien hatte ich mit meinem Enkel Michael ein interessantes Gespräch, das mich sehr bewegt hat. Wir unterhielten uns über seinen künftigen Beruf, seine Vorstellungen von seinem Leben. Michael ist 10 Jahre alt und besucht seit 3 Jahren die Musikschule. In seinem Leben soll die Musik eine große Rolle spielen. Es gibt aber auch viele andere Berufe, die ihn locken. Im Spaß haben wir seinen Lohn aufgeteilt und gemeinsam überlegt, wie lange man für eine größere Sache sparen muß. Plötzlich sagte Michael: 'Wir haben das Geld für den Mitgliedsbeitrag vergessen, denn bis dahin bin ich Genosse.' Ist das nicht ein schönes Ergebnis der gemeinsamen Erziehung zu Haus und in der Schule?
Hanni Weber, 725 Wurzen (Originally published in *Leipziger Volkszeitung*, 8 September 1973)

In the holidays, I had an interesting conversation with my grandson Michael, which moved me a great deal. We were talking about his future occupation, his ideas about his life. Michael is 10 years old and has been going to music school for three years. He wants music to play an important part in his life. But there are also many other careers that appeal to him. Just for fun, we divided up his wages and worked out together how long one would have to save up for a large item. Suddenly, Michael said: 'We've forgotten the money for the membership subscription, I'll be a comrade by then.' Isn't that a splendid result of the shared upbringing at home and in school?

The subordination of the apparently individual voice in this letter to the aims of the state is surely evident in the crude pathos of the barely credible 'punchline' of the final sentence. Text 3, by contrast, expresses a challenge to the first government of unified Germany on behalf of what the author sees as a disadvantaged section of the population, but in passionately personal terms.

Text 3 Leserbrief 3

Nachdem nun in rasantem Tempo die Erhöhungen der Preise und Tarife in allen Varianten vollzogen sind und noch werden, muß ich doch fragen, was haben wir mit unserem Ruf 'Wir bleiben hier' wohl erreicht? Es ist doch himmelschreiend, was die damaligen Wahlredner der CDU (ich höre sie heute noch) den 'Hiergebliebenen' zumuten. Was ist eigentlich der Einigungsvertrag noch wert, wenn man an die geplanten Mieterhöhungen ab Juli 1991 denkt? Was sind die Rentner wert im Vergleich mit den Asylanten? Was hat das Sparen von Energie für Anreiz, wenn man dafür mehr zahlen muß? Was hat ein Rentner für Chancen bei den geplanten Kohlepreisen? Betriebskosten bis eine DM pro Quadratmeter—sind wir Freiwild? Sollte die Regierung vergessen haben, daß in vier Jahren wieder Wahlen sind? Die 'Hiergebliebenen' vergessen die Enttäuschung nicht!

Lothar   Kunze,   7022   Leipzig   (Originally   published   in   *Leipziger   Volkszeitung*, 15 February 1991)

Now that prices and charges of all kinds have been increased, and continue to rise, at a great rate I have to ask: what have we achieved with our cry 'we're staying here'? It is simply outrageous what the CDU election campaigners at that time (I can still hear them now) expect of those who 'stayed put'. What is the unification treaty worth now, if you think about the rent increases planned for July 1991? What are pensioners worth in comparison with asylum-seekers? What incentives are there to save energy if you have to pay more for it? What chance has a pensioner got with the planned coal prices? Overheads of up to DM 1 per square metre—are we fair game? Can the government have forgotten that there will be elections again in four years? Those who 'stayed put' won't forget being let down like this!

The author constructs a critical category of the east German electorate—'those who stayed put', based on the familiar *Wende* slogan 'Wir bleiben hier' (we're staying here) (see 3.3)—in which he evidently situates himself, and delivers a stinging accusation of betrayal to the CDU-led government with a series of blunt rhetorical questions.

Authors of *Leserbriefe* in a democratic press have the opportunity to address a general readership in their own style, and by and large are constrained only by limits of space and the requirement of relevance to an issue of topical interest or public concern. In other genres, however, individualization may be as much an imposition as an opportunity. For example, apparently trivial texts such as *Wohnungsanzeigen, Stellengesuche*, or *Kontaktanzeigen* (small ads seeking accommodation or jobs, or in the personal columns) may be subject to the rules of the marketplace and demonstrate in their own way the tensions between competing social systems. Consider the following two examples of *Wohnungsanzeigen* from Reiher (1997b):

Text 4 Wohnungsanzeige (GDR source)

Biete gr. 3-Raum-Whg., 96 m², Dimitr.str., VH., Balkon, gefl. Dusche, IWC, verkehrsg.
Suche 2-Raum-Komf.-Whg., auch Altneubau, mit mod. Hzg. Tel. 449 75 29, ab 18 Uhr.

Offer large 3-room flat, 96 m², Dimitroffstrasse, facing the street, balcony, tiled shower, inside WC, convenient location.
Seek 2-room flat with modern conveniences, post-war block considered, with modern heating.

Text 5 Wohnungsanzeige (*Dresdener Neueste Nachrichten*, 1990)
Jg., christl. Familie (Dipl.-Ing., Musikpäd.) mit kleinem Clown (6 Monate) sucht dringend
eine 3-Raum-Wohnung o. größere mit Bad. Zahle Miete auf westdeutsch. Niveau. Auch
Kaufangebote angenehm.

Young Christian family (qualified engineer, music teacher) with little rascal (6 months old)
urgently seeks 3-room flat, or bigger, with bathroom. Will pay rent at west German rate.
Offers to purchase also welcome.

On the lexical level alone, these texts provide material for comparative analysis
of the kind we considered in the previous section, such as the typical eastern
terms *Komfortwohnung, Altneubau,* and *3-Raum-* instead of the normal western
3-Zimmerwohnung. As texts, however, they offer more striking and more significant contrasts. With its GDR-typical vocabulary and its exclusive focus on the
characteristics of the accommodation offered or sought, Text 4 could only be from
an east German source. The only things that 'betray' Text 5 as also being from an
eastern context are the retention of *Raum* for *Zimmer* and the willingness to pay
at 'west German rates': in every other respect, the structure of the advertisement
is different. The features of the required flat are now reduced in favour of personal
details of the flat-hunters: age, profession, marital/family status, income. In a controlled economy, where most housing is publicly owned and where moving from
one flat to another is usually a matter of seeking an exchange, the only issues of
any significance have to do with the nature and location of the accommodation.
In a market economy, however, seeking rented accommodation in the private sector entails competing with other potential tenants and, since landlords are entitled
to establish their own selection criteria, entering a kind of 'beauty contest'.
The function of the advertising text is therefore quite different in the western
discourse: instead of merely specifying essential factual information concerning
the flat in order to enable a suitable match to be found, it is now necessary to construct a positive verbal image of the flat-seeker in order to make them maximally
desirable as tenants and give them an advantage over potential rivals (see also
Teidge 1990).

The same applies in job-seeking advertisements, where in the GDR the emphasis was on declaring qualifications, and the norms of the genre included the
acceptability of stating required social conditions: compare Texts 6 and 7 (both
from Barz 1997: 83).

Text 6 Stellengesuch (*Leipziger Volkszeitung*, 13 November 1981)
Junge Frau, Abitur, sucht wegen Wohnortw. neuen Wirkungskrs. mit Qualifizierungsm.,
zwei Kindergartenpl. erforderlich., Zuschr. m. ausführl. Angaben an ...

Due to move, young woman with *Abitur* (university entrance qualification) seeks new
sphere of activity with opportunities for further training, two kindergarten spaces
required, write with full details to ...

Text 7 Stellengesuch (*Leipziger Volkszeitung*, 13/14 April 1996)
Bin zuverlässig, techn. bewandert, habe Bürokenntnisse mit PC und bin vielleicht Ihre neue
Mitarbeiterin. Ich, 30 J., suche Arbeit mit Festeinstellung.

Am reliable, familiar with technology, have office skills including PC and may be your new
colleague. Am 30 years old and seek permanent post.

While the writer of Text 6 feels able to stipulate the provision of two places in a
nursery for her children, the author of Text 7 makes no demands and highlights
her personal qualities and experience. Barz (1997: 87–8) lists many examples
of self-evaluating attributes found in post-1990 job-seeking advertisements in
this major regional newspaper ('*Allround-Bürokraft*', all-round office worker;
'*hochkarätige Chefsekretärin*', top-class senior secretary; '*versierter Computerfreak*',
experienced computer freak), and concludes that the new ground rule is to declare
not 'was ich bin' (what I am) but 'wie ich bin' (what I'm like) and 'was ich kann'
(what I can do).

Perhaps the ultimate manifestation of the discourse of individualism and self-
marketing is the personal ad. Here too, as Galler (1993) and Weydt (1993) have
shown, the market exerts its pressure to conform to the textual conventions of
the genre, which in turn require writers to present themselves in a very different
way and to occupy a different position in relation to the reader. Unlike in
Wohnungsanzeigen, it is obviously in the nature of *Partnerschaftsanzeigen* (personal ads) that the authors of the advertisements present personal details.
However, as Texts 8 and 9 (both from Weydt 1993) show, there is considerable
scope for contrasts in the way in which this self-image is constructed.

Text 8 Personal ad (from *Berliner Zeitung*, published in East Berlin, 16/17 September 1989)
Bin 31/1,86, schlk., suche ehrl., aufgeschl., jg. Frau f. dauerh. Partnersch. Int.: Musik, Reisen,
Kino u. all. Schöne. Halte viel v. Treue, Geborgenh. u. Liebe. Bin Optimist, um mit Dir ein
gemeins. Leben aufzubauen. Jede ernstgem. Zuschrift (mit Bild bevorz., n. Bed.) w. beantw.

Am 31, 1.86 m tall, slim, looking for honest, open-minded young woman for lasting relationship. Interests: music, travel, cinema, and all things beautiful. Value loyalty, security,
and love. Am optimistic about building a life together with you. All serious responses
(preferably, but not necessarily, with photo) will be answered.

Text 9 Personal ad (from *Tip* magazine, published in West Berlin, no date)
Eine Frau, Anfang 40, häßlich, gefühllos, uninteressant und -beweglich, mit Neigungen zu
Abhängigkeit, Langeweile und Verdruß begegnet dem sinnlichen, an vielem interessierten,
humorigen, selbständigen Mann. Nur wo?

A woman, early 40s, ugly, insensitive, uninteresting, and undynamic, with tendency to be
dependent, bored, and frustrated, wants to meet sensuous, humorous, independent man
with many interests. But where?

Text 8 gives a straightforward list of the author's personal characteristics and
the features he is looking for in a potential partner; the guiding principle of text

construction here appears to be 'be factual and be frank'. Text 9 turns this principle on its head and requires the reader to generate their own picture of the author based on the ironic formulation and the contrast between the first part of the text and the second; the guiding principle in this case seems to be 'be different and be memorable'.

The texts we have explored so far in this section illustrate in different ways how the analysis of textual patterns and strategies of text construction can contribute to an understanding of the complexity of sociolinguistic difference. By focusing on conventions associated with particular genres, and by situating these genres within competing or at least contrasting discourses, I have tried to steer a course beyond the study of lexical variation and change in order to show how the study of 'language in use' needs to be rooted in an understanding that contexts are created and negotiated rather than merely being static 'backdrops' to linguistic action. The limitation of the material I have drawn on up to this point—apart from methodological doubts about its quality as representative data in some cases—is that written texts of the kinds discussed here are by their nature monologic or at best pseudo-dialogic forms.[15] They lack the spontaneity of many spoken texts, are capable of editing or repair before being made available to a reader or addressee, and are not subject to modification through interaction with other 'text-producers' in the course of production (for discussions of contrasts between written and spoken texts, see, for example, Biber 1991, Carter 2001, Coulmas 1985, Halliday 1989).

Since our concern here is with the roles played by language in periods of social change, it is logical to place greater emphasis on processes of change than on their products. Furthermore, it will be more interesting and more revealing to investigate undirected processes that occur in the course of spoken interaction, rather than directed processes such as language instruction. In other words, what can an analysis of spoken interaction reveal about the linguistic habits, assumptions, and practices that speakers from different social backgrounds bring with them into personal encounters, and what can it show about how changes in language behaviour are brought about in the course of such encounters?

One of the contexts in which the most direct confrontations occurred between east and west Germans after unification was in the relatively public domains of work and employment. These domains are characterized by many different communicative genres, such as meetings, briefings, consultations, interviews, and presentations, some of which may have been peculiar to one society or the other, but more often it was the case that the same or similar genres were realized differently. The problem with any attempt to analyse potentially contrasting behaviours, however, is the lack of empirical material still available from GDR times, so that analysts have had to rely on the assumption that patterns of speech and interaction

---

[15] Electronic communication in the form of e-mails, chatroom exchanges, and text messages, for example, is a different matter, but it is a form of communication that has developed only since 1990.

observed and recorded in the period immediately after the *Wende* were much the same as those routinely used within GDR settings: since we know that language change is a gradual process, this is not an unreasonable assumption, but it is unverifiable and this necessarily relativizes the validity of some of the research results.

A good example of early disruption in the communicative repertoires of the eastern speech community was the challenge to accustomed ways of doing (especially talking) business. Buying and selling were not in themselves new practices for east Germans, of course, but, as Sabine Ylönen (1992) shows, westerners often appeared to attribute to their eastern neighbours a complete ignorance of market principles. Moreover, her study demonstrates how communicative dissonance could arise not only from different practices but also from the adoption by west Germans of discursive strategies that establish them in a position of dominance over their eastern interlocutors. At the Leipzig Trade Fair in September 1990— after the introduction of economic and monetary union in July of that year, but just before political union in October—she observed negotiations between the west German representative of a Finnish construction company and an east German businessman who wanted to build houses in the Dresden area. After the customer (C) has explained what he wants to do (build detached family houses), the sales representative (SR) launches into a lengthy and fluent sales pitch:

SR: Wir ham jetzt hier nur ein' Teil da und äh, es kommt ja immer darauf an, wir könn ja keine maßgeschneidertn Lösung' anbietn für das, was sie jetz hier konkret in der DDR brauchen. In der DDR sind Sie vor eine neue Situation gestellt und wir bzw. unsre Mandanten aus Finnland auch, so daß Sie uns im Prinzip sagn müßten, welche Leistung' Sie erbring' könn', wie Sie den Markt beurteiln—soweit Ihn' das jetz schon möglich ist— und dann müßtn wir'n Weg findn, unter unsren Mandantn jetz die richtign mit Ihn' zusamm'zubring' und vor alln Ding' auch das richtige Produkt zu entwickeln. Äh smuß ja nich immer das gleiche sein, was den Finn'
C: Nein
SR: gefällt und was den Deutschn gefällt, ja? Vielfach sind Änderung' nötig, aber der Markt is da.
C: 's klar.
SR: Grade im Gewerbebereich. Wir ham hier diese Holzhäuser als Kiosk oder Imbißstand, stelln
C: Ja
SR: sich'n Naherholungsgebiet vor, was entwickelt werdn soll. Wir könn' also ohne weitres in jeder Größe'n Golfklub oder irgendwas baun und die ganzn Einfamilienhausbebauung', die jetz komm'.
C: Das is das, äh wo wir die Hauptintresse hätten, was hier ganz aktuell wird äh, was bisher ja
SR: Ja
C: ouch anders gelaufn is, wo jeder sein Haus irgendwie selber baun mußte [*lachend*]
SR: Ja
C: äh, wo doch off die Baufirm' jetz äh ouch diese Markt... dieser Marktbereich zukommt.
(Ylönen 1992: 18–19)

SR: We haven't got everything here, and er it always depends, we can't provide any tailor-made solutions for what you need here in the GDR. You're in a new situation in the GDR, and so are we and our clients in Finland, so you really need to tell us what you can achieve, how you assess the market—to the extent that that's possible for you at this stage—and then we'll have to have a look at our clients and find a way of getting you together with the right ones and above all of developing the right product. Er, it doesn't always have to be the same thing, that appeals to the Finns
C: No
SR: and the Germans, does it? Many changes have to be made, but the market is there.
C: Sure.
SR: Especially in the commercial sector. We have these wooden huts here as kiosks or fast-food stands, think of
C: yes
SR: everything that has to be developed for a recreational area. We can easily build a golf club or something like that in any size, and all these new developments with detached family houses.
C: That's where, er, our main interest would be, what's happening now, which used to be
SR: Yes
C: quite different, everyone had to build their own home [laughing],
SR: Yes.
C: er, this area of the market that's opening up for construction companies now.

In the absence of comparative data showing either the customer or the sales representative operating in what would, for either of them, have been their 'own' social setting, we cannot read from this exchange how the respective participants 'normally' behave in the context 'conducting a sales negotiation'. However, a number of significant features of their behaviours in this specific context can be established: for example, in quantitative terms, SR dominates the conversation until C is able to find an opening, and when C does finally manage to do this, his explanation of his interests is more hesitant and less fluent than SR's exposition (greater frequency of the hesitation marker *äh*, reformulations, nervous (?) laughter). It may be tempting to see in this an indication of C's lack of experience in a 'western' genre and therefore his limited communicative competence, and no doubt he would have had grounds for feeling somewhat insecure under the circumstances. But his relative taciturnity could well have an alternative explanation.

SR makes it clear at the beginning of his long speech that he considers C's belonging to the social category 'GDR citizen' to be a relevant factor in their relationship. From SR's perspective, C is not just a potential customer, nor even just a customer from another country, but a customer from one particular country with special and as yet not determined needs. However, rather than seeking to establish exactly what the customer wants, SR delivers a lecture on the nature of 'the market' ('*smuß ja nich immer das gleiche sein, was den Finn' gefällt und was den Deutschn gefällt, ja?*', it doesn't always have to be the same thing that appeals to the Finns and the Germans, does it?) and what he expects C to do, before going on to expatiate on the range of products he can supply, regardless of whether this has any relevance for C. By adopting a discourse of instruction (*'In der DDR sind Sie vor eine neue Situation gestellt, . . . so daß Sie uns im Prinzip sagen müßten'*, You're in a new situation in the GDR, so you really need to tell us . . .), SR situates C in the position not of valued client, as he might have expected, but of novice or tutee with little experience relevant to the matter in hand and limited ability to make appropriate judgements (*'. . . wie Sie den Markt beurteilen—soweit Ihn' das jetz schon möglich ist'*, how you assess the market—to the extent that that's possible for you at this stage). C therefore has little alternative other than to listen patiently and indicate with minimal responses (*'nein, 's klar, ja'*, no, sure, yes) that he is following the lecture, until he sees his opportunity to intervene. When this eventually arises, with SR's mention of the key word *Einfamilienhausbebauung* (developments with detached family houses), C seizes it and redirects the conversation in the direction he wants to take it.

If this interpretation of this speech event is justified, then this episode is a good illustration of a broader pattern of discursive monopolization of the rules of language use and interaction by west German speakers. We have already seen (in 2.3) the thoroughness with which names of streets, schools, and other public institutions in eastern Germany were changed after unification in order to eradicate irritating traces of the GDR and to incorporate the territory of the former GDR firmly into the Federal Republic by imposing topographical conformity. The introduction of the western legal system and its attendant bureaucratic structures of implementation brought with it the issue of what patterns of language use would be considered appropriate in public administration. On the one hand, of course, the law requires a technical register in order to enable the precise and unambiguous formulation of legal texts; this may be rebarbative and impenetrable for the non-specialist, but that applies to west Germans as much as to easterners. On the other hand, there is no necessary requirement for a particular, conventional form of language use in bureaucratic communication: registers of this kind generally serve the purpose of restricting access to decision-making processes and protecting the 'expert' status of officials within their area of competence.

Ironically enough, perhaps, extensive exposure to official discourse in the GDR and experience of manipulating it in order to achieve a goal may well have been invaluable for east Germans confronted with the often tortuous (and tortured) language of western bureaucratic texts. The mayor of a small town in Sachsen-Anhalt, for example, showed his expertise in this area by deftly reformulating an application for project funding to meet the requirements of the funding body in Brussels (see Antos 1997: 160):

Wir haben für diesen Weinberg zuerst den Antrag gestellt 'Förderung des Weinbau im nördlichen Unstrut-Saale-Gebiet un und und'. Magdeburch meldet an Brüssel, Brüssel meldet: 'Weinbau fördern wir nich!' So, und jetzt passen Sie mal jut uff. Magdeburch hat dieses Schreibn der Brüsseler Beamten jenommen und uns zujeschickt, 'tut uns leid, Weinbau fördern wir nicht'. So, und dann bin ich nach Machdeburch un den Leuten klargemacht, ich sach: 'Ich will doch jar keen Weinbau jefördert haben, ich will eine *dausenjährige Weinbaukultur im Saale-Unstrut-Jebiet erhalten* [italics added] mit dieser Förderung'. Nach Brüssel jeschrieben: 'Dausenjährige Weinbaukultur erhalten'—'Das fördern wir.'

Originally, we put in an application for this vineyard [the town had inherited a run-down vineyard] 'promoting wine growing in the northern Unstrut-Saale region etc.'. Magdeburg [the state capital] passes it on to Brussels, Brussels says 'we don't provide support for wine growing!' OK, so listen carefully to this. Magdeburg took this letter from the bureaucrats in Brussels and sent it to us, saying 'sorry, we don't provide support for wine growing'. Right, so then I went to Magdeburg and explained to the people, I said 'But I don't want to have support for wine growing, I want support for *maintaining a thousand-year-old wine-growing culture in the Saale-Unstrut region*.' They write to Brussels: 'Thousand-year-old wine-growing culture'—'We'll support that.'

Through a small demonstration of political pragmatism the crafty mayor was able to achieve his aim: by applying for funding to 'maintain a thousand-year-old wine-growing culture' instead of simply to 'promote wine-growing', he secured the funding he needed. At a more general level, this shows how success in communicative encounters can depend on more than one kind of knowledge: the mayor needed to know not only what to ask for and where, but also how to ask for it.

The acquisition and constant updating of different kinds of knowledge are characteristic requirements of complex societies, but there is a limit to the amount of knowledge that individuals can store for themselves. So as Antos, Palm, and Richter (2000: 21) point out, the increasing specialization of everyday life increases our dependency on having access to expert knowledge, where access implies both availability and attainability: in other words, we have to be able to locate sources of expert knowledge and be able to make sense of it. This in turn imposes a communicative burden on both parties in the transfer of knowledge: seekers of knowledge must articulate their needs comprehensibly, and providers of knowledge must convey the information required comprehensibly and in an appropriate manner. Furthermore, these conditions for understanding go beyond linguistic issues: linguistic comprehension is necessary but not sufficient for a 'meeting of minds'. A satisfactory outcome of a consultation requires a shared understanding of the purpose of the event and of the participants' respective roles in it, as well as a willingness to negotiate an understanding of each other's position: successful communication is not merely a process of identifying the 'correct' answer to a given question, it has to be achieved interactionally. Where the participants bring with them into the encounter quite different expectations and different frames for understanding what is said (what Antos, Palm, and Richter 2000: 23–6 call 'cultural and communicative presuppositions'), there is therefore at least the potential for an unsatisfactory outcome.

The need for east Germans to acquire knowledge about all aspects of the business and work environment in the Federal Republic was obviously great in the early years after unification. As well as official advisory bodies, advice columns in newspapers and telephone hotlines were available in abundance—but how can knowledge be transferred interactionally when the interlocutors share neither background knowledge nor expectations of the consultation, and if such consultations are unsatisfactory, to what do we attribute the failure? These questions have been explored in detail by Gerd Antos and his team in Halle using data gathered in the mid-1990s from telephone calls to the advice line of a regional newspaper (see Antos and Schubert 1997*a,b* for a detailed account of the methodology). Their thesis is that there *is* a relationship between linguistic behaviour and communicative outcomes in this setting, but that it is indirect and mediated by other factors:

> Ost- und Westdeutsche orientieren sich in ähnlichen Situationen an verschiedenen sprachlichen Handlungsmustern. Die sich daraus ergebenden Divergenzen in der Diskursorganisation führen zu kommunikativen Verunsicherungen und Verständigungsproblemen, in deren Folge es zur Bestätigung soziopolitisch begründeter Stereotype und damit zu Belastungen der Kommunikation zwischen Ost und West kommt. (Antos, Palm, and Richter 2000: 22)

> In similar situations, east and west Germans operate according to different patterns of linguistic behaviour. The divergent patterns of discourse organization that result from this lead to communicative uncertainty and comprehension problems, which in turn result in the confirmation of socio-political stereotypes and therefore to obstacles to communication between east and west.

The 350 telephone calls they monitored consisted of conversations between east German advice-seekers and both east and west German advisers, which enabled them to explore both potential contrasts in terms of assumptions and expectations between western advisers and eastern advice-seekers, and differences in the 'Inszenierung von Expertentum' (performance of expertness—Antos and Schubert 1997*b*: 326) of eastern and western advisers.[16] Their analysis rests on the use of two contrasting behaviour patterns adopted by the advisers and the impact this has on the interaction with the advice-seekers. They argue that the genre *Beratungsgespräch* (advice session, consultation) is characterized by a particular structure, which consists of a sequence of four steps:

- presentation of the problem (advice-seeker);
- exploration and specification of the problem (advice-seeker and adviser);
- proposal of solution(s) (adviser);
- ratification of the proposed solution(s) (advice-seeker).

Individual advice sessions may or may not adhere to this sequence, but this is the common underlying structure. Where they may differ is in the patterns of behaviour and interaction with which they are realized.

---

[16] The potential weakness in the research design, that pattern conflicts might derive from other variables than 'east–west'—such as age, gender, or dialect use—was acknowledged (Antos and Schubert 1997*b*: 320, 326–7) but not taken further into account.

Antos, Palm, and Richter (2000) propose two basic patterns of problem-solving that can be identified in their corpus: BERATUNG (ADVICE) and AUSKUNFT (INFORMATION) (see also Palm and Richter 2000). It is important to emphasize that all the advice sessions share the same objective, which is to find suitable solutions to the problems presented; however, the course the sessions take depends on the perspective of the individual advisers (their interpretation of their role) and how this relates to the perspective of the advice-seekers. The resulting differences in discourse organisation arise mainly in the two central phases of the structure. If the adviser adopts the ADVICE pattern, he or she typically reformulates the problem as presented by the advice-seeker in terms of a more general set of issues, then situates the particular problem in this broader context, before putting forward a range of options and therefore leaving the final decision on action to be taken to the advice-seeker. Where the adviser adopts the INFORMATION pattern, however, he or she typically narrows the problem down to a very specific issue and proposes a single solution and often spells out concrete steps to be taken. In other words, the adviser understands his or her role either as interpreter of the interlocutor's life situation and as educator, or as friend and instructor.

For example, one woman rings the helpline and speaks to a west German adviser with a question about how to finance the modernization of her parents' house, which she is about to inherit. She poses a specific question about how much money she needs to have saved in the terms of her savings contract with her building society in order to be able to use this to finance the building work. Instead of offering a direct answer to this question, however, the adviser interprets it as an opening to a more general discussion on financing building. Having converted a specific question into a complex problem, he then goes on to outline a bewildering array of possible solutions: in other words, he reconfigures the interaction from the INFORMATION model to the ADVICE model. The discrepancy between the expectations of the advice-seeker and the position adopted by the adviser results in an unsatisfactory conclusion to the session:[17]

Ratgeber: Dann würden Sie also sagen wir mal fünfzigtausend Mark KFW-Mittel bekommen, würden dann äh zwanzigtausend Mark äh hier erstmal zwischenfinanzieren mit Schwäbisch Hall, und hätten dann nochmal zwanzigtausend Mark normal Hypothekenkredit, den Sie einfach mit Tilgung bedienen sollten.
Ratsuchende: Oh je.
Ratgeber: Ja, 's doch gar nich so schwierig.
Ratsuchende: [*Lacht*]

Adviser: Then you would get let's say a DM 50,000 loan from the KFW [Kreditanstalt für Wiederaufbau—bank providing funding for reconstruction], then you'd get er DM 20,000 bridging finance from a building society, and then you'd have a normal mortgage loan for another DM 20,000, which you should just service through repayments.

---

[17] As explained in the Preface, I have adopted a simplified form of transcription here (and throughout the book) in order to make the material accessible to the more general reader.

Advice seeker: Oh dear!
Adviser: Well, it's really not difficult.
Advice seeker: [*Laughs*]

By contrast, in another session an advice-seeker speaks to an east German adviser and explicitly asks about what options are available to her for financing the building of a new house. Although the adviser initially appears to pursue the ADVICE route that this opening move invites ('*Ja, es gibt kein Idealrezept, muß ich Ihnen erst sagen*', Well, there's no ideal recipe, I have to tell you), she then goes on to focus on one specific aspect of the question and develops a single concrete solution.

The corpus does not show a clear one-to-one relationship between the origin of the advisers and the pattern they adopt, but there seems to be a definite preference among western advisers for the ADVICE model and among eastern advisers for the INFORMATION model. Antos *et al.* (2000) are at pains to point out that both models were perfectly familiar both in the GDR and in the 'old' Federal Republic but argue that their distribution across contexts was different.[18] While the ADVICE model was widespread in the west except in certain official contexts where only specific answers were sanctioned, in the GDR it was largely confined to private and non-institutional contexts:

[Es] gab in der DDR allein schon aus Mangel an alternativen Handlungsmöglichkeiten (z.B. in den Bereichen Konsum, Versicherung, Finanzen usw.) keine dem heutigen Beratungswesen vergleichbare soziale Praxis, nimmt man private und inoffizielle Bereiche (z.B. Kirche) ebenso wie Medizin und Technik aus. Durch diesen Mangel an Handlungsalternativen gab es auch keine Notwendigkeit für die Herausbildung des Konzepts Beraten im öffentlichen Raum. Zum Erreichen eines gewünschten Handlungsziels (im Rahmen staatlich geregelter Handlungswege etwa bei Kreditvergabe, Abschluss einer Versicherung usw.) reichte weithin das Muster AUSKUNFT. Zwar kannten DDR-Bürger Formen privater BERATUNG, nicht aber im öffentlichen Raum angesiedelte professionelle oder gar institutionalisierte Beratungsformen. (Antos and Richter 2000: 88).

In the GDR, for lack of alternative opportunities (e.g. in the areas of consumer affairs, insurance, finance, etc.), there was no social practice comparable to the current advice system, if you exclude private and unofficial spheres (e.g. the Church) and medicine and technology. Given this lack of alternative forms of action, there was also no need to develop the concept of 'advice' in the public sphere. In order to achieve a desired outcome (in the context of state-regulated procedures such as granting loans, taking out insurance etc) the INFORMATION pattern was generally sufficient. GDR citizens were familiar with forms of

---

[18] This is important, because some eastern linguists, such as Wolfdietrich Hartung (forthcoming) and Jörg Pätzold (personal communication), have criticized the 'two models' approach on the grounds that exclusively attributing one pattern to each speech community in complementary distribution was simply wrong, but also that the particular attribution of ADVICE to the western and INFORMATION to the eastern community could be taken to imply passivity in eastern citizens, which they understandably reject.

private ADVICE, but not professional or institutional forms of advice established in the public sphere.

It is then precisely in the intermediate areas of semi-public contexts such as consultations that a clash may occur in terms of the patterns anticipated by east-erners and westerners respectively: they share the same knowledge of the two pat-terns, but not the same knowledge about 'appropriate' contexts of use for the two patterns (Antos, Palm, and Richter 2000: 41). In other words, their communicative competence is constituted differently in this respect—but because they are unaware of this, their interpretations of unsatisfactory interactions will differ. The west German advisers, for example, may be surprised by the dissatisfied reaction of east Germans to their detailed and authoritative but 'arm's length' approach, while the advice-seekers may be irritated by the loquacity and non-committal responses of the western adviser. It could well be, of course, that western advisers would articulate their 'expertness' in exactly the same way to west German non-experts, who in turn might well be as disenchanted by such conversations as their eastern counterparts. However, since the advisers know from the situation that their interlocutors on this occasion are easterners, that fact must be relevant in their approach to their task (see also Birkner and Kern 2000: 56–7 on this point), and the argument that in adopting the ADVICE model western advisers are operat-ing within the hegemonic discourse of 'western superiority' is plausible, if not necessarily demonstrable.

The inequality that is inherent in the consultation—the advice-seeker wants something that the adviser is in a position to reveal or to withhold—should not in itself constitute an obstacle to a successful outcome, since it can be assumed (in the absence of ulterior motives) that both parties are equally interested in achieving a satisfactory result: if the advice-seeker gets what they want, the adviser can feel they have done their job. In other interpersonal encounters, however, the participants do not necessarily share the same objective and this fundamental imbalance has a decisive effect on the conduct of the exchange. In a parallel project to the research on consultations, Peter Auer and his colleagues in Hamburg (later Freiburg) studied just such a genre, the *Bewerbungsgespräch* (job interview).[19]

These two genres have certain features in common: they represent everyday events, have a real impact on people's lives, are characterized by an unequal dis-tribution of power, and can be analysed in terms of clearly specifiable, conven-tional patterns of interaction. They are also both discourse types (Fairclough 1989: 29) which belong (albeit not exclusively) to the larger discourse of 'work in a mar-ket/capitalist economy'. However, there are also important differences between the

---

[19] Together with Ulla Fix's projects on ritualization and on language biographies (see 3.2 and 5.1), these constituted perhaps the most significant empirical research (collectively entitled *Fremdheit in der Muttersprache*, Foreignness in the Mother Tongue) on the east–west language question in the 1990s.

genres. First, as I have just argued, the unequal distribution of power between participants is more transparent in the job interview: even when the surface style is relatively informal, the 'asymmetry of the underlying agenda' (Auer 1998: 10) is understood by both parties. Secondly, in a job interview the interest in a particular outcome—the offer of a job—is generally greater on the part of the applicant than on the part of the employer: if one applicant cannot offer what the employer is looking for, they can usually interview another candidate. It seems, then, that a good outcome in a consultation is best assured where both parties are sensitive to each other and between them negotiate the desired result, but in a job interview the burden of success rests more firmly on the applicant.

In a competitive job market, it is often the case that several applicants have comparable qualifications and experience, so that the selection of one over another will be determined by other criteria that will emerge only in the context of the interview. The object of the exercise is to find out things about the applicants that cannot be gleaned from their documentation. This is where 'genre knowledge', in the sense of knowing 'the rules of the game', should be critically important, and it is here that the crucial contrast with the consultation lies. Auer (1998: 10–11) argues that the job interview is a specifically western genre—this means that unlike in the consultation, there is only one acceptable model. There is no inherent linguistic or even communicative problem in a consultation—difficulties arise from different expectations in terms of which choices are made, and when, from the shared repertoire of behaviour patterns. However, in a job interview, if Auer is right about its exclusivity as a western genre (or perhaps even if he is not), there is an in-built communicative problem because the genre does not admit alternatives. For example, it is at least conceivable that an eastern advice-seeker could redirect a consultation away from the ADVICE pattern towards the INFORMATION pattern, if that is what they want, but an eastern job applicant has no alternative but to adopt the western model, since that is taken as a precondition of suitability for employment (and they anyway have no other model, as opposed to an individual style, to choose instead).

Some eastern observers reject this argument on the grounds that it is predicated on the fixed idea of a deficit in the competence of east Germans which can be overcome only by their accommodating to the western model, and that employers are unaware of differences between eastern and western behaviour patterns in this context (for example, Hartung forthcoming, Jörg Pätzold pers. comm.). They argue instead that employers are less concerned than Auer believes with the ability of applicants to perform in accordance with particular genre conventions: employers want to identify, for example, a good computer programmer, not a good interviewee. Furthermore, they argue that while the linguistic and communicative differences Auer and his collaborators identify may exist, they are not relevant in determining the outcome of the interviews—the problem has its roots not in communicative (in)competence but in social prejudice. According to this view, it is precisely not the interview that provides the decisive information, as eastern journalist Frank Rothe claims to have found when being interviewed for a job with the (west German) broadcasting network NDR:[20]

Als ich dann da so saß und das Tafelwasser in der Tafelrunde öffnete, überkam es mich kalt. Ich sprach wohl nicht ihre Sprache, obwohl ich meinen Berliner Akzent herunterschraubte und mich ihrem uniformen Hochdeutsch anpaßte. Heute glaube ich, daß es sowieso egal war. Klar war, daß ich auf der Abschußliste stand, schon bevor ich meinen Mund öffnete. Ich sah es an diesen Blicken, die gegen mich gerichtet waren. Sie hielten alle eine Kopie meines Lebenslaufes in der Hand. Dort stand, daß ich die POS (Polytechnische Oberschule) und die EOS (Erweiterte Oberschule) besucht hatte und in Berlin-Mitte geboren war. Spätestens jetzt hätte ich ahnen müssen, daß ich mein Hochdeutsch verschwendete. (Rothe 2000: 57–8)

Then as I sat there and opened the bottle of water in front of this group around the table I went cold. I probably wasn't speaking their language, even though I played down my Berlin accent and adapted to their uniform standard German. Now I don't think it really made any difference. It was clear that I was done for even before I opened my mouth. I saw this in the looks that were directed at me. They all had a copy of my CV in their hands. It stated that I had attended the POS and the EOS and was born in Berlin-Mitte [a district in east Berlin]. By then I should have realized that speaking standard German was a waste of time.

The relative weight attached to linguistic/communicative discrepancies between western interviewer and eastern interviewee on the one hand and to the social identities of the respective participants on the other is therefore an important issue, and it would be imprudent to draw significant conclusions from this data about the impact of communicative dissonance on the outcome of such encounters. Nevertheless, the data from Auer's job interviews does make an important contribution to our understanding of sociolinguistic difference in terms of expectation and performance in this speech event. How, then, did eastern job applicants reveal their unfamiliarity with the rules of this 'western genre' in the early period of their exposure to it, and how was this interpreted by the interviewers?[21]

The data is drawn from two main sources: role-played interviews conducted in 1993 as part of a training exercise in Rostock (in eastern Germany), and actual interviews carried out in 1995. Unlike in Antos's project, comparative data (for the role-played interviews) is available from a similar training programme conducted with west Germans. We can categorize the features that appear to distinguish western from eastern speakers in this context broadly in two ways: first, there are linguistic and stylistic features, most of which can be subsumed in the notion of formality; secondly, there are strategic features, which have to do with how applicants present themselves in terms of their responses to particular challenges.

[20] For a counter-example, drawn from an actually recorded job interview, see Birkner and Kern (2000: 49–50).
[21] I shall give just a few illustrative examples here. For a detailed account of the project, see Birkner (2001), Kern (2000); concise discussions in English are in Auer (1998, 2000a).

As might be expected, especially in the light of our earlier discussion of lexical change in written texts (see 4.1), the earlier interviews frequently show evidence of mixing, where speakers readily adopt lexical items that belong, for example, to the register of business and commerce but embed them in a highly formal grammatical style that would arguably not be expected in this context:

Interviewer: Also, mit welchen Erwartungshaltungen gehen Sie an eine eventuelle Anstellung in unserer Firma?
Interviewee: Ich gehe grundsätzlich an die Erwartungshaltung diesbezüglich ran: daß ich sage, ich möchte in meiner Position gefördert und gefordert werden. Das heißt also aufbauend auf den Fähigkeiten und Kenntnissen, die ich schon besitze, die nun auch vorliegen, das heißt Kundengespräche, Arbeitsorganisation, Bankgeschäfte, daß ich dahingehend die Unterstützung habe, durch die Filialleitung bzw. den Bankdirektor bzw. den Filialleiter, daß dort Möglichkeiten geschaffen werden der Weiterbildung. (Auer 1998: 18)

Interviewer: So, what expectations would you have of a position in our company?
Interviewee: I approach my expectations in this respect fundamentally by saying that I would like to be supported and challenged in my position. That is to say that building on the abilities and knowledge that I already possess, which are there, that is to say discussions with clients, organization of work, banking transactions, that I have support in this sense, through the branch management or the bank manager or branch manager, that opportunities for further training will be created.

Auer argues that words like *Kundengespräche* (discussions with clients), *Arbeitsorganisation* (organization of work), *Bankgeschäfte* (banking transactions), and *Filialleitung* (branch management) belong to western business discourse and would therefore have been in this sense 'new' to the applicant, but that they are transported into a highly formal speech style more characteristic of eastern public discourse, with features such as the gerundial '*aufbauend auf*' (building on), the nominal construction '*Unterstützung durch die Filialleitung*' (support through the branch management), and the passive construction '*daß Möglichkeiten geschaffen werden*' (that opportunities will be created) (ibid.: 19, 29). Perhaps the most striking aspect of this style is this tendency to use depersonalized structures, such as the passive but also for example the avoidance of personal pronouns and an emphasis on functions of a post-holder rather than individual activities. Contrast the styles of the interviewer and the interviewee in the following passage in this respect:

Interviewer: Wir haben die Absicht, in absehbarer Zeit nach Osten hin zu expandieren, weil wir der Meinung sind, der Markt ist für uns noch offen und erschließbar, da wir aus Ihren Unterlagen entnehmen, daß Sie auch Russischkenntnisse besitzen, ist unsere Frage dahingehend: Würden Sie bereit sein, ein Servicenetz in den baltischen Staaten, oder in Rußland aufzubauen, oder mithelfen, dieses aufzubauen.
Interviewee: Da kann ich Ihnen erst mal ein grundsätzliches 'Ja' auf Ihre Frage entgegenhalten. Natürlich, ich habe Russischkenntnisse, die aber vervollständigt werden müssen, weil momentan meines Erachtens nach nicht in der Lage bin, mich fließend in Russisch zu verständigen, aber wenn Ihre Firma angedacht hat, das Servicenetz in Richtung Osten

auszubauen, dann darf ich vielleicht mal fragen, dann müßte eigentlich angedacht sein, um einen Niederlassungs- oder Betriebsleiter im Osten, ob angedacht ist von Ihrer Firma, einen Qualifizierungs-, Fortbildungslehrgang in Russisch anzubieten, wo ich meine Bereitschaft natürlich sofort signalisiere, um dort ein gutes, funktionierendes Service- und Vertriebsnetz aufzubauen. (Ibid.: 12)

Interviewer: We intend to expand into the east in the foreseeable future, because we believe that the market is still open for us and can be developed. We see from your application that you speak Russian, so our question in this respect is: would you be willing to build a service network in the Baltic states or Russia, or at least help to build this up?

Interviewee: Well, first of all I can answer your question with a definite 'yes'. Of course, I do speak Russian, although it needs to be perfected because at the moment in my opinion I am not in a position to communicate fluently in Russian, but if your company has been thinking about expanding the service network towards the east then perhaps I might ask, then there ought to be plans for a branch manager in the east, whether it is intended by your company to offer in-service training in Russian, in which case of course I indicate at once my willingness to develop a good functioning service and sales network there.

While the interviewer uses active constructions throughout and consistently selects personal pronouns both for self-reference (*wir, unser*, we, our) and to refer to the interviewee (*Sie*, you), the interviewee oscillates between using pronouns and indirect forms of reference ('*Ihre Firma*', your company) and uses passive constructions ('*die vervollständigt werden müssen*', which must be perfected; '*ob dort angedacht ist von Ihrer Firma*', whether it is planned by your company). However, this example is taken from a role-played interview, in which both participants were east Germans, and so a preference for either personal or impersonal styles cannot be attributed to the speakers' social origins but rather, if anything, to their perception of what is appropriate to the respective roles they are playing.

I shall consider possible motivations for variation and change in style in such contexts in the next section, but we can see here a suggestion of discomfort that is reinforced by eastern interviewees' strategic behaviour. Auer (1998: 28–9) sees a 'clash between the demands of the new communicative genre and the linguistic and other communicative resources available to deal with these demands' resulting from an incompatibility between western and eastern models of interaction in this context. In addition to prescribed stylistic patterns, he identifies forms of self-presentation and engagement with the interviewer which are part of the 'hidden agenda' of the interview. For example, it is a routine aspect of job interviews for applicants to be invited to assess their strengths and weaknesses frankly, but in a way that shows not only self-awareness but also an ability to address and counteract weaknesses that could impair competence in fulfilling the demands of the particular job. However, an eastern applicant in one of the authentic interviews was clearly taken aback by the question (this and the following examples are taken from Auer 2000a: 171–4):

Interviewer: Wo liegen Ihre Stärken? Und wo meinen Sie liegen Ihre Schwächen?
Interviewee: Das ist aber 'ne Frage.

Interviewer: Das 'ne Frage. Stimmt's, die is Ihnen noch nie begegnet. [general amusement among the interviewers] Und dann kriegen Sie sie hier in Xberg zum erschten Mal zu hören.
Interviewee: Nu ja, was will mer darauf sagen.

Interviewer: Where do your strengths lie? And where do you think your weaknesses lie?
Interviewee: What a question!
Interviewer: Quite a question, I know, and you've never come across it before. [general amusement] And now you get to hear it for the first time here in X-berg.
Interviewee: Well, what can you say.

The same awkwardness occurs on another occasion when an applicant is asked, conversely, to identify what her colleagues would assess as her strengths:

Interviewer: Was würden die sagen, wenn wir sie fragen würden, was sie besonders an Ihnen schätzen?
Interviewee: Ja, das is 'ne gute Frage. Man muß eigentlich, wie jesacht, wie alle andern auch, pünktlich sein, man muß natürlich, wie jesacht, weil ja auch jeder seine Arbeit hat, seine Kunden, daß man dran interessiert is, diese alle anzurufen, und es hat jeder sein festes Aufgabengebiet....Es is auch würklich 'ne tolle Teamarbeit, muß ich sagen. Also, jeder probiert da wirklich jedem zu helfen.

Interviewer: What would they say if we were to ask them what they particularly value in you?
Interviewee: Well, that's a good question. You must really, as I said, like everyone else, be punctual, you must of course, as I said, because after all everyone has their job to do, it's in your interest to ring them all up, your customers, and everyone has their own area of responsibility....It really is a great team effort, I must say. So, everyone really tries to help everyone else.

The interviewee deflects the interviewer's attempt to get her to talk about herself, first by using the impersonal pronoun *man* (you, one) with implied self-reference, then by praising the collective qualities of her colleagues. In a feedback session following this interview, the applicant makes it clear that she would find it very difficult to engage in self-praise, but the interviewer impresses on her that the strategy of 'modesty' in this context is inappropriate: 'Bescheidenheit ist eine Zier, aber wenn Sie einen Job haben wollen, müssen Sie ein bißchen mehr auf den Punkt kommen' (modesty is a virtue, but if you want to get a job you must get to the point a bit more) (Birkner and Kern 2000: 62–3).

The relative informality of the typical interviewer's style appears to encourage the more 'honest', less strategically calculated approach apparently preferred by eastern applicants, but this kind of behaviour may be taken as an indication of what we might call 'communicative innocence': the interviewee tends to take questions at face value. Birkner and Kern (ibid.: 70–1) illustrate this with an exchange in which the applicant is implicitly expected to disagree with a proposition put by the interviewer but prefers to respond to the surface invitation to agree:

Interviewer (the interviewee has explained that he is studying as well as working full-time): Belastet das nich? Also so Abitur und arbeiten?
Interviewee: Gut, der Tag is ziemlich volljepackt, aber ich wohne noch zuhause, und gehe morgens aus dem Haus, und komme abends gegen zehn wieder, esse noch was.
Interviewer: Abends um zehn wieder, ach so, dann von de Schule dann schon.
Interviewee: Ja ja, genau.
Interviewer: Is das jeden Abend?
Interviewee: Jeden Abend.
Interviewer: Oijoijoi, puh, meine Güte. Eh, meinen Sie nicht, dass das vielleicht Probleme bereiten könnte, wenn man sich irgendwo neu einarbeitet, also jetzt in so einer Phase zu wechseln?
Interviewee: Wäre möglich, ja.
Interviewer: Hm.

Interviewer: Isn't that a bit much? Doing *Abitur* and working?
Interviewee: Well, the day is pretty packed, but I still live at home and I leave the house in the morning and get back in the evening around ten, and have something to eat.
Interviewer: Back around ten in the evening, oh right, from college then?
Interviewee: Yes, exactly.
Interviewer: Is that every evening?
Interviewee: Every evening.
Interviewer: Wow, goodness me. Er, don't you think that that could cause problems if you're trying to settle into a new job, to change at a time like that?
Interviewee: It could do, yes.
Interviewer: Hm.

The interviewer makes it clear that he sees a potential problem in the double burden that the applicant has taken on himself, and offers him the opportunity to deny that this would pose an obstacle to his being able to carry out his new job satisfactorily. However, he appears to read the challenge as an expression of sympathy and instead of disagreeing opts for a moderate agreement with the interviewer.

Such exchanges illustrate the potential for communicative dissonance which Auer claims is inherent in genres that are defined by behavioural patterns prescribed in terms of western norms. Whether the sociolinguistic differences manifested in the 'performances' of eastern and western participants are symptoms or causes of friction and conflict in these situations is another matter: I shall return to questions of interpretation in Chapter 6.

My principal purpose in this section was to consider the evidence for potential communicative conflict in terms of incongruity of textual patterns and conversational dissonance arising from different expectations and practices associated with specific everyday communicative genres. The emphasis was on contrasts that can be identified between patterns and behaviours that could be seen as characteristic of eastern and western speakers in public and semi-public contexts. But to what extent, and in what ways, have they adapted or accommodated their language use since 1990? What instrumental or affective/symbolic motivations might there be for accommodation (or lack of it)? These are the questions I shall pursue in the next section.

4.3   Linguistic variation and social mobility

Writing in 1992–3, the veteran east German sociolinguist Helmut Schönfeld identified Berlin as a microcosm in which the problems of German unity were concentrated, and set out a list of broad objectives for research on language in Berlin (and so, by extension, in Germany as a whole):

Unterschiede im Sprachsystem, das unterschiedliche kommunikative Verhalten, der damit zusammenhängende differenzierte Sprachgebrauch und seine soziale und situative Determiniertheit sowie die Wirkung und Bewertung der sprachlich-kommunikativen Verschiedenheiten müssen bei sozialen Gruppen in Berlin erforscht sowie die ablaufenden und zu erwartenden Angleichungen beschrieben werden. (Schönfeld 1993: 188–9)

Differences in the linguistic system, different communicative behaviour, the associated differences in language use and their social and situational determination as well as the effects and evaluation of linguistic-communicative differences must be explored in relation to social groups in Berlin and both current and likely future processes of accommodation must be described.

As we have seen in 4.1, the differences in the language system were confined almost exclusively to the vocabulary and some idiomatic expressions, and their description need not occupy us any further here. We have also considered some of the differences in communicative behaviour and language use, and made some initial observations on the extent to which they are socially and situationally conditioned (see 4.2). At the end of the previous section, we began to explore some of the effects and evaluations of these differences and I shall focus on these issues now more in this and the following section.

The final element of Schönfeld's prescription relates to what many observers no doubt saw as an inevitable consequence of contact between the previously diverging 'communication communities': processes of accommodation. He goes on to emphasize the agency of social groups in any such process of change and the inextricable link between this and political, economic, and social developments, but also the significance of individual psychological factors:

Wieweit sind die verschiedenen Gruppen [der Berliner] willens und in der Lage, sprachlich-kommunikative Unterschiede zu überwinden? Von welchen Gruppen wird die Ausbildung gemeinsamer sprachlicher Normen bestimmt, wie verläuft die Entwicklung dahin, welche Rolle spielen dabei politische, wirtschaftliche sowie soziale Faktoren und Erfolge des

Zusammenwachsens? Welchen Einfluß haben bei den einzelnen Personen psychische Faktoren und ihre Biographie? (Ibid.)

To what extent are the various groups [of Berliners] willing and able to overcome linguistic-communicative differences? Which groups are going to determine the development of common linguistic norms, how will this process occur, what role will political, economic, and social factors and outcomes of the process of growing together play in this? What influence will psychological factors and personal life histories have on individual people?

He is stressing here that change is not automatic but also that it is not dependent solely on the influence of external forces, a salutary reminder that, in the words of Derek Bickerton's famous dictum, 'speaking, after all, is not done by ... the lower middle class of Upper Middletown—it is done by Irma and Ted and Basil and Jerry and Joan' (Bickerton 1971: 483). In our context, we need to keep reminding ourselves that speaking in Germany is not 'done' by homogeneous groups of 'easterners' and 'westerners', although the salience of being eastern or western (as opposed to being male or female, young or old, working class or middle class) may be heightened in certain situations.

From the outset, there has been a tension on both sides between reducing and maintaining the differences between them and for many this is felt as strongly now as it was then. For some easterners, for example, a desire to distance themselves from negative aspects of their past and to stake a claim to belonging in their new environment may vie with a need to assert positive associations of 'old' values and to reject the need to conform to western norms in order to qualify for membership of the new society. Westerners, for their part, may feel torn between an aspiration to be part of the revolutionary enterprise of constructing a new Germany and an unwillingness to concede equal entitlement to the credit for this achievement to their eastern compatriots. It is this continuing tension that may account, on the surface, for both change and lack of change in patterns of linguistic behaviour. However, sociolinguistic analyses of change in language and language use have consistently shown that the relationship between social and linguistic change is rarely direct, but rather has to be mediated by other factors.

In her pioneering study of language shift in a small community on the Austrian–Hungarian border, for example, Susan Gal (1980) showed how the progressive attrition of Hungarian, which on the macro level could be read as an inevitable effect of modernization, depended crucially on the intervening variable of individual evaluations of social categories (such as 'rural' versus 'urban'). Since the publication of this study, and the simultaneous appearance of Lesley Milroy's equally groundbreaking investigation of language variation and change in the monolingual context of Belfast, it has been clear that convincing explanations of change in language use require us to take account of *individual* motivations deriving from evaluations of *social* relationships and conventions. So, for instance, the general shift from Hungarian to German in eastern Austria was preceded by a revaluation of the two languages as 'traditional, rural, backward-looking' versus 'modern, urban, progressive' respectively, as opposed to the previous, evaluatively neutral contrast 'local' versus 'non-local'. In this context, individual choices could be interpreted as neither random nor automatically triggered by the identity of the interlocutor but as conscious selections that represented projections of the speaker's self—not every inhabitant of the small town was in favour of the modernization process and individual attitudes towards social change could not necessarily be predicted on the basis of objective or observable criteria such as occupation, gender, or age.

Viewed from this perspective, change in language use or behaviour is an indicator of social mobility—not necessarily in the vertical sense of social advancement, but in the sense of realignment with a social group or category to which you had not previously felt yourself to be bound and from the association with which you hope to gain some benefit. In the terms of communicative accommodation theory (see, for example, Giles 1994), depending on individual motivation speakers may choose to converge towards a target model, to diverge from it, or more neutrally to pursue a policy of non-convergence: in other words, through my speech choices I either seek to locate myself more closely to you, to distance myself from you, or to avoid using you as a point of reference at all. This process of relocation, which may be either temporary (tactical) or long-term (strategic), can be seen to operate most clearly where the relevant social categories constitute a dichotomy (e.g. black–white, male–female, native–non-native) rather than a continuum, and the east–west relationship is generally perceived in this way, even though it is cross-cut by many internal differences (I shall return to this point in Chapter 6).

So where changes in language use appear to be to attributable to this variable, we can see them as the result or expression of either a metaphorical or a literal move or 'migration' from east to west or vice versa. Conscious avoidance of shibboleths from the official discourse of GDR times could, for an easterner, be a declaration that 'I have left that place behind me' (divergence or non-convergence), and the deliberate use of western terms or linguistic patterns a sign that 'I have moved to this new place' (convergence) (I shall deal with another, less conscious aspect of this in 5.3). In a monolingual context, where there is no possibility of a complete shift from one discrete code to another, this process is more likely to be observable as a tendency than as a total change: we can identify features of various kinds that may be indicative of a willingness to migrate, or to stay put, or even (as we shall see) to remigrate.

Schönfeld (1993) concludes his catalogue of research questions by asking whether 'die sich aus der Vereinigung Deutschlands ergebenden sprachlichen Prozesse ein Ost-West-Problem oder nur ein Ost-Problem sind' (the linguistic processes resulting from the unification of Germany are an east–west problem or just an eastern problem), and all the evidence subsequently gathered certainly seems to support his implicit assumption that west Germans have been spared the difficulties that easterners have had to confront; to put it another way, it is only east Germans for whom sociolinguistic migration has been considered a possibility. With the exception of very recent work by Jennifer Dailey-O'Cain and Grit Liebscher (forthcoming), the counter-phenomenon of west-to-east migration has not been investigated, even though the actual movement of population in that direction has been not inconsiderable,[22] and reports of western journalists suggest there is a topic here waiting to be explored (see, for example, the articles by Stephanie Wätjen and Wiete Andrasch in Simon *et al.* 2000).

During the transitional period of the early 1990s, more or less random studies of language use by east Germans (particularly in 'western' settings) revealed an abundance of apparently mixed patterns, especially what we might call 'collocational blends', where a word that is associated specifically with either eastern or western usage is collocated with a word that is characteristic of the 'other' discourse. For example, even in late 1989, Burkhardt (1992: 189) captured a reference in a debate in the Volkskammer (GDR parliament) to 'eine an den Marktbedingungen orientierte Planwirtschaft' (a planned economy based on market conditions) (see also Kronenberg 1993: 83, 87); Roche (1991: 305) quotes an east German conservative politician describing freedom to travel as 'eine Errungenschaft der freiheitlich-demokratischen Grundordnung' (an achievement [using a term characteristic of official discourse in the GDR: see 4.1] of the fundamental constitutional order based on freedom and democracy); and Birkner and Kern (1996: 59) cite an eastern interviewee referring to '*unsere* Bundesanstalt für Angestellte' (*our* Federal Institute for Social Security and Pensions) (see also 4.1). Expressions such as these may be deliberate choices, but they are at least as likely to be slips of the tongue or ad hoc formulations and so of no consequence. To be able to talk of accommodative behaviour, we would need to have more systematic or at least more consistent manifestations of change, perhaps reinforced by evidence of intentionality such as conversational repairs.

Evidence of convergence and divergence at the lexical level, of acceptance and rejection of change, is supplied at length by Schönfeld (1993) himself for the Berlin 'microcosm', but while the research on which this is based may be credible, in that it would almost certainly be corroborated by many Berliners, it is largely anecdotal. A more systematic investigation of change, albeit focusing on a single lexical pair, is offered in Dittmar and Bredel's study of the modal particles *halt* and *eben* (1999: 153–64), which they take to be a sociolinguistic indicator of social transformation (Dittmar 2000: 212; for a critique, see Hartung forthcoming). The data for their study consists of transcripts of interviews carried out between 1993 and 1996 with thirty-one east Berliners and twenty-five west Berliners. Their argument rests on the fact that the two particles were, until relatively recently, geographically speaking in complementary distribution: they were synonyms,

---

[22] According to the official figures of the *Statistisches Bundesamt* (Federal Office for Statistics), the overall numbers for population movements between 'old' and 'new' *Bundesländer* in the ten years from 1990 to 1999 inclusive were as follows: from west to east—1,238,780; from east to west—2,059,816.

both used with the function of intensifying the force and plausibility of an utterance (as in '*das ist eben/halt nicht mehr möglich*', 'that just isn't possible any more'), but *halt* was generally found in the south and *eben* in the north (see Eichhoff 1978, Map 103).

By the 1980s, however, *halt* appears to have spread into urban areas in the north. When lexical diffusion brings two synonymous forms into contact in a particular area, it is likely to result either in the incoming form displacing the 'resident' form or in semantic differentiation (see Barbour and Stevenson 1990/1998: 3.5.2 and 3.5.3). Since both *eben* and *halt* continue to be used in Berlin and other northern areas, Dittmar (1997: 22, 2000: 218–20) follows Hentschel (1986) in postulating a developing distinction between the 'harder, more fact-oriented' *eben* and the 'softer, friendlier, more subjective' *halt*—a distinction reinforced by the fact that the two can co-occur in the same utterance, almost exclusively in the sequence *eben halt*, with *halt* supposedly softening the impact of *eben*. The relevant sociolinguistic questions then would be: is there a clear distinction in the use of these two particles between east and west Berliners; if so, is this remaining constant or is there a discernible trend towards a levelling out or accommodation; and how can we explain the answers to these two questions?

Table 4.1 shows, in simplified form, the distribution of the two particles in the interviews. Taking the data at face value, we could draw the following tentative conclusions: *halt* has entered the repertoire of some east Berliners but is not used at all by others, and *eben* is still used far more often overall; in the speech of west Berliners, however, *halt* now seems to occur at least as frequently as *eben*. However, the data on which Dittmar and Bredel base their analysis is (as they concede) unreliable in that there were more east Berliners than west Berliners in the corpus, the interviews were of quite different lengths (in general, the east Berlin interviews were longer than the west Berlin ones), and global conclusions

Table 4.1 *Frequency of use of* halt *and* eben *by speakers from east and west Berlin (based on Dittmar 1997: 23)*

	Occupation	Age	eben	halt	eben halt	halt eben
Eastern informants (male)						
EM1	Lighting technician	43	21	0	0	0
EM2	Electrician/student	26	19	17	0	0
EM3	Old people's nurse	38	1	2	0	0
EM4	Nurse	40	6	31	0	0
EM5	White collar worker	30	100	0	0	0
EM6	Musician	33	36	0	1	0
EM7	Fitter	33	7	0	0	0
EM8	Teacher/nurse	44	13	0	0	0
TOTAL			203	50	1	0

Table 4.1 *Continued*

	Occupation	Age	eben	halt	eben halt	halt eben
Eastern informants (female)						
EF1	Kindergarten supervisor	48	2	0	0	0
EF2	Student	23	20	5	0	0
EF3	Dentist's assistant	23	67	35	10	0
EF4	Paediatrician	36	15	11	0	0
EF5	Teacher	38	11	0	0	0
EF6	Social psychologist	59	17	0	0	0
EF7	Teacher	53	5	0	0	0
EF8	Doctor's receptionist	27	4	28	0	0
TOTAL			141	79	10	0
TOTAL (male and female)			344	129	11	0

	Occupation	Age	eben	halt	eben halt	halt eben
Western informants (male)						
WM1	Law student	30	1	24	0	0
WM2	Student	27	0	6	0	0
WM3	Teacher	37	14	14	17	1
WM4	Nurse	34	8	6	0	0
WM5	Salesman	28	7	2	0	0
WM6	Nursery teacher	39	0	1	3	0
WM7	Sales rep	57	3	2	0	0
WM8	Nursery teacher	35	0	15	0	0
TOTAL			33	70	20	1

	Occupation	Age	eben	halt	eben halt	halt eben
Western informants (female)						
WF1	Social psychologist	46	0	0	0	0
WF2	Student	27	10	8	0	0
WF3	Old people's nurse	51	3	12	0	0
WF4	Nurse/student	29	5	4	0	0
WF5	Head teacher	48	1	0	0	0
WF6	Dentist	50	8	10	2	0
WF7	Nursery teacher	55	2	0	0	0
WF8	Housewife	41	3	0	0	0
TOTAL			32	34	2	0
TOTAL (male and female)			65	104	22	1

about the usage of east- and west-Berliners conceal radical variations within each population. The quantitative analysis therefore has to be taken as no more than broadly suggestive.

In terms of studying language change, the data for this study was gathered over too short a time to permit any conclusions about trends, and there is no comparable data from an earlier period which could serve as a comparison. Moreover, since the innovation of *halt*-usage is historically very recent, the strong claim (Dittmar 2000: 220) that the softening effect of *halt* constitutes a 'socio-psychological advantage' which confers prestige on this form and therefore leads to language change, is really no more than speculation. Dittmar and Bredel (1999: 160–4; also Dittmar 2000: 225–9) do attempt a cautious evaluation of the data in terms of types of speaker and argue that different patterns of use are both linguistically and sociolinguistically motivated. However, the evidence is thin, and the interpretation of the fact that six younger east-Berliners in the corpus use *halt* relatively frequently as 'dieser durch Anpassung an den westlichen Sprachgebrauch hervorgerufene Sprachwandel' (this linguistic change brought about by accommodation to western language use) (Dittmar 2000: 227) is scarcely justified by the evidence. Nevertheless, it does seem reasonable to conclude from this study that the use of these two common forms could be in the process of change and that there may be grounds for exploring their status as sociolinguistic markers (in the sense of Labov 1972b), since the informants were evidently aware of them as competing alternatives and were able to make judgements about their own usage (ibid.: 229–31). Even then, though, it might be difficult to determine whether a trend towards greater usage of *halt* by easterners was part of a process of accommodation to *western* norms or rather part of a 'catching up' exercise, following the general northern tendency to adopt this *southern* form.

That differences in knowledge of social history are perceived as relevant by participants in east–west encounters is clear from metacommunicative behaviours, such as those described by Wätjen (2000) and more analytically by Birkner and Kern (2000). As a western journalist working in the east, Stephanie Wätjen was routinely taken to be a westerner, whether she identified herself as such or not, and explanatory 'footnotes' were a regular part of eastern interviewees' conversational style with her:

'Wissense, junge Frau, bei uns früher, da haben wir ja noch...' So fängt es meistens an, wenn ich mal wieder DDR-Unterricht bekomme. Wenn mir der Abteilungsleiter eines ehemaligen Kombinats erklärt, wie die Brigade früher zusammenhielt und daß die Kollegen sich auch privat auf der Datsche trafen. Wo man sich Kacheln für ein neues Badezimmer organisieren konnte oder wie das mit den begehrten Plätzen in Betriebsferienobjekten an der Ostsee geregelt war. Diese Erklärungen sind meistens freundlich gemeint; nur eine kleine Aufklärung für die Unwissende aus dem Westen. (Wätjen 2000: 45–6)

'You know, young woman, in the old days here we still used to...' This is how it usually starts whenever I get 'GDR lessons'. When the section head of a former combine explains how the work team used to stick together and colleagues also used to meet outside work time in their *dachas* (country cottages). Where you used to be able to get hold of tiles for a new bathroom or what the system was for getting sought-after places in the employees' holiday camp on the Baltic. These explanations are generally well meant; just a little enlightenment for the ignorant woman from the west.

'Enlightenment' was presumably not an end in itself in such situations: the purpose of providing 'GDR lessons' was not merely to fill gaps in the westerner's knowledge, but also to warn them against making false judgements about the present based on ignorance of the past, as well as to keep the past alive by 'telling it'. It is a strategy of continuity and self-assertion.

Birkner and Kern illustrate a more tactical form of accommodation in their analysis of ways in which eastern applicants and western interviewers in job interviews foreground the difference in their social (Birkner and Kern say cultural) backgrounds.

Bewerber: Ja gut, damals eh nannte sich das Erweiterte Oberschule, und hier eh mittlerweile heißt das Gymnasium.

Applicant: Yes, well, in those days it was called *Erweiterte Oberschule*, and here it's now called *Gymnasium*.

By 'translating' the GDR-specific term into a more or less equivalent 'western' term, the speaker removes any potential grounds for misunderstanding that could arise if the interviewer is unfamiliar with the GDR term, but more importantly proclaims his own knowledge of the social environment in which he is seeking employment. That comprehension is not necessarily the principal issue in such situations seems clear from the second example:

Bewerberin: Eh, mei Mann is dann zur Armee jejang', also hier heißt das ja wohl Bund?

Applicant: Er, then my husband joined the army, here it's called the *Bund* [short for *Bundeswehr*], isn't it?

Since *Armee* is bound to be comprehensible to the interviewer, the translation in this case is superfluous unless the real purpose is the speaker's declaration of their knowledge of appropriate western terms. By the same token, western interviewers may display knowledge of GDR-specific terms, presumably as a gesture of recognition and acceptance:

Bewerber: Also eh in Potsdam eigentlich das das war 'ne 'ne Außenstelle.
Interviewer: In in Potsdam an der Fachhochschule? Oder Ingenieurschule nannte sich die bei Ihnen?

Applicant: Well, in Potsdam that was actually a branch unit.
Interviewer: In Potsdam at the *Fachhochschule* [a particular kind of higher education institution]? Or *Ingenieurschule* (College of Engineering) is what you would have called it, isn't it?

None of these practices, of course, constitutes accommodative behaviour as it is generally understood in sociolinguistics (i.e. in the sense of adapting some aspect of your speech to that of an actual or 'virtual'—i.e. ideal, imagined—interlocutor), but in a looser sense of the term this does show a willingness on the part of a speaker to accommodate to the level of knowledge, relevant to the immediate speech situation, that can be assumed of the interlocutor: to mediate *between* your own discourse and that of the other, rather than to make the move *from* your own *to* that of the other.

But is there evidence of linguistic and/or communicative change that could be interpreted as accommodation to norms or patterns associated with the 'other' community? Research on changes in patterns of language use from those associated with either community before the *Wende* has been hampered by the lack of accessible relevant data from the GDR. There is no shortage of material recorded in the west before 1989 (see Wagener and Bausch 1997), but comparable material from the east has largely been overlooked (and in some cases even destroyed: Wolfdietrich Hartung, pers. comm.), although there are recordings from GDR media sources (radio, television, film: see Schlosser 1990a/1999: 145–9) that can be used to stand in for authentic spontaneous speech, *faute de mieux*. Retrospective impressionistic accounts of everyday speech styles of the GDR, whether delivered by east or west Germans, are at best indicative of what may or may not have been the case. West German Horst Dieter Schlosser (1999: 245), for example, refers to the post-*Wende* persistence of stylistic features familiar to him as a seasoned observer in the past: 'etwa ein stärkeres Bemühen um präzise Formulierungen, das teilweise noch mit einem langsameren Sprechtempo einhergeht, oder ein weitgehender Verzicht auf Signale individueller Selbstdarstellung' (for example, a greater effort to formulate things precisely, sometimes accompanied by a slower speech tempo, or generally not using any indicators of individual self-presentation). Similarly, in early encounters after the *Wende*, east German Dagmar Barth (1997: 396) detected differences in conversational management between what she was accustomed to amongst east Germans and what she observed amongst west Germans: '[Auch] die Art und Weise der Problembehandlung unterschied sich: Während sich der Tenor der Wessiäußerungen in einem "ich habe die Lösung für Dein Problem" zusammenfassen ließ, müßte dieser für die Ossis eher lauten: "ich habe ein Problem, wir überlegen gemeinsam" ' (There were also different ways of dealing with problems: while the tone of typical *Wessi* remarks could be summed up as 'I know how to solve your problem', for the *Ossi* it would have to be 'I've got a problem, let's talk about it together').[23]

Both Schlosser's and Barth's observations accord with comments made by eastern school students I interviewed in Cottbus in 1992 on the basis of their first

---

[23] It is worth noting that this observation from personal experience contradicts the finding from the project on *Beratungsgespräche* (advice sessions/consultations: see 4.2) that westerners tend to adopt a negotiating ADVICE-type approach and easterners a directive INFORMATION-type.

exposure to young west Germans. They expressed a strong sense that west Germans know how to project a powerful personal image: 'Die Westdeutschen sprechen viel mehr, sie wissen genau, wie sie sich geben sollen, gestisch und mimisch, und das schüchtert dann die Ostdeutschen ein bißchen ein' (The west Germans talk a lot more, they know exactly how to present themselves, using gestures and facial expressions, and that is a bit intimidating for east Germans) (Stevenson 1995: 55). And more generally they argued that for west Germans spoken interaction is more about establishing personal credentials in terms of 'experiences consumed' than about establishing personal relationships in terms of 'feelings experienced' (see also Beneke 1993): 'Die Westler erzählen mehr, was sie gehört haben und was sie erfahren haben, während die Ostler mehr so Gefühle äußern' (The west Germans tend to talk about what they've heard and what they've done, while the east Germans tend to express their feelings) (Stevenson 1995: 55).

Barth (1997) also refers to what she reluctantly perceived as a clear need to adapt to the western style of self-promotion in semi-public contexts if she was to survive in the competitive job market. She characterizes this globally as 'Ich denke, den Anforderungen gerecht zu werden und *die* ideale Person für Ihre Stelle zu sein' (I think I meet your requirements and am *the* ideal person for your post), but of course in the absence of recordings of job interviews or similar interactions in the GDR we have no concrete basis for analysing specific ways in which east Germans' speech behaviour in such contexts might have changed.

Peter Auer (2000*a*,*b*) has attempted to get around the apparently intractable data problem by drawing on a series of interviews conducted by west German journalist Erika Runge in 1970 in Rostock (the same city as his role-played interviews were recorded in: see 4.2). Together with the two sets of interviews he and his colleagues recorded themselves, this gave him material from three points in the development of the east German speech community: an initial point of reference in the GDR period, a moment in the *Umbruch* phase after unification in 1992–3, and a point only slightly later (1995), by which time however a substantially increased amount of contact with western speakers can be assumed. The drawback to this exercise in linguistic archaeology is that it was not possible to compare like with like: Runge's interviews were different in nature from Auer's (Runge's were journalistic interviews dealing with aspects of life in the GDR), and they were not transcribed but processed by the author into a more readable format. There is therefore no guarantee that her representation of the interviewees' language is accurate, which makes it an insecure basis for comparison; that in itself does not render the exercise invalid, but the results clearly need to be treated with caution. It is also worth emphasizing that none of the three sets of data (neither Runge's nor Auer's interviews) constitutes *Alltagssprache* in the sense of unconstrained, private, spontaneous speech: they all belong to similar semi-public genres of structured interaction. To that extent, although personal traits obviously still come into play, we can anticipate a degree of patterned behaviour.

Auer's procedure is to begin with the lowest layer in the stratigraphy, the Runge interviews, in which he isolates seven stylistic features that meet the criteria of frequent occurrence in the data and of being in his view characteristic of speech in semi-public contexts in the GDR (I shall outline them very briefly here, as they are discussed in detail in Auer 2000*a*, *b*; the examples used here are taken from these sources unless otherwise indicated).

1 use of *unser* (our) with reference to public or state institutions and organizations (*unsere Regierung*, our government; *unsere Republik*, our republic), where the definite article would be adequate and probably more normal in western usage;
2 *ich möchte sagen* (I would like to say) as an introductory formula to add weight to a statement: 'Ich möchte sagen, die Aufgabe der Liberal-Demokratischen Partei ist es, den Mittelstand mit einzubeziehen in den Aufbau, also in den Aufbau des Sozialismus' (I would like to say that it is the task of the Liberal Democratic Party to include the middle class in the construction of socialism);
3 use of 'generic' masculine forms for occupations even with individual female referents: 'Meine Frau ist Wirtschaftsleiter beim RDGB-Feriendienst' (My wife is a manager in the RDGB [a trade union]holiday service);
4 use of expressions such as *den Beruf/ die Funktion eines X ausüben* (carry out the occupation/function of X) instead of simply *X sein* (to be an X): 'In der FDJ-Sektionsleitung hatte ich die Funktion des Kulturfunktionärs' (In the FDJ section leadership I had the function of culture officer);
5 use of 'rhetorical doublets' (synonymous pairs of terms, such as *erziehungswirksam und bildungseffektiv*, educationally effective—see 3.2 above);
6 use of complex syntactic structures creating a sense of solidity and earnestness in the statement;
7 use of nominalization in place of simple verb forms; the following example illustrates features 5, 6 and 7: '. . . wird die gegenseitige *Hilfe und Zusammenarbeit* (5) aller Bürger durch den Wohnbezirksausschuß als wichtige Aufgabe *in Angriff genommen* (6), um neue *Impulse zur Entfaltung der sozialistischen Gemeinschaft* (7) zu geben' (mutual *support and cooperation* of all citizens will be *taken on board* as an important task by the district housing committee, in order to give new *impetus to the development of the socialist community*).

The data from the other two sources was then searched for occurrences of these features. Since none of the material had been gathered with quantitative analysis in mind, it would have been impossible to construct a precise statistical comparison, so the results in Table 4.2 are no more than a rough guide to trends.

The striking contrast in Table 4.2 is not, as might have been expected, between Runge's interviews and the post-*Wende* material, but between the two sets of job interviews. Why should this be? On the one hand, it might be anticipated that if east German interviewees were keen to 'make the right impression' they would make considerable efforts to adapt their speech behaviour to meet the requirements of the

Table 4.2 *Frequency of occurrence of 'east German' stylistic features in three sources (from Auer 2000a: 184)*

Feature	Runge interviews 1970	Role plays 1992	Job interviews 1994–5
1st person pl. poss. pronoun	very frequent	rare (?)	absent (?)
'I'd like to say' routine	very frequent	occasionally used	absent
masc. forms for names of occupations used by female speakers	very frequent	very frequent	rare
rhetorical doublets	very frequent	frequent	absent
'the occupation/function of' formula	very frequent	occasionally used	rare
complex syntax: *Funktionsverbgefüge*	frequent	very frequent	in only 3 out of 20 speakers
complex syntax: nominalizations	frequent	very frequent	in only 3 out of 20 speakers

setting: resistance to adaptive pressure in this context, in the form of overtly divergent behaviour, might be counter-productive. On the other hand, the role plays were precisely part of a training programme with participants who were by definition relatively inexperienced in the genre. More importantly, perhaps, since the interviewers in the role plays were also easterners, this attribute may well have mitigated or even eliminated the formal aspect of the role they were playing from the perspective of the interviewees. It is therefore probable that the interviewees' incentive to converge towards their actual interlocutor outweighed the pressure to converge towards the role they were playing. By contrast, in the authentic interviews, the interviewers were 'real' west Germans and the interviewees were often younger and had had greater exposure to western norms. Since the participants are not automata, this fact would not in itself explain the apparent abandonment of the 'eastern' features in the later data. Much will rest first on these features being identified by the eastern speakers as sociolinguistic markers deriving, for the most part, from official discourse patterns of the GDR (see 3.1 and 3.2), and secondly on the speakers then deciding that the benefits of deleting these components from their style repertoires outweigh the costs, in the sense that doing this represents a loss of 'self', a potential threat to their 'face' (see Hudson 1996: 113–16).

All acts of accommodation are potentially face-threatening: convergence entails a risk to your own 'independence' or 'negative face', divergence represents a threat to your interlocutor's 'involvement' or 'positive face'. The process of accommodation is therefore always a balancing act between conflicting interests (Scollon and Scollon 1995: 38). In job interviews, it is generally in the interests of both parties to confine the potential for conflict within strict limits. In openly confrontational situations such as political debates, however, conflict is of the essence. Yet we have seen in 3.1 the essentially preordained and non-combative nature of this genre in the GDR, and in his analysis of proceedings in the final Volkskammer of 1990 Burkhardt (1992: 192–3) comments on what he sees as the continuing passivity of the participants, compared to their counterparts in the west German Bundestag, interpreting the delegates' 'excessive politeness', the lack of interjections and of responses to provocative remarks, as signs of an unwillingness to engage in open controversy. When east German politicians entered the domain of western dominated politics, therefore, the question of contrasting or even incompatible traditions or styles did arise.

The majority of eastern politicians elected to the Bundestag and to the regional state parliaments (*Landtage*) in and after 1990 were new to parliamentary politics, and the only ones with previous experience of public speaking had generally gained this through involvement in the Church or reform movements during the *Wende*. Most of them therefore brought with them not only relatively little political baggage but also none of the bland and formulaic debating style characteristic of GDR politics. At the same time, west German politics had long been dogged by growing public disenchantment (*Politikverdrossenheit*) with the practices and processes of their stale political culture, and west German politicians and public figures were in no position to preach to their eastern counterparts about appropriate styles of public speaking. Dagmar Blei (1992: 51), for example, quotes the frank and hopeful words of east German Social Democrat MP (and former member of the Volkskammer) Richard Schröder shortly after unification:

Wir haben viel zu erläutern über unsere Verhältnisse. Bei der Fahrt zum Flughafen sagt die Fahrerin, sie fahre am liebsten Ost-Abgeordnete, denn wenn die von Politik reden, verstünde sie auch was; bei West-Abgeordneten dagegen wüßte sie hinterher nie, was sie eigentlich gesagt haben. Wir hören solche Komplimente natürlich gern. Vielleicht stimmen sie sogar. Dann könnte die noch ausstehende wirkliche Vereinigung, die Vermischung der Deutschen, wirklich was Neues bringen. In den Ostländern jedenfalls ist die gestanzte Bonzensprache tot. Wir müssen neue Worte finden und normal reden. Wir werden auch im vereinten Deutschland eine neue, gemeinsame Sprache erst noch finden müssen. (Originally in: 'In ein fremdes Land geraten? Am meisten überrascht die kühle Perfektion des Bonner Parlamentsbetriebes', in *Die Zeit*, 23 December 1990: 8)

There are a lot of things we need to get straight. On the journey to the airport, the driver says she prefers driving eastern members of parliament because when they talk about politics she can understand some of what they say; with western members of parliament she never has any idea what they've said. Of course, we like getting compliments like this. Perhaps they are even true. In that case, the real unification, which has still to take place, the blending together of the Germans, may really bring about something new. In the eastern states at any rate the hackneyed language of the Party bosses is dead. We must find new words and speak normally. We have still yet to find a new, common language in the unified Germany.

In the same vein, she also cites Schröder's political opponent and fellow easterner, the then up-and-coming Christian Democrat Minister for Youth and Family Affairs (now leader of her Party) Angela Merkel:

Obwohl häufig Argumente parteiübergreifend seien, so Jugend- und Familienministerin Angela Merkel (CDU), 'bemühen sich viele um zuviel Polemik'. Sie selbst sei nicht bereit zu glauben, daß das der einzige Weg ist, um Politik zu machen im Sinn der Bürger, die wohl mehrheitlich der Meinung sind, daß sich die Politiker zuviel streiten. Sie sei zwar auch dafür, daß in einer Demokratie um den richtigen Weg gerungen wird, doch solle das ein 'konstruktiver Streit' sein. (Originally in: 'Zu viel Streit und Polemik. Ossis fühlen sich im Bundestag zuwenig vertreten', in *Die Union*, 131/1991: 3.)

Although, according to Angela Merkel (CDU), Minister for Youth and Family Affairs, arguments are often not a matter of party politics, 'many politicians engage in too much polemic'. She herself was not willing to be believe that this was the only way of doing politics as the public would like to see it done, the majority of whom think that politicians argue too much. She was certainly in favour of there being a debate about the right way in a democracy, but it should be a 'constructive argument'.

No doubt, allowances have to be made for the understandably over-optimistic tone and content of such remarks, and with the cynicism that hindsight allows it is easy to dismiss them as no more than naïve and pious hopes of inexperienced performers on the public stage. However, there was at the same time a unique opportunity here to achieve a change for the better in German political culture, to revive the declining reputation of political processes in Germany and to allow the fresh air of new voices to breathe new life into the parliamentary practices of the Bundestag. No one in the east can have regretted the passing of the ritually consensual political style of the GDR, but few in the west would have argued that the ritual hostility of the disputes between the political dynasties of the Federal Republic were an ideal realization of parliamentary democracy either.

Here again, though, there are no signs that the dominant majority of western politicians saw any value in questioning, let alone moving away from, traditional practices and making a genuinely fresh start. On the contrary, the onus was once more clearly on the easterners to adapt to what was evidently taken to be the only appropriate mode of behaviour: the interruption of an eastern MP's speech by a western MP during a speech in the Bundestag, crudely 'correcting' his German, is an early indication of this assumption (the east German MP had used the term *Zielstellung*, 'objective, aim', and the west German interjected: 'Das heißt hier *Zielsetzung!*' (Here we say *Zielsetzung!*); see Hellmann 1997*b*: 83–4). Furthermore, Biege and Bose (1997: 127), quoting a politician interviewed in a study by Schaaf (1995), suggest that the growing use of personal attacks by eastern politicians in debates in east German state parliaments in the mid-1990s was a device to demonstrate their 'competence' in the (for them) newly defined genre:

Man muss meiner Meinung nach bestimmte Redetricks auch drauf haben, glaube ich, und vielleicht auch ein paar Sprüche.... Wenn ein Abgeordneter spricht, der kann alles vom

Leder ziehen, der kann auch unter die Gürtellinie gehen.... Und ich wurde oft unter der Gürtellinie angegriffen, wissen Sie, und von Leuten, wo ich das nicht erwartet hätte; das hat mich oft enttäuscht, muss ich sagen.... Ich bin der Meinung, Sachlichkeit, Fachbezogenheit, auch ruhig über ein bestimmtes Maß, aber nie unter der Gürtellinie. Das ist unheimlich wichtig. Erst recht, wenn wir in einer neudemokratischen Ordnung zueinander finden sollen,... sollten wir wenigstens den Ton wahren, wenn man das schon in den alten Bundesländern nicht so kann, aber hier.

In my opinion, you have to have certain rhetorical tricks up your sleeve, and perhaps a few witty sayings.... When a member of parliament speaks, he can really let rip, he can even go below the belt.... And I've often been attacked below the belt, you know, and by people I wouldn't have expected it from; I've often been disappointed by that, I must say.... In my opinion, objectivity, dealing with the issues, even a bit over the top, but never below the belt. That is extremely important. Especially if we are to try to get on with each other in a new democratic order,... we should at least maintain a certain tone, even if that's not really possible in the old Federal states, we can here.

This impression is further reinforced by a brief exchange between the west German chair of a studio discussion on the east German television channel ORB and an east German panellist. The chair, Günter Gaus (who had been the first leader of the 'permanent representation' of the Federal Republic in the GDR in the 1970s), after trying repeatedly but in vain to get Manfred Stolpe (Prime Minister of Brandenburg) to give a direct answer to a question, declares ironically: 'Sie könn' das inzwischen fabelhaft. Sie könn' das inzwisch'n wie ein westdeutscher Politiker.' (You've learned to do that brilliantly. You've learned to do that like a west German politician.) (Läzer 1996b: 170)

More detailed exploration of accommodation to the western norms of debating style comes in a quantitative study by Stephan Elspaß (2000). He analyses speeches made by ten east German MPs and ten west German MPs (all women, to remove gender as a variable) in the Bundestag, first in 1991 and then again in 1997. He focuses on one specific feature of speech styles, which he refers to as 'communicative uncertainty' (see also Kreutz 1997a,b) and which is considered a negative attribute in the western tradition of public rhetoric, a tradition that places the highest value on expressions of clarity and fixity. He identifies a set of markers of this feature and undertakes a quantitative analysis of the speeches in order to determine whether any changes in this respect can be discerned. The markers include, for example, introducing statements with a verb of saying or thinking (*ich glaube/denke/nehme an, daß...*, I think/assume that...) or verbal phrases with a similar function (*es scheint/es sieht so aus, daß...*, it seems/looks as if...), modal adverbs (*vielleicht*, perhaps; *wahrscheinlich*, probably; *im Grunde*, basically), and adverbial phrases expressing modality (*meines Erachtens/meiner Meinung nach*, in my opinion). The premise on which the study is based is that the western parliamentary style demands that speakers avoid such expressions of uncertainty and vagueness, which are interpreted as signs of weakness and lack of resolve. At issue, then, is whether east German politicians use more of these markers than west

Germans in the early debates and, if so, whether they modify their behaviour in the course of the intervening six years by converging to the western norm.

The sample is relatively small, and Elspaß (2000: 215) concedes that the results cannot be conclusive. However, what they appear to show is that in 1991 there was in fact no significant difference between the eastern and western MPs in his sample in terms of their use of markers of uncertainty. Furthermore, both groups show a substantial reduction in the use of these markers in the later data. Although this reduction is most dramatic in the case of the east German MPs (about 50 per cent compared to about 34 per cent for west German MPs), the discrepancy between the two groups at the later stage appears to be attributable mainly to a single feature (verbs of saying and thinking). It is therefore difficult to draw firm conclusions from this study, but it does provide some very interesting data and Elspaß's analysis throws up some important questions for further research. On the one hand, the results do seem to suggest that the east German MPs as a group have adapted to the western conventions. On the other hand, the west German MPs also seem to have adapted their speech behaviour in much the same way, albeit to a lesser extent. It could therefore be that the relative inexperience of the majority in *both* groups, rather than their origin, is accountable for the initial similarity in performance and for the direction of change. At least as important, perhaps, is first the fact that the features studied here may have more than one function in discourse, and secondly the fact that individual characteristics of the speakers may be concealed by the way the data is represented. Both of these issues (the 'form and function' problem, and the distorting effects of grouping the results from individual speakers according to one of several possible variables) are common problems in studies of sociolinguistic variation (see, for example, Holmes 2001: 286–93, Wardhaugh 1998: Chapters 6 and 7).

In the present context, it is the second of these issues—how to explain variation and change in language use—that is of greater interest. Having had to abandon his initial hypothesis (that east and west German politicians differ significantly in their language behaviour in the context of Bundestag debates), Elspaß tries to identify an intermediate category between the 'individual' and the 'group', since the latter appears to conceal important internal differences, while if we tie variation to the former we have to accept that there is no social basis for patterns of variation. He seeks instead to redistribute the members of his sociogeographically defined groups into three behavioural types, based on the relative frequency with which they use the 'uncertainty' markers. This turns out to provide both a more subtle and a more revealing explanation for variation and for change, since it potentially allows us to integrate all three categories in one model: we can account for similarities and differences between *individual* members of (apparently) objectively defined *groups* in terms of the ways in which they align themselves behaviourally with one or other *type*.

This suggests a modification, or an extension, to Bickerton's maxim (see above). Speaking may be done by Irma and Ted and Basil and Jerry and Joan, but if we want to find explanations for the similarities and differences between their speech patterns, we need to ask questions like: who else speaks like Irma, and when and why? When and why does Irma speak like Ted, when and why does she speak more like Basil? In other words, there is a fundamental problem in starting from assumptions of homogeneity in constructs such as 'east' or 'west' Germans, not only because we ought to know that not all members of such groups will behave alike, but also because some members of one group may well behave more like most members of the other group than they do of their 'own'. The recognition of this fact has profound implications for the methodology of sociolinguistic research. Rather than allocating informants to predetermined groups on the basis of variables such as age, gender, or occupation and then seeking to attribute differences in linguistic behaviour to these variables, informants can be selected on the basis of a single common characteristic (such as 'being MPs' or 'migrating from one place to another place'), they can then be clustered according to their linguistic behaviour in terms of particular linguistic variables, and we can finally seek an appropriate explanation for the constitution of these self-defining groups.

Much early sociolinguistic work shunned the individual in favour of the social group on the grounds that the group concept would have greater explanatory power in the context of an understanding of language use as a social phenomenon. At least since the late 1970s, however, the need has been widely accepted in sociolinguistics to rehabilitate the individual as a social agent who, amongst other things, constructs 'a more or less unconscious mental map of the community in which they live, in which the people around them are arranged in a "multidimensional space", i.e. showing similarities and differences relative to one another on a large number of dimensions or parameters' (Hudson 1996: 11). According to this view, individuals construct a floating model of the speech community which they inhabit and which is subject to change as their perceptions of their relationships with other constituents or members of the community change:

Each individual creates the systems for his [sic] verbal behaviour so that they shall resemble those of the group or groups with which from time to time he may wish to be identified, to the extent that
  a. he can identify the groups,
  b. he has both opportunity and ability to observe and analyse their behavioural systems,
  c. his motivation is sufficiently strong to impel him to choose, and to adapt his behaviour accordingly,
  d. he is still able to adapt his behaviour.
(Hudson 1996: 26, adapted from Le Page and Tabouret-Keller 1985: 182)

In one form or another, this view, which makes room for individual psychological motivation for action within a social model of language behaviour, has informed most sociolinguistic research on variation and change over the last twenty years or more. It is very much the foundation of Birgit Barden's and Beate Großkopf's longitudinal study of the changing speech behaviour of inhabitants of

Saxony in eastern Germany, who 'migrated' to parts of west and south-west Germany in the early 1990s (Barden and Großkopf 1998; for a detailed summary of the project in English, see Barden 2000). While the other studies I have discussed in this section investigate the consequences of making a metaphorical journey from east to west, the subjects in this study literally migrate. The second crucial difference between this and other research is that by observing the same set of speakers at intervals over a two-year time span (from 1990 to 1992) Barden and Großkopf were able to identify patterns of change in 'real' individuals (rather than comparable groups) in real time.

The methodology employed here was to select fifty-six people aged between 12 and 52, whose one common feature was that they were east Germans who had moved to western Germany after the *Wende,* and to interview them at regular intervals (eight times in total) over the two-year period. The interview data was then analysed on the basis of the realizations of twelve phonological variables, whose non-standard variants were considered to be distinctive features of the Upper Saxon Vernacular (USV). USV has relatively high prestige on its own territory, but in western Germany it is not only readily identified as an eastern speech form but associated irrevocably with the GDR: since many of the leading political figures in the GDR were from this region, the 'Saxon voice' was for many in the west the 'voice of the GDR'. USV was therefore heavily stigmatized in the west, and it could be assumed that there would be a strong incentive for USV-speakers to accommodate their speech on arrival in the west, either through convergence with the local or regional varieties of their new place of residence or through non-convergence, i.e. a more evasive strategy that entails moving away from their normal speech form but changing in the direction of the regionally neutral standard German rather than a localized variety (Barden 2000: 227).

For the group as a whole, this anticipated result was indeed what seems to have occurred: on average, the speakers reduced their use of non-standard, USV forms by about 11 per cent over the two-year period. This is an interesting finding in itself, providing as it does concrete, quantified evidence of linguistic change. However, the important issue here is not merely to establish the fact of change, but to identify the reasons for change and to construct a convincing analytical model to capture and account for it. If it is to be convincing, the model will need to be able to show both whether there are patterns of behaviour common to sub-groups within the overall population of the study and to what extent (and why) individual behaviours conform to, or diverge from, these patterns. Barden and Großkopf seek to do this by developing a hybrid model that integrates objective and subjective dimensions of variation and change. The objective dimension is the measurement of the linguistic variables, and the subjective dimensions have to do with how the individual speakers locate themselves in the 'multi-dimensional space' (see above) of their communicative and social environment.

Using a version of the social network concept, first deployed in sociolinguistic analysis in Milroy (1980/1987) and since applied to many other contexts (see

Milroy 1987: Chapter 7, Hudson 1996, Wardhaugh 1998), the researchers invited each speaker to represent, in the form of a simple diagram, their relationships with other people who played some kind of role in their lives. An example is shown in Fig. 4.1.

The size of the circles indicates the relative frequency of contact the speaker claims to have with each individual member of their network, and the distance between their 'ego' and the other circles represents the emotional distance the speaker perceives between them and the individuals concerned. Lines were then drawn around those circles representing people who knew each other. Finally, the origins of each individual in the network were indicated by variable shading. In this way, a picture was constructed of the unique pattern of each informant's network.

Unlike in Milroy (1987), where a 'network strength score' was calculated for each informant on the basis of the relative 'density' (number of contacts within the network) and 'multiplexity' (number of ties *between* contacts) of the networks, there was no attempt here to quantify the strength of the networks. Density and multiplexity are significant variables in the German study, but Barden and

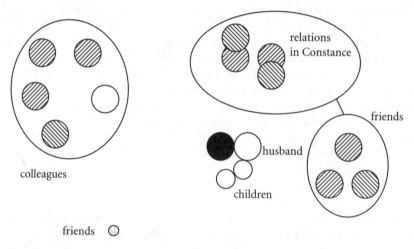

The origin of the persons in the network is symbolized by the hatching:

● = Ego   ⊘ = Locals from the new place of residence
⊕ = Saxon living in Saxony   ⊘ = Other persons
○ = Saxon not living in Saxony

The lines around the small circles symbolize a cluster: the persons within a cluster know each other

Figure 4.1 *Example of a social network: a Saxon living in Constance*
(from Barden 2000: 230)

Großkopf were more interested in the nature and quality of the networks than in measuring them on a scale of strength and weakness, believing that patterns of variation and change in language use could be related more readily to fluctuations (or lack of them) in the formation of networks. In order to achieve this, it was necessary to construct a higher level of description than the individual network, the 'network type'. Based on the perceived density of the networks, the relative importance attached to contacts with other Saxons, and informants' degree of satisfaction with their network, eight theoretically possible network types were devised (see Fig. 4.2).

A second step was to allocate each speaker to one of nine 'attitude types', based on their own comments on their regional affiliation and their evaluation of their experience of migration (see Barden 2000: 231–4). To piece the whole puzzle together, it was then necessary to show how the three dimensions (linguistic variation, social network types, attitude types) interacted to provide an explanation of the interdependence of linguistic and social accommodation. This was done by constructing a further tier of abstract types, 'integration types', which subsumed the network and attitude variables and which could then be related to patterns of language use. These show that there is no single parameter that can account for any particular pattern of linguistic accommodation, but rather a complex picture of interaction between factors emerges. For example, of the four main and two intermediate integration types, Types A and D are similar in that they both show significant levels of convergence towards standard German and towards the local dialect of the new location. However, while they share certain characteristics (contact with other Saxons considered unimportant, affiliation with the new location or lack of specific regional loyalty), they also differ in important ways: Type A has a dense network, is highly satisfied with its social contacts, is positive about the experience of migration, and has a generally 'optimistic' attitude, but Type D has

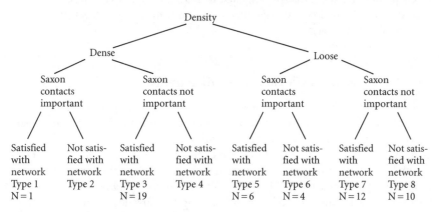

Figure 4.2 *Possible combinations of networks*
(from Barden 2000: 231)

a loosely structured network, is not satisfied with its social contacts, and generally takes a negative attitude towards life after migrating.

At the same time, as well as constructing a general framework of accommodative prototypes, the methodology allows us to track changes in individual behaviours. For example, one informant's linguistic behaviour initially follows the general trend of convergence towards the standard and new local forms, but after the first year it begins to diverge again so that at the end of the time he is linguistically even further removed from his new location than he was at the outset. He has metaphorically 'remigrated' back to Saxony, and Barden is able to explain this in terms of changes in his personal circumstances (he loses his job following an injury), which result in a reconfigured and subjectively less satisfactory social network and in a more negative attitude and realignment of his affiliation from his new location back to Leipzig.

I have dwelt on Barden and Großkopf's use of social types at some length here because it seems to me to offer a particularly persuasive account of accommodative behaviour through its ability to propose explanations that are both psychologically realistic and socially coherent: it combines individual motivation with the social conditions of personal experience. I shall return to this question in Chapter 6.

In this section, I have considered patterns of change and accommodation at different linguistic levels (lexis, style, metacommunication, accent) and in different contexts (personal/private, semi-public, public), but following the more descriptive emphasis in previous sections there has been a generally increasing emphasis on interpretation and explanation. In a highly sensitized speech community, there is relatively little random or 'free' variation in the kinds of feature discussed here. Surface patterns of variation and change are tied, as we have begun to see here, to deep-rooted evaluations of language forms and their users; these 'language attitudes' are the fuel of language ideologies, and this is the subject of the final section of this chapter.

4.4   Language ideologies and social discrimination

Attitudes towards language have been a minor theme running through the earlier parts of this chapter: the stigmatization by western speakers of words, textual patterns, and speech behaviours associated with east Germans and/or the GDR, the avoidance by east Germans of words and expressions that were perceived as eastern shibboleths, the reluctance of easterners to adopt linguistic forms and communicative patterns sanctioned by west Germans as authoritative and correct. We have seen how Helmut Schönfeld (1993), amongst others, documented the rise of a small-scale 'complaint tradition' (see Milroy and Milroy 1999, and 2.1 above), in which indignant east Germans voiced their resentment at the elimination of familiar words and concepts and at the imposition of unfamiliar ones, complementary features of what they saw as a devaluation of their past and enforced cultural and social assimilation. We have also considered ways in which individual speakers may or may not have adapted their speech (behaviour) in accordance with their perceptions of what is positively evaluated. In this final section, I want to shift attitudes into the centre of our attention and examine more closely how social evaluations of language act as the motivating force for linguistic change— or resistance to it. More specifically, I shall explore how language ideologies function as a 'mediating link between social structures and forms of talk' (Woolard and Schieffelin 1994: 55).[24]

In perceptual terms, accent outweighs other features of speech in interaction, not because it is necessarily decisive in terms of comprehensibility but because it is what speakers rely on most heavily to place their interlocutor (socially, ethnically, geographically) and so constitutes the primary basis on which they make judgements about the other person and decisions on how to behave towards them: whether to be friendly or hostile, cooperative or obstructive, in other words whether to be willing to accept their share of the responsibility for making the communication work. However, other linguistic features such as vocabulary can operate in the same way, especially in a negative sense, as when the use of even a single word provokes a hostile reaction in the hearer so that they effectively close down their communicative systems. West German journalist Wiete Andrasch gives a clear, if ingenuous, account of this process in a reflection on her own behaviour under such circumstances. At a party in east Berlin in the early 1990s, she found herself in a fractured conversation with a local woman, who at one point enthuses about the practice of socializing on rooftops, using a characteristically eastern expression: 'urst schau da oben!' (really cool up there). Andrasch recounts her reaction like this:

Ich hielt mindestens das dritte Glas Wein fest umschlossen in meinen Händen, als ich merkte, daß sich zwei Worte in meinen Gedanken verfangen hatten, deren Bedeutung mir rätselhaft war. Was heißt 'urst'? Und was 'schau'? Während der gesamten Unterhaltung fielen diese Worte unzählige Male. Abgesehen davon, daß ich fand, sie klangen ein bißchen russisch und ziemlich albern, konnte ich nichts mit ihnen anfangen. Ich verriet dieser Frau nicht, *daß mir ihre Sprache fremd war.* Die Selbstverständlichkeit, mit der sie jene Worte in den Mund nahm, schüchterte mich ein. (Andrasch 2000: 69; my italics)

I was holding at least my third glass of wine firmly in my hand when I noticed that two words had got entangled in my thoughts, whose meaning was a mystery to me. What does

<hr>

[24] Attitudes and identities together constitute a vast area of critical analysis, and there is a very substantial literature on social attitudes and general questions of social and political identity in Germany since unification: see, for example, the titles listed under 'Literatur aus Nachbargebieten' in Hellmann (1999) and the website www.wiedervereinigung.de. Here and in Chapter 5 I shall deal only with linguistic and communicative aspects of these issues, and with ways in which attitudes and identities are realized, projected, processed, and contested in discourse and interaction.

urst mean? And *schau*? During the whole conversation these words cropped up over and over again. Apart from the fact that they sounded a bit Russian and rather silly to me, I couldn't make any sense of them. I didn't let on to the woman *that her language was foreign to me.* The way she uttered these words so naturally intimidated me.

Although the rest of the context makes it quite clear that she understood the woman perfectly well, she claims that two words were sufficient to make the other person's language strange or alien to her. The only way to make sense of such a statement, it seems to me, is to understand it as a concealed declaration of her feeling of alienation or detachment from the woman herself: it is her, not really her language, that Andrasch perceives as *foreign*. But if this is the case, why does she not say so? After all, she is not speaking directly to the other woman, this is an 'interior dialogue'. What seems to be happening here is a specific form of a general practice in social relations, which is to articulate what could be an offensive opinion about an individual or social group in terms of a particular attribute: the intention is to mitigate the underlying proposition ('easterners are strange people') by expressing it as an observation about an apparently isolated aspect of their behaviour ('easterners speak strangely'). In this particular case, the anecdote is not intended merely as a portrayal of an 'amusing' incident but as an illustration of the broader thesis of the article: 'Wir sind außen ähnlicher, aber innen nicht gleicher geworden' (on the outside, we have become more similar to each other, but on the inside, we have not become more alike) (ibid.: 77). So the party guest is standing in for 'exotic easterners' in general, and the 'two words' that trigger Andrasch's reaction represent a whole 'way of speaking'. This can then be seen as part of the process that Woolard and Schieffelin (1994: 61–2) describe like this:

Language varieties that are regularly associated with (and thus index) particular speakers are often revalorized...not just as symbols of group identity, but as emblems of political allegiance or of social, intellectual, or moral worth....Moreover, symbolic revalorization often makes discrimination on linguistic grounds publicly acceptable, whereas the corresponding ethnic or racial discrimination is not.

This is spelled out most clearly in another journalistic essay, this time about other Americans' attitudes towards New Yorkers, in an article quoted by Rosina Lippi-Green (1997: 175):

No matter how many [linguistic] habits New Yorkers consciously unlearn, they will still unconsciously say some things differently from the rest of the country. They will still sound like New Yorkers, and they will still be ashamed. They will discover, despite all their efforts, the fundamental truth about the national hatred of the New York accent: America doesn't really hate us for the way we tawk [*sic*]. America hates us for who we are.

Strictly speaking, there is more to 'the way we talk' than what is normally understood by 'accent' (patterns of pronunciation) or even by 'dialect' (a variety defined in terms of grammatical, phonological, and lexical differences from other related varieties): people also make judgements about the way we talk that refer to 'manners of speaking', generally using impressionistic terms such as 'brash', 'musical', 'vulgar', or 'ponderous'. However, attitudes towards linguistic variation most commonly make reference to accents and/or dialects, because they can be named and because they have the important symbolic function of identifying the speaker's social location (whether this be geographical, class, ethnic, or whatever). Since some such locations seem to be more significant in the general value systems of communities than others, some linguistic varieties appear to be more available for the focused perceptions and evaluations that are typically characterized as 'attitudes'. Speakers of British English, for example, may be able to identify a New York City accent but will not normally be in a position to distinguish between individual 'southern' US accents, and similarly speakers of American English may pick out a London accent but will not be able to distinguish between individual Scottish accents.

As a recent survey in Germany has shown, selectivity in perception can apply within a speech community too: the five 'least favoured' varieties (Bavarian, Berlinish, Plattdeutsch, Saxon, and Swabian) also occupy five of the top six places in the list of 'most favoured' varieties (Stickel and Volz 1999: 31–2). The reasons for these particular varieties being selected are a matter for conjecture, although the geographical distribution may give a clue: the list includes a south-eastern form, a south-western one, a central one, and two northern ones. Research on language attitudes has consistently shown that evaluations of linguistic varieties are in fact evaluations of speakers (see, for example, Holmes 2001: Chapter 14, Fasold 1984: Chapter 6), and while there may be an aesthetic component to individual assessments, the systematic acclaim for or denigration of particular speech forms has much more to do with the positioning of social groups than with indicating how pleasing their speech is felt to be. It is therefore likely that this survey is reinforcing what we already know: that there is a fierce tradition of regional loyalty in Germany, and that there is a particularly strong mutual dislike between southerners and northerners.

However, in the context of east–west relations, two of these varieties deserve closer attention: Saxon, which in the west has connotations not simply of 'eastern' but of 'GDR' (see 4.3, and this section, below), and Berlinish, which straddles the east–west divide.[25] It may or may not be legitimate to consider Berlin as a microcosm of social and political developments in Germany as a whole since 1945, but it is not difficult to see why it was a magnet for social dialectologists (see, for example, Dittmar *et al.* 1986, Dittmar and Schlobinski 1988, Johnson 1995, Schlobinski 1987, Schönfeld 1986, 1989, 1993, 1995, 1996*a,b*, and Schönfeld and

---

[25] The same is true of other varieties, including one of those listed here—Plattdeutsch—but the unique position of Berliners as a divided urban speech community justifies the degree of attention devoted to this case.

Schlobinski 1997). Here was an ideal opportunity to study the effects of the abrupt division of a speech community that had developed over centuries, although comparative work was obviously severely hindered by the constraints on access imposed by the political situation.

Labov's claim (1972b: 248) that 'social attitudes towards language are extremely uniform throughout a speech community' may be exaggerated and difficult to sustain even in relatively stable communities, but it is a useful contention to bear in mind when tracing the development of Berliners' evaluation of Berlinish. From its emergence in the sixteenth century until the early part of the twentieth century, Berlinish appears to have enjoyed considerable prestige throughout the speech community, but increased social mobility and demographic changes in the years before the Second World War made the linguistic landscape of Berlin more complex and the standing of Berlinish as the predominant speech form of the city and the surrounding region became less secure (Schönfeld 1986: 287–8, 1996b: 71–3). This process of differentiation was greatly accelerated by the effects of the physical destruction of the city in the War and by the massive subsequent migration, both within Berlin and into and out of it. Even before the physical division of the city in 1961, therefore, the Berlin speech community had been disrupted and fragmented, so that we cannot postulate a uniform, homogeneous starting point against which to measure later developments, either during the years of division or following unification.

Very broadly speaking, however, significant trends can be isolated in the development of the social evaluation of Berlinish before 1989, which do provide a context to give meaning to the comparative empirical studies that were possible for the first time in the early 1990s (see Barbour and Stevenson 1990/1998: 4.4.5). Many west Berliners expressed conflicting views: on the one hand, there appears to have been a widespread sense of negative social prestige attached to Berlinish, but on the other hand, they would defend its use in what they considered to be appropriate contexts (Schlobinski 1987: 196). This widely declared acceptance of a functional distribution of non-standard and standard speech forms rests on a tacit allegiance to what Dailey-O'Cain (1997, 2000) calls the 'standard language ideology', according to which the standard variety is granted the status of 'legitimate language' and hence becomes, in evaluative terms, the yardstick against which other varieties are to be measured.

Although a similar ideology existed in the GDR and was officially promoted by the state, however, the public acceptance of it amongst east Berliners was very low and the prestige of Berlinish correspondingly higher than in west Berlin. In the less hierarchically organized society of the GDR, the potential for linguistic varieties to be invested with differing levels of social prestige in the sense of 'vertical' differentiation was much weaker than in the more highly stratified and competitive social environment of the west (see Hartung 1981b: 69–71, Reiher 1997a: 182, Schmidt-Regener 1998: 161). It was therefore possible to 'recontextualize' Berlinish (in the sense of Gal 1993) as the 'language of the capital of the GDR', and empirical studies confirmed its overwhelmingly positive evaluation by east Berliners (see, for example, Peine and Schönfeld 1981). Moreover, this emblematic elevation of the 'local' variety was further enhanced by the hostility of many east Berliners towards the Saxon variety, due to their resentment at the domination of Saxons in many state organizations:

Kommste inne Kaufhalle, ja, sprichste mit der Fleischabteilung, weil du da [?] worden bist, eene aus Sachsen, so 'ne sture und dämliche, von Tuten und Blasen keene Ahnung. Und, biste denn uf die Dame anjewies'n, wa, du fühlst dich als Berliner da irgendwie fremd, ja. (East Berliner, cited in Dittmar *et al.* 1986: 131)

You come into the supermarket, you know, and talk to the woman in the meat department because you've been [?], one of those women from Saxony, pig-headed and stupid, hasn't a clue. And if you have to rely on this lady, you know, as a Berliner you feel sort of foreign.

The shop assistant can only have been identified as coming from Saxony by virtue of her speech, and that appears to be sufficient to allocate her to a category ('*eene aus Sachsen*', one of those women from Saxony), which in turn seems to be associated almost self-evidently with negative personal traits ('*stur*', pig-headed; '*dämlich*', stupid).

So even if we adopt a weak version of Labov's perspective on the speech community and take 'widely shared social attitudes towards language' as a defining criterion, we have at best two discrete communities in Berlin by 1989 (Schönfeld 1996*b*: 74–8). If Berlinish was actually used more widely and in a more 'marked', conservative form in east Berlin, as Schlobinski (1987) claims to have shown, and if it was more positively evaluated there, what impact would these facts have on the outcome of the encounter between the two speech communities? Would increased exposure to Berlinish as a highly valued speech variety encourage greater acceptance of it amongst west Berliners and therefore pave the way for a unified speech community on the basis of the former eastern model? Would this eastern model succumb to the pressure of market forces in the new social and economic environment where Berlinish was widely stigmatized and a premium was placed on 'talking correctly'?

Not surprisingly, perhaps, studies by Ruth Reiher, Helmut Schönfeld, Irena Schmidt-Regener, and others,[26] that have tracked Berliners' awareness of their language and their attitudes towards it since 1990, offer no simple answer to these questions. Rather than becoming clearer, the picture seems to have become more complex, but this was probably to be expected in a transitional period, and it may well be that a definite trend will begin to emerge in the course of the second decade after unification. However, it is also possible that the social differences between east and west Berliners are so deep-rooted that their articulation in attitudes towards language will resist change for much longer.

[26] For example, Vogel (forthcoming).

In his questionnaire survey, Schönfeld (1996*a,b*) classified his informants into three main groups—school students, teachers, and other adults—and posed questions about their feelings about Berlinish, their tolerance of its use by others, and their perceptions of differences between east and west Berliners in their use of it (i.e. in terms of situation, frequency, manner, style, authenticity etc.) (see Table 4.3).

Age seems to have been a more significant variable than geographical origin as far as the popularity of the dialect is concerned: the responses for both teachers

Table 4.3 *Attitudes towards Berlin vernacular speech (answers in per cent of those asked) (Based on Schönfeld 1996: 91)*

1 *Do you like Berlinish?*

	Teachers		Other adults		School students	
	east	west	east	west	east	west
yes	23	26	47	50	31	17
no	20	19	14	12	12	26
sometimes	50	48	25	36	36	36
indifferent	7	7	14	2	21	21

2 (Teachers only) *How do you react when other people speak a strong form of Berlinish?*

	Children and young people		Adults	
	east	west	east	west
positively	12	25	12	25
negatively	37	32	50	41
mixed	28	34	27	26
neutrally	23	9	11	9

3 *In your opinion, is there such a thing as bad Berlinish?*

	Teachers		Other adults	
	east	west	east	west
yes	60	51	41	57
no	18	25	19	21
don't know	22	24	40	22

4 *Do east and west Berliners differ in their use of Berlinish?*

	Teachers		Other adults		School students	
	east	west	east	west	east	west
yes	27	59	44	72	14	37
no	27	17	4	7	58	26
sometimes	22	7	29	19	28	37
don't know	24	17	23	2	0	0

and other adults were more or less identical in east and west, with the teachers being generally less enthusiastic and a small minority expressing indifference; a rather larger proportion of students from both sides were indifferent, but almost twice as many eastern students gave a positive response, while western students were the least positive of all sub-groups. The numbers of teachers expressing intolerance of dialect use by others was roughly the same on both sides, but more western teachers were willing to accept its use either conditionally or under certain circumstances. Finally, western respondents seemed much more convinced than the easterners that there were differences in the use of Berlinish by east and west Berliners (see also Schmidt-Regener 1998: 175).

The bare quantitative results of such studies have to be treated with caution, especially since some of the questions may be open to various interpretations and simple answers reveal nothing about individual motivations and experiences. Schönfeld's survey was backed up with a series of semi-structured interviews, which reveal a wide range of personal and very specific responses (see Schönfeld 1996*b* for representative examples), but it is difficult to synthesize these in any meaningful way. Irena Schmidt-Regener's more refined quantitative study (1998) is an attempt to fill this gap by integrating in a statistical model several key variables: self-reported language use, evaluation of Berlinish and standard German, evaluation of the speech behaviour of other Berliners, and opinions on the acceptance of Berlinish. For example, she establishes four groups in relation to the assessment of speech behaviour of Berliners in the 'other' part of the city:

Group 1 is the largest group and is dominated by west Berliners and standard speakers; they clearly dislike the speech behaviour of the 'other' Berliners, but believe that acceptance of Berlinish has grown since 1989.
Group 2 is dominated by east Berliners and many are Berlinish speakers; they are 'firmly undecided' in their attitudes towards other Berliners' speech, but believe that acceptance of Berlinish is declining.
Group 3 is evenly balanced between east and west Berliners; the majority are non-Berlinish speakers; they are generally very undecided in their opinions.
Group 4 consists mainly of Berlinish speakers and east Berliners, and this group expresses the highest level of tolerance towards the 'other side'.

From this complex picture, Schmidt-Regener (1998: 180–1) draws a number of conclusions. In particular, she sees a greater polarization of views in the west than in the east: Berlinish is more strongly stigmatized by west Berliners, but there are also signs of growing acceptance there too; east Berliners seem to be becoming less emphatic and more uncertain in their views, and she attributes this to the fact that Berlinish now represents for them not the 'variety of the capital city' (or, since Berlin is of course the capital city of Germany, it might be better to say 'of *their* capital city'—i.e. of east Germany) but the 'variety that divides the city' (ibid.: 175). In Gal's terms, Berlinish and the relationship between it and the standard variety is again being recontextualized within the broader political economy of the unified Germany. Schmidt-Regener also identifies a close relationship between the degree of familiarity and contact between east and west Berliners and their level of acceptance of the other's speech behaviour, but at the same time a tendency for contact to decline rather than increase. However, as she concedes (ibid.: 181), her detailed analysis may reveal a speech community that is as non-homogeneous as it was before 1989, but it does not provide an explanation for the picture that emerges. The more complex patterns of behaviour defy reduction to an explanatory model based on the solidarity–status dichotomy that seemed adequate for the earlier context.

Yet, solidarity and status as 'orientations' did not in themselves provide explanations for language practices or attitudes before 1989 either. For example, studies such as Schlobinski (1987) appear to show convincingly that Berlinish was used more extensively by working-class inhabitants of the Wedding district than by middle-class inhabitants of the more affluent Zehlendorf district. However, to attribute this difference in behaviour to the pull of solidarity (or 'covert prestige') amongst the former and the pull of status (or 'overt prestige') amongst the latter may be an elegant description of sociolinguistic contrasts in west Berlin, but this does not explain why the respective populations behaved in the way they did. Similarly, we can establish that Berlinish enjoyed greater positive prestige in east Berlin than in the west, but there is no necessary connection between different evaluations of language varieties in east and west and different patterns of use. Solidarity and status are important dimensions of the motivations underlying individual behaviour and interpersonal relations, but they need to be understood as elements within the overall apparatus or workings of the life of a society. Again, Gal (1993: 337) argues that

patterns of linguistic variation that express status or solidarity not only coordinate interpersonal relations, they also provide evidence about the workings of 'symbolic domination' or 'cultural hegemony' in social life.... This analytical move... conceptualizes the use of a nonauthoritative variety not simply as a way of expressing different interpersonal meanings, but as a type of social practice that constitutes 'resistance' to the dominant values and institutions of a society.

Put simply, in our context this would mean that—where there is a choice—speaking Berlinish is not merely declaring that 'I am a Berliner, I want you to see me as such, and I value the association with this low-prestige social category more than the benefits I might gain by aligning myself through language choice with a high-prestige category'. More than this, Gal implies, you would be declaring that 'I reject the prevailing evaluation of Berlinish, and therefore of its speakers, as inferior'. In other words, language choice is not merely a personal decision or preference, but a social practice, and linguistic resistance is a form of social resistance. As Gal also points out though, both domination and resistance may take on various forms, and their realization in actual social behaviours may be more complex and less clear-cut than the simple dichotomy might suggest (see also Gal

1987, 1995). Furthermore, resistance is not the only response of less powerful social groups to attempts by more powerful ones to impose their values: indeed it is precisely the converse reaction, the complicity or collusion of non-dominant groups in their own domination, that requires explanation. Why do non-dominant groups sometimes comply with the pressure to conform to the values and norms of dominant groups? Can acceptance of the ideology coexist with continued non-conforming practices, and conversely, can changed behaviour coincide with resistance to the ideology?

As an attempt to find out whether east Germans have responded to western language values in a very general sense, Jennifer Dailey-O'Cain (1997, 2000) has explored their reactions to what she calls the 'western standard language ideology'. This term is rather ambiguous, and I shall deal with a further aspect of it shortly, but what Dailey-O'Cain is referring to is a value system widely accepted in western Germany, according to which the 'best German' is spoken in the northern city of Hanover. This does not mean that speakers from other parts of western Germany attempt to emulate what they perceive as Hanover speech, but rather that they accept it as the yardstick of quality against which their own speech and that of others can legitimately be measured. As Woolard (1985: 741) argues,

> a variety may be said to be hegemonic [that is, legitimizing the cultural authority of a dominant social group] even if a large part of the population does not control that variety.... The test of legitimacy is the extent to which the population that does not control that variety acknowledges and endorses its authority, its correctness, its power to convince, and its right to be obeyed, that is, the extent to which authority is ceded to those who do control that variety.

The question for Dailey-O'Cain then was: will east Germans sign up to this ideology (and therefore consent to the cultural authority of west Germans) or will they resist it? Her conclusion, based on two sets of quantitative and qualitative studies conducted with subjects from all parts of Germany in 1994 and 1995, was that there was evidence to suggest that there was an ongoing process of acceptance, although—as with Schmidt-Regener's study—it was far from uniform, and in the light of the more general reassertion of eastern values detected by many observers since the mid-1990s (see 5.3) it may not have continued. While the earlier study appeared to show a continuing divergence between easterners (who located the most 'correct' German in the whole of northern Germany) and westerners, the later study showed a greater degree of convergence towards the western perception (Dailey-O'Cain 2000: 258). Not only did easterners show an increased tendency to identify Hanover as the 'home' of 'correct' German, they often reacted uncomfortably when asked specifically about this perception.

> They often protested, saying that they had 'no way of knowing' that the most correct German is spoken in Hanover, since they were not allowed to go there until 1989. In other

words, they had accepted the idea that Hanover was the centre of spoken standard German as a 'fact' to 'know', not something that westerners believed but which they disagreed with. (Ibid.: 257)

In a slightly different, more conventional sense of the term, a standard language ideology had existed in both German states: although individual speech repertoires remained in many cases highly diverse, official policies and institutions of cultural authority (schools, universities, broadcast media) rigorously promoted the standard variety as a supposedly cohesive force of national bonding and cultural transmission. It was precisely this ideologization of the standard that was exploited in the debates on language discussed in Chapter 2. However, because the substance of the respective standard varieties was virtually identical, there would appear to be no basis for either party to contest the validity of the 'other' standard. Yet as we also saw earlier, substance is not always necessary in ideological debates on language—if difference is needed, it can always be invented—and as the various forms of 'verbal hygiene' that we have discussed (training in interview talk, for example, or prescriptions on 'correct' vocabulary) show, language ideology opens up many routes for asserting the superiority of the 'western way'.

At issue here then is not only the function of the western standard language ideology of locating the 'source' of the standard variety in the west, the siting of what is correct and therefore good, but also the deeper function of disparaging eastern social traditions by denying the validity of 'its' language. One of the reasons why the Saxon dialect was (and still is) so strongly stigmatized in the west (it was by far the most disfavoured variety in Stickel and Volz's survey: see above) is that it was a convenient way of reifying and pinning down the abstract and amorphous quality of 'eastness'. So the ideological process here operates on two fronts simultaneously (see also Lippi-Green 1997: 65): the 'good' is located in the west, and the 'bad' is located in the east. As Dailey-O'Cain (2000: 265) puts it:

eastern Germans, and particularly central eastern Germans [i.e. Saxon dialect speakers], are not only told that their way of speaking is wrong, but that there is a particular right way of doing so *in the west*, and that they must change their language in order to overcome an inferior social position. (Italics in the original)

and Rosina Lippi-Green (1997: 173) generalizes this process, arguing that 'standard language ideology is concerned not so much with the choice of one possible variant, but with the elimination of *socially unacceptable* difference [italics in the original]. This is externalized in the targeting of particular variants linked to specific social identities.' From what we have seen, this could well be what has been happening in Germany.

However, this process would pose a double threat. For the easterners, of course, it would mean abandoning a core distinctive feature and undermining their sense of self-worth, but westerners' own highly valued distinctiveness would also be at risk. It is here that the psychological connects with the social. The paradox of individual and group relations is that perceived similarity is likely to increase attractiveness between individuals but it represents a threat for groups, since the possibility of a group's positive self-evaluation is in a direct relationship to the number of dimensions on which it sees itself as distinct from other groups (Bickes 1992, and Tajfel and Turner 1986 on social identity theory). What west Germans value most highly is their prosperity, and the principal complaints about the unification process in the west are about economic issues ('*we* had to work hard for our success while *they* were feather-bedded', '*our* taxes are paying for *them* to catch up', 'are *they* grateful for the financial sacrifices *we're* making?'). The concentration on this dimension is likely to exacerbate conflict between the two social groups, but so long as you can identify a scapegoat for your problems—real or imagined—you have a way of dealing with them.

The situation that developed in the early post-unification period is therefore characterized by contradictions. The belated consensus in the 1980s on the fundamental linguistic unity of the 'German people' (see 2.2), which should have facilitated integration under the banner of a common standard, was rapidly superseded by a popular discourse of difference: as the costs of unification (in every sense of the term) became ever more apparent, integration became less attractive to large parts of both populations, and so if palpable differences did not exist they had to be invented. However, as we have seen, the discourse of difference was not neutral but evaluative: 'our' talk is better than 'their' talk. The authority invested in what was perceived as 'western' speech forms and styles by the hegemonic effect of the western standard language ideology meant that only westerners were in a position to demand change, conformity to their norms of behaviour, from easterners and not the other way round.

The underlying refrain 'if you want to join our club, you'll have to learn our rules' is articulated in many ways: in terms of 'appropriate' language use ('die ha'm die Einheit jewollt un müssen sich nun unsren Jargon aneignen', they wanted unity so now they must learn our language—Schönfeld and Schlobinski 1997: 134), as much as other 'correct' behaviours ('die müssen erst mal arbeiten lernen', first of all they'll have to learn to work properly—Reiher 1996: 51). Yet the demand for conformity, expressed from a position of perceived superiority and as an exercise of social control, carries within it a potential risk to the distinctiveness and thus the exclusivity of the dominant group. The success of the ideological process depends therefore on the acceptance by the non-dominant group that the values and norms of the dominant group are 'naturally the right ones', but equally on their inability or unwillingness to change their behaviour accordingly.[27]

---

[27] This is illustrated graphically by the cartoon from *Eulenspiegel* 12/1991 reproduced in Bickes (1992: 124). Two *Wessis* are in conversation:

'Those *Ossis*, they're everywhere, it really gets on my nerves!'
'But how can you tell? They're not so easy to spot any more.'
'Exactly, that's what most annoys me about them!'

However, this may not be an entirely one-sided process. Consider the following passage from Ayers's analysis of relations between north and south in the United States (quoted, once again, from Lippi-Green 1997: 205):

The South plays a key role in the nation's self-image: the role of evil tendencies overcome, mistakes atoned for, progress yet to be made. Before it can play that role effectively, the South has to be set apart as a distinct place that has certain fundamental characteristics. As a result, Southern difference is continually being recreated and reinforced. Americans, black and white, somehow need to know that the South is different and so tend to look for differences to confirm that belief. This is not something that is only done to the South by malevolent, insensitive non-Southerners. The North and the South have conspired to create each other's identity as well as their own. The South eagerly defines itself against the North, advertising itself as more earthy, more devoted to family values, more spiritual, and then is furious to have things turned around, to hear itself called hick, phony, and superstitious. The South feeds the sense of difference and then resists the consequences. (Ayers 1996: 66)

I would not want to force the analogy, but it seems to me that up to a point at least we could substitute 'west' for 'North' and 'east' for 'South' and produce a plausible analysis of social relations in post-unification Germany. The dominant way in which unified Germany has been constructed as a new nation depends heavily on casting the east in the role of 'evil tendencies overcome, mistakes atoned for, progress yet to be made'. In order to achieve this, the east 'has to be set apart' and eastern difference is 'continually being recreated and reinforced', and, as we shall see in Chapter 5, the east is not a passive participant in this process but is 'eager to define itself against the west'. In doing so, it inevitably exposes itself to the risk of being denigrated by the dominant social group, and this could be one explanation for the tendency of easterners to make less of supposed linguistic differences than westerners (see Table 4.3, and also Schmidt-Regener 1998: 175, Stickel and Volz 1999: 33).

On the other hand, as with American southerners who have no desire to live elsewhere, for east Germans who stay in the east 'threats of exclusion and gate-keeping [should] be less effective' (Lippi-Green 1997: 212) than they typically are for, say, migrant ethnic minorities, and the western language ideology should be less likely to prevail. A crucial difference between the two cases, however, is precisely the fact that most public institutions and private enterprises in the east since unification have been dominated by westerners, and that the east has therefore not remained as discrete within the nation state as the American south appears to have done within the union: the Mason-Dixon Line seems to have remained a less permeable partition than the Elbe in terms of political, economic, and cultural control.

Lippi-Green concludes her analysis of north–south linguistic subordination in the US by arguing that 'the south has resources to call on, ways to deflect subordination tactics, but only so long as it keeps itself intact and separate' (1997: 216). The east German struggle to 'keep itself intact and separate' will be one of the central issues in the next chapter. The main emphasis in Chapter 4 has been on the relationship between language use and social identities. In Chapter 5, I shall develop the issues that have begun to come into focus in the final part of the present chapter: the discursive use of language as a topic, and the role of discourses on 'east' and 'west' in establishing, contesting, and reshaping eastern and western social identities.

5

The Discursive Construction
of Difference

5.1 Narratives of collective memory

In Chapter 2, I contrasted the idea of history as an object awaiting discovery with the notion of history as a work in progress. According to this 'process' view of history, it is not simply a matter of different interpretations of the 'same' reality but of the manufacture of different realities. Writing history is therefore making history. When we talk of the history of a language, and of the role of language in history, we need to ask which history and which language is at issue or, more precisely, whose history and whose language? In my earlier discussion, I was concerned with public historiography and with conceptions of 'the German language' and its role in the development of 'the German question': with the big picture, in other words. Here I want to sharpen the focus of our enquiry and zoom in from the broad perspective of the speech or language community to the perspective of the individual participants or actors in the language-making process.

This is a further move away from a monolithic history towards individual biographies, from the public to the personal. In this case, the principal 'history writers' are not academics and political publicists but 'ordinary people'—the 'observed' are simultaneously the 'observers'. We do not need to go so far as the anthropologist Clifford Geertz (1995: 2, cited in Dittmar and Bredel 1999: 60) in completely rejecting the possibility of constructing a 'common history', a 'synoptic picture', to accept the importance of this alternative project, which he defines as 'hindsight accounts of the connectedness of things that seem to have happened: pieced-together happenings, after the fact'. For, as we have seen in Chapter 4, the meaning of social life can only be derived from studying the actions of both the collectivity and the individual.

Oral histories emphasize 'the story in history' (Linklater 2000: 151), and in German the same word—*Geschichte*—is used for both. By telling the story of their lives, individuals do exactly what academic historians do: select, evaluate, order, synthesize, explain, and try to 'make sense'. The difference is that the raw material is their own experience, even though this may include things they have heard, read, or been told, as well as things they have witnessed or undergone. Their narratives are an opportunity for them to process their experience, to establish a coherence in their lives, which in the normal course of events often appear to be fragmented and diffuse. The need to do this is felt particularly keenly at times of turbulence, when our lives seem to have been disrupted by massive and unexpected events and diverted from the meandering but generally consistent track they had been following until that point. A common response to such moments is to try to hold onto things of value that seem to be slipping away or to have been forcibly removed, but this can be a constructive process, not necessarily a despairing act of salvage. The past as the place we have left behind may be a source of regret, but it may also provide an anchor and a point of orientation in the present. In principle, at least, openly confronting the differences between past and present conditions offers an opportunity to resist being swept along by the tide and

einen konstitutiven Teil der *Ich-* und *Wir*-Identität aus einer vergangenen Lebens- und Gesellschaftsphase nicht als 'falsch' oder 'nicht existent' abzuspalten, sondern als noch gegenwärtige, lebendige Erfahrungen und Ressourcen in veränderte Orientierungen und Identifizierungen konstruktiv zu integrieren. (Dittmar and Bredel 1999: 59)

not to split off one constitutive part of our *I-* and *We*-identity from a past period in our life and of society as 'wrong' or 'non-existent', but rather to integrate it constructively into changed orientations and identifications as still present, living experiences and resources.

To achieve this in a context such as the period following the *Wende*, it is necessary to (be able to) reject the conception of the 'catastrophic event' as a caesura, a complete break with the past. The change in circumstances may be irreversible, but this does not necessarily mean that the past cannot be reclaimed. For this, we need a concept of memory that is analogous to the process view of history: memory not as a set of snapshots, which collectively constitute a fixed record of the past, but as an active process of assembling recalled experiences into a coherent story, of tracing back and picking up again the narrative thread of your life, and therefore of relocating yourself in the changed present.[1]

If oral histories are the opportunity for individuals to take charge of their own pasts, the task of the historian is not merely to act as facilitator but to intervene at the level of collective analysis: individual narratives are unique, in the same way that individual utterances are unique, but there are bound to be points of contact (repeating patterns) between them which open up the prospect of identifying a location of community. Individual memory is also unique, but since it is conditioned by social circumstances (by our exposure to, and interaction with, family, friends, and colleagues, and with institutions such as the media and the school), it is plausible to postulate the notion of 'collective memory', not in the sense of identical visions of the past but as common patterns of extracting from a shared pool of resources—including events, institutions, popular culture (folk tales, comics, television programmes, advertising slogans, and so on), and communicative practices (Dittmar and Bredel 1999: 58).

---

[1] There has been an explosion of interest in theories of memory over the last ten years or so: see, for example, Assmann and Harth (1991), Assmann (1997). For the present context, Burke (1997: Chapter 3) and Prins (2001) are particularly relevant.

Just a few years after the *Wende*, it was claimed that 'citizens of the former German Democratic Republic had become the world's most interviewed population' (Ostow 1993: 1, cited in Linklater 2000: 163). From our point of view, there are two issues—one to do with substance, the other to do with form— on which such interview material might throw some light. First, since both linguists and non-linguists (albeit in different ways, of course) regard language use as an index of social change, it would be interesting to know how east Germans in particular reflect on their experience of language across the prism of the *Wende*, what changes there have been in their awareness of language, how their evaluations of the changes in their social circumstances are articulated in terms of their attitudes towards language. Secondly, given our perspective on personal histories as the narration of experience we should want to know what techniques and organizational principles individuals use to construct their narratives.

The first set of questions has been explored by Ulla Fix and her colleagues in Leipzig in a project on 'language biographies'. The biographies are in fact twenty-four interviews (and one monologue) conducted between 1994 and 1996 with east Germans of different ages and social backgrounds, focusing principally on language and language use both in the GDR and after unification. Most of the interviewers were east German students, which meant that there were no immediate obstacles between them and the interviewees, and the sheer volume of material suggests that the informants were able and willing to discuss issues of language use at length. Some of the questioning shows an inexperience in ethnographic interviewing (leading questions and intrusion of the interviewer's personal experience and opinions), but most of the interviewees appear to have well-formed and robust views that were not excessively influenced by this (see Fix and Barth 2000 for lengthy edited transcripts).

One of the most frequently recurring topics was the supposed *Doppelsprachigkeit* in the GDR, the practice of code switching between the official discourse and 'ordinary speech' according to context. Western observers tend to take for granted this virtually diglossic situation, in which an official and a private speech variety were said to have operated in complementary distribution, but eastern commentators have often expressed irritation at the inadequacy of this description (see 3.2). Fix's interviewees, who were not selected as representatives of particular constituencies but as randomly chosen 'experts' in language use, collectively reveal a much more complex and subtle picture of GDR speech repertoires and considerable sensitivity towards the conditions and consequences of language behaviours.

Some speakers, such as H.G. (a retired music lecturer), appear to accept the code switching thesis and apply it in a very general way across the speech community (although this statement was prompted by a question setting up this dichotomy rather than offering H.G. an opportunity to make his own judgement):

H.G.: Naja, es gab einen offiziellen Sprachton, den sprachen alle Verantwortungsträger, und das kann also von Regierungsebene ab bis…zur kleinsten Parteiorganisation oder im

Betrieb der Meister,...sobald er auf der offiziellen Ebene sprach, da hatte er eine andere Sprache, als wenn er dann zu Hause...mit seinen Leuten oder wenn die Arbeiter untereinander sprachen, auch den Meister eingeschlossen, da veränderte sich die Sprache von der offiziellen Ebene in die Umgangssprache. (Fix and Barth 2000: 272)

Well, there was an official manner of speaking, everyone in a position of responsibility used it, and that can...from government level down to the smallest Party organization or the foreman in the factory,...as soon as he started speaking on the official level he used a different language than when he was at home...with his people or when the workers spoke amongst themselves, even including the foreman, then the language changed from the official level to everyday casual speech.

Others, such as A.D. (a student in his twenties), identify more subtly graded layers of speech:

A.D.: Ich hab' weniger die Erfahrung gemacht, daß das also weniger die Ideologiesprache war, also die ganz offensichtlich, das ganz offensichtliche Parteichinesisch, das einen zur Anpassung sozusagen forderte. Sondern es war so ein Zwischenglied zwischen dieser, in der DDR typische [*sic*] Sprache der Intimität, und dieser hochoffiziösen Ideologiesprache. Es gab so eine Sprache der Gemeinplätze, die zwischen diesen beiden Sphären vermittelte, die zwischen Ideologie und Intimität kompatibel war. (Ibid.: 637)

I didn't so much have the experience that, well, it was not so much the ideological language, the really blatant Party jargon that as it were demanded that you conform. It was more a sort of intermediate form between that typical GDR language of intimacy and that highly official ideological language. There was a kind of language of commonplaces, which mediated between these two spheres, which was compatible with ideology and intimacy.

Whichever view individual interviewees subscribed to, there is throughout these texts a highly developed awareness of the social significance of different manners of speaking, a conscious and explicit knowledge about how language use was sanctioned as acceptable or not and of the potential consequences of violating sociolinguistic norms. For many of the speakers what we might call the local politics of spoken interaction occupies an important place in their recollections of life in the GDR. For example, W.H. (a 58-year-old master craftsman), claimed:

W.H.: Das habe ich am eigenen Leib erfahren, daß ein Durchbrechen dieses uniformen Sprachstils sogar gefährlich war. Wenn einer ganz individuelle Formulierungen benutzte in der DDR, die bewußt den Parteijargon mieden, machte er sich verdächtig, galt er als Individualist und wurde schärfer beobachtet als andere....Es war gefährlich, anders zu sprechen. (Ibid.: 321)

I experienced that for myself, that violating this uniform speech style could even be dangerous. If you used individual formulations in the GDR, and consciously avoided Party jargon, you made yourself suspicious, you would be considered as an individualist and be observed more closely than others....It was dangerous to speak differently.

Some of the speakers claimed to have deliberately transgressed these unwritten rules, more as a means of self-assertion than as a form of political resistance, but they are then vague about the repercussions:

H.G.: Nein... also ich bin an dem Punkt vielleicht 'n bißchen sehr sensibel... ich habe mich immer bemüht, wenn ich Inhalte... übernehmen mußte oder übernehmen wollte, weil sie mir sinnvoll erschienen, die dann selbst zu formulieren. Und das enthielt natürlich immer ein gewisses Risikopotential, denn... mit der eigenen Formulierung... zeigte man unter Umständen einen zusätzlichen Gedanken oder eine Richtung eines Gedankens, die nicht der offiziellen Festlegung entsprach, und das wurde registriert. (Ibid.: 277)

No... well, perhaps I'm rather sensitive about that... if I had to take on ideas, or if I wanted to because they seemed sensible to me, I always tried to formulate them myself. And of course that always contained an element of risk, because... with your own formulation... you might reveal an additional thought or an angle which did not correspond to the official position, and that was noted.

A.P. (45-year-old academic and artist): Ich erinnere mich, daß ich manchmal ganz bewußt bestimmtes Wort- oder Sprachmaterial gebraucht habe, um mich zu distanzieren. [*Interviewer: Um zu provozieren?*] Auch zu provozieren. Weil ich wußte, das ist jetzt nicht angemessen, das wollen die nicht hören. (Ibid.: 499)

I remember sometimes quite deliberately using certain words or language in order to distance myself. [Interviewer: To be provocative?] That too. Because I knew that that's not appropriate, they don't want to hear that.

In order to distil these individual representations of experience with language into more general social attitudes, Fix (1997*a*, *b*, 2000*a*) examines how the interviewees rationalize their past behaviour, locating themselves in relation to the political structures of the GDR through their narratives about language use. She proposes two basic categories, not in terms of self-affiliation, but on the basis of their remarks about language and the way in which they represent their past from the perspective of the present: 'conformists', who appear to offer an image of themselves as having been more or less involved in the social and political development of the GDR, and 'non-conformists', who project a relatively detached attitude. The interpretation is arbitrary but Fix seeks to support it through an analysis of the speakers' discursive behaviour. She argues that 'conformists' tend to express a degree of alienation in the new circumstances and a continued attachment to their past, but at the same time a need to justify this. 'Non-conformists', on the other hand, seem basically at ease with the new context of their lives and are content to reflect relatively dispassionately on the past, describing how things were and explaining why they were the way they were (Fix 1997*a*: 35–7, 2000*a*: 23, 32 ff.).

The claim of A.P. (cited above), that she deliberately sought to shrug off the restrictive mantle of—in the GDR context—politically correct language use, could be seen as an example of the 'non-conformist' pattern in the interviews, and her reassessment of her past in the light of recent experience lends further weight to this:

A.P.: Ich habe geglaubt, in meinem Denken und Fühlen und Sprechen ziemlich unabhängig zu sein und habe erst nach der Wende an diesem Befreitheitsgefühl oder an einer anderen Rede, die ich plötzlich geführt habe, gemerkt, daß ich weniger frei war, als ich je glaubte.... Ich würde sagen, ich habe vorher nach dem Maßstab gelebt, nur zu sagen, was ich denke, aber nicht alles zu sagen, was ich denke. (Fix and Barth 2000: 500)

I used to think that I was fairly independent in my thinking, feeling, and speaking, and it was only after the *Wende* that I realized from that feeling of liberation or from suddenly speaking in a different way that I was less free than I had believed....I would say I used to live according to the rule of saying what I think but not saying everything I think.

H.G.'s remark (also above) seems to belong in the same category, and it is reinforced by his comments on different forms of address:

[*Interviewer: Hans, Du arbeitest im Museum. War das—sprachlich gesehen—eher eine Nische, ein Stück weg von dieser offiziellen Sprache?*]
H.G.: Ja....Ja, z.B. in der von vielen belächelten Praxis, daß wir Kollegen, die wir...also in den fünfziger Jahren studiert haben, daß wir untereinander immer beim 'Sie' geblieben sind. Auch also 'Herr Kollege' und 'Sie'. Das war etwas, was...eine ganz deutlich spürbare, aber nicht ausdrücklich formulierte Kritik an dem 'Du' der Genossen. Die SED-Genossen untereinander waren ja im Grunde genommen zum 'Du' fast verpflichtet, die mußten also auch 'Genosse Minister, Du ...' sagen, wenn's drauf ankam. (Ibid.: 273)

[*Interviewer: Hans, you work in a museum. Was that—from a linguistic point of view—a kind of niche, a step away from this official language?*]
H.G.: Yes...yes, for example in the practice that many people made fun of, that those colleagues who had studied in the 50s continued to say 'Sie' [formal 'you'] to each other. And 'Herr Kollege' and 'Sie'. That was something that...a clearly perceptible but not explicitly formulated criticism of the 'Du' [informal 'you'] of the comrades. Among themselves, the SED comrades were more or less obliged to use 'Du', they even had to say for example 'Comrade Minister, Du...'.

However, H.G.'s distancing of himself from some of the practices he encountered in the GDR is not simply matched by an uncritical acceptance of the western communicative environment. Dealings with GDR authorities, for example, may have been marked by a brusqueness of tone, but the new bureaucracy seems to him not an unqualified improvement:

H.G.: Der Umgangston ist freundlich aber es gibt...eine neue Form der Allmacht, der bürokratischen Allmacht,...die ist völlig unbeweglich, die ist freundlich, aber unbeweglich....Es gibt eben Mitteilungen von Behörden, da steht drin: 'Ein Einspruch gegen diese Regelung ist nicht statthaft.' Das ist etwas, woran ich mich aus der alten Behördensprache nicht so richtig erinnern kann. (Ibid.: 283)

Their way of speaking is friendly but there is . . . a new form of all-pervading power, of all-pervading bureaucratic power. . . . It is completely inflexible, it's friendly, but inflexible. . . . Authorities send out notices saying 'Objections to this ruling are not permitted'. That is something that I can't really remember from the old bureaucratic language.

As a Party member, E.P. (a 37-year-old teacher) explicitly committed herself to the cause of developing a socialist society ('Ich habe daran geglaubt, daß der Sozialismus eine gute und gerechte Gesellschaft ist', I believed that socialism was a good and just society; ibid.: 518) and repeatedly expresses her present insecurity and fear for her future. She uses these personal positions to explain her respective language behaviours, then and now:

E.P. (talking about life in the GDR): Irgendwo ist das im Kopf bzw. auf Abruf parat. Wir hatten ja alle dieses offizielle und das inoffizielle Gesicht. Und damit auch die offizielle und die inoffizielle Sprache. Da hat man das ganz einfach abgerufen. Aber wie gesagt, das waren Phrasen. Ich muß das ehrlich so sagen. Man mußte das schreiben, es gehörte dazu. (Ibid: 526)

It's somehow just in your head, ready for use. We all had this official and the unofficial face. And the official and unofficial language to go with it. You quite simply just called it up. But as I said, it was just empty phrases. I honestly have to put it like that. You had to write it, it was part of the job.

E.P. (talking about life after the *Wende*): Ja, ich meine, ich darf heute nicht alles sagen, und heute wird das—jedenfalls in meinen Augen—wesentlich schwieriger für einen . . . kreativen Menschen als früher. . . . Heute kann ich zwar alles sagen—theoretisch—muß es mir aber genau überlegen, weil es dann nämlich um meine eigene Existenz geht. . . . Also, die Zwänge sind immer da. (Ibid: 517)

I mean, I'm not allowed to say everything today, and today—as I see it, at least—it's considerably more difficult for a . . . creative person than it used to be. . . . OK, I can say everything today—theoretically—but I have to think very carefully about it because my own livelihood is on the line. . . . So the constraints are always there.

E.P. therefore appears to be a particularly clear example of Fix's 'conformist'. However, not all speakers who adopt 'conformist' positions at times in their interviews maintain them consistently. For example, M.Z. cannot be allocated unambiguously to the 'conformist' camp any more than H.G. can to the 'non-conformists'. A 59-year-old working in the public relations department of an energy concern, M.Z. offers a picture of herself as having been 'involved' in the past (as a Party member) and largely in agreement with the overall political programme of the state. She is also critical of many more recent developments such as the intrusion of western speech patterns and the increased use of anglicisms, and she explicitly links what she perceives as a general deterioration in the quality of language use with other undesirable social developments, such as the frantic pace of life allowing no time for, or tolerance of, casual conversation and dictating a more unrefined and unreflective style of writing. However, although she acknowledges the pressure in the past to conform to official norms and a general public–private contrast in terms of the possibilities of language choice, she rejects the rigid code-switching model from the perspective of her own practice. She also insists that language use in semi-public contexts such as Party meetings was informal and not necessarily constrained by the official nature of the context: she distinguishes between the requirements imposed by the content of the discussions, and the general speech style in which business was conducted. In other words, while she does to some extent seek to justify conforming to official language use, she is also at pains to dispel the stereotypical image implied by the interviewer's questions:

[*Interviewer: Wie war das auf Parteiversammlungen, wurde da mit Schablonen hantiert oder wurde da tatsächlich auch eigen formuliert?*]
M.Z.: Also…natürlich mußte man sich, was den Inhalt der Versammlung belangte, nach vorgegebenen…Beschlüssen, Orientierungen, Direktiven usw. handeln, das war ja nun Bestandteil der Parteidisziplin [*sehr leise*] muß man sagen [*wieder laut*]….Und ich muß sagen,…war eigentlich der Umgangston und die Sprachwelt der Parteiversammlungen offen und unverblümt. Das muß ich sagen. Und wir haben uns da auch recht gut verstanden. Es war keiner, wo wir gesagt haben, dieser Holzkopf, den müssen wir aber nun mal geraderücken, nee, das war Gott sei dank nicht. (Ibid.: 315)

[*Interviewer: What was it like at Party meetings, did they use fixed patterns all the time or did people actually use their own words?*]
M.Z.: Well…of course, as far as the business of the meeting was concerned, you had to operate according to predetermined…resolutions, instructions, directives etc., that was just part of Party discipline [*very quietly*] it has to be said [*louder again*]…And I must say, the manner of speaking and the language used at Party meetings were open and pretty blunt. I have to say that. And we understood each other very well. There was no one that made us think 'that blockhead, we're going to have to sort him out', no, thank God, there was none of that.

The model of two sets of east German individuals who belong to the same 'communication community' but to distinct 'communities of memory' (Fix 1997*a*) is attractive to the extent that it offers a possibility of constructing social groups based on shared interpretations of experience rather than merely shared circumstances. However, it has so far not been developed beyond the level of a preliminary sketch, and the brief discussion here suggests that it would be difficult to sustain on the basis of the Leipzig interviews alone. It would seem more plausible to analyse the interviews in terms of orientations or positions that speakers adopt at different moments, in ways that are often inconsistent and even contradictory. A typically 'non-conformist' orientation is relatively straightforward to identify in declarations of detachment from practices that could be seen from the present social perspective as deviant (see, for example, the remarks by

A.P. or H.G. above). 'Conformist' positions are more complex, in that they may be articulated in different ways, from the defiant assertion of principles to which the speaker still adheres, to the more defensive deployment of what Fix (2000*a*: 35–6) calls 'immunization strategies'. These strategies are approaches to the processing of experience which entail situating past behaviours in a context in which they may be seen to be legitimate, or creating an explanatory context for past actions that renders them harmless. In other words, people immunize themselves against criticism by acknowledging potentially 'deviant' behaviour but rehabilitating it by bringing it within the framework of what is 'normal' or morally defensible: 'yes, we did do that but it's just the same now', 'people do that everywhere, it's normal', 'I did that because I thought what the state was doing was basically correct'.

Barth (2000) claims that these explanatory frames are reinforced by the use of the linguistic strategy of 'defocusing', in her view the key narrative technique in the realization of immunization strategies. This brings us to the second set of issues identified above: the ways in which these narratives are constructed.[2] Given that they are essentially autobiographical accounts, we should expect them to concentrate on actions and experiences of the narrators and therefore that they would be expressed predominantly using first person pronouns and related forms (I/we, my/our, etc.). Where depersonalizing forms such as the indefinite pronoun *man* (one/you) and passive constructions with no explicit agent occur, some explanation appears to be called for: are the speakers using these forms in order to stress the general validity of the statement, to focus on the action rather than the agent, or to distance themselves from the action? Barth's quantitative analysis shows that these depersonalizing forms in fact occur much less frequently than the personal pronouns, but she argues that their distribution in individual texts can be explained in functional terms and related to the ways in which speakers seek to place themselves in relation to the actions they are recounting. In particular she claims they are used to suspend the relationship of identity between the narrator and the agent when dealing with past actions that the narrator might expect to be evaluated negatively in the present social context. For example, S.S. is a teacher talking about her use of language in different contexts:

S.S.: … und noch mal darüber dann diese offizielle Ebene, und da geht eigentlich nichts Privates, da hab' ich mich zumindest sehr zurückgenommen. [*Interviewer: War das dann 'n Lügen?*] … Ein Lügen mit Sicherheit nicht. Es läuft eher auf die die Richtung schweigen und sich zurücknehmen hinaus, bei mir also, die Dinge, die ich vertreten konnte, die hab' ich gesagt und geschrieben und die Dinge, die ich nicht wollte, die hab' ich nach Möglichkeit weggelassen, nach Möglichkeit. Sicher verbiegt man sich, aber so wenig wie möglich. (Barth 2000: 71)

… and then again above that this official level, and you couldn't do anything private there, at least I held myself back a lot. [Interviewer: Was that lying?] … Certainly not lying. It was more a question of remaining silent, of withdrawing. I mean, in my case, I said and wrote

---

[2] On this question, see also Sobotta (2000).

those things that I found acceptable, and as far as possible the things I didn't want I left out, as far as possible. You do bow to the pressure, but as little as possible.

When pressed by the interviewer to redefine her (legitimate) practice of reticence or withdrawal as (non-legitimate) lying, S.S. resists by adopting the interviewer's impersonal formulation ('Was that lying?' as opposed to 'Were you lying?') and extending it ('It was more a question of remaining silent, of withdrawing'). When she refocuses on herself, she couches her actions in terms that are unlikely to elicit censure, but when she then refers to potentially 'reprehensible' behaviour, she adopts the defocusing strategy of expressing it in terms of common practice ('You do bow to the pressure, but as little as possible').[3]

The apparent avoidance of personal pronouns is not automatic in contexts where the recounting of a particular action is face-threatening. If the speaker's intention is self-criticism, or conversely if they want to insist that they have no need to justify their past actions, their accounts are generally expressed in first-person terms: W.B., for example, presents himself unapologetically as a supporter of the system in the GDR and uses virtually no non-personal forms with reference to himself (ibid.: 172). H.S., by contrast, uses a very high proportion of non-personal forms, although he was a former editor of *Junge Welt* (the official news-paper of the FDJ, the youth movement of the communist party) and like W.B. acknowledges his active involvement in the development of the state. In spite of this general position of support for the system, however, H.S. takes every oppor-tunity to express his distaste for the prescriptive rules of journalistic practice that he and his colleagues had been required to observe and to illustrate his own occa-sional non-conformist behaviour. On this basis, Barth (ibid.: 128–9) interprets his exceptionally frequent use of impersonal forms specifically in relation to actions that might be negatively evaluated in the present context as a conscious defocus-ing strategy.

Similar effects of shifting between personal and impersonal forms are identified by Auer (2000*a*: 166–7) in his east German job interviews, and by Dittmar and Bredel (1999: 175–82) in their interviews with east and west Berliners on experi-ences of the *Wende*. While Barth interprets defocusing primarily as an immuniza-tion strategy, however, the other studies suggest a broader range of motivations. Dittmar and Bredel, for example, do see some evidence for an association between the use of impersonal forms and the expression of problematic issues, but they also emphasize both the solidary function of *man* (representing the view of the

---

[3] Barth acknowledges the vulnerability of eastern interviewees, in that even though the interview-ers were other easterners, the interviewees knew their statements would be published and therefore made available to other, unknown, and potentially less sympathetic eyes. This is part of a general prob-lem of research in this area, as easterners are in a double bind: as subjects of western research, they are analysed in terms of western expectations and norms, and therefore often found wanting from a deficit perspective, but even as subjects of eastern research they run the risk of being accused of concealing or excusing the supposedly 'negative' aspects of their past.

speaker but permitting them to enlist support from others by retreating into the generalized impersonal form) and the potential of pronoun-switching as a narrative resource. In the following extract, for instance, a west Berlin woman highlights the new possibility of travelling outside the confines of the city:

Dafür könn' wa endlich mal ein bißchen weiter rausfahren, können uns mal, können da hinfahren, wo man ehm früher nicht hinkonnte. Also hat man zuhause gesessen am Wochenende und so kann man öh kannst de jetzt mitn [*sic*] Auto hinfahren und kannst beim Bauern das Gemüse kaufen frisch ausm Garten. (Dittmar and Bredel 1999: 179)

But then we can at least travel a bit further out at last, we can go where you er didn't use to be able to go. At the weekends, you used to sit around at home and now *you*[4] can er drive out there in the car and buy vegetables on the farm fresh from the garden.

The main point of this passage is the contrast between 'then' and 'now', and the speaker appears to underline this by using *wir* (we) and *du* (you) to refer to the present, and the impersonal, distancing *man* (one, you) to refer to the past (the repair from '*kann man*' to '*kannst de*' when reverting to the present from the past makes this particularly clear).

Like the east Germans Fix and Barth, the west Germans Dittmar and Bredel use biographical interviews to gain access to communities of memory, but in this case from a comparative perspective. Between 1993 and 1996 they collected interview material with east and west Berliners, and to reduce the inherent tension of the interview situation the members of each constituency were recorded by fieldworkers from their 'own' territory (east Berlin primary school teachers and west German students respectively).[5] The interviews were loosely structured around two key questions: how did individuals experience the 'fall of the Wall' on 9 November 1989, and what were their reflections on the *Wende* from the perspective of the present? The focus on a single moment that everyone 'knows', makes it possible to identify similarities and differences in content and structure of the (hi)stories that people want to tell: 'das Gemeinsame des wiedervereinigten Deutschland ist nicht der Konsens der öffentlichen Geschichte, sondern der Dissens persönlicher Geschichten' (the common factor in the united Germany is not the consensus of public history but the divergence of personal histories) (Dittmar and Bredel 1999: 61).

Although the material deals specifically with this 'German' event, the broader relevance lies in the attempt to discover what narrative techniques people affected by profound and irreversible changes use to model their experience of these

---

[4] Since 'impersonal you' (i.e. used with non-specific reference, equivalent to 'one', as opposed to specific second-person reference) would probably be used here for both *man* and *du*, I have distinguished between the two in the translation by italicizing the 'you' that stands for the *du* in the original.

[5] The analysis is based on a final selection of thirty-one eastern interviewees and twenty-five westerners. For full details on the data, see Dittmar and Bredel (1999: 23–30); for discussion of further aspects of the study see 4.3 above, and also Dittmar (1997) and Dittmar and Glier (2000).

changes, since, as Linklater (2000: 163) argues, 'oral testimony is not just a source of information, it is "an event in itself"' (Portelli 1990)'. Autobiographical accounts, or personal histories, are therefore not merely individual interpretations of historical events but representations of events with the narrator as central participant. Furthermore, individual constructions of the past are not fixed but subject to change across time (and, as Meinhof 2000 shows in her analysis of television representations of the fall of the Wall on successive anniversaries of the event, this can apply also to media discourses). We may ask then on what basis the informants in this study assembled their images of the *Wende* in the mid-1990s, but it would also be interesting to invite them to offer 'remakes' of their stories ten or twenty years later.

As an analytical perspective, Dittmar and Bredel (1999: 64–91) start from the analogy of narrator as film director, who selects which scenes to 'shoot', from what angle to film them, and in which sequence to edit them together. On this basis, they identify the filmic techniques adopted by their informants and allocate individual narratives to a range of film genres: short film, feature film, reportage, montage, even horror film. Broad contrasts between responses of east and west Berliners to the events they portray appear to correspond to preferences in terms of genres of representation. Eastern narrators typically focus on their direct experiences of the *Wende*, the confrontation between familiar and unfamiliar values and norms, and the resulting conflicts; westerner narrators are concerned less with actual events than with new opportunities that arose for them and with observations on the eastern 'others'. For westerners, the fall of the Wall typically represents the resolution of the disruptive event (or 'skandalon') that provides the dramatic impetus for their stories; for easterners, however, the fall of the Wall is itself the disruptive event. Consequently, preferred western genres are the personal adventure of the feature film and the detached format of the reportage, such as Alfred's account (ibid.: 88–9), which echoes the impersonal observation of television news reports. For many easterners, on the other hand, the need to process and contextualize the events gives rise to the more reflective essay approach or the montage, such as Dolly's complex story (ibid.: 72–3), with its frequent flashbacks to life in the GDR interspersed in her narrative on 9 November.

In allowing individuals to speak for themselves, oral histories provide ordinary witnesses of massive social change with a means of 'finding a voice' (Jackman and Roe 2000): they are for once not 'being written' but 'writing themselves'. These autobiographies are uniquely focused on the self, for even when the narrators talk about others, they are telling us something exclusively about themselves. This also gives them the chance to make sense of their past, and to use this process of 'meaning making' as a way of connecting past with present, of fashioning a coherence and continuity in their curriculum vitae that may not be apparent to an outside observer. Where these individual trajectories intersect, where we can detect points of contact between personal histories, common perspectives in individual memories, there may be some justification in assembling collective memories as the basis for postulating communities whose members actually recognize each other.

In this section, I have examined some of the ways in which individual reflections on past experiences of language and the narrative processing of individual biographies may contribute to the process of forming 'communities of memory'. In the next section, I shall explore ways in which perceptions of language use in the present form the basis for identifying easterners and westerners as 'other' and for constructing stereotypical representations of them in the 'symbolic space East–West' (Dittmar and Bredel 1999: 33), the social space within contemporary Germany that subsumes and sustains the divisions of the past.

5.2   Representations of self and other

In earlier chapters I have referred a number of times to the emblematic or diagnostic quality of individual words and phrases: the occurrence of a word marked in the public lexicon as specific to either the GDR or the Federal Republic (for example, *Kader* or *Gastarbeiter* respectively) in an otherwise unmarked sequence was often sufficient to identify the source of the text and therefore to categorize the speaker or writer in terms of origin. This applied both before 1989 and in the early years of the new speech community, and in principle is no more than an extension of the general practice of placing a speaker in terms of their regional origin, just as using *Schlachter* (butcher) marks the speaker as northern, and *Metzger* as southern (see Barbour and Stevenson 1990/1998: Chapters 2 and 3, Clyne 1995: Chapters 2 and 4). Where such contrasts are perceived as examples of 'variation within a system', values may be associated with individual variants that speakers identify as different from their own, but this need not have significant social consequences. Where they are considered as 'differences between systems', however, they may acquire a more powerful status as boundary markers separating 'right' from 'wrong'. As the *Zielstellung/Zielsetzung* example showed (see 4.3), fine distinctions in linguistic form can be potent weapons in constructing social difference, and when 'different' means 'wrong' the use of different terms is read as deviant behaviour.

Recent evidence suggests that the concrete basis for such discrimination, on lexical grounds at least, has more or less vanished, since GDR-specific terms have been either abandoned or divested of their historical connotations and absorbed into the broader spectrum of regional variation (see 4.1, and Hellmann 1997*b*, Stickel and Volz 1999, Stickel 2000, Reiher 2000). Furthermore, as I argued in Chapter 4, the extent of actual differences in linguistic forms and practices between east and west Germans may well have been exaggerated and to some degree an artefact of research design. However, *perceptions* of linguistic difference do seem to have played a major role in the negotiation of relationships between east and west Germans in the period of social transformation in the 1990s, and it follows from everything that we have seen so far that in times of uncertainty and upheaval people will resort to language use as a secure means of orientation. How widespread then was the belief that easterners and westerners could be identified by their language use? What kinds of feature did people use to achieve this? How did they represent the language use of the 'other' Germans? What were the motives and the consequences of these acts of categorization? How can negative consequences be overcome, especially if it is true, as Margita Pätzold (forthcoming) maintains, that there is no eastern *Öffentlichkeit*, no adequate public context in which these issues can be debated without prejudice?

In their reflections on personal experiences, many individuals in east and west corroborate west German linguist Hans-Werner Eroms's identification of a different *Diktion* (style or manner of speaking) within each of the two broad communities (1997: 8), although there is not necessarily agreement on what constitutes these different styles.[6] For example, east German students in Ruth Reiher's surveys expressed various degrees of admiration for their western counterparts' apparent fluency, confidence in public speaking, and sophisticated rhetorical skills, but at the same time there is a thin line between this and a sense of pomposity, condescension, and superciliousness (1996: 50–3). Their praise for western students' abilities implies deficits in their own, but these perceived deficiencies are offset by other, more positive attributes: a more open, honest, and direct manner in discussions, a greater willingness to engage in genuine dialogue rather than concentrating on self-presentation. Western students often concurred with this contrast:

Da würd' ich schon sagen, hab' ich festgestellt, daß im Osten äh die Kommunikation einfacher läuft. Also es is' mir meistens aufgefalln, daß die Leute viel offener sind und viel direkter auf auf Leute zugehn äh. . . . Ich hatte schon das Gefühl, daß man leichter Leute kennengelernt hat und daß sie ebn auch nich' so dieses, zu Anfang jedenfalls nich' so dieses Imponiergehabe hattn, was also was man hier [i.e. in the west] oft hat, wenn man Leute kennenlernt, daß man erstmal durch 'ne unheimlich harte Schale durch muß, um überhaupt zu den Menschn vorzudringn. Und da hatt' ich das Gefühl, daß sie etwas natürlicher warn, und das hat sich natürlich in der Sprache niedergeschlagn. (Reiher 1996: 52)

Well, I'd certainly say I've found that communication is easier in the east. I mean, it's generally struck me that people are much more open and they approach people much more directly. . . . I had the feeling that you got to know people more easily and that they didn't, at least at the start they didn't do all this posturing, like you often get here [i.e. in the west] when you meet people, the way you have to break through an incredibly hard shell just to get through to the real person. And I had the feeling that they were a bit more natural, and that obviously came through in their language too.

This commonly perceived distinction led to a succinct representation in the form of the wry coining by easterners of a new version of an old proverb: 'Ein Ossi— ein Wort, ein Wessi—ein Wörterbuch' (One *Ossi*—one word, one *Wessi*—a whole dictionary) (ibid.).

[6] See also Wachtel (1991) on different *Sprechkulturen* (cultures of talk) in east and west.

These mixed perceptions are shared by many of the east Germans interviewed by Fix and Barth (2000) (see 5.1). W.B., for example, acknowledges the greater apparent fluency of west German speakers, but attributes this to different educational traditions and considers the surface impression misleading:

W.B.: Ich glaube,...daß der Westdeutsche scheinbar fließend spricht, aber mit sehr viel Worthülsen operiert; während der Ostdeutsche stolpernder spricht, aber sorgfältiger auf die Wortwahl achtet, mühsamer drum ringt, was er sagt. (Fix and Barth 2000: 359–60)

I think that west Germans appear to speak more fluently but they use a lot more empty words; while east Germans speak more awkwardly but choose their words more carefully and struggle more laboriously over what they say.

Similarly, D.B. identifies a 'special manner of speaking' in western students in particular: they talk and talk but always say the same thing, while eastern students speak more slowly but what they say 'hatte Hand und Fuß' (made sense) (ibid.: 393). This is seen as part of a more general superficiality in the public performance of the self in west German contexts and the exclusively western communicative genre of small talk: 'Sprechen ohne Informationen,...Aneinanderreihen von Worten.... Was die alten Bundesländer uns als, wie sagen sie, Funktionärssprache ankreiden—sie haben 'ne Wohlstandssprache' (speaking without information,... stringing words together.... What people in the old Federal states hold against us as, what do they call it, the language of functionaries—well, they have a language of affluence) (M.K.; ibid.: 305–6). For S.S., a teacher in her late forties, this feeling that 'Konversation spielt 'ne größere Rolle als bei uns' (chatting/small talk is more important than it is for us), and the sense of helplessness and inferiority that overcame her amongst her western relatives, were so extreme that they had the effect of making her feel positively dysfunctional (ibid.: 414–15).

It is important to emphasize that not only are these comments a random selection of views with no strictly representative status, but they are also all expressions of perceptions based on recollections of experience: in other words, the statements are at several removes from direct observation and analysis. Furthermore, they reveal nothing about the actual speech behaviour either of the observed or of the observers—they are highly subjective assessments which rarely identify specific features that could be quantified. Nevertheless, it is striking how similar so many of these remarks from different sources are, both in their substance and in the ways they are formulated. This suggests two things: first, that they may have a relatively high degree of validity *as perceptions*, in the sense that they would be acknowledged as legitimate by many members of the relevant population, and secondly, that they are only in part personal evaluations, that they derive to some extent from what Jäger (1997) calls 'inter-discourse'—the discursive flow of ideas, opinions, and representations within a society, typically in the form of interaction between media products and media consumers. Newspaper and magazine commentaries and reports on public opinion surveys, for example, characteristically generate a battery of standard expressions that can be recycled both in further journalistic texts and in conversations based on them. As ideas are circulated in this way, opinions become crystallized into 'facts', contestable claims are naturalized as 'common sense' notions that have an axiomatic quality and therefore require no further justification (see Fairclough 1989): 'easterners don't know the meaning of work', say, or 'westerners are arrogant and insincere'.

Whether evaluations of 'typically' western and eastern speech behaviour are predominantly internalized from discursive sources or derive primarily from first-hand experience, it is likely that observers will bring with them into direct contact assumptions and expectations both about what is appropriate in a given context and about what is characteristic of specific 'other' forms of behaviour. For example, Pätzold and Pätzold (1995) report on comments made by a group of observers on a televised discussion between an east German writer and a west German presenter, in which the interviewee was pressed to justify the relationship he had had with the state in the GDR. The writer objected to the way in which the presenter was conducting the interview and consistently refused to be drawn on the main issue. Non-Germans asked to comment on the interview were clearly struck by what for them was the surprisingly defensive behaviour of the interviewee ('Warum läßt er sich das gefallen?', Why does he put up with that?), but west German (and even some east German) judges characterized his behaviour as 'typically east German':

Das ist typisch ostdeutsch, sie lassen es mit sich machen und sind dann sauer darüber, wie die Westdeutschen mit ihnen umgehen. Zum Verhör gehören immer zwei.

That's typically east German, they let themselves be pushed around and then get annoyed about the way the west Germans treat them. It takes two to make an interrogation.

...eben ganz Ossi, denn wenn er gewollt hätte, hätte er sie doch ganz schön auflaufen lassen, an einigen Stellen zumindest.

...typical *Ossi*, because if he'd wanted to he could easily have dropped her in it, in some places at any rate.

Since the judges knew who the participants were and where they came from, they were not being asked to identify them on the basis of their speech behaviour, but merely to comment on the behaviour. There is therefore no means of knowing to what extent the judges' assessments were preformed through their knowledge about the participants and their expectations, but their responses strongly suggest that the German observers were predisposed to take a generic rather than an individual perspective. In other words, they know they are observing an east German and so 'call up' their east German 'template' and map the actually observed behaviour onto that. Since the non-Germans presumably had no such template available to them, they resorted to their default position of setting the observed behaviour against their own personal norms and expectations.

In real-world contexts, you may or may not know where your interlocutor or the speaker on television is from: either way, as research on language attitudes has repeatedly shown (see Holmes 2001: Chapter 14), it is common practice, consciously or unconsciously, to search your personal database, built up through previous encounters, for a match in terms of salient parameters (colouring of eyes, hair, or skin; style of hair or dress; use of gestures or facial expressions; aspects of language use). A clear regional accent and the use of marked lexical items are obvious signposts in this respect, but in the absence of such transparent features do east and west Germans feel confident that they can allocate a speaker to an eastern or a western background on the basis of their speech? As we have already seen from survey data (Stickel and Volz 1999: 33–5—see Chapter 4.4), only about 50–60 per cent of those asked expressed the view that there were any noteworthy differences between 'eastern' and 'western' language use, and of those only about 20 per cent said they could always tell where someone was from on the basis of their speech. This may have something to do with the passage of time—the survey was conducted in 1997–8—but it may also have to do with the nature of the exercise: the questions were very abstract and relied on the respondents' powers of recall and their ability to generalize from specific experiences.

The situation is rather different when individuals are confronted with actual speech material. Pätzold and Pätzold (1998: 73) found, for example, that many east and west Germans considered it necessary to be able to identify their interlocutors in terms of their origin in order to ensure successful communication and found it perfectly natural to be asked to identify speakers on a tape. This, again, accords with the experience of language-attitude researchers, and the important point is not whether people can make accurate judgements but rather the fact that they believe they can, as this shows that 'east' and 'west' are salient social categories for them. Furthermore, while direct questions on the nature of east–west differences generally elicit predictable responses focusing on vocabulary and accent, experimental data reveal a greater range of features that people refer to in order to navigate their way through the evaluation of speech.

At a relatively trivial level, Weydt's experiment with personal ads (Weydt 1993—see Chapter 4.2) shows that this can apply to written texts. Most of his judges correctly identified Text 9 as written by a westerner, but for quite different reasons. East German judges typically expressed a hostile reaction: 'Unsere Frauen haben sich nicht so erniedrigt' (our women didn't demean themselves like that), for example, and 'So'n Quatsch wurde in unseren Anzeigen nicht gedruckt' (Rubbish like that wasn't printed in our ads). West Germans, on the other hand, made comments such as 'Meiner Meinung nach haben Ost-Bürger Schwierigkeiten mit Ironie' (in my opinion, easterners have problems with irony), and remarked on the author's 'Selbstbewußtsein zu ihrer Person' (self-confidence). In other words, the same text was variously interpreted as an expression of self-abasement and of self-confidence. However, while the judges disagree in their assessments of the respective texts, they share a sense of distinct communicative styles and attribute characteristics to these styles which in reality seem to refer to people rather than texts:

Ost- und Westinformanten haben ein deutliches und weitgehend identisches Profil von Ost- und Westanzeigen vor Augen. Als negativ wird an der westlichen Selbstpräsentation empfunden, daß sie oberflächlich, künstlich, übertrieben und unnatürlich sei. Ostdeutsche fragen sich, warum Wessis sich in Anzeigen so verstellen. Tendenziell überwiegen negative Urteile in den Begründungen der Ostinformanten. 'Blödsinnige Übertreibung', 'oberflächliche Ironie', 'entspricht der allgemeinen aufgesetzten Lockerheit (coolness)'. Die gleichen Merkmale können auch positiv gewertet werden, vorwiegend von Westinformanten, nämlich als phantasievoll, ironisch, witzig, selbstbewußt, interessant, locker. 'Respektlosigkeit' wird dem Westen zugeschrieben und offenbar unterschiedlich bewertet. Dagegen erkennen Ost- wie Westinformanten Ostanzeigen an der 'normalen, nicht übertriebenen Ausdrucksweise', an Sachlichkeit, Korrektheit, Ernsthaftigkeit: als typisch empfinden sie die genaue Aufzählung 'vielfältiger' Interessen; die wird manchmal im Westen als 'Obergenauigkeit', als 'reine, relativ stupide Aufzählung der Qualifikation' empfunden. (Weydt 1993: 215–18)

Informants from both east and west have a clear and largely identical profile of eastern and western ads in their minds. The western manner of self-presentation is considered negatively in that it is felt to be superficial, artificial, exaggerated, and unnatural. East Germans wonder why *Wessis* put on such an act in ads. Eastern informants tended to give negative assessments in their judgements. 'Ridiculous exaggeration', 'superficial irony', 'characteristic of their general insincere "cool" manner'. The same features may also be evaluated positively, especially by western informants, for example as imaginative, ironic, witty, self-confident, interesting, cool. 'Lack of respect' is attributed to the west and is evidently evaluated in different ways. On the other hand, both eastern and western informants recognize eastern ads in the 'normal, not exaggerated form of expression', in their matter-of-factness, correctness, seriousness: a typical feature is felt to be the careful listing of 'diverse' interests, which in the west is sometimes considered to be 'excessive precision', 'nothing but rather mindless listing of qualifications'.

In a study conducted in the middle of the *Wende* period itself, Julia Liebe Reséndiz carried out a similar experiment using spoken material with remarkably similar results (Reséndiz 1992). The texts in this case consisted of extracts from broadcasts from east and west Berlin radio stations, and the judges were east and west Berliners and a group of *Übersiedler* (easterners who had moved to the west before the *Wende*). While vocabulary was naturally referred to by the judges as a means of identifying the extracts, individual lexical features were only rarely taken in isolation and typically led indirectly to an eastern or western attribution: for example, unconventional, creative, and playful use of words and phrases was often deemed characteristic of western speakers. However, syntactic and prosodic features and aspects of textual structure seemed to be at least as important. Reflecting Weber's (1989) empirical analysis of morphosyntactic contrasts between east and west German radio texts, which showed that GDR radio texts typically used longer, grammatically more complex sentences, the judges distinguished between the 'written style' of the east German extracts and the more 'oral style' (even of scripted passages) of western texts (see also Holly 1997 on the trend towards increasing orality in German television language). Compare, for example, these two descriptions (both by *Übersiedler*) of an east and a west German doctor respectively:

Ich hab' gemerkt, daß die Sätze sehr sehr verschachtelt waren durch Wortverbindungen, durch 'und, obwohl, trotz' wurden Sätze miteinander verbunden und wirkten teilweise langweilig. Und man hat nach 'ner Weile ooch nich' mehr hingehört.

I noticed that the sentences were very very complex because of the way words were joined, sentences were linked with 'and, although, in spite of' and sometimes seemed boring. And after a while you didn't listen any more.

Dieset Lockere, dis der einfach so erzählt hat. Also ick kann mir vorstellen, dis ick vor ihm stehe und dis er mir genau so wat erzählt. (Reséndiz 1992: 131)

That easy-going manner, the way he just talked. I mean, I can picture myself standing in front of him and he's telling me something just like that.

Similarly, they distinguished between what they perceived as the relatively mono-tonous, disengaged speech rhythms of eastern broadcasters and the more lively, spontaneous articulation of their western counterparts. Here again are two *Über-siedlerinnen* on an eastern and a western presenter respectively:

Dis fällt mir urst oft auf, dieses lalalalalala, also man merkt irgendwie so wenig Interesse an diesem Thema...und da is' es, man merkt, wie se die Fragen irgendwie so auswendiglernen,...also man merkt, *sie* wissen von dem Thema genauso wenich wie jeder andere. Also ich weeß nich', irgendwie dieses Langweilige.

That really strikes me a lot, that lalalalalala, I mean you can sort of tell they have so little interest in the subject...and you can tell that they sort of learn the questions off by heart,...you can tell that *they* know as little about the subject as anyone else. I don't know, just that sort of boring effect.

Hier geht es irgendwie fließender, wird mehr betont, was sie/worauf sie Wert legt, betont sie auch irgendwie. Also man merkt bei den DDR-Sprechern nie, was sie nun/sie können über alles mögliche sprechen, man weiß aber nie, was sie denken. (Ibid)

Here it's sort of more fluent, they emphasize more what they/what they think is important is more sort of emphasized. I mean, with the GDR speakers you can never tell/they can talk about all sorts of things but you never know what they think.

Not only do we find consistent images of 'eastern' and 'western' manners of speaking in all of these studies, what is also common to them all is the association between perceptions of linguistic patterns or behaviours and of social practices: for the informants in the various studies, a particular way of speaking is indicative of a particular way of being. Pätzold and Pätzold (1998) adopt a concept of Karl Bühler's to account for the way this process occurs—the process of relating properties of speech to properties of speakers and so to the social and historical contexts in which these speech practices are taken to be habitually situated. Bühler's metaphor of the *Sphärengeruch*, the 'scent' of particular 'spheres' or domains such as cooking or politics (Bühler 1934: 172, cited in Pätzold and Pätzold 1998: 75), is intended to indicate how certain words or other linguistic features are invested with an indelible marker, which not only activates certain associations in the hearer's mind but constrains the possibilities of interpretation or understanding of the texts in which they occur by specifying the context in which they 'normally' appear. The 'release' of the 'scent' that is attached to the word or phrase has the effect of directing the hearer towards the linguistic—and thus social—practices in which it is generally to be found. For example, a word such as *Solidarität* may have general associations with notions such as cooperation and mutual support, but for someone socialized in the GDR it carries the 'scent' of 'struggle' and the cause of socialism through ritualized collocations such as the 'internationale Solidarität der Arbeiterklasse' (international solidarity of the working class). The *Sphärengeruch* of words or phrases therefore has the effect that Gumperz (1982) attributes to 'contextualization cues'. Beyond merely triggering specific associations with other ideas or concepts, they contribute towards the way in which the hearer structures their whole understanding of the speaker's text. To continue the previous example, the use of *Solidarität* (under certain circumstances at least) might direct the hearer towards a particular set of linguistic and social practices, which in turn conditions the way in which the rest of what the speaker says is interpreted (Pätzold and Pätzold 1998: 76–7, 84–5).

In their project, organized along similar lines to Liebe Reséndiz's study, Pätzold and Pätzold try to show how hearers respond to the *Sphärengeruch* of individual words (such as *Solidarität*) to identify a particular sub-context (the solidarity of the working class) and then extrapolate from this to construct a larger context (social practices and norms of the GDR). A video recording was made of psychology students at the Humboldt University in Berlin taking part in a role play as teachers and students at a school meeting. The recording was then played to a group of linguistics students, who were asked to judge whether the 'teachers/school students' were from east or west Germany and to justify their judgement on linguistic grounds; both groups of students contained easterners and westerners.

Example 1
'*School student*' 3: Ja, das würde ich auch noch bestätigen wollen, das ham wa vorher zwar nich' gesehen, aber das Bild hier vom Zeichenunterricht, wo man wirklich kreativ sein kann, das finde ich schon sehr positiv, daß dieses/die Möglichkeit der Individualität auf jeden Fall im Unterricht erhalten bleiben sollte.
Judge (east German): Drei halte ich, denke ich, fürn fürn Wessi: Zeichenunterricht, kreativ, Individualität—also, viel Schrütz um Nüscht.

'*School student*' 3: Yes, I would like to confirm that too, admittedly we didn't see that before but the picture that we have here of art lessons where you can be really creative, I find it

very positive that this/the possibility of individuality should definitely be maintained in lessons.
Judge (east German): I'd say number 3 is a *Wessi*, I think: art lessons, creative, individuality—a lot of waffle in other words.

The east German judge reacts to the *Sphärengeruch* attaching to the words *Zeichenunterricht* (art lessons), *kreativ* (creative), and *Individualität* (individuality) and collocates them in an associative bundle that represents for him/her a particular speech practice (*viel Schrütz um Nüscht*, a lot of waffle), which he/she considers characteristic of westerners. In the second example, another eastern judge identifies a 'teacher' as a fellow east German:

Example 2
'*Teacher*' 2: Es geht auch darum, erstmal rauszufinden, wieviel Leute das Fotolabor überhaupt nutzen. Wenn ich daran vorbeigeh', dann seh' ich 'n eingeschworenes Grüppchen von drei vier Leuten, die immer dieselben sind. Es macht, es hat keinen Zweck, wenn es nur 'n paar Leute sind, die ihre Privatfotos entwickeln, ja, es sollen 'n paar mehr Leute daran beteiligt sein und es ist wichtig rauszufinden, wieviel Leute das sind, auch um die Mittel besser planen zu können und die Effektivität erstmal.
Judge (east German): Dit is' ooch wieder typisch ossihaft, also man kann nicht etwas einrichten, was nur zwei Leute nutzen, sondern das muß von der gesamten Gemeinschaft genutzt werden, hm, und 'die Effektivität erstmal', also irgendwas muß effektiv sein, also dis kann nicht aus Spaß an der Sache einfach, sondern das muß effektiv sein, genau wie wa äh wie wa unsern Plan immer erfüllen mußten, so muß dieses auch effektiv sein und nicht nur von zwei bis drei Leuten genutzt werden. Also L2 is' Ossi.

'*Teacher*' 2: What we need to do is first of all find out how many people actually use the darkroom. Whenever I go past it I see a closely knit little group of three or four people, always the same ones. There's no point if it's just a few people developing their private photos, there should be a few more people involved and it's important to find out how many there are, also so that we can plan the use of resources better and the effectiveness in the first place.
Judge (east German): This is typically *Ossi*-like again—you can't set up something that is only used by two people, it must be used by the entire community, hmm, and 'the effectiveness in the first place', so things have to be effective, they can't just be because people enjoy doing them, they have to be effective, just like we always had to fulfil our plan, so this has to be effective too and not just be used by two or three people. So 'Teacher 2' is an *Ossi*.

Here, the east German judge responds first to the general proposition that 'resources must be used effectively', but this seems to have been prompted by the specific formulation 'die Effektivität erstmal' (the effectiveness in the first place), which he/she quotes. This in turn triggers associations with the requirement to 'unseren Plan erfüllen' (fulfil our plan; quite possibly in reaction also to the teacher's use of *planen*), which, as the use of the past tense form (*mußten*, had to) clearly implies, is a linguistic and social practice rooted in the social and historical context of the GDR.

Reactions such as these, elicited under experimental conditions with the participants explicitly required to search for linguistic markers of difference, clearly should not be understood as a reflection of everyday behaviour. What they do suggest is that 'east' and 'west' have a psychological reality for many individuals as primary, discrete categories, and that people believe that these social categories are discoverable through patterns of linguistic behaviour. The accuracy of the judgements made in such exercises is not the issue, nor is the question of whether there 'really is or was' a distinctive eastern or western manner of speaking. What we seem to have from a range of different sources is evidence of a belief that the ability to distinguish an easterner from a westerner is a part of a speaker's communicative competence.

This becomes potentially significant when the isolated characteristics that people identify in the ways we have seen are rolled up or assembled into complete images of whole beings—Dittmar and Bredel's western interviewees, for example, collectively supply the defining features of the *Ossis*: '*unsicher*' (insecure), '*autoritätshörig*' (obedient to authority), '*würdelos und unselbständig*' (undignified and lacking in independence), '*unfreundlich*' (unfriendly), '*ausländerfeindlich*' (xenophobic), '*hart und unpersönlich*' (hard and impersonal), '*unqualifiziert und arbeitsscheu*' (unqualified and workshy), '*schlechte Autofahrer*' (bad drivers), '*Zerstörer ihrer selbst*' (self-destructive) (1999: 122–5). While specific features have a diagnostic function (he/she said/did X, so he/she must be an *Ossi*/a *Wessi*), complete images have a predictive function (he/she is an *Ossi*/a *Wessi*, so he/she must be lazy/arrogant, etc.). The indeterminacy of reality is supplanted by sharply defined contrasts, and the individual disappears behind the stereotype. Furthermore, the role of linguistic features or practices in the formation of stereotypes is precisely so important because, as Pätzold and Marhoff (1998) argue, they function as a primary 'interpretative resource' in interaction: the identification of a particular linguistic form as habitually belonging to a particular discourse or context is the first step in constructing a frame for processing the interaction—'people who speak like that probably think XYZ'.

The importance of binary oppositions in the process of stereotype formation is that the attribution of negative qualities to the other implies the possession of corresponding positive qualities by the self: if social group A is considered to be 'humourless', social group B will be considered to be 'amusing'—but only if A and B constitute a fundamental dichotomy within the society (see also Chapter 6). Dittmar and Bredel (1999: 126–7) argue that the westerners in their study rely on this first-order contrast to develop and stabilize a positive self-image: the list of features attributed to easterners in the narratives of the west Berliners represents the exact opposite of what the westerners believe themselves to be or aspire to be. Furthermore, these sets of opposing qualities did not appear out of the blue but derive from global prejudices towards 'the east' before 1989: the previously shapeless image of the eastern other, associated abstractly with the 'system' in the GDR, now developed clear contours in the form of the *Ossi* (this term did exist before

1989, but was used within west Germany to refer to another 'minority' social group, the *Ostfriesen* (East Frisians): see Küpper 1987).

As both direct and mediated contact between easterners and westerners grew following the *Wende*, some of the negative qualities attributed by each to the other became further distilled into the complementary stereotypes of the *Jammerossi* (whingeing easterner) and the *Besserwessi* (a pun on *Besserwisser*, 'know-all'). The development of a joke genre (*Ossi-Wessi* jokes) based on this conceptual pair was a characteristic response to social tension or conflict, and it is evidence of a perceived need to harden diffuse perceptions into distinct representations, but it also served to shore up the popular belief in the fundamental east–west contrast and reinforced the perception of difference as 'common sense' or 'common knowledge' (see, for example, Heringer 1991, Schiewe and Schiewe 2000, Staininger 1995). To a certain extent, the *Ossi* (=east German) replaced the *Ossi* (=East Frisian) as the butt of western jokes, but this new target provided a convenient and apparently socially acceptable alternative to ethnic and national minority groups such as the Turks to fulfil the socially dominant group's need to assert itself by disparaging and humiliating a socially less powerful population. *Ossi* jokes may be perceived as legitimate, in a way that 'Turkish jokes' are not, since the humorous attacks are 'kept within the family' (just as the same jokes may be told with relative impunity by Dubliners about 'Kerry men' as the English tell more controversially about 'the Irish'). Ironically, perhaps, this also has the no doubt unintentional effect of ratifying easterners' membership of the larger category of 'Germans'. *Wessi* jokes grew out of a more subversive tradition in the GDR, and now the SED regime and its agents were replaced as targets by representative members of the affluent and domineering west. Unlike western jokes, these are an opportunity for easterners to salvage dignity and reassert self-esteem in the face of a dominant other that cannot be countered effectively by other means, but at the same time they imply an acknowledgement of their own subordination.

So the existence of a 'joke culture' that gives expression to mutually held prejudices and antipathy also gives a misleading sense of equilibrium. The consequences of the petrified representations *Jammerossi* and *Besserwessi* are clearly not evenly distributed, for while the westerners in general enjoy a more satisfactory social situation and can disown the behaviour patterns that underpin 'their' stereotype without creating suspicion about their motives and without any risk to face, many easterners remain socially disadvantaged and are in a double bind: they can either suffer in silence or air their grievances and thereby confirm the prejudice underlying 'their' stereotype. Wolf (1995) shows how easy it is for self-justification to result in unwitting self-condemnation (see 5.3), so is there a way out of this dilemma—a way of articulating a grievance without making yourself vulnerable to accusations of self-pity?

Bredel and Dittmar (1998) suggest that there are narrative devices which provide speakers in this situation with the possibility of foregrounding their own problems while at the same time embedding them in a broader context. Borrowing the analytical concept of polyphony from Bakhtin's theoretical writing on literary style, they argue that 'polyphonic speaking'—integrating a repertoire of different 'voices' in a single narrative—allows the speaker or narrator to bring different perspectives to bear on problematic or disrupted aspects of their experience and therefore to make different interpretations of them available. They distinguish between inter- and intra-subjective polyphony, depending on whether 'other' voices are integrated into the speaker's own utterance (for example, by quoting or through indirect speech) or other 'guises' of the speaker are merged with the speaker's own principal narrative voice (such as in the form of an inner dialogue). How intersubjective polyphony can work to immunize the narrator against criticism can be seen in the following passage, which is an extract from a narrative interview in which Dirk, a professional musician in his early thirties, talks about his unemployment and his lack of job prospects (taken from a longer extract in Bredel and Dittmar 1998: 137–8):

Dirk: Hier vom Rundfunksinfonieorchester die Fusion, dit hat ja oo ni jeklappt, und die hatten ja schon alle so jut wien Vertrach inne Tasche. Die sitzen ja nun ooch alle off der Straße, ne. Naja, dit is, hab' mich grad jes/heute mit dem eenen unterhalten, der is' so na ick weeß nich', wie alt der is', ick schätze mal so Mitte vierzich, Trompeter von da. Sagt er, wat soll ickn machen, sagt da, ick brauch' doch nich' mehr ürgendwo vorblasen zu gehen, kannste doch vergessen. Dit steht. Da brauch icke ja nich' ma mehr hingehen, und weeß ick, wenn de drezich überschritten hast, dann is' schon bloß, naja, wir werden sehen . . . .

The merger of the Radio Symphony Orchestra here, that didn't work out either, and they all as good as had a contract in their pockets. They're all out on the street now too. Well, I was just talking to one of them yes/today, he's about, I don't know how old he is, I'd say about mid-forties, trumpeter. He says, what am I supposed to do, there's no point going to audition anywhere, you can forget about that. That's true. There's no point me going any-where, and if you're over thirty, then it's already, well, we'll see . . . .

As well as contextualizing his own position by referring to an entire orchestra being made redundant, Dirk uses a number of narrative techniques to situate his case as typical rather than as extraordinary or unique: for example, he uses the generalizing, impersonal *du* in place of the first person to make the point that at thirty-three he is already old in job market terms ('*wenn de drezich überschritten hast*', if you're over thirty). He also 'imports' the voice of another musician, who is unemployed too, to substantiate the nature of his own situation and validate his assessment of it: '*Sagt er, wat soll ickn machen, sagt da, ick brauch' doch nich' mehr ürgendwo vorblasen zu gehen, kannste doch vergessen*' (He says, what am I supposed to do, there's no point going to audition anywhere, you can forget about that). His principal concern in his narrative is to portray both the injustice and the hopelessness of his situation, but by transferring this evaluation to another voice within his narrative, he is able to insulate himself from the charge of self-pity.[7]

---

[7] Whether such techniques are successful or not in achieving this effect would have to be tested empirically, of course.

Like all clichés and stereotypes, *Ostjammer* is a portmanteau term that means different things to different people, but once coined, such terms provide an off-the-shelf label for all sorts of utterances and a convenient means of avoiding the need for analysis. One of Dittmar and Bredel's west Berlin informants, for example, clusters several characteristic topics (freedom to travel, material possessions, sacrifice, hard work) around the central image of *Jammern*:

Alfred: Und dann sagn wir och, guck mal uns an, sagn se, jammern se rum, und sagen, sie hättn kein Geld. Reisen in jedes Land, wo wir noch nich' mal warn. Die wolln in drei vier Jahrn, wolln die 'n Haus und 'n Auto ham wie wir. Mensch, deine Eltern ham auch zwanzich dreißich Jahre jespart, dit is' nich' drinne, und da sagn wir natürlich och, die solln sich das erstmal erarbeiten und erkämpfen. (Dittmar and Bredel 1999: 126)

And then we say, look at us, they say, they start whingeing and say they haven't got any money. Trips to every country we haven't even been to yet. In three, four years they want to have a house and a car like us. I mean, damn it, your parents saved for twenty or thirty years too, that's not on, and of course we say they should work for it and fight hard to get it.

Shethar and Hartung (1998: 45–6) give a similar example from media discourse. They argue that the authority to determine the preferred interpretation of an utterance or a narrative derives from what Fairclough (1989) calls 'power behind discourse'—the power to establish and police the conventions within which specific discourses are framed—and they conclude:

Eine Diskursideologie, die den 'Ost-Diskurs' als jammernd identifiziert, privilegiert klar einen bestimmten Typ von Erfahrung, Autorität und Berechtigung und schafft so eine 'separate Öffentlichkeit', deren Rede weniger mächtig ist. (Shethar and Hartung 1998: 50)

A discourse ideology that identifies the 'eastern discourse' as whingeing clearly privileges a particular kind of experience, authority, and legitimacy, and in this way creates a 'separate public', whose talk is less powerful.

The problem this creates for this 'separate public' is that it has to find a way within the constraints imposed by the dominant discourse ideology of making itself heard and having its own experience acknowledged by the other, dominant public. The task is to construct a context in which easterners can participate in debating issues that concern them directly without having their arguments marginalized as purely personal and therefore not legitimate. Shethar and Hartung found the same kind of framing strategy in the narratives of their informants that Bredel and Dittmar found in their data: to avoid 'sounding like an *Ossi*' when expressing critical judgements about their experience since unification, speakers in their interviews package their personal criticisms in a general analysis of the current social and political situation. In the following extract, an engineer in his forties, who has been made redundant and is being retrained, talks about his experience:

Insofern is' also det 'ne sehr anjenehme Atmosphäre, muß sagen, ooch aus dem Grunde macht det mir Spaß, hier täglich herzukommen, äh wobei det is' die Kehrseite jetzt dazu, äh so eigentlich seh' ick also eigentlich diese janzen Umschulungsmaßnahmen als großen Trick an... die Arbeitslosigkeit zu kaschieren und die Leute von der Straße zu holn. 'Ne andre Funktion hat det nich', denn eigentlich ham wa alles Berufe, die sofort in dem Beruf ooch wieder einsetzbar wärn, und dit is also 'ne Sache, die die Bundesregierung äh seit Jahrzehnten ja offensichtlich geschickt betreibt, indem se nämlich also an die die irgendwie äh durch die wirtschaftliche Entwicklung also äh an den Rand jebracht worden äh irgendwie zu beschäftjen mit sinnvollen und ooch teilweise sicherlich mit nich' so sehr sinnvollen Dingen und damit also Ruhe in der Bevölkerung zu halten, weil äh also sich sozusagen andre Strukturen dadurch nich' bilden können.... Diese Umschulungsmaßnahme is' also sicherlich nicht zu unserm Nachteil, äh weil wa also erstens geistig beweglich bleiben, weil wir zweetens natürlich trotzdem ooch einjes dazulernen,... aber wie jesagt, äh möchte ma sagen, für für die Entwicklung insjesamt mal weltpolitisch jesehn, ja, äh könnte eigentlich die vorhandene Intellijenz der alten DDR eingesetzt wern, um Probleme dieser Welt zu lösen, und das wird überhaupt nich' in Griff jebracht, und det is' eigentlich ooch mein mein großes Problem und und det, wat ick also der äh jetzigen politischen Führung da also äh nachtrage. (Ibid: 61–2)

To that extent it's a very pleasant atmosphere, I must say, for that reason too I enjoy coming here every day, although that's the other side of the coin now, I actually see all these retraining measures as a big trick... to conceal unemployment and get the people off the street. It's got no other function, because we've actually all got skills and qualifications, which could be put into use again straight away, and that's something that the government has obviously been doing very cleverly for decades, by finding some way of occupying those who have been marginalized as a result of the economic development with useful and in some cases certainly not so useful things, and in that way maintain calm in the population, because then other structures so to speak can't develop.... So this retraining measure is certainly not to our disadvantage, because firstly it keeps our minds active and secondly we do of course learn the odd thing too,... but as I said, I'd like to say that for the overall development from the global point of view, the intelligentsia of the old GDR could actually be employed to solve the problems of this world, and this is simply not being tackled, and that is actually my big problem, that's what I hold against the present political leadership.

The speaker positions himself clearly as an easterner through his reference to the unexploited potential of the GDR intelligentsia (of which, we can infer, he counts himself a member), and the thrust of his narrative is an indictment of the current employment policy of the German government, which he sees as a cynical manoeuvre to conceal the real extent of unemployment and maintain public order. However, the criticism is couched in terms of an objective and (through his status as a highly trained and experienced professional) authoritative assessment of the global situation, and he forestalls accusations of whingeing by framing the critical passages with positive remarks about his own situation. Since the policy to which he refers directly affects him and he clearly sees himself as belonging to the 'wasted resources' from the GDR, there cannot but be an ironic edge to his comments on his own situation (and this is supported by his faint praise for the retraining course: '*weil wa... geistig beweglich bleiben, weil wir... ooch einjes dazulernen*', it keeps our minds active and we do learn the odd thing too), but he does not explicitly complain about this.

In this section, I have tried to show how individual perceptions of east–west differences in language use develop reciprocally with public representations to form complex stereotypes, and to explore some of the ways the negative consequences of these stereotypes can be avoided in and through talk. The emphasis has been on perceptions of self and other as articulated in individual utterances, on what constitutes particular images. However, my discussion of 'problem-solving' strategies adopted by eastern speakers to evade the discursive trap of permanent association with negative images of the past points towards the subject of the final section in this chapter, which is how individual and collective identities are proposed and contested interactively and how old and new identities are manufactured in public discourses.

5.3   Manufacturing and contesting identities

Ingwer Paul (1995: 306) argues that when they were first coined as a conceptual pair after the *Wende*, the categories *Ossi* and *Wessi* were 'empty vessels', signifiers devoid of content other than the vague attribution of generalized contrasting social and political origins. They were as yet forms with no specific contours, a simple one-dimensional dichotomy pressed into service when the need arose for a concise means of labelling what was suddenly 'discovered' as a fundamental semantic distinction. From what we have seen in the previous section, this claim needs to be qualified, since the Germans in east and west interviewed by Dittmar and Bredel (1999), Beneke (1993), Schönfeld (1996*b*), and others appear to draw on images of the 'other' Germans in each case that do not derive entirely from their experience in the early 1990s, but rather—in part, at least—from stereotypical conceptions carried over from the pre-*Wende* period and based on assumptions about what someone socialized in the GDR or the Federal Republic 'must be like'.

These, then, are images that emerge from introspective accounts, narratives that are conscious reflections on knowledge and experience (direct and indirect), memories or reconstructions of past events: images that have a more or less fixed, axiomatic quality, and are stored as part of what Fairclough (1989: 11) calls 'members' resources' (MR): 'prototypes for a very diverse collection of things—the shapes of words, the grammatical forms of sentences, the typical structure of a narrative, *the properties of types of object and person*, the expected sequence of events in a particular situation type, and so forth' (my emphasis). These resources are part of the apparatus we use for participating in and interpreting the processes of social interaction, including the production and interpretation of texts:

The MR which people draw upon to produce and interpret texts are cognitive in the sense that they are in people's heads, but they are social in the sense that they have social origins—they are socially generated, and their nature is dependent on the social relations and struggles out of which they were generated—as well as being socially transmitted and, in our society, unequally distributed. People internalize what is socially produced and made available to them, and use this internalized MR to engage in their social practice, including discourse. (Ibid.: 24)

If we accept this argument, if, in particular, we accept that our MR include what we consider to be knowledge about such things as the properties of types of person, about the typical structure of a narrative, and about the expected sequence of events in a given situation type, how does this condition our perceptions and behaviour in actual interaction? How exactly are these resources mobilized and brought into play in encounters with other people? How do we select from our MR, how do we determine what is relevant in a given situation? How is the communicative load distributed between participants in interaction, and who determines this? How do we use these prototypes to categorize each other, and how are the prototypes themselves modified as a result of new experiences and encounters? How are identities proposed and projected, contested and reworked in the process of interaction? All of these questions have more to do with the process than with the product of interaction, and I want to focus in this section on different ways in which the concepts of east and west, *Ossi* and *Wessi*, are made relevant in different social contexts—private, semi-public, public.

The relevance of locating your interlocutor is sometimes made explicit, almost to the extent that a continuation of the interaction seems to be conditional upon it. In the following extract from a radio phone-in programme on the subject of *Ostwerbung* (advertising for the east German market: see below), for example, an eastern caller tries to reposition himself by using the geographical term 'in the north' to situate his home town, but the presenter insists on placing him socially as 'from the east' (i.e. 'so you are an *Ossi* then').

Presenter: Wo kommst du her?
Caller: Aus Neustrelitz, das is' im Norden, wollt' ich grad' sagen [laughs].
Presenter: Ah ja, das is' also quasi Werbung für dich.

Presenter: Where are you from?
Caller: From Neustrelitz, that's in the north, I was going to say [laughs].
Presenter: Oh right, so that's sort of advertising for you then.

Having rejected the caller's manoeuvre, the presenter relentlessly pens him in like a sheepdog with a wayward sheep, even though he tries to respond as an individual rather than as a representative *Ossi*:

Presenter: Kaufst du eher Ostprodukte, bist du so'n traditionsbewußter Ostler oder is' dir das egal, woher das kommt?
Caller: Nö, eigentlich nich' so, ich probiere das aus und wenn's schmeckt oder wenn's gut is', dann wird das gekauft, und wenn nich', dann halt nich'....
Presenter: Is' das denn auch so gewesen bei dir, daß da im Laufe der Zeit sich was geändert hat, und daß du anfangs schon ersmal die ganzen Westsachen ausprobiert has' und dann überlegt, ach Mensch, eigentlich schmeckt dir ja die Marmelade, die wir damals hatten, doch besser....
(Paul 1995: 308–9)

Presenter: Do you tend to buy eastern products? Are you a tradition-conscious easterner, or is it all the same to you where things come from?
Caller: No, not really, I try things out and if they taste nice or they're good then I buy them, if not then I don't . . . .
Presenter: Have you found that things have changed in the course of time, that at first you tried out all the western things and then you thought, actually I like the jam we used to have better . . . .

Of course, the presenter is pursuing an agenda determined by the topic of the programme, but while another caller is also identified by origin—this time as a *Wessi*—he is invited to give a personal opinion. Moreover, Shethar and Hartung (1998) show that the converse situation can arise: when east German callers on another phone-in programme try to make their experience in the GDR relevant, these attempts are ignored by the presenter because on this occasion the variable 'origin' conflicts with her intended emphasis on the variable 'gender'.

Everyday encounters are generally not constrained by these kinds of considerations, but here too social categorization in terms of the east–west dichotomy can be perceived as crucial. Undine Kramer (1998: 281–2), for example, cites the experiences of an east German journalist, Heide-Ulrike Wendt:

Situation 1: Im Frühling traf ich am Piccadilly Circus einen Mann aus Düsseldorf, der von mir wissen wollte, woher ich komme. 'Aus Berlin', sagte ich. 'Ost oder West?' fragte er. 'Lichtenberg', sagte ich. 'Wo liegt das?' fragte er. 'In der Mitte Berlins', sagte ich. 'Am Tiergarten?' fragte er. 'Am Alex', sagte ich. 'Ah, also doch im Osten', sagte er. Dann ging er, als wüßte er nun genauestens über mich Bescheid. Wie viele Stadtbezirke hat eigentlich Düsseldorf, und wen interessiert das?
Situation 2: Vier Wochen später fragte mich im Weserbergland noch ein Mann, woher ich komme. Ich kam wieder aus Berlin. Und wieder fragte er: 'Woher aus Berlin?' Ich sagte diesmal, denn wir sind ja bekanntlich umgezogen: 'Aus Berlin-Tegel', und er war sofort zufrieden. Und? Was hat er davon? Ich bin immer noch ein Ossi. (Originally in *Spiegel special*, 6/1997)

Situation 1: In the spring, I met a man in Piccadilly Circus who wanted to know where I came from. 'From Berlin', I said. 'East or West?' he asked. 'Lichtenberg', I said. 'Where is that?' he asked. 'In the centre of Berlin', I said. 'By the Zoo? [i.e. in the west]' he asked. 'Near Alexanderplatz [i.e. in the east]', I said. 'Oh, so that *is* in the East then', he said. And then he went, as if he knew everything about me. How many districts has Düsseldorf got, and who cares anyway?
Situation 2: Four weeks later, in the Weserbergland, another man asked me where I came from. Again, I came from Berlin. And again he asked: 'Where in Berlin?' We've moved now, of course, so this time I said: 'Berlin-Tegel [i.e. in the west]', and he was perfectly satisfied. So? Where has that got him? I'm still an *Ossi*.

As Wendt suggests, this not uncommon kind of spontaneous exchange was motivated virtually exclusively by westerners' need to place easterners (see also

Rothe 2000), and this asymmetrical burden on east Germans to locate themselves corresponds to the continued isolation of the east even after the *Wende* as the marked location in (western) media discourse. The tendency to treat 'Germany' as synonymous with 'West Germany' in the later period before the *Wende*, which I referred to in 2.3, did not end after unification: individuals are still identified in news stories as 'east German' but never as 'west German'. For example, references to 'the first German foreign minister to visit Vietnam' or 'the first German in space' (in both cases meaning west Germans) conveniently overlook the fact that east Germans had already reached both destinations (Kramer 1996: 59–64).

In situations where the speakers' social identities are already known and therefore do not need to be elicited as was the case in the examples above, this knowledge still may or may not be relevant to the participants in terms of how they interact (although it is always potentially relevant for the purposes of interpretation). However, even where it is not made overtly significant, a point is often reached in the course of a conversation when a reference of some kind, either to present or to past circumstances, brings the latent question of social belonging to the surface. This is relatively unlikely to occur in interaction between western speakers, but frequently comes about in conversations between easterners (especially those who have memories of life experiences in the GDR available to them) and in east–west encounters. For example, in a casual conversation between a west German teacher (T) and an east German secretary (S) at a language school in west Berlin in 1993 (see Drescher and Dausendschön-Gay 1995), the question of belonging to different social categories is never explicitly raised—it is never established as a topic—but it does impose itself implicitly on the otherwise inconsequential exchange, with a potentially disruptive effect.

They are discussing the difficulties of travelling within Berlin due to extensive reconstruction and repair work on the public transport system, and although S's description of her journey makes it clear that she lives in the east (as T already knows) this does not become significant in the conversation for some time. The first indication of the geographical locations possessing a social relevance for either of the speakers comes when S says 'das [the disruption to the urban rail network] fängt bei uns im Ostteil irgendwo schon an' (that starts somewhere over with us in the east). The collocation of the two elements *bei uns* and *im Ostteil* strongly suggests both a local and a social identification, through which S implicitly allies herself with a social group to which T does not belong. This potential contextualization cue creates an opening for a context in which S and T are not merely two people with a common problem but rather members of two distinct social communities with quite different perspectives on this and on other problems.

Although this cue does not in fact appear to establish a new context immediately, a short time later T reintroduces the topic by declaring that she is glad she did not accept a post that she had been offered in the east of the city as she would then have had the same difficult journey as S, only in reverse. She then continues:

'Aber Sie haben nich' irgendwie vor, mehr hier in die Gegend zu ziehn oder so?' (But you're not planning to move sort of more into this area here?). While '*hier in die Gegend*' (into this area here) certainly includes the idea 'nearer to the school', the textual location of this utterance suggests the additional component 'in the west'. Again, S's response gives no indication of how she interprets the question, but in addressing the question of a possible move she mentions a visit to an estate agent: 'Der hat in Forsthaus Mietshäuser aufgekauft; (leiser) Forsthaus, das is' bei uns' (He's bought up some blocks of flats in Forsthaus; [more quietly] Forsthaus, that's in our part of town). Gradually, the social demarcation between S and T seems to be resurfacing, and at this point T brings it abruptly into focus with her next remark: 'Ja, da war ich schon mal, . . . da hab' ich schon mal diese (lachend) KGB-Siedlungen angeguckt' (Yes, I've been there, . . . I've had a look at those [laughing] KGB estates). This rather flippant designation of former military buildings as 'KGB estates' clearly irritates S, who then tries to correct this assertion, drawing on her knowledge of the area and what went on there during the GDR period. Since S also makes it clear that she finds the area attractive as a potential place to live, it is evident that T's remark has had a face-threatening effect, and both speakers then have to invest considerable conversational effort in order to recover the situation (ibid.: 91–4). The tacit awareness of each other as a member of a different social category is therefore activated only in the process of interaction, but when this occurs it has significant consequences.

In this exchange, the function of local deictic terms such as *hier* (here) and *da* (there) is extended beyond the geographical to the social: 'there' means not only 'in the east' but also 'that place that used to be in the GDR/occupied by the Russian Army / very run down, etc.'. The same can apply to temporal deictics such as 'now' and 'then', so that for an east German, for example, *damals* (then, in those days) may indicate distance not only in time but also in social space: *damals* means a place that no longer exists. Hausendorf (2000a: 88) refers to this as 'social deixis' and it is a potent discursive resource. It can be used in subtle and complex ways to position people in talk, and especially in periods of major social and political change the relationship between the place in which talk occurs and past and present social spaces is often not fixed but subject to manipulation and negotiation (Liebscher 2000: 190).

This is particularly evident in east–west interactions and above all when the two dimensions of eastern speaker/western speaker, on the one hand, and of past/present, on the other, intersect. An example of this can be seen in the communicative process of 'translating' social institutions peculiar to one political system or another, as in this passage from one of the job interviews discussed in 4.2 and 4.3:

Applicant (east German): Ja gut, damals eh nannte sich das Erweiterte Oberschule, und und hier eh mittlerweile heißt das Gymnasium. (Birkner and Kern 2000: 47)

Applicant (east German): Yes, well, in those days it was called *Erweiterte Oberschule*, and here it's now called *Gymnasium*.

The interview is taking place in eastern Germany but the setting is interpreted as a western-dominated one, since *hier* refers to a new social space ('the east which is now part of the west': see also below) by contrast with *damals*, which refers to the GDR—the same geographical territory but a different and now defunct social space. Such 'translations' may not be strictly necessary for the purpose of comprehension (in this instance, it is highly likely that the interviewer would know perfectly well what an *Erweiterte Oberschule* was), but speakers use this conversational move to reposition themselves—however fleetingly—in the same social location as their interlocutor.[8]

Encounters such as these are a good test of Grice's cooperative principle, according to which participants in a conversational exchange will, all else being equal, perform whatever communicative work is necessary to ensure that successful communication is achieved (see Grice 1975). In terms of face, they show how a mutually satisfactory outcome depends on each participant attending to the face needs of the other without neglecting their own, or, from the perspective of social psychology, the degree of convergence required in patterns of talk to achieve attraction without arousing suspicion about your motives. In practice, of course, achieving a mutually satisfactory outcome is not always the aim of all participants, and even when it is, initially stable conversations can be derailed. Furthermore, the potential for derailment is greater when interlocutors are conscious of tensions between social categories to which they may be considered to belong and which condition the interaction. How this potential conflict is managed in individual encounters will depend very much on both short-term and long-term objectives of the participants: what do they want to accomplish with this particular interaction, and how do they want it to contribute to their cumulative image of, and relationship with, the other social category?

In her painstakingly detailed analysis of television talk shows involving east and west Germans, Grit Liebscher (2000) demonstrates the intricacy and the potency of apparently innocuous features of talk such as social deictics, and how difficult it was (and perhaps still is) to avoid the communicative undertow which they mark on the surface. In the following two passages, the communicative conditions are very similar but small linguistic choices are sufficient to construct very different contexts.

Extract 1
Setting: Talk show on MDR (TV station based in Dresden and broadcasting to mainly east German audience), 23 April 1993
Host: Jan Hofer (west German)
Guest: Marijam Agischewa (east German, escaped from GDR in summer 1989)

---

[8] Birkner and Kern (2000: 48) give an illustration of the same thing happening the other way round—a western interviewer translates a west German term into a GDR-specific one for the benefit of an interviewee.

Host: Sie waren eines der großen Talente der DDR und 1989 haben Sie sich dann trotzdem entschlossen (pause) rüberzumachen (pause) sind Sie in den Westen gegangen. Hat Ihnen das gut getan?
Guest: Ja, das hat mir, glaube ich, sehr gut getan.
(Liebscher 2000: 195)

Host: You were one of the big talents in the GDR and then in 1989 you nevertheless decided to [pause] go across [pause] you went (or: moved) to the west. Was that good for you?
Guest: Yes, I think that was very good for me.

Extract 2
Setting: Talk show on MDR, 5 March 1993
Host: Christel Cohn-Vossen (west German)
Guest: Peter Hick (east German, escaped from GDR before 1989)

Host: Aber Sie kommen aus der ex-DDR.
Guest: Richtig.
Host: Sie sind auf ziemlich schwierigem Wege hierhergekommen: Wie war das?
Guest: Ich bin bei irgendeiner Produktion mal abgehauen, weil ich einfach mal die Nase voll hatte.
(Ibid.: 198–9)

Host: But you come from the ex-GDR.
Guest: That's right.
Host: You came here by a rather difficult route: what happened?
Guest: I got away (or: cleared off) during some production or other because I'd just had enough.

In the first extract, the western host describes the eastern guest's move from the GDR to the Federal Republic in the summer of 1989 in terms that an east German would have used (*rübermachen*, go across; *in den Westen gegangen*, go or move to the west). In doing so, he adopts the perspective both of his guest and of his audiences (studio and viewers) and therefore pursues what Scollon and Scollon (1995: 38–41) call an 'involvement strategy'. However, although he lived in the east at the time of the interview, he had not lived there at the time under discussion (1989). So while he positions himself verbally in the social space of the GDR, he uses paralinguistic features (a smile and pauses around *rübermachen*) to mark the deictic expressions as 'quotations' and therefore to acknowledge his outsider status and avoid encroaching on his listeners' 'independence face' (Scollon and Scollon 1995: 38–41).

In the second extract, another western host is again talking to an eastern guest with predominantly eastern audiences. This guest had also left the GDR for the Federal Republic before the *Wende*, but this time the host appears to adopt a different perspective. By saying 'Sie sind . . . hierher gekommen' (You came here), she is overriding the present location (Dresden) and situating her guest's point of arrival either in the social space 'former (pre-1990) Federal Republic'—and thus privileging space over time—or in the social space 'unified Germany understood as an expanded version of the old Federal Republic'. In other words, 'you moved to the place that I, as a *Wessi*, am accustomed to think of as *here'* or else 'you moved to a place that we would now think of as being *here'*. Either way, by implicitly importing a western perspective, the host is—perhaps unwittingly—posing a threat to her listeners' face.

In the final extract, the same linguistic signs occur but this time with an overtly conflictual force:

Extract 3
Setting: Talk show on N3 (west German TV station with mixed western and eastern audience), 25 August 1995
Huber: Ellis Huber, west German President of the Ärztekammer (Medical Board) Berlin
Grunert: Horst Grunert, former GDR Ambassador

Huber: Dann löst doch endlich die PDS auf und kommt hier an.
Grunert: Zu Ihnen, meinen Sie?
Huber: Nein zu—in dieses Land.

Huber: Well then, dissolve the PDS and come here.
Grunert: To you, you mean?
Huber: No, to—to this country.

The west German, Huber, makes the dissolving of the PDS (the successor party to the SED) a condition for the east Germans' 'arrival' in the new unified Germany. However, he is careful to avoid the explicit formulation of the 'you–we' dichotomy which Grunert seems to see as the implied reference and which would foreground too strongly the idea that *we* (westerners) are already in the new social space of unified Germany ahead of *you* (easterners).

The first passage from Liebscher's material shows that accommodation is possible and that when westerners are willing to make the communicative effort easterners can be relieved of the onus of being required to justify themselves. However, the historical circumstances have dictated that 'eastern' is the marked origin (against 'western' as the unmarked norm), and east Germans bear a double burden of identification: the challenge from westerners to locate themselves in relation to their past and to the present, and the internal interrogation of their own sense of belonging. This social imbalance is manifested in asymmetrical communicative situations, where it is expected

daß die eine Seite ständig erzählt und die andere einordnet, bzw.—noch deutlicher—daß die eine Seite erwartet, daß die andere sich mit ihren Erzählungen sozusagen pflegeleicht verhält und sich selbst, erzählend, einordnet. (Pätzold and Pätzold 1995: 253, footnote 4)

that one side constantly tells stories and the other categorizes, or—even more clearly—that one side expects the other to tell its stories in a way that is, so to speak, easy to handle and, in telling its stories, to categorize itself.

In this context, it again becomes clear that problems which occur in east–west communication are not (necessarily) communicative problems. They arise not as a result of different uses of language—let alone as a result of different linguistic forms—but because within specific contexts of interaction the two perspectives are not equally valued: the expectations built into the framework of the interaction give preference to the western perspective, so that eastern speakers have to work harder to have their perspective acknowledged.

This is particularly transparent in openly confrontational contexts such as the television interview between the west German presenter and the east German writer discussed briefly in 5.2. It is also designed in to apparently less personal, more objective scenarios such as the television debate analysed by Ingwer Paul (1995, 2000*a*). In this programme (broadcast in August 1992), one east German and five west German commentators have been invited to discuss the state of the German economy, with the specific issue of measures to revive and restructure the eastern economy ('Aufschwung Ost') identified as a particular problem to be addressed. From the outset, the potential not only for differences of opinion— without which there would be no programme—between participants representing different political interests and presented, for example, as 'government minister', 'bank director', 'alternative economist', and 'trade union official', but also for conflict along social lines, since the sole east German participant is the only one to be identified in terms of where he comes from.

At first, this asymmetry remains tacit and the potential for conflict is contained for a time by the 'rules' of the genre, according to which the host acts as presiding umpire ensuring a fair distribution of conversational rights (number and length of turns, for example). In other words, a 'working consensus' (Paul 2000*a*: 119, following Goffman 1963) is established, within which participants can agree to disagree without provoking a breakdown or collapse in communication. However, the latent conflict proves too explosive to be subdued for long, and the working consensus is disrupted by the east German, Wagner, interrupting the west German government minister, Möllemann, and seizing the floor.

Möllemann: Es wird sich ein einheitlicher Wirtschaftsstandort Deutschland...nur entwickeln können, wenn es uns gelingt, eine Art neuen Konsens zur Sicherung unserer Zukunft des Standorts Deutschland zu bilden, der weit übergreifend sein muß, über Regierung und über Tarifpartner hinaus.... Ich glaube, wir brauchen die Bündelung der Kräfte, und das ist möglich, was in den letzten Tagn...
Wagner: (schnell, erregt) Aber in der Zwischenzeit ändern wir erst mal das Grundgesetz Artikel drei, daß alle Menschen vorm Gesetz gleich sind, denn wir ham ja jetz' die Ostgleichen und wir ham die Westgleichen, und das für viele viele Jahre. Man kann doch nun hier nicht mehr davon sprechen, daß wir unter den gleichen Verhältnissen leben. Ich mein', ich muß mich jetzt einfach mal einmischen Herr Böhme [der Moderator], denn ich bin ja in dieser erlauchten Runde der einzige, der hier bißchen die ostdeutschen äh Interessen vertritt.... (Paul 2000*a*: 143)

Möllemann: A unified 'business location Germany' will only be able to develop if we succeed in forming a kind of new consensus on securing the future of 'location Germany'

which must go way beyond government and both sides of industry.... I think we need to consolidate the various forces, and that is possible, what has recently...
Wagner: [quickly, agitated] But in the meantime we're changing Article 3 of the Constitution, that everyone is equal in the eyes of the law, because now we've got the eastern equals and the western equals, and that will be the case for many many years. You really can't say any more that we're living under the same conditions. I mean I just have to butt in here Herr Böhme [the presenter] because I'm the only one in this illustrious panel who represents east German interests a bit.

Wagner acknowledges that in doing this he has flouted the rules, but justifies his conversationally 'illegitimate' behaviour on the grounds that he is the only participant who can 'legitimately' represent eastern interests. This claim is coupled with an accusation that the other participants are denying east Germans their constitutional right to equality and with an implicit insult ('*diese erlauchte Runde*', this illustrious panel).

Taken together, these elements of Wagner's behaviour represent a challenge to what Paul (2000*a*: 127) calls the western 'ethos' of the debate. The composition of the panel makes it clear that Wagner has been invited to occupy the subject position of subordinate 'minority representative', whose voice has a correspondingly minor role in the discussion in relation to those of the western 'experts'. The debate on the economy is a 'discourse within a discourse', in both of which he is relatively powerless: the power behind the 'economy discourse' lies with the western political and social establishment (government, industry, bankers, academics), and the power behind the 'talk show discourse' lies with the western media establishment. Wagner therefore seems to see himself as doubly disabled: first, his expert status as someone experiencing at first hand the conditions under discussion is not recognized, or at best is attributed less weight than the theoretical expertise of the west Germans (see also the patronizing 'advice' of another participant, ibid.: 133), and secondly, he can assert his own authority only by violating the conventions of the genre (and thereby, moreover, running the risk of confirming the *Jammerossi* stereotype—see 5.2).

The discursive power to claim expertise in terms of relevant social knowledge and to deny it to others both depends on and reinforces social inequality. From his position of social dominance, the president of the German industry confederation, Heinrich Weiß, is able to 'correct' Wagner's characterization of the social situation and advise him, in a familiar refrain, 'Wohlstand muß man sich auch erarbeiten' (prosperity has to be worked for—from a later part of the debate, not transcribed here), and by asserting his qualification to 'know' this, he is reasserting his social superiority. Furthermore, the more secure one party is in possession of this power, the less forcefully it needs to be deployed: Weiß couches his remarks in overtly considerate and conciliatory terms ('*ich möchte Sie herzlich bitten,...*', I would very much like to ask you to...; '*ich gebe zu,...*', I admit/concede...).

As we have seen on a number of occasions, the subject Weiß touches on here—working practices, material prosperity, and the relationship between the two—has been one of the most sensitive and contentious issues in the unfolding relationships between east and west Germans since 1990. In particular, the common western prejudice that east Germans 'don't know how to work', and the equally strongly held counter-contention amongst easterners that 'we had to work hard too', constitute a major impediment to mutual acceptance. This tension often operates insidiously below the level of the openly expressed prejudices I discussed in 5.2, through the more subtle mechanisms of discursive practices which categorize and situate individuals in social groups and ascribe characteristics to them without making overt criticisms. Consider, for example, the delicate communicative manoeuvres in the following passage:

Job centre representative (west German):...und dat muß ich den Frauen in aller Deutlichkeit sagen, weil eigentlich gerade hier im Osten die Frauen ja auch immer so gearbeitet haben. Aber wenn Kinder dahinterstandn oder Familie, dann hattn sie soziale Vorteile, und die haben wir jetzt nicht mehr, und diese sozialen Vorteile, die kann ich dann auch nich' mehr in Anspruch nehmen, un' deswegen würd' ich sie/Sie gerne so 'n bißchen (?hüten) davor, daß sie/Sie das immer in den Vordergrund stellen, wenn sie/Sie arbeiten wollen, und wenn sie/Sie darauf pochen, daß sie/Sie gleichberechtigt werden wollen. (Hausendorf 1997: 138)

...and I must say that to the women very clearly because precisely here in the east women have always worked like that. But when there were children or family involved, then they had social benefits and we don't have them any more, and these social benefits, I can't claim them any more and so I'd warn them/you against emphasizing that all the time, if they/you want to work, and if they/you keep insisting that they/you want to have equal rights.

This extract is taken from the early part of a talk by a west German job centre representative to a group of long-term unemployed east German women. She has just emphasized the need to be punctual and to be committed to their work. In this passage, she develops an instructional, 'moralizing' discourse, but rather than addressing her message explicitly to her audience, she directs it at a social category—'eastern women'—and it is left up to them to transfer the reference to themselves. She achieves this by exploiting the ambiguity of the homophonous personal pronouns *sie* (= they) and *Sie* (= you): the first instance seems clearly to refer back to 'die Frauen hier im Osten' (i.e. 'they'), but the remaining ones could equally well refer to the women in the room (i.e. 'you'). At the same time, she positions herself in a relationship of apparent solidarity with the 'women in the east' by using the first person forms *ich* (I) and *wir* (we) in contexts that cannot strictly apply to her as a west German ('die [= soziale Vorteile] haben wir jetzt *nicht mehr*', we don't have those social benefits *any more*; 'die kann ich auch *nicht mehr* in Anspruch nehmen', I can't claim them *any more*). She then slips into a different position with the next *ich*, which is explicitly in contrast with *sie/Sie* and which is the voice of authority.

What seems to be common to west Germans in such episodes is the certainty of being able to speak with conviction, confident that their position is legitimized by the unquestionable superiority of 'their' social and political system. They speak with eloquence, in the sense in which I used the term in Chapter 3. They present what they (feel they can) take for granted, since they have not had occasion to subject their assumptions to scrutiny. East Germans, on the other hand, enter encounters with their western compatriots under different conditions. What they may have taken for granted in the past has now been put in doubt, which means that in order to find their bearings they have to reflect on and analyse their assumptions, and in order to keep a secure hold on what they have brought with them from their past lives they find themselves having to make a case.

To the extent that social identities are, or become, relevant in an east–west encounter, both parties will have some 'image work' to do, but creating a positive self-image will require a greater communicative effort from easterners, since their identities were generated within the moral context of a society that has collapsed and which their interlocutors will not have the opportunity to experience for themselves at first hand. Furthermore, the process often entails dealing with negative handed-down images, which is as likely to confirm prejudices as to dismantle them (see Dittmar and Bredel 1999: 129 ff., and below).

This asymmetry of communicative conditions offers an unpromising prospect for attempts to build well-balanced and tolerant relationships, and even well-intentioned efforts can easily go awry. For example, a conversation (recorded and analysed in 1993 by Ricarda Wolf) between women from east and west, with the explicit purpose of exchanging information and breaking down prejudices, becomes problematic when the initial identification of the participants on the basis of individual occupations (mother, teacher, social worker, etc.) is supplanted by a reformation of the twelve speakers into two groups—east and west: 'Die Teilnehmerinnen "konstruieren" sich interaktiv um' (the participants 'reconstruct themselves' in interaction) (Wolf 1995: 207). Since stereotypical images of these groups were, especially at that time, part of a common store of resources for interpreting experience, it is not surprising that they surface even in a setting designed to overcome them. The following passage shows how easily under such circumstances the very mention of a negative image can divert a conversation from a harmonious course.[9]

C *(west German):* Ick habe nämlich ein, ein dickes Vorurteil von mir, mit dem ick hier sitze, is: Kreativität war nich' jefragt. Dit hör ick jetzt irgendwo, ich weeß nich'...
G *(east German):* Ich ich war mein Leben lang, kann ich behaupten, eigentlich kreativ, und ich kann es, ich kam damit nich' durch,... ich war richtig tot am Schluß.
C: Eben, also et gibt doch nicht...'ne Wand, die sacht, da sind die kreativen Menschen und da nich',...

---

[9] In this particular case, my simplification of the original transcript removes some telling details which are necessary to demonstrate fully the force of Wolf's analysis. However, I hope that the reduced version is adequate for the present purposes.

G: Nein, aber das war's ja eben, daran haben wir uns zum größten Teil totgelaufen, so daß sich die meisten sachten, ich fang's doch erst gar nich' an, ich setz' mich, ich bau' mir meine Datsche.... (Wolf 1995: 208–9)

C (west German): You see, I've got a, I'm sitting here with a big prejudice: there was no demand for creativity. I've heard that somewhere, I don't know...
G (east German): My whole life, I can say, I was creative, and I can, that wasn't enough to get me through,...I was completely dead by the end.
C: Exactly, so there isn't...a simple dividing line, with the creative people here and not there,...
G: No, but that was just it, that's what really ground us down, so that most people said, I'm not even going to try, I'm just going to settle down and build my dacha.

C acknowledges that the proposition 'creativity was not required' (in the GDR) is a prejudice that she is aware of and that she has brought with her into the discussion, and she also indicates her doubts about its validity ('*ich weeß nich*'...', I don't know...). Before she can proceed further, however, G takes the floor, apparently to contradict the proposition. Her rebuttal suggests that she has interpreted it not only as a critique of the GDR system, but also (in spite of C's reassurance that you cannot say 'one group is creative and the other is not') as an implied slur on individual east Germans. In defending herself against this accusation, G falls into what Wolf (1995: 210) calls 'die Falle der Selbstverortungsaufgabe' (the trap of taking on the job of positioning yourself): she seeks to salvage her own reputation but this is achieved at the expense of the 'majority', who—in her account—simply gave up. Feeling obliged to justify herself, she constitutes herself as an exception that appears to confirm the stereotype.

G's reconstruction of 'creativity' as a quantitative concept (meaning 'industriousness' rather than 'inventiveness') is subsequently taken up by another *west* German participant (M), who relates at length how 'creative' she had to be to juggle her various roles as businesswoman, housewife, and mother in an 'eighteen-hour day'. Unlike G, M uses her heroic self-presentation as evidence of a general model of behaviour in 'her' society ('ich denke schon, daß wir mehr kreativ sein konnten, mußten', I certainly think that we were able to be more creative, we had to be) and contrasts this with the 'less demanding' life in the GDR ('das war ja viel besser im Osten gelöst, da war man ja versorgt', that was dealt with much better in the east, you were looked after there).

The dynamics of this interactively generated pair of complementary images—west Germans had/have to be creative, i.e. work hard; east Germans were not expected to be creative, i.e. did not have to work hard—is completed by another *east* German woman's attempt to refute M's construction of easterners as less industrious.

W *(east German):*...Ich fahre dort gerne hin [to the west German village where her son is living], ich freue mich schon auf die nächste Begegnung, ja weil alle Leute in diesem kleinen Dorf, und die wenigsten hatten Ostverbindungen, und sie haben uns mit offenen Armen dort aufgenommen, hart arbeiten, zum Teil haben zwei Berufe, äh arbeiten acht Stunden im Betrieb, arbeiten nebenbei, äh und das hat dort mein Sohn getan, als er dahinkam, und deshalb war der sofort in diesem Ort integriert, ja die habn jesacht, wenn dein Mario anders reagiert hätte und versucht hätte, hier sich durchzuschlauchen,... sich auf die faule Haut zu legen, wäre der hier nicht so anerkannt gewesen, und das find' ich in Ordnung, solln se mehr haben, wenn se mehr gearbeitet haben. (Ibid.: 226–7)

I like going there [to the west German village where her son is living], I'm looking forward already to our next meeting, because everyone in that little village works hard—and very few of them had any connections with the east, and they welcomed us with open arms— some of them have two jobs, work eight hours in the factory and then do another job, that's what my son did when he went there, and that's why he was integrated there straight away, in fact they said if your Mario had reacted differently and had tried to scrounge his way through here,... to just lounge around doing nothing, he wouldn't have been so well accepted, and I think that's right, why shouldn't they have more if they've worked more.

Like G, W paints a picture of a hard-working easterner (her son), but the yardstick by which his excellent behaviour is measured in her presentation is his acceptance by the phenomenally diligent west German host community in which he now lives. Her final remark in this passage confirms that she has bought into the west German value system, and so her narrative ultimately has a stabilizing rather than a disruptive effect on the stereotype that has evolved in the course of the discussion.

There is, of course, nothing inevitable about what occurs in these exchanges, and they should not be read as a 'typical' outcome of east–west encounters. I have dwelt on them at some length here because they seem to me to show two things exceptionally clearly; first, what *can* happen as a result of the one-sided pressure on east Germans to position themselves in their new social and communicative environment, and secondly, the hegemonic effects of dominant western discourses on everyday interactions. The pervasiveness and durability of these phenomena depend in large measure on the ways in which the ideas that underpin them are circulated through media sources of all kinds and in private and public forums from breakfast table through bus stop to classroom, work place, and pub. That different responses are possible, that ideological pressure to conform to dominant values can be resisted, is nowhere more transparent than in advertising discourse, the site where public meets private most directly.

For western producers of consumer goods, unification represented not a problem but an opportunity, the east German population a potentially lucrative market—and one that could be developed relatively easily and cheaply, since it would be possible to appeal to it through common traditions and a common language. Early signs seemed to confirm that easterners would be docile consumers with a pent-up demand for western goods, so that they would be both desperate to conform to western norms of consumption and 'obedient' in adjusting to western discourses of consumption. However, these assumptions had to be revised quite rapidly, when the initial appetite for the 'new' had been satisfied and market research revealed a new demand for eastern products: by late 1991, nearly three quarters of east German households claimed to prefer them (Läzer 1996a: 213) and newspapers reported a 'more discriminating' approach to buying, resulting in renewed interest in 'local' products (Gläser 1992: 192). In many cases, of course, the *Ostprodukte* (eastern products) demanded by eastern consumers were now actually produced and marketed by western firms which had taken over the eastern brands—so it would seem that eastern consumers were motivated less by loyalty to eastern businesses than by an aspiration to cultivate an eastern identity, for which the brand was more important than the ownership.

Furthermore, not only were western products treated more sceptically, but western advertising was considered inappropriate and irritating. Advertising strategists had to recognize that the eastern market was as complex and internally differentiated as the western one (Kelly-Holmes 2000: 96), but some argued—and continue to argue—that there were two fundamentally different 'consumer communities' in east and west, which demanded to be spoken to in their own way (see Shethar forthcoming on the idea of 'Dolmetscher der Träume', interpreters of dreams).[10] The east German petrol company MINOL, for example, declared in its 1993 advertising: 'Uns finden Sie fast überall, wir sind Ostmeister im Modernisieren und sprechen die Sprache unserer Kunden' (You'll find us almost everywhere, we are the eastern masters of modernization and we speak our customers' language) (Läzer 1996a: 216). In this context, the commonplace sales pitch 'we speak your language' clearly takes on extra resonance.

However, constructing an 'acceptable' marketing strategy for the eastern market posed a problem. For a short while, it was possible to offer a sense of stability and security in turbulent and uncertain times through the revival of familiar brands from the popular perspective that 'things weren't all bad in the old days'. But this reassuring *Ostalgie* could only be short-lived and would not have universal appeal across all the segments of the east German market. As in personal interaction, the dilemma was how to (re)construct a positive eastern image that neither painted the recent past in a falsely rosy glow nor devalued it. Läzer (1996a: 214–15) cites two examples of marketers' attempts to tread this fine line. In the first, a kitchen equipment manufacturer (FORON) implicitly acknowledges the demands and opportunities in the new market context, while resolutely affirming that its commitment to quality and careful workmanship has always been its hallmark:

Wir wissen, was wir können. Aber erst jetzt können wir endlich zeigen, was wirklich in uns steckt. Natürlich war nicht alles schlecht, was wir früher gemacht haben. Aber es gibt nichts, was man nicht noch verbessern kann. Das haben wir getan. Mit neuem Schwung

[10] This contrasts with earlier assumptions that advertising in the east simply needed to be adapted to the western 'model'. Schmider (1990: 7), for example, says that his comparative study of eastern and western advertising, conducted before the *Wende*, 'dient ... ostdeutschen Werbern als schnelle Hilfe zur Angleichung an den westdeutschen Standard' (serves as a rapid means of assisting eastern advertisers to adapt to the west German standard).

und neuen Ideen, aber mit der alten Liebe zu hoher Qualität und sorgfältiger Arbeit haben wir unsere Kühlschränke, Waschmaschinen und Herde gründlich verbessert. Erstklassige Verarbeitung, überaus faire Preise und ein zuverlässiger Kundendienst: das ist die neue Foron.

We know what we can do. But now we're finally able to show what we're really made of. Of course, not everything we used to make was bad. But there's nothing that can't be made even better. That's what we've done. With new energy and new ideas, but with our old love of high quality and careful work, we have thoroughly improved our refrigerators, washing machines, and cookers. First-class workmanship, extremely fair prices, and reliable customer service: that's the new Foron.

In the second text, an advertisement promoting the lignite industry, the sensitive subject of hard work is highlighted once again, this time insisting that the miner in the picture can be proud of his past achievements but can also adapt to the demands of the new economy:

Er hat allen Grund, selbstbewußt zu sein. Er hat sich nie gedrückt vor Arbeit und Verantwortung. Das brachte ihm früher den Verdienst ein, sich Held der Winterschlacht[11] nennen zu dürfen. Doch heute ist nicht mehr Quantität oberstes Gebot, sondern Qualität. Und die kann nur er garantieren.

He has every reason to be self-assured. He has never shirked either work or responsibility. In the past, that earned him the right to call himself 'hero of the winter battle'. But today the top priority is no longer quantity, but quality. And only he can guarantee that.

Advertisers responded to this dilemma in different ways, but the profound importance of place—especially in the guise of the German folk tradition of *Heimat*—established itself as the common denominator in selling the east to the east. For example, a crispbread produced near Magdeburg in Sachsen-Anhalt was sold as 'ein knackiges Stück Heimat' (a crunchy piece of *Heimat*), and a radio advertisement for *Freiberger Pils*, a popular beer brewed in Saxony, featured a domestic dialogue in Saxon dialect (Gläser 1992: 193, 206). *Heimat* suggests more than a mere geographical locality though, it implies a real attachment to the soil (see Bastian 1995, Boa and Palfreyman 2000). Food and drink in particular have therefore often been identified closely with place, and consumption of particular brands is portrayed not just as a matter of taste but as a cultural practice and a declaration of belonging. The advertising for one east German beer—*Glückauf Bier*, brewed in the Erzgebirge (in Saxony, on the border with the Czech Republic)—is targeted at a very specific market, as the slogans depend for their effect on local knowledge: for example, 'Wo mit Glückauf gegrüßt wird, wird auch *Glückauf* getrunken' (Where they say 'Glückauf', they drink *Glückauf*) (Kelly-Holmes 2000: 99; 'Glückauf' is a form of greeting used by miners in the region). Another brewery, in Görlitz on the Polish border, combined the standard sense of

[11] A term used in the GDR to refer to the 'battle' to mine brown coal under difficult winter conditions.

'eastness' as location and the new sense of a mark of quality in its campaign: 'Landkron—aus der östlichsten Privatbrauerei Deutschlands' (*Landkron*—from Germany's most eastern private brewery) (Läzer 1996*a*: 221).

The underlying theme of all these campaigns is that, with familiar products produced on eastern territory, 'you know where you are'—both literally and metaphorically. Whether the appeal was directed at a local or at a regional market, the common project was to reinvest 'eastness' with positive values and to reconnect it with cultural traditions reaching back beyond the GDR period. The emphasis was on asserting that 'here' had not been divested of its historical and social content—after all, 'here' as the site of past and present conflicts and contradictions, and as the product, imperfect though it was, of two generations of social struggle, was where millions of east Germans had chosen to stay in 1989. In this context, in the market created by those who had declared 'wir bleiben hier' (we're staying here; see 3.3), the spare and simple slogan of yet another beer—'Berliner Pilsener, das Bier von hier' (Berliner Pilsener, the beer from here)—opens up a whole range of connotations, but there is clearly a confidence that only positive ones will be selected. *Ostalgie* has been replaced by *Ostimismus*, a sense of confidence in eastern identities.[12]

The core value for credibility in this market is encapsulated in the term *bodenständig*, which carries the sense of both 'long-established (on this territory)' and of 'straightforward, uncomplicated, down-to-earth'. The significance of this was not lost on political strategists either, as Ruth Geier (1996) shows in her analysis of the 1994 general election campaign. Opposition Social Democrats, in particular, recognized that incumbent Chancellor Helmut Kohl still had sufficient credit as the architect of unification to be difficult to dislodge, and their candidate, west German Rudolf Scharping, could only hope to succeed amongst eastern voters if he could be sold as 'one of us'. Accordingly, the visual imagery in advertisements placed him alongside well-known eastern Social Democrat politicians, one of whom (Regine Hildebrandt) supplied the complementary textual validation of his candidacy:

Mit Rudolf Scharping tritt jetzt ein Mann an, der in Deutschland für mehr Gerechtigkeit sorgen will. Ich kenne ihn, ich vertraue ihm und ich traue ihm zu, unser Land nun wirklich zu vereinen.... Er schwafelt nicht, er packt an. Nutzen wir die Chance. Er ist einer für uns. (Geier 1996: 241)

With Rudolf Scharping, a man has now stepped into the ring who wants to see to it that there is more justice in Germany. I know him, I trust him, and I believe he is capable of really uniting our country.... He doesn't waffle, he gets stuck in. Let's take this opportunity. He's the one for us.

He may not be an easterner, but he has the trust of a prominent easterner, he has positive 'eastern' qualities ('*er schwafelt nicht, er packt an*', he doesn't waffle, he gets stuck in), and so he is 'the one for us'.

---

[12] For a detailed analysis of advertising for eastern products in the 1990s, see Hennecke (1999).

By the end of the first decade of the politically unified society, writers of both consumer and political advertising campaigns had come to realize that there were still—indeed, increasingly—two distinct audiences that they had to address. They had also had to acknowledge that the eastern consumer-voter was neither naïve nor unsophisticated but critical and sceptical. The success of a campaign therefore depended on placing the 'product' (whether washing powder or political party) in the respective audiences' social and historical domain. Eastness and westness did not need to be referred to explicitly, but text producers understood that these categories existed in the minds of their target readerships and that they had a 'shape' which could be invoked but also developed.

In this section, I have explored some of the ways in which eastern and western identities have been proposed, negotiated, and contested in the process of interaction between east and west Germans since the *Wende*. Especially in the early years following unification, eastness and westness as social categories—however diffuse and ill-defined—were often perceived to be sufficiently significant and troubling to be foregrounded in many interpersonal encounters in both public and private contexts. Even where this aspect of individual social identities was not obviously relevant to the conduct of such interactions, it seemed to lurk just below the surface of social intercourse. The first decade of the supposedly unified German speech community witnessed a great deal of uncomfortable discursive manoeuvring amongst participants, as east Germans above all were challenged to (re)locate themselves in relation to their past and to their present circumstances. At the same time, this process of relocation represented an opportunity for discovery and for self-discovery, a chance to articulate what east and west might mean or might come to mean in the future.

6

Conclusions

Although the political division of Germany into east and west after the Second World War was unprecedented, as was the conception of a major linguistic divide along this axis, both political disunity and the role of language as a political factor in the shaping of German identities were not: the *questione della lingua* had repeatedly surfaced in different guises in connection with the question of nationhood throughout the history of modern Germany. Moreover, the tension between the idea of 'the German language' as a cultural constant and the fact of continuous linguistic change is just as old, and after 1945 it formed the basis of the ideological contestation of the German cultural heritage during the Cold War, as well as underlying the independent development of the study of 'language in society' in the GDR and in the Federal Republic. These discursive struggles over language and the evolution of different patterns of language use were an integral part of the historical process of separate social and political development in the two German societies. The discrete trajectories of these two societies continued to be a source of tension and then of conflict when political unification forced the underlying disunity of the 'German people' to the surface, and the collision between political aspirations of harmony on the one hand and discordant social realities on the other revealed itself very palpably in the clash between the supposedly unifying impulse of the 'common language' and the tenacity of perceived sociolinguistic difference.

The founding of the Federal Republic and of the GDR represented the beginning of two parallel experiments in seeking a solution to the German question in the new era. Part of this process was the development of distinct political discourses. But unlike in the Federal Republic, political conditions in the GDR both favoured and depended on the consistent propagation and elaboration of a single discourse that monopolized the public sphere and simultaneously permeated many domains of everyday life. The political aim was not to create a separate language—'GDR German' was neither an objective nor a reality—but to harness the communicative potential of language to realize the objective of building a cohesive social body grounded in a shared set of moral values and political principles, a project in which the *German* language was ultimately irrelevant. However, this discursive thoroughness in the end contributed to the collapse of the social and political enterprise of the GDR, and the people's 'special relationship' with language equipped them with more flexibility and resourcefulness than had been imagined by western observers: while complex economic and political factors were what made the position of the SED leadership unsustainable in the context of global political conditions in 1989, the *Wende*, when it came, was enacted as a sequence of intersecting speech events—the chanting of slogans and the waving of placards at demonstrations, public speeches by Party leaders, intellectuals, and ordinary people alike, interviews, press conferences, televised talks to the nation.

After the *Wende*, the importance of language did not diminish but shifted onto new territory. While the emphasis had previously been on the conflictual relationship between competing political systems, the focus now was on the painful consequences of attempts to merge two societies. Experience of life and of language had been different in many ways in the GDR and the Federal Republic, but for most people the nature of the contrast remained largely abstract until the opening of the borders. Contact with the 'other' Germans confirmed the possibility of communication, but easterners were confronted with linguistic and communicative challenges and required to adapt since westerners were, in general, unwilling to make this effort. As social difference re-emerged as a potent force quite soon after the *Wende*, easily identifiable measures of difference were sought and once again language seemed one of the most readily available.

What began to develop, quite early, was an initially diffuse consciousness of categorical difference between east and west. Social encounters between easterners and westerners frequently served as opportunities to flesh out these competing identities: 'being different' was perceived as being manifested through 'talking different'. At the same time, stereotypes were constructed in the course of interaction and through public discourses, so that difference was not brought out solely in forms of language or in talk about language, but also through the conduct of linguistic and communicative activities in which east and west were produced and reproduced as essential categories.

So with the formal act of unification on 3 October 1990, the political opposition 'GDR versus Federal Republic' was dissolved but the social opposition 'east versus west' remained. The history of the decade that followed was marked by the parallel but contradictory processes of harmonizing political and economic structures on the one hand and substantiating and elaborating social differences on the other. What began as simple generic labels for a one-dimensional contrast to designate belonging to one 'camp' or another—*Ossi* and *Wessi*—developed in the course of the 1990s into complex social categories, heavily laden with evaluative characteristics subsumed in the concepts of *Ossizität* and *Wessizität*. We could dismiss this familiar contrast as a crude generalization or stereotype, as an ephemeral product of the destabilized social conditions following the *Wende*. But as Jürgen Streeck (1995: 434) mischievously suggests: 'Wie an anderen dichotomen Menschenklassifikationen (z.B. Schwarz/Weiß oder Abendland/Morgenland) besticht an dem Kategorienpaar Ossi/Wessi seine einfache, aber perfekte poetische Konstruktion. Das Paar ist zu schön, um nicht zuzutreffen.' (As with other ways of classifying people in terms of dichotomies—e.g. Black–White or Occident–Orient—the categorical pair *Ossi–Wessi* is almost irresistible in its simple but perfect poetic construction. The pair is too beautiful not to be true.) Indeed, Margot Heinemann (1995: 392) argues that in early encounters between east and west

Germans after the *Wende,* eastness and westness came to constitute first-order criteria of identification, more significant than occupation, age, or gender. Even
today, many Germans' conviction of belonging to discrete social traditions does
not appear to have diminished.

Is it possible, then, from an analytical perspective to retain the intuitively satis-
fying but broad distinction between east and west, while distinguishing groups
within these populations that are more narrowly specified inter alia in terms of
linguistic and communicative practices? Unlike the pair GDR vs Federal Republic,
Ossi vs *Wessi* constitute, as Streeck suggests, a dichotomy rather than merely an
opposition: 'Federal Republic', for example, could also stand in opposition to
'France' or 'Japan', and has meaning independently of these oppositions, but *Ossi*
and *Wessi* have meaning only in relation to each other and as sub-categories of the
larger entity 'German'. Therefore, they will presumably continue in use only so
long as they represent a perceived need to distinguish between two significantly
different social groups. However, the social groups represented by the *Ossi–Wessi*
dichotomy are global categories constituted by social origins, family history, and
personal experiences, with which people identify in a general way, but they are too
ill-defined to act as analytical categories to which personal or social characteristics can be attributed and of which in turn particular linguistic and communicative practices are surface markers.

A more differentiated analysis may be possible through the more highly specified
clustering of individuals within 'interpretative prototypes' in terms of characteristic
responses to their experiences as easterners or westerners in unified Germany. We
have already seen this approach used in relation to self-representation (Wolf 1995),
accommodation and social networks (Barden 2000), speech styles (Elspaß 2000),
and language attitudes (Schmidt-Regener 1998) (see Chapters 4 and 5), while
Heinemann (1995: 393), for example, proposes a range of prototypical interaction
patterns rather than speakers. Such prototypes may offer a means of constructing
a relatively refined descriptive categorization of groups within the broad populations 'east' and 'west', but this still does not help us towards an explanation of communicative dissonance—what Ingwer Paul (2000*b*) calls 'Verständigung ohne
Verstehen' (communication without understanding).

Again, we have seen that this may be attributable to many causes, and the search
for a single overriding explanation risks reducing a complex phenomenon to a
caricature (see Fritze 1996: 921). In the early stages of contact, for example, inadequate knowledge of the respective social systems undoubtedly contributed to
problems of comprehension, but while this may have been manifested linguistically it was typically rooted in different social experience, and as Paul (2000*b*) and
Hellmann (1998) show (with the examples of the complex connotations of the
terms *Aufbau Ost* and *Reisekader* respectively), the degree of ignorance amongst
west Germans about the life experiences of their eastern compatriots was—and
arguably still is—at least as great as the converse, even though far less attention
has been paid to this by researchers. Moreover, communicative difficulties might

be attributed to exaggerated expectations of understanding (Fraas 1994: 88) but also, conversely, to the anticipation of incomprehension: there are none so deaf as those that will not hear.

Auer and Hausendorf (2000*b*) also emphasize the importance of context as the site where linguistic and communicative differences can be linked with language users' biographical or cultural origins, both synchronically in terms of difference and diachronically in terms of change. However, virtually all of the research that has been conducted on actual language use since the *Wende* has been based on relatively formal and/or public contexts (interviews, radio phone-ins, television talk shows, advice sessions), which impose their own constraints on the kinds of choices speakers make, so that even now relatively little can be said with any certainty about similarities and differences in the everyday, casual speech of east and west Germans. Furthermore, in many of these contexts the participants are pitched against each other in circumstances that carry the potential for conflict and in some cases conflict is positively designed into the context. This was especially true in the early years after the *Wende*, when, as Claudia Fraas (1994: 89) points out, east–west encounters constituted 'eine von vorn herein emotional sehr aufgeladene Kommunikationssituation' (a communication situation that was highly emotionally charged from the outset). In these situations, participants' roles are also almost always allocated on the same basis, with the western speaker occupying the dominant position of interrogator or expert and the eastern speaker that of the subject or novice. The construction of the communicative encounter and the distribution of roles inevitably condition the participants' behaviours, and where their otherness is known and either foregrounded from the outset or made relevant in the course of the interaction, difference may be more an artefact of the situation than a consequence of a fundamental opposition between the two parties.

There is therefore a risk of exaggerating the extent of communicative dissonance by focusing on particular contexts in which difference is at least anticipated and in many cases brought about as a consequence of the setting or the way in which the interaction is staged. As both Manfred Hellmann (1997*b*) and Wolfdietrich Hartung (forthcoming) point out, our perception of difference is selective: speakers tend to notice only those (relatively few) things that are different or problematic to them, not the many things that present no difficulties to either party, and what strikes an observer in either west or east as noteworthy in the language use of the other may not seem at all remarkable to that other.[1]

Intergroup differences are easier to accommodate where the social groups concerned do not perceive grounds for conflict or antagonism between them. Where a

---

[1] An example might be the use of first person plural pronouns *wir* (we) and *unser* (our) in political texts, which is often considered to have been a dominant characteristic of official GDR discourse and a potential marker of 'eastness' in formal usage after the *Wende* (see 3.1 and 4.3) but which east Germans consider no less typical of west German political discourse (see again Hartung forthcoming). Fleischer (2001) offers a comparative empirical analysis of pronoun usage in the *Leipziger Volkszeitung* before, during, and after the *Wende*.

conflict of interests does exist, it may be rationalized by exaggerating signs of allegedly inherent behavioural contrasts, which then serve as clear boundary markers. As Antos and Richter (2000: 77) rightly warn: 'Der ökonomische und soziale Wettbewerb zwischen Ost und West könnte durchaus dazu führen, dass durch die Fokussierung und Überbetonung von angeblichen Sprachunterschieden eine Stabilisierung von Ingroup-Outgroup-Differenzen versucht wird' (The economic and social competition between east and west could well lead to an attempt to stabilize differences between ingroup and outgroup by focusing on and over-emphasizing supposed linguistic differences). But the emphasis in this explanation of the source of continued conflict lies less in the psychological mechanisms of group differentiation than in the social origins of the conflict. As Woolard and Schieffelin (1994: 61) argue, in a passage I referred to earlier (see 4.4), 'language varieties that are regularly associated with (and thus index) particular speakers are often revalorized—or misrecognized—not just as symbols of group identity, but as emblems of political allegiance or of social, intellectual, or moral worth'. This is the process that Irvine and Gal (2000: 37) refer to as 'iconization', whereby 'linguistic features that index social groups or activities appear to be iconic representations of them', and which they see as one of the key processes by which 'people construct ideological representations of linguistic differences'. The identification of these processes as ideological is important, because it exposes the constructed nature of what becomes represented as natural or inherent properties of language use or behaviour: it 'reminds us that the cultural conceptions we study are partial, contestable and contested, and interest-laden . . . , that cultural frames have social histories' (Woolard and Schieffelin 1994: 58).[2]

Nevertheless, some commentators interpret encounters between east and west Germans in general terms as intercultural communication and accordingly attribute complications in interactions to the fact that the participants operate within different cultural frames. Such interpretations derive logically enough from characterizations of east and west Germans as inhabitants of different 'cultural communities' who bring different 'cultural presuppositions' into their encounters. However, even some of those analysts who use such terms are sceptical about classifying 'German–German' communication as 'intercultural' (see, for example, Antos and Richter (2000: 95), footnote 16). For one thing, it presupposes two discrete but internally homogeneous cultural entities, but how long does it take for 'a culture' to evolve, and in what sense can we postulate 'east' and 'west' German cultures as distinct from 'German' culture (see Satzger 1994: 62–3)? Cultural differences are easier to identify where they are felt to be categorical rather than gradual—Poles and Indonesians, for example, share virtually no salient cultural characteristics and their histories do not intersect or even touch—and pairs such as this permit what Streeck (1995: 431) calls the prototypical conception of culture

---

[2] See Kroskrity (2000*b*) for definitions and a broad discussion of language ideology. I am grateful to Alissa Shethar for drawing may attention to this and the other contributions in Kroskrity (2000*a*).

as an island. But this evidently does not apply in the German context, and if communicative obstacles are found to be no greater and no more systematic between east and west Germans than, say, between Hamburgers and Bavarians, the grounds for claiming 'interculturality' in the one case but not the other are not clear. As Schmitt and Keim (1985: 414) warn, other factors such as participants' roles in the interaction, their respective status, and institutional hierarchies need to be eliminated first, since otherwise there is the risk of 'obliterating general and non-culture-specific structural phenomena of communication with "the sledgehammer of interculturality"' (allgemeine und kulturunspezifische Strukturphänomene von Kommunikation mit 'dem Hammer der Interkulturalität' zu erschlagen).

Moreover, interculturality is not merely a rather blunt weapon for tackling complex social interactions. The very conception of culture as a static, monolithic inventory of features, which seems to underlie many intercultural models, is itself problematic: the idea of *Kulturberührung* (contact between cultures: see, for example, Fiehler 1995) appears to be predicated on the existence of two discrete entities which come into contact through the interaction of individual 'representatives', who are thereby apparently stripped of their individuality and trapped within a fixed assemblage of prescribed behaviours and beliefs. Auer and Kern (forthcoming) summarize common criticisms of this conception of culture as something separate from social individuals and to which they are perceived to 'belong'—i.e., to which they are allocated by the analyst—and argue instead for a dynamic understanding of culture that focuses on action in context, on the creation of 'culturality':[3] 'intercultural communication is not what happens when two people of different cultural-biographical backgrounds meet, but rather it is a brought-about... feature of an encounter', and cultural belonging is not attributed to participants but instead they 'may choose to categorise each other as members of two different cultures, thus "talking each other into" cultural differences' (cf. Wolf 1995, and 5.3 above). From this point of view, being east or west German is therefore not a sufficient condition for interaction between two parties to be construed as intercultural, nor is it merely a matter of identifying different communicative practices between the participants: the differences have to derive from, and be actively associated with, incompatible features of the participants' respective life experiences.

A final problem with the 'intercultural' position is that it seems to be favoured more by west German observers than by east Germans or non-Germans, and this may be because in this conception of interculturality there is at least an implicit assumption that 'difference' is not merely a neutral, descriptive notion but an evaluative category. If east Germans do not perform particular communicative genres in the same way as west Germans, especially in mixed east–west interactions, there are various conclusions that could be drawn from this: for example, where west German observers, consciously or unconsciously taking western norms as their

---

[3] For a stimulating and wide-ranging critique of 'the idea of culture', see Eagleton (2000).

frame of reference, see the east Germans' 'lack of appropriate knowledge', 'lack of relevant experience', or 'inability to meet the requirements of the situation', east German observers may see the west Germans' 'unwillingness to recognize other ways of enacting the speech event' and their 'arbitrary imposition of their own practices as "normal"'.[4] An outsider, on the other hand, might take the view that both parties in such encounters are participating in a new kind of interaction in a new context and that both therefore have the opportunity and the necessity to negotiate a mutually satisfactory modus operandi. However, this presupposes a shared recognition of the historically contingent nature of communicative practices and social relations, an understanding that living under radically different social conditions inevitably entails the development of different forms of social behaviour, different expectations, and different interpretations of other people's actions. Where such reciprocity is lacking, difference is perceived not as a balance between equally valid if contrasting patterns, but as an imbalance in the possession of necessary knowledge—either knowledge of the world or communicative competence, or indeed both. Difference is then indistinguishable from deficit, and when the communicative genres that are studied are characterized in terms of a 'western model', the deficit is inevitably on the side of the easterners.

In this case, regardless of whether there are grounds for identifying a 'cultural' collision between the two participants, the decisive factor is an unequal distribution of power that permits one party, but not the other, to determine what may be considered normal or relevant, in other words, legitimate. This results in the classic double bind created by what we might call 'hegemonic contextualization': the ability of western members of the German speech community to establish and police the parameters of discourse challenges eastern members either to collude in their own subordination by conforming to these 'other' norms and thereby lose face, or to resist this process but still lose face by being cast in the role of 'bad loser', 'whinger', 'ungrateful', or even 'disruptive element'. From this perspective, therefore, it could be argued that we are dealing not with the 'discovery', but with the manufacture, of difference.

The issue is then one of social inequality that does not arise through linguistic or communicative differences: language is neither the problem nor the solution. But since language is perceived as a salient component of group identity especially strongly in the German context—for all the historical reasons we have explored in the course of this book—and since communicative interaction is the primary site of self-representation and for forming and developing perceptions of others, the burden of achieving social integration and of explaining the failure of this goal of unification, is frequently transferred onto this level:

Man projiziert die politischen, ökonomischen und soziokulturellen Probleme, die durch die Vereinigung vor allem für den Osten relevant waren und sind, also die Unterschiede in

---

[4] And as Margita Pätzold (1995: 404) points out, analysts are as prone as the participants in interactions to taking their own norms and experiences as a measure of others' performance.

der Sache, auf den Diskurs, der darüber geführt wird, also auf Unterschiede in der Sprache. (Antos and Richter 2000: 77; and see again in this respect Hartung forthcoming.)

The political, economic, and sociocultural problems that as a result of unification were and still are of particular relevance for the east, in other words material differences, are projected onto the discourse that is conducted about them, that is, onto linguistic differences.

Many east German observers rightly criticize the attribution of social and economic problems to 'cultural' differences articulated and sustained through language, since this can be taken to imply that social discord can best be resolved by east Germans adapting to western patterns of behaviour. To argue that social and economic problems can be alleviated or overcome if easterners would only accommodate more fully to western linguistic and communicative norms is either disingenuous or naïve. Social problems and inequality can be addressed only by the adoption of appropriate social policies and practices. But at the same time easterners tend to underrate the importance of language in the long-term development of social relations within Germany. Shethar and Hartung (1998: 42), for example, are surely right to argue that changing judgements of language use in east and west reveal 'weniger eine sich kontinuierlich vertiefende Divergenz der Redeweisen selbst als vielmehr wechselnde *Interpretationen* von Wahrnehmungen und Erfahrungen' (not so much an ever deepening divergence between the manners of speaking themselves as changing *interpretations* of perceptions and experiences; italics in original), but the evidence seems to me to suggest that diverging speech patterns did nevertheless exist and had a significant impact. Perhaps more importantly, however, part of the continuity in the history of debates on sociolinguistic difference in Germany is that their significance has always rested primarily in perceptions and their interpretation more than in the objective existence of difference. Since language has always been a contentious issue in the German context, it is unrealistic to expect perceptions of linguistic difference to be relegated to the margins during a period of social upheaval, either by 'ordinary' language users or by 'professional' observers.

It may turn out that one of the ironies of the *Wende* was that the less hysterical, more rational, analysis of 'the language question', which in the 1980s had led to the critical consensus on the fundamental sameness of the communication communities in east and west, concealed, rather than expunged, the latent ideology in the west that held western norms and practices as authentic and legitimate and eastern ones as corrupt and debased. If this is true, then we should see the *événement* of 1989–90 not as a turning point but as a temporary suspension of the conviction which many ordinary people—as opposed to experts—shared: that there were (and still are) deep-seated differences between easterners and westerners. These differences were not (primarily) linguistic but rather differences in attitudes and expectations, conditioned by radically different historical experiences. But language is a convenient metaphor for social difference, because of its materiality, because it is abundantly available in its concrete realizations in spoken and written texts, and because it is the one common resource that a society has at its disposal.

These attributes of language are also what has made it possible to construct a history of disunity in modern Germany from the perspective of language-in-history: not a linear, evolutionary 'history of the language', but a multi-layered and complex history of the uses and users of language. Jan Blommaert (1999c: 426) insists that 'the story of language must not be an abstract *histoire d'idées* in which developments are narrated as sequences of phases.... Rather, it should be a story of different, conflicting, disharmonious practices performed by identifiable actors, in very specific ways, and by means of very specific instruments.' This is what I have tried to present in the course of this book. More than any other issue, the 'German question', as it re-emerged in the aftermath of the Second World War, defined the history of Europe in the second half of the twentieth century, and, as I hope to have shown, the unifying and divisive potential of language was a constant feature of this history—in debates about the German language, in discourses of Germanness, and in interactions between Germans.

Bibliography

AHLZWEIG, CLAUS (1994). *Muttersprache—Vaterland. Die deutsche Nation und ihre Sprache* (Opladen: Westdeutscher Verlag).

AHRENDS, MARTIN (ed.) (1986). *Trabbi, Telespargel und Tränenpavillon. Das Wörterbuch der DDR-Sprache* (Munich: Heyne).

—— (ed.) (1989). *Allseitig gefestigt. Stichwörter zum Sprachgebrauch in der DDR* (Munich: Heyne).

ALTER, PETER (1994). *Nationalism*, 2nd edn (London: Arnold). [Originally published in 1985 as *Nationalismus* (Frankfurt/Main: Suhrkamp).]

AMMON, ULRICH (1991). *Die internationale Stellung der deutschen Sprache* (Berlin, New York: de Gruyter).

—— (1995). *Die deutsche Sprache in Deutschland, Österreich und der Schweiz. Das Problem der nationalen Varietäten* (Berlin, New York: de Gruyter).

—— (1997). 'Schwierigkeiten bei der Verbreitung der deutschen Sprache heute', *Muttersprache* (1), 17–34.

—— (2000a). 'Die Rolle des Deutschen in Europa', in Gardt (2000a), 471–94.

—— (2000b). 'Sprache—Nation und die Plurinationalität des Deutschen', in Gardt (2000a), 509–24.

—— and SIMON, GERD (1975). *Aspekte der Soziolinguistik* (Weinheim, Basle: Beltz).

ANDERSON, BENEDICT (1991). *Imagined Communities* (London: Verso).

ANDRASCH, WIETE (2000). 'Mitten im Niemandsland. Wieso es in Brandenburg keine netten Westler gibt', in Simon, Rothe, and Andrasch (2000), 65–77.

ANTOS, GERD (1997). 'Sprachregelung. Zur Einführung der Verwaltungssprache in den neuen Ländern am Beispiel von "Förderprogrammen Ost"', *Deutsche Sprache* 25 (2), 157–64.

—— JÖRG PALM, and STEFAN RICHTER (2000). 'Die diskursive Organisation von Beratungsgesprächen. Zur unterschiedlichen Distribution von sprachlichen Handlungsmustern bei ost- und westdeutschen Sprechern', in Auer and Hausendorf (2000a), 21–43.

—— and STEFAN RICHTER (2000). '"Sprachlosigkeit" Ost? Anmerkungen aus linguistischer Sicht', in Jackman and Roe (2000), 75–96.

—— and THOMAS SCHUBERT (1997a). 'Existenzgründung nach der Wende. Verbalisierungsprobleme von Präsuppositionen bei der sprachlichen Bearbeitung des Wissenstransfers in telefonischen Beratungsgesprächen', in Barz and Fix (1997), 233–62.

—— —— (1997b). 'Unterschiede in kommunikativen Mustern zwischen Ost und West', *Zeitschrift für germanistische Linguistik* 25, 308–30.

ARNDT, ERNST MORITZ (1813). *Über Volkshaß und über den Gebrauch einer fremden Sprache* (Leipzig: Fleischer).

ASENG, CHRISTINA (1998). 'Zur Entwicklung der Sprache der Wende', in Rösler and Sommerfeldt (1998), 123–7.

ASHER, R. (ed.) (1994). *The Encyclopaedia of Language and Linguistics* (Oxford: Pergamon).

ASSMANN, ALEIDA, and DIETRICH HARTH (eds.) (1991). *Mnemosyne. Formen und Funktionen der kulturellen Erinnerung* (Frankfurt/Main: Fischer).

ASSMANN, JAN (1997). *Das kulturelle Gedächtnis. Schrift, Erinnerung und politische Identität in frühen Hochkulturen* (Munich: C. H. Beck).

AUER, PETER (1992). 'Intercultural discourse without intercultural communication: a preliminary investigation of role-played job interviews in east Germany', paper delivered at 17th International LAUD Symposium, Duisburg.

——(1995). ' "Hegemonialer" Geltungsanspruch und konversationelle Realität: Anmerkungen zu einer vernachlässigten Perspektive auf die Ost/West-Daten der Forschungsgruppe *Nationale Selbst- und Fremdbilder*', in Czyzewski *et al.* (1995), 379–83.

——(1998). 'Learning how to play the game: An investigation of role-played job interviews in East Germany', *TEXT* 18 (1), 7–38.

——(2000*a*). 'Changing communicative practices among east Germans', in Stevenson and Theobald (2000*a*), 167–88.

——(2000*b*). 'Was sich ändert und was bleibt: Vorläufiges zu stilistischen Konvergenzen Ost-West am Beispiel von Interviews', in Auer and Hausendorf (2000*a*), 151–75.

——, BIRGIT BARDEN, and BEATE GROSSKOPF (1993). 'Dialektwandel und sprachliche Anpassung bei "Übersiedlern" und "Übersiedlerinnen" aus Sachsen. Bericht über eine laufende Langzeitstudie', *Deutsche Sprache* 1993 (1), 80–7.

——, KARIN BIRKNER, and FRIEDERIKE KERN (1997*a*). 'Der Spiegel der Wende in der biographischen Selbstdarstellung von ostdeutschen Bewerbern und Bewerberinnen', *Deutsche Sprache* 25 (2), 144–56.

————(1997*b*). 'Wörter—Formeln—Argumente. Was in Bewerbungsgesprächen "Spaß" macht', in Barz and Fix (1997), 213–32.

——and HEIKO HAUSENDORF (eds.) (2000*a*). *Kommunikation in gesellschaftlichen Umbruchsituationen* (Tübingen: Niemeyer).

————(2000*b*). '10 Jahre Wiedervereinigung. Hauptrichtungen linguistischer Untersuchungen zum sprachlichen und gesellschaftlichen Wandel in den neuen Bundesländern', in Auer and Hausendorf (2000*a*), 3–17.

——and FRIEDERIKE KERN (forthcoming). 'Three ways of analysing communication between east and west Germans as intercultural communication', in Günthner *et al.* (forthcoming).

AUGST, GERHARD, and WOLFGANG W. SAUER (1992). 'Der Duden—Konsequenzen aus der Wende?', in Welke *et al.* (1992), 71–92.

AULERICH, GUDRUN, and RUTH HEIDI STEIN (1998). 'Sind ostdeutsche Handlungsmuster unter westdeutschen Bedingungen lebbar? Studierende in Dresden nach der Wende', *Deutsche Studien* (138), 145–73.

AYERS, EDWARD (1996). 'What we talk about when we talk about the South', in Ayers *et al.* (1996), 62–82.

——, PATRICIA LIMERICK, STEPHEN NISSENBAUM, and PETER ONUF (eds.) (1996). *All Over the Map: Rethinking American Regions* (Baltimore: Johns Hopkins Press).

BADENOCH, ALEC (forthcoming). 'Radio and reconstruction in occupied Germany', Ph.D. dissertation, University of Southampton.

BARBOUR, STEPHEN (1993). ' "Uns knüpft der Sprache heilig Band": reflections on the role of language in German nationalism, past and present', in Flood *et al.* (1993), 313–32.

——(2000*a*). 'Nationalism, language, Europe', in Barbour and Carmichael (2000), 1–17.

——(2000*b*). 'Germany, Austria, Switzerland, Luxembourg: the total coincidence of nations and speech communities?', in Barbour and Carmichael (2000), 151–67.

——(2000c). 'Sociolinguistics in the GDR: the study of language in society in East Germany', in Jackman and Roe (2000), 115–27.

——and CATHIE CARMICHAEL (eds.) (2000). *Language and Nationalism in Europe* (Oxford: Oxford University Press).

——and PATRICK STEVENSON (1990). *Variation in German: A Critical Approach to German Sociolinguistics* (Cambridge: Cambridge University Press). [2nd edn publ. in 1998 as *Variation im Deutschen: soziolinguistische Perspektiven* (Berlin, New York: de Gruyter).]

BARDEN, BIRGIT (2000). 'The influence of attitudes and social networks on long-term linguistic accommodation in Germany', in Stevenson and Theobald (2000a), 226–47.

——and BEATE GROSSKOPF (1992). '"Ossi meets Wessi": social and linguistic integration of newcomers from Saxony', paper delivered at 17th International LAUD Symposium, Duisburg.

——————(1998). *Sprachliche Akkommodation und soziale Integration. Sächsische Übersiedler und Übersiedlerinnen im rhein-/moselfränkischen und alemannischen Sprachraum* (Tübingen: Niemeyer).

BARTH, DAGMAR (1997). 'Arbeitsweltliche Kommunikationsprobleme zwischen Ost und West', in Barz and Fix (1997), 395–9.

——(2000). 'Die Brisanz der eigenen Rolle. Referenzmittel und Selbstdarstellung in Sprachbiographien ehemaliger DDR-Bürger', in Fix and Barth (2000), 55–201.

BARTHOLMES, HERBERT (1991). 'Sogenannte DDR-Wörter', *Der Sprachdienst* 1991 (4), 115–19.

BARZ, IRMHILD (1992). 'Aktionen, Aktivitäten, Initiativen. Beobachtungen zum euphemistischen Sprachgebrauch in der wirtschaftspolitischen Berichterstattung in der DDR', in Lerchner (1992a), 143–65.

——(1997). 'Was ich kann und wie ich bin. Individualitätsgewinn und Identitätsverlust beim Umgang mit Berufen und ihren Bezeichnungen', in Barz and Fix (1997), 75–91.

——and ULLA FIX (eds.) (1997). *Deutsch–deutsche Kommunikationserfahrungen im arbeitsweltlichen Alltag* (Heidelberg: Winter).

——and MARIANNE SCHRÖDER (eds.) (1997). *Nominationsforschung im Deutschen. Festschrift für Wolfgang Fleischer zum 75. Geburtstag* (Frankfurt/Main: Lang).

BASTIAN, ANDREA (1995). *Der Heimat-Begriff. Eine begriffsgeschichtliche Untersuchung in verschiedenen Funktionsbereichen der deutschen Sprache* (Tübingen: Niemeyer).

BAUER, DIRK (1993). *Das sprachliche Ost–West-Problem. Untersuchungen zur Sprache und Sprachwissenschaft in Deutschland seit 1945* (Frankfurt am Main: Peter Lang).

BAUER, GERHARD (1988). *Sprache und Sprachlosigkeit im Dritten Reich* (Cologne: Bund-Verlag).

BAULE, BERNWARD (1995). 'Sprache und Struktur der Staatssicherheit', *Deutschland Archiv* 1995 (8), 864–7.

BAUMANN, ANTJE (2000). 'OstWind aus NeuLand. Zur Debatte um doch nicht ganz einfache Geschichten', in Reiher and Baumann (2000), 194–221.

BAUSCHKE, CHRISTIAN (1995). 'Arroganter Wessi, bescheidener Ossi. Endlich. Eine wissenschaftliche Untersuchung zeigt uns, wie Westdeutsche und Ostdeutsche wirklich sind. Wirklich?', *Wochenpost*, 23 February 1995, 3.

BENEKE, JÜRGEN (1993). ' "Am Anfang wollten wir zueinander . . ."—Was wollen wir heute? Sprachlich-kommunikative Reflexionen Jugendlicher aus dem Ost- und Westteil Berlins zu einem bewegenden Zeitthema', in Reiher and Läzer (1993), 210–38.

BERGMANN, CHRISTIAN (1990). 'Anmerkungen zur Sprache und Gesellschaft in der DDR. Von der Wirkung und Wahrheit des Wortes', *Wirkendes Wort* 1990 (1), 1–3.

BERGMANN, CHRISTIAN (1991). 'Neues Denken und neue Sprache', in Pohl and Bartels (1991), 45–59.

—— (1992). 'Parteisprache und Parteidenken. Zum Sprachgebrauch des ZK der SED', in Lerchner (1992*a*), 101–42.

—— (1995). 'Semantische Destruktion als Methode der Manipulation', in Reiher (1995*b*), 299–304.

—— (1996). 'Über das "Herausbrechen" und "Zersetzen" von Menschen', *Muttersprache* (4), 289–301.

—— (1997). 'Über das "Herausbrechen" und "Zersetzen" von Menschen', *Deutsche Sprache* 25 (2), 98–102.

—— (1999). *Die Sprache der Stasi* (Göttingen: Vandenhoeck & Ruprecht).

BERGSDORF, WOLFGANG (1993). 'Die Wiedervereinigung der deutschen Sprache', *Deutschland Archiv* 26 (10), 1182–91.

BERNSTEIN, BASIL (ed.) (1971*a*). *Class, Codes and Control* (London: Routledge & Kegan Paul).

—— (1971*b*). 'A socio-linguistic approach to social learning', in Bernstein (1971*a*), 118–43.

BERSCHIN, HELMUT (1979). *Deutschland—ein Name im Wandel* (Munich, Vienna: Olzog).

—— (1994). 'Kontinuität oder Wandel? Deutsch als internationale Sprache seit 1989. Anläßlich des Erscheinens von: Ulrich Ammon, Die internationale Stellung der deutschen Sprache', *Zeitschrift für Dialektologie und Linguistik* 61 (3), 308–24.

BESCH, WERNER (1998). *Duzen, Siezen, Titulieren. Zur Anrede im Deutschen heute und gestern* (Göttingen: Vandenhoeck & Ruprecht).

——, ARNE BETTEN, OSKAR REICHMANN, and STEFAN SONDEREGGER (eds.) (2000). *Sprachgeschichte: Ein Handbuch zur Geschichte der deutschen Sprache und ihrer Erforschung*, 2nd edn (Berlin, New York: de Gruyter).

——, OSKAR REICHMANN, and STEFAN SONDEREGGER (eds.) (1985). *Sprachgeschichte. Ein Handbuch zur Geschichte der deutschen Sprache und ihrer Erforschung* 2 vols. (Berlin, New York: de Gruyter).

BIBER, DOUGLAS (1991). *Variation Across Speech and Writing* (Cambridge: Cambridge University Press).

BICKERTON, DEREK (1971). 'Inherent variability and variable rules', *Foundations of Language* 7, 457–92.

BICKES, HANS (1992). 'Sozialpsychologisch motivierte Anmerkungen zur Rolle der deutschen Sprache nach der "Einigung"', in Welke *et al.* (1992), 111–26.

—— and ANNETTE TRABOLD (eds.) (1994). *Förderung der sprachlichen Kultur in der Bundesrepublik Deutschland: Positionsbestimmung und Bestandsaufnahme* (Stuttgart: Bleicher).

BIEGE, ANGELA, and INES BOSE (1997). 'Untersuchungen zur Redeweise in Landtagen', *Deutsche Sprache* 25 (2), 123–31.

BIERE, BERND ULRICH, and HELMUT HENNE (eds.) (1993). *Sprache in den Medien nach 1945* (Tübingen: Niemeyer).

BIRKNER, KARIN (2001). *Bewerbungsgespräche mit Ost- und Westdeutschen: Eine kommunikative Gattung in Zeiten gesellschaftlichen Wandels* (Tübingen: Niemeyer).

—— and FRIEDERIKE KERN (1996). 'Deutsch–deutsche Reparaturversuche. Alltagsrhetorische Gestaltungsverfahren ostdeutscher Sprecherinnen und Sprecher im westdeutschen Aktivitätstyp "Berwerbungsgespräch"', *Zeitschrift für angewandte Linguistik* 1996 (25), 53–76.

—— —— (2000). 'Ost- und Westdeutsche in Bewerbungsgesprächen', in Auer and Hausendorf (2000*a*), 45–81.

BLEI, DAGMAR (1990). 'Ist die "Sprache der Wende" eine "gewendete Sprache"? Bemerkungen zum Sprachgebrauch in der (ehemaligen) DDR', *Info DaF* 17 (4), 391–401.

—— (1992). 'Deutsch versus "DDRsch"? Stand der Perspektiven einer nationalsprachlichen Variante', *Info DaF* 19 (3), 326–34.

—— (1993). 'Ein Deutschland—eine deutsche Sprache? Ein Beitrag zu den sprachlichen Anpassungsleistungen der Ostdeutschen', *Germanistische Mitteilungen* 37, 105–112.

—— (1994). ' "Altbundesdeutscher" Spracherwerb in Ostdeutschland? Gemischtes und Vermischtes im Wortschatz der Ostdeutschen', in Bungarten (1994a), 38–60.

BLOMMAERT, JAN (ed.) (1999a). *Language Ideological Debates* (Berlin, New York: Mouton de Gruyter).

—— (1999b). 'The debate is open', in Blommaert (1999a), 1–38.

—— (1999c). 'The debate is closed', in Blommaert (1999a), 425–38.

BOA, ELIZABETH, and RACHEL PALFREYMAN (2000). *Heimat—a German Dream. Regional loyalties and national identity in German culture 1890–1990* (Oxford: Oxford University Press).

BÖHM, CARL (1992). 'Der Broiler lebt. Die deutsche Sprache im Wandel zwischen DDR und BRD. Ergebnisse einer interdisziplinären Untersuchung im Bereich Jugendsprache in der mecklenburgischen Landeshauptstadt Schwerin im Sommer 1991', *Zeitschrift für Germanistik* 1992 (2), 320–40.

BÖKE, KARIN, MATTHIAS JUNG, and MARTIN WENGELER (eds.) (1996). *Öffentlicher Sprachgebrauch* (Opladen: Westdeutscher Verlag).

BORN, JOACHIM, and GERHARD STICKEL (eds.) (1993). *Deutsch als Verkehrssprache in Europa* (Berlin, New York: de Gruyter).

BRAUDEL, FERNAND (1958a). *Ecrits sur l'histoire* (Paris: Flammarion).

—— (1958b). 'Histoire et sciences sociales: la longue durée', in Braudel (1958a), 41–83.

BRAUN, PETER (1992). ' "Erichs Krönung" im "Palazzo Protzi"—Zur Rolle alltagssprachlicher Kritik vor der Wende', in Welke *et al.* (1992), 35–42.

—— (1993). *Tendenzen in der deutschen Gegenwartssprache* (Stuttgart, Berlin, Cologne: Kohlhammer).

BREDEL, URSULA (2000). 'Erzählen vom Umbruch. Zu einer Form narrativer Konversion', in Auer and Hausendorf (2000a), 177–98.

—— and JEANETTE DITTMAR (1997). 'Strukturelle Planbrüche als Hinweise auf Registerkonflikte im Sprachgebrauch von Ostberlinern nach der Wende', *Deutsche Sprache* (1), 39–53.

—— and NORBERT DITTMAR (1998). ' "naja dit sind allet so + verschiedene dinge die einem da so durch-n kopp gehen ... zuviel neues mit eenem schlach". Verfahren sprachlicher Bearbeitung sozialer Umbruchsituationen', in Reiher and Kramer (1998), 129–52.

BRESGEN, BERT (1993). 'Grenzgänger und Wiedergänger. Zur Berichterstattung des "Neuen Deutschland" über die Öffnung der ungarischen Grenze im September 1989', in Reiher and Läzer (1993), 53–86.

—— (1995). 'Als das Wünschen noch geholfen hat. Semantische und symbolische Strategien im Gründungsaufruf des Neuen Forums', in Reiher (1995b), 277–98.

BRUNNER, MARGOT, and KARIN FRANK-CYRUS (eds.) (1998). *Die Frau in der Sprache. Gespräche zum geschlechtergerechten Sprachgebrauch* (Wiesbaden: Gesellschaft für deutsche Sprache).

BÜHLER, KARL (1934). *Sprachtheorie* (Jena).

BUNGARTEN, THEO (ed.) (1994a). *Deutsch–deutsche Kommunikation in der Wirtschaftskooperation* (Torstedt: Attikon Verlag).

BUNGARTEN, THEO (1994*b*). 'Kommunikationspsychologische Barrieren in interkulturellen Managementkontakten', in Bungarten (1994*a*), 24–33.

BURKE, PETER (1997). *Varieties of Cultural History* (Cambridge: Polity Press).

—— (ed.) (2001). *New Perspectives on Historical Writing* (Cambridge: Polity Press).

—— and ROY PORTER (eds.) (1987). *The Social History of Language* (Cambridge: Cambridge University Press).

BURKHARDT, ARMIN (1992). 'Ein Parlament sucht(e) seine Sprache—Zur Sprache der Volkskammer', in Burkhardt and Fritzsche (1992), 155–98.

—— (1993). 'Vergangenheitsüberwältigung. Zur Berichterstattung über die "Affäre Fink" in deutschen Medien', in Reiher and Läzer (1993), 126–46.

—— (1996). 'Palast versus Schloß oder: Wem gehören die Symbole?', in Reiher and Läzer (1996), 137–68.

—— (2000). 'Vom "Akklamations- zum Abwicklungsparlament". Zur Sprache der Volkskammer', in Reiher and Baumann (2000), 73–98.

—— and KLAUS PETER FRITZSCHE (eds.) (1992). *Sprache im Umbruch* (Berlin, New York: de Gruyter).

BUSCH, RAINER (ed.) (1993). *Gemischte Gefühle. Einheitsalltag in Mecklenburg-Vorpommern* (Bonn: Dietz).

BUSSE, DIETRICH (1993). 'Deutschland, die "schwierige Nation"—Mythos oder Wirklichkeit?', in Reiher and Läzer (1993), 8–27.

—— (1995). 'Deutsche Nation. Zur Geschichte eines Leitbegriffs in Deutschland vor und nach der Wiedervereinigung', in Reiher (1995*b*), 203–31.

——, FRITZ HERMANNS, and WOLFGANG TEUBERT (eds.) (1994). *Begriffsgeschichte und Diskursgeschichte. Methodenfragen und Forschungsergebnisse der historischen Semantik* (Opladen: Westdeutscher Verlag).

CAMERON, DEBORAH (1995). *Verbal Hygiene* (London, New York: Routledge).

——, ELIZABETH FRAZER, PENELOPE HARVEY, BEN RAMPTON, and KAY RICHARDSON (1992). *Researching Language: Issues of Power and Method* (London: Routledge).

CARTER, RONALD (2001). *The Language of Speech and Writing* (London: Routledge).

CHAMBERS, J. K., and PETER TRUDGILL (1998). *Dialectology*, 2nd edn (Cambridge: Cambridge University Press).

CHILTON, PAUL, MIHAIL ILYIN, and JACOB MEY (eds.) (1998). *Political Discourse in Transition in Europe 1989–1991* (Amsterdam, Phildelphia: Benjamins).

CLYNE, MICHAEL (1993). 'The German language after unification: adapting assumptions and methodologies to the "new world order"', *International Journal of the Sociology of Language* (100/101), 11–27.

—— (1995). *The German Language in a Changing Europe* (Cambridge: Cambridge University Press).

COLE, PETER, and JERRY L. MORGAN (eds.) (1975). *Syntax and Semantics*, vol. 3, *Speech Acts* (New York: Academic Press).

COULMAS, FLORIAN (1985). 'Reden ist Silber, Schreiben ist Gold', *Zeitschrift für Literaturwissenschaft und Linguistik* 15, 94–112.

—— (1990). 'The status of German: some suggestions for future research', *International Journal of the Sociology of Language* (83), 171–85.

—— (1997). 'Germanness: language and nation', in Stevenson (1997), 55–68.

CROWLEY, TONY (1996). *Language in History. Theories and Texts* (London: Routledge).

CZYZEWSKI, MAREK, ELISABETH GÜLICH, HEIKO HAUSENDORF, and MARIA KASTNER (eds.) (1985). *Nationale Selbst- und Fremdbilder im Gespräch. Kommunikative Prozesse nach der*

Wiedervereinigung Deutschlands und dem Systemwandel in Ostmitteleuropa (Opladen: Westdeutscher Verlag).

DAHL-BLUMENBERG, MICHAEL (1987). 'Zum Podiumsgespräch "Nationale Varianten der deutschen Hochsprache" auf dem IDV-Kongreß in Bern', *Deutsche Sprache* 15, 358–66.

DAILEY-O'CAIN, JENNIFER (1997). 'Geographic and socio-political influences on language ideology and attitudes toward language variation in post-unification Germany', Ph.D. dissertation, University of Michigan.

——(2000). 'Competing language ideologies in Germany: when east meets west', in Stevenson and Theobald (2000*a*), 248–66.

——and GRIT LIEBSCHER (forthcoming). 'Interacting identities in dialect and discourse: migrant western Germans in eastern Germany'.

DANN, OTTO (1992). *Nation und Nationalismus in Deutschland* (Munich: C. H. Beck).

DEBUS, FRIEDHELM (1991). 'Zur Entwicklung der deutschen Sprache seit 1945', *New German Studies* 16 (3), 173–206.

——MANFRED W. HELLMANN, and HORST DIETER SCHLOSSER (eds.) (1985). *Sprachliche Normen und Normierungsfolgen in der DDR* (= *Germanistische Linguistik* 82/83) (Hildesheim: Olms).

DIECKMANN, WALTHER (1967). 'Kritische Bemerkungen zum sprachlichen Ost–West Problem', *Zeitschrift für Deutsche Sprache* 23, 136–65.

——(1969). *Sprache in der Politik. Einführung in die Pragmatik und Semantik der politischen Sprache* (Heidelberg: Winter).

——(1983). 'Diskontinuität? Zur—unbefriedigenden—sprachkritischen und sprachwissenschaftlichen Behandlung der Nachkriegssprache in Deutschland 1945–1949', *Argument*, Special Issue 116, 89–100.

——(1989*a*). 'Die Untersuchung der deutsch–deutschen Sprachentwicklung als linguistisches Problem', *Zeitschrift für germanistische Linguistik* 17, 162–81.

——(ed.) (1989*b*). *Reichthum und Armut der deutschen Sprache* (Berlin, New York: de Gruyter).

DIEHL, ELKE (1992). '"Ich bin Student." Zur Feminisierung weiblicher Personen- und Berufsbezeichnungen in der früheren DDR', *Deutschland Archiv* 25 (4), 384–92.

DIEKMANNSHENKE, HAJO (1997). 'Sprachliche Ostidentität? Ostprofilierung bei Parteien in den neuen Bundesländern', *Deutsche Sprache* 25 (2), 165–75.

DITTMAR, NORBERT (1983). 'Soziolinguistik, Teil II', *Studium Linguistik* 14, 20–57.

——(1997). 'Sprachliche und kommunikative Perspektiven auf ein gesamtdeutsches Ereignis in Erzählungen von Ost- und Westberlinern', in Barz and Fix (1997), 1–32.

——(2000). 'Sozialer Umbruch und Sprachwandel am Beispiel der Modalpartikeln *halt* und *eben* in der Berliner kommunikationsgemeinschaft nach der "Wende"', in Auer and Hausendorf (2000*a*), 199–234.

——and URSULA BREDEL (1999). *Die Sprachmauer. Die Verarbeitung der Wende und ihrer Folgen in Gesprächen mit Ost- und WestberlinerInnen* (Berlin: Weidler).

——and MELANIE GLIER (2000). 'Abbruch, Aufbruch, Umbruch!? Im Schatten der alten und im Flutlicht der neuen Sprache', in Reiher and Baumann (2000), 241–72.

——and PETER SCHLOBINSKI (eds.) (1988). *Wandlungen einer Stadtsprache. Berlinisch in Vergangenheit und Gegenwart* (Berlin: Colloquium Verlag).

——, PETER SCHLOBINSKI, and INGE WACHS (1986). *Berlinisch. Studien zum Lexikon, zur Spracheinstellung und zum Stilrepertoire* (Berlin: Arno Spitz).

DOCEN, BERNHARD JOSEPH (1814). 'Über die Selbständigkeit und Reinerhaltung unserer Literatur und Sprache: Rückerinnerungen und Wünsche', in *Nemesis: Zeitschrift für Politik und Geschichte* 2.

DONATH, JOACHIM (1974). 'Soziolinguistische Aspekte der sprachlichen Kommunikation', in Ising (1974), 37–74.

——RUTH PAPE, MARION ROLOFF, and HELMUT SCHÖNFELD (1981). 'Beschreibung einer empirischen Untersuchung zur Sprachvarianz', in *Kommunikation und Sprachvariation* (1981), 308–440.

DRESCHER, MARTINA, and ULRICH DAUSENDSCHÖN-GAY (1995). '*Sin wer an son immobilienmakler da eh gekommen.* Zum Umgang mit sozialen Kategorien im Gespräch', in Czyzewski *et al.* (1995), 85–119.

DROSDOWSKI, GÜNTHER (1991). 'Deutsch—Sprache in einem geteilten Land', *Sprache und Literatur in Wissenschaft und Unterricht* (67), 21–35.

DURRANI, OSMAN (2000). 'Language and subversion in GDR rock music', in Jackman and Roe (2000), 145–70.

EAGLETON, TERRY (1991). *Ideology: An Introduction* (London: Verso).

——(2000). *The Idea of Culture* (Oxford: Blackwell).

EBERLE, HENRIK (ed.) (1998). *Mit sozialistischem Gruß! Parteiinterne Hausmitteilungen, Briefe, Akten und Intrigen aus der Ulbricht-Zeit* (Berlin: Schwarzkopf & Schwarzkopf).

EICHHOFF, JÜRGEN (1978). *Wortatlas der deutschen Umgangssprache* (Berne, Munich: Francke).

EICHHOFF-CYRUS, KARIN M., and RUDOLF HOBERG (eds.) (2000). *Die deutsche Sprache zur Jahrtausendwende. Sprachkultur oder Sprachverfall?* (Mannheim, Leipzig, Vienna, Zurich: Dudenverlag).

EICHLER, ERNST, and GEORG HILTY (eds.) (1995). *Namenforschung* (Berlin, New York: de Gruyter).

EIFLER, GÜNTHER, and OTTO SAAME (eds.) (1992). *Gegenwart und Vergangenheit deutscher Einheit* (Vienna: Passagen Verlag).

ELSPASS, STEPHAN (2000). ' "Es ist so; jedenfalls erscheint es mir so": markers of uncertainty and vagueness in speeches of east and west German politicians', in Stevenson and Theobald (2000*a*), 206–25.

ENGLER, WOLFGANG (2000*a*). *Die Ostdeutschen. Kunde von einem verlorenen Land* (Berlin: Aufbau).

——(2000*b*). 'Sie sprechen doch Deutsch. Trotzdem verstehen Ost und West einander nicht', *Die Zeit*, 24 August 2000, 9.

ENSEL, LEO (1995). *'Warum wir uns nicht leiden mögen . . .'. Was Ossis und Wessis voneinander halten* (Münster: Agenda Verlag).

EPPLER, ERHARD (1992). *Kavalleriepferde beim Hornsignal. Die Krise der Politik im Spiegel der Sprache* (Frankfurt/Main: Suhrkamp).

ERMERT, KARL (ed.) (1994). *Sprache zwischen Markt und Politik: Über die internationale Stellung der deutschen Sprache und die Sprachenpolitik in Europa* (Rehburg-Loccum: Evangelische Akademie).

EROMS, HANS-WERNER (1994). 'Die deutsche Sprache hüben und drüben—drei Jahre nach der Wiedervereinigung', in Heringer *et al.* (1994), 23–40.

——(1996). 'Streitpunkte politischer Sprache in der Bundesrepublik Deutschland', in Böke, Jung, and Wengeler (1996), 38–50.

——(1997). 'Sprachliche "Befindlichkeiten" der Deutschen in Ost und West', *Der Deutschunterricht* (1), 6–16.

ETZOLD, SABINE (1993). 'Was Stasi-Namen verraten', *Die Zeit*, 1/1993, 43.

FAIRCLOUGH, NORMAN (1989). *Language and Power* (London, New York: Longman).

—— (1992). *Discourse and Social Change* (Cambridge: Polity Press).

FALKENBERG, GABRIEL (1989). 'Zur Begriffsgeschichte der deutschen Spaltung zwischen Deutschem Reich und zwei Deutschen Republiken', *Sprache und Literatur in Wissenschaft und Unterricht* (64), 3–22.

FASOLD, RALPH (1984). *The Sociolinguistics of Society* (Oxford: Blackwell).

FIEHLER, REINHARD (1995). 'Die Wiedervereinigung als Kulturberührung', in Czyzewski *et al.* (1995), 328–47.

FINK, HERMANN, LIANE FIJAS, and DANIELLE SCHONS (1997). *Anglizismen in der Sprache der Neuen Bundesländer: eine Analyse zur Verwendung und Rezeption* (Frankfurt: Lang).

FIX, ULLA (1990). 'Der Wandel der Muster—Der Wandel im Umgang mit den Mustern. Kommunikationskultur im institutionellen Sprachgebrauch der DDR am Beispiel von Losungen', *Deutsche Sprache* 18/4, 332–47.

—— (1992a). ' "Noch breiter entfalten und noch wirksamer untermauern." Die Beschreibung von Wörtern aus dem offiziellen Sprachverkehr der DDR nach den Bedingungen ihres Gebrauchs', in Große, Lerchner, and Schröder (1992), 13–28.

—— (1992b). 'Rituelle Kommunikation im öffentlichen Sprachgebrauch der DDR und ihre Begleitumstände. Möglichkeiten und Grenzen der selbstbestimmten und mitbestimmenden Kommunikation in der DDR', in Lerchner (1992a), 3–99.

—— (1993). 'Medientexte diesseits und jenseits der "Wende". Das Beispiel "Leserbrief" ', in Biere and Henne (1993), 20–55.

—— (1994a). 'Die Beherrschung der Kommunikation durch die Formel. Politisch gebrauchte rituelle Formeln im offiziellen Sprachgebrauch der "Vorwende"-Zeit in der DDR. Strukturen und Funktionen', in Sandig (1994), 139–53.

—— (1994b). ' "Gewendete" Texte—"gewendete" Textsorten', in Heringer *et al.* (1994), 131–46.

—— (1995). 'Texte mit doppeltem Boden? Diskursanalytische Untersuchung inklusiver und exklusiver personenbeurteilender Texte im Kommunikationskontext der DDR', in Wodak and Kirsch (1995a), 71–92.

—— (1997a). 'Die Sicht der Betroffenen. Beobachtungen zum Kommunikationswandel in den neuen Bundesländern', *Der Deutschunterricht* (1), 34–41.

—— (1997b). '*Erklären* und *Rechtfertigen*. Die Darstellung der eigenen sprachlich-kommunikativen Vergangenheit in Interviews. Ein Analyseansatz', *Deutsche Sprache* 25 (2), 187–94.

—— (1997c). ' "Bewältigung" von Vergangenheit und Gegenwart beim Erzählen über Sprache. Strategien des Darstellens sprachlich-kommunikativer Erinnerungen an die DDR und Erfahrungen mit der gegenwärtigen Sprachsituation', in Barz and Fix (1997), 33–43.

—— (1997d). 'Wortzuteilung, Wortverknappung, Wortverweigerung, Wortverbot. Die Rolle von Benennungen bei der Steuerung des Diskurses', in Barz and Schröder (1997), 345–59.

—— (ed.) (1998). *Ritualität in der Kommunikation der DDR* (Frankfurt/Main: Lang).

—— (2000a). 'Fremdheit versus Vertrautheit. Die sprachlich-kommunikative Befindlichkeit von Sprachteilnehmern der DDR und ihre Reaktion auf die Destruktion der kommunikativen "Selbstverständlichkeiten" des Alltags durch die politische Wende von 1989', in Fix and Barth (2000), 15–54.

—— (2000b). ' "Sprachverwendung im Klasseninteresse": Philosophische, sprachwissenschaftliche und sprachpraktische Äußerungen von Wissenschaftlern der DDR zum Gebrauch von Sprache im "Klassenkampf" ', in Jackman and Roe (2000), 97–113.

FIX, ULLA and DAGMAR BARTH (eds.) (2000). *Sprachbiographien. Sprache und Sprachgebrauch vor und nach der Wende von 1989 im Erinnern und Erleben von Zeitzeugen aus der DDR* (Frankfurt am Main: Lang).

FLEISCHER, HOLM (2001). *Wandlungen im Sprachgebrauch. Referenz und Pragmatik der Pronomen in ostdeutschen Zeitungskommentaren, am Beispiel der Leipziger Volkszeitung vor, während und nach der 'Wende'* (Mannheim: Institut für Deutsche Sprache).

FLEISCHER, WOLFGANG (1983). 'Die deutsche Sprache in der DDR: grundsätzliche Überlegungen zur Sprachsituation', in *Linguistische Studien (Reihe A). Arbeitsberichte* 111, 258–75.

——(ed.) (1987). *Wortschatz der deutschen Sprache in der DDR* (Leipzig: Bibliographisches Institut).

——(1992). 'DDR-typische Benennungen und ihre Perspektive', in Welke *et al.* (1992), 15–34.

FLOOD, JOHN L., PAUL SALMON, OLIVE SAYCE, and CHRISTOPHER WELLS (eds.) (1993). *'Das unsichtbare Band der Sprache'. Studies in German Language and Linguistic History in Memory of Leslie Seiffert* (Stuttgart: Akademischer Verlag).

FOWLER, ROGER (1991). *Language in the News. Discourse and ideology in the press* (London: Routledge).

FRAAS, CLAUDIA (1990). 'Beobachtungen zur deutschen Lexik vor und nach der Wende', *Deutschunterricht* 43 (12), 595–9.

——(1994). 'Kommunikationskonflikte vor dem Hintergrund unterschiedlicher Erfahrungswelten', *Zeitschrift für germanistische Linguistik* 22, 87–90.

——(1996). *Gebrauchswandel und Bedeutungsvarianz in Textnetzen. Die Konzepte* IDENTITÄT *und* DEUTSCHE *im Diskurs zur deutschen Einheit* (Tübingen: Narr).

——(1997). ' "Die *sozialistische Nation*—sie war eine Chimäre." Interpretationsmuster und Interpretationskonflikte', *Deutsche Sprache* 25 (2), 103–13.

——and KATHRIN STEYER (1992). 'Sprache der Wende—Wende der Sprache? Beharrungsvermögen und Dynamik von Strukturen im öffentlichen Sprachgebrauch', *Deutsche Sprache* 20 (2), 172–84.

FRICKE, CORINNA (1990). 'Überlegungen zu einem Neuansatz der gesellschaftswissenschaftlichen Linguistik, ihren Aufgaben und Quellen', *Osnabrücker Beiträge zur Sprachtheorie (OBST)* 43, 141–60.

FRIEDRICH-EBERT-STIFTUNG (ed.) (1989). *Politik und Sprachentwicklung in der DDR. Zu neuen Ufern* (Bonn-Bad Godesberg: Friedrich-Ebert-Stiftung).

FRIEL, BRIAN (1981). *Translations* (London: Faber).

FRITZE, LOTHAR (1996). 'Gestörte Kommunikation zwischen Ost und West. Erscheinungen—Ursachen—Folgen', *Deutschland Archiv* 6, 921–8.

FRITZSCHE, K. PETER (1992). 'Auf der Suche nach einer neuen Sprache. Schulbücher in der DDR', in Burkhardt and Fritzsche (1992), 199–210.

FULBROOK, MARY (1990). *A Concise History of Germany* (Cambridge: Cambridge University Press).

GAL, SUSAN (1980). *Language Shift* (New York, London: Academic Press).

——(1987). 'Codeswitching and consciousness in the European periphery', *American Ethnologist* 14 (4), 637–53.

——(1993). 'Diversity and contestation in linguistic ideologies: German-speakers in Hungary', *Language in Society* 22, 337–59.

——(1995). 'Cultural bases of language use amongst German-speakers in Hungary', *International Journal of the Sociology of Language* 111, 93–102.

GALLER, KATRIN (1993). 'Die Heiratsannonce im deutsch–deutschen Wandel', Diplomarbeit, Humboldt-Universität Berlin.

GANSEL, CHRISTINA, and CARSTEN GANSEL (1993). 'Aspekte der deutschen Sprache in der DDR als Unterrichtsgegenstand', *Deutschunterricht* 46 (3), 140–51.

—— —— (1997). 'Zwischen Karrierefrau und Hausmann. Aspekte geschlechterdifferenzierenden Sprachgebrauchs in Ost und West', *Der Deutschunterricht* (1), 59–69.

GARDT, ANDREAS (1999). 'Sprachpatriotismus und Sprachnationalismus. Versuch einer historisch-systematischen Bestimmung am Beispiel des Deutschen', in Gardt, Haß-Zumkehr, and Roelcke (1999), 89–113.

—— (ed.) (2000a). *Nation und Sprache. Die Diskussion ihres Verhältnisses in Geschichte und Gegenwart* (Berlin, New York: de Gruyter).

—— (2000b). 'Sprachnationalismus zwischen 1850 und 1945', in Gardt (2000a), 247–71.

——, ULRIKE HASS-ZUMKEHR, and THORSTEN ROELCKE (eds.) (1999). *Sprachgeschichte als Kulturgeschichte* (Berlin, New York: de Gruyter).

GÄRTNER, DETLEV (1992). 'Vom Sekretärsdeutsch zur Kommerzsprache—Sprachmanipulation gestern und heute', in Lerchner (1992a), 203–61.

GAUDIG, RICHARD (1958–9) 'Die deutsche Sprachspaltung', *Neue Deutsche Hefte* 5 (55), 1008–14.

GEERTZ, CLIFFORD (1995). *After the Fact: Two Countries, Four Decades, One Anthropologist* (Cambridge, MA: Harvard University Press).

GEIER, RUTH (1996). 'Die Welt der schönen Bilder. Wahlwerbung in Ostdeutschland—Wahlwerbung für Ostdeutsche?', in Reiher and Läzer (1996), 229–44.

—— (1997). 'Festreden in sozialistischen Betrieben', in Barz and Fix (1997), 339–47.

—— (1998). 'Reden als rituelle Ereignisse', in Fix (1998), 321–68.

—— (2000). ' "Alle Jahre wieder...". Zehn Reden zur deutschen Einheit', in Reiher and Baumann (2000), 115–30.

GESELLSCHAFT FÜR DEUTSCHE SPRACHE (ed.) (1993). *Wörter und Unwörter: Sinniges und Unsinniges der deutsche Gegenwartssprache* (Niedernhausen/Taunus: Falken-Verlag).

GILES, HOWARD (1994). 'Accommodation in communication', in Asher (1994), 12–15.

GLÄSER, ROSEMARIE (1992). 'Gestalt- und Stilwandel in der kommerziellen Werbung der neuen Bundesländer', in Hess-Lüttich (1992), 189–211.

GLASEROW, VERA (1996). 'Die Vorurteile verhärteten sich. Schulklassen aus Ost und West sind sich in einem Punkt einig: sie finden sich blöd', *Die Zeit*, 31 May 1996, 21.

GLÜCK, HELMUT (1992). 'Aktuelle Beobachtungen zum Namen Deutsch', in Welke *et al.* (1992), 141–71.

—— (1995). 'Westdeutsch + Ostdeutsch = Gesamtdeutsch? Die deutsche Sprache fünf Jahre nach der "Wende" ', *Sprachwissenschaft* 20, 187–206.

—— and WOLFGANG W. SAUER (1997). *Gegenwartsdeutsch*, 2nd edn (Stuttgart: Metzler).

GOFFMAN, ERVING (1963). *Behavior in Public Places. Notes on the Social Organization of Gatherings* (New York: Free Press).

GOOD, COLIN (1991). 'Der Kampf geht weiter oder Die sprachlichen Selbstrettungsversuche des SED-Staates', *Sprache und Literatur in Wissenschaft und Unterricht* (67), 48–55.

—— (1993). 'Die sprachliche Inszenierung der Hauptstadtdebatte. Oder: "Wie kann es Konsens in einer Frage geben, die eine klassisch-klare Entscheidung erfordert?" ', in Reiher and Läzer (1993), 117–25.

—— (1995). 'Sprache im totalitären Staat: der Fall DDR', in Reiher (1995b), 263–76.

—— (1996). 'Über die "Neuen Linken": der Versuch der PDS, eine neue Sprache des Sozialismus zu finden', in Reiher and Läzer (1996), 265–85.

GRAMSCI, ANTONIO (1985). *Selections from Cultural Writings* (London: Lawrence and Wishart).

GRASSL, SIGRID (1991). 'Zur Sprache der Sportberichterstattung in der ehemaligen DDR und BRD', in *Zum Sprachgebrauch unter dem Zeichen von Hammer, Zickel und Ährenkranz* (1991), 57–72.

GREWENIG, ADI (ed.) (1993). *Inszenierte Information. Politik und strategische Kommunikation in den Medien* (Opladen: Westdeutscher Verlag).

GRICE, H. P. (1975). 'Logic and conversation', in Cole and Morgan (1975), 41–58.

GRIMM, JACOB (1847). 'Einleitender Vortrag des Vorsitzenden über die wechselseitigen Beziehungen und die Verbindung der drei in der Versammlung vertretenen Wissenschaften', published in *Verhandlungen der Germanisten zu Frankfurt am Main am 24., 25. und 26. September 1846* (Frankfurt am Main: J. D. Sauerländer's Verlag), 11–18.

—— (1864). *Über den Ursprung der Sprache* (Berlin: Dümmler).

GROSSE, RUDOLF, and ALBRECHT NEUBERT (eds.) (1974a). *Beiträge zur Soziolinguistik* (Munich: Hueber).

—— —— (1974b). 'Thesen zur marxistisch-leninistischen Soziolinguistik', in Grosse and Neubert (1974a), 9–22.

——, GOTTHARD LERCHNER, and MARIANNE SCHRÖDER (eds.) (1992). *Phraseologie, Wortbildung, Lexikologie: Festschrift für Wolfgang Fleischer zum 70. Geburtstag* (Frankfurt am Main: Lang).

GRUNER, PAUL-HERMANN (1992). 'Kontinuität oder Innovation? Zur Frage konstanter formaler und inhaltlicher Prägung des Sprachkampfes anläßlich der ersten gesamtdeutschen Bundestagswahl vom 2.12.1990', in Burkhardt and Fritzsche (1992), 267–86.

GÜGOLD, BARBARA (2000). ' "Höher, schneller, weiter": Deutsch als Fremdsprache in der DDR', in Jackman and Roe (2000), 129–43.

GUMPERZ, JOHN (1982). *Discourse Strategies* (Cambridge: Cambridge University Press).

GÜNTHNER, SUSANNE, ALDO DI LUZIO, and FRANCA ORLETTI (eds.) (forthcoming). *Language, Culture, and Interaction: New Perspectives on Intercultural Communication* (Amsterdam, Philadelphia: Benjamins).

HAHN, SILKE (1995). 'Vom *zerrissenen Deutschland* zur *vereinigten Republik.* Zur Sprachgeschichte der "deutschen Frage"', in Stötzel and Wengeler (1995), 285–353.

HALLIDAY, MICHAEL (1989). *Spoken and Written Language* (Oxford: Blackwell).

HAMPEL, ANJA (1998). 'Zum Gebrauch und zur Rezeption von Anglizismen in regionalen Werbeanzeigen', in Rösler and Sommerfeldt (1998), 109–22.

HARTUNG, WOLFDIETRICH (1981a). 'Differenziertheit der Sprache als Inhalt kommunikativer Erfahrung', in *Kommunikation und Sprachvariation* (1981), 11–26.

—— (1981b). 'Differenziertheit der Sprache als Ausdruck ihrer Gesellschaftlichkeit', in *Kommunikation und Sprachvariation* (1981), 26–72.

—— (1981c). 'Eine hohe Sprachkultur: Aufgabe in der sozialistischen Gesellschaft der DDR', *Deutschunterricht* 6, 292–303.

—— (1990). 'Einheitlichkeit und Differenziertheit der deutschen Sprache', *Zeitschrift für Germanistik* 90, 447–66.

—— (ed.) (1991a). *Kommunikation und Wissen* (Berlin: Akademie Verlag).

—— (1991b). 'Linguistische Zugänge zur sprachlichen Kommunikation', in Hartung (1991a), 13–90.

—— (forthcoming). 'Über die Wahrnehmung sprachlicher Unterschiede. Methodologische Anmerkungen zu "Ostdeutsch" und "Westdeutsch"', in Hartung and Shethar (forthcoming).

——and ALISSA SHETHAR (eds.) (forthcoming). *Kulturen und ihre Sprachen. Die Wahrnehmung anders Sprechender und ihr Selbstverständnis* [= Abhandlungen der Leibniz-Societät, Band 7] (Berlin: Trafo Verlag).

HAUSENDORF, HEIKO (1995). '*Man spricht zwar eine Sprache aber*. . . Die Wiedervereinigung als Kommunikationsproblem', in Czyzewski *et al.* (1995), 120–44.

—— (1997). '*Gerade hier im osten die frauen.* Soziale Kategorisierung, Macht und Moral', *Deutsche Sprache* 25 (2), 132–43.

—— (2000*a*). 'Ost- und Westzugehörigkeit als soziale Kategorien im wiedervereinigten Deutschland', in Auer and Hausendorf (2000*a*), 83–111.

—— (2000*b*). *Zugehörigkeit durch Sprache. Eine linguistische Studie am Beispiel der deutschen Wiedervereinigung* (Tübingen: Niemeyer).

HEINEMANN, MARGOT (1995). '*Vorher war das alles irgendwie organisiert:* Verhaltensmuster im deutsch–deutschen Diskurs', in Czyzewski *et al.* (1995), 389–95.

—— (ed.) (1998). *Sprachliche und soziale Stereotypen* (Frankfurt/Main, Berlin, New York: Peter Lang).

HEINRICH-BÖLL-STIFTUNG (ed.) (1996). *Die Sprache als Hort der Freiheit* (Cologne: Heinrich-Böll-Stiftung).

HELLMANN, MANFRED W. (ed.) (1973). *Zum öffentlichen Sprachgebrauch in der Bundesrepublik Deutschland und in der DDR. Methoden und Probleme seiner Erforschung* (Düsseldorf: Schwann).

—— (ed.) (1976). *Bibliographie zum öffentlichen Sprachgebrauch in der Bundesrepublik Deutschland und in der DDR* (Düsseldorf: Schwann).

—— (ed.) (1984). *Ost–West-Wortschatzvergleiche. Maschinell gestützte Untersuchungen zum Vokabular von Zeitungstexten aus der BRD und der DDR* (Tübingen: Narr).

—— (1989*a*). 'Die doppelte Wende: Zur Verbindung von Sprache, Sprachwissenschaft und zeitgebundener politischer Bewertung am Beispiel deutsch–deutscher Sprachdifferenzierung', in Klein (1989), 297–326.

—— (1989*b*). 'Zwei Gesellschaften—zwei Sprachkulturen? Acht Thesen zur öffentlichen Sprache in der Bundesrepublik Deutschland und in der Deutschen Demokratischen Republik', *Forum für interdisziplinäre Forschung* 1989 (2), 27–38.

—— (1990). 'DDR-Sprachgebrauch nach der Wende—eine erste Bestandsaufnahme', *Muttersprache* 100/2–3, 266–86.

—— (1991). ' "Ich suche eine Wohnung." Zur vergleichenden Untersuchung alltagssprachlichen Handelns in den beiden deutschen Staaten', in Schlosser (1991*b*), 19–32.

—— (1993). 'Die Leipziger Volkszeitung vom 27.10.1989—eine Zeitung im Umbruch', *Muttersprache* 103 (3), 186–218.

—— (1994*a*). 'Ostdeutsch–Westdeutsch im Kontakt. Brücke oder Schranke der Verständigung?', *Terminologie et Traduction* 1994 (1), 105–38.

—— (1994*b*). ' "Rote Socken"—ein alter Hut?', *Der Sprachdienst* 1994 (5), 170–2.

—— (1997*a*). 'Wörter der Emotionalität und Moralität in Texten der Wendezeit—sprachliche Revolution oder Kommunikationsbarriere?', in Barz and Fix (1997), 113–52.

—— (1997*b*). 'Sprach- und Kommunikationsprobleme in Deutschland Ost und West', in Schmirber (1997), 53–87.

HELLMANN, MANFRED W. (1997c). 'Das "kommunistische Kürzel *BRD*". Zur Geschichte des öffentlichen Umgangs mit den Bezeichnungen für die beiden deutschen Staaten', in Barz and Schröder (1997), 93–107.

——(1997d). 'Tendenzen der sprachlichen Entwicklung seit 1989 im Spiegel der Forschung', *Der Deutschunterricht* (1), 17–32.

——(1998). '"Durch die gemeinsame Sprache getrennt"—zu Sprache und Kommunikation in Deutschland seit der Wende 1989/90', *Das Wort (Germanistisches Jahrbuch)* 1998, 51–69.

——(1999). *Wende-Bibliografie. Literatur und Nachschlagewerke zu Sprache und Kommunikation im geteilten und vereinigten Deutschland ab Januar 1990* (Mannheim: Institut für Deutsche Sprache).

——(2000). 'Divergenz und Konvergenz: Sprachlich-kommunikative Folgen der staatlichen Trennung und Vereinigung Deutschlands', in Eichhoff-Cyrus and Hoberg (2000), 247–75.

——(ed.) (forthcoming). *Wörter in Texten der Wendezeit. Alphabetisches Wörterverzeichnis zum "Wendekorpus" des IDS—Mai 1989 bis Ende 1990* (Tübingen: Narr).

HENNE, HELMUT (1995). 'Hassen. Legendieren. Abschöpfen. Das Wörterbuch der Staatssicherheit', *Zeitschrift für germanistische Linguistik* 23 (2), 210–14.

HENNECKE, ANGELIKA (1999). *Im Osten nichts Neues? Eine pragmalinguistisch-semiotische Analyse ausgewählter Werbeanzeigen für Ostprodukte im Zeitraum 1993 bis 1998* (Frankfurt: Peter Lang).

HENTSCHEL, ELKE (1986). *Funktion und Geschichte deutscher Partikeln: ja, doch, halt und eben* (Tübingen: Niemeyer).

HERBERG, DIETER (1991). 'Ost-Deutsch. Betrachtungen zum Wortgebrauch in der Noch- und in der Ex-DDR', *Sprachpflege und Sprachkultur* 40 (1), 1–5.

——(1997). '*Beitritt, Anschluß* oder was? Heteronominativität in Texten der Wendezeit', in Barz and Schröder (1997), 109–16.

——STEFFENS, DORIS, and ELKE TELLENBACH (eds.) (1997). *Schlüsselwörter der Wendezeit. Wörter-Buch zum öffentlichen Sprachgebrauch 1989/90* (Berlin, New York: de Gruyter).

HERDER, JOHANN (1770). *Abhandlung über den Ursprung der Sprache* (Munich: Hanser).

HERINGER, HANS JÜRGEN (1990). *'Ich gebe Ihnen mein Ehrenwort.' Politik, Sprache, Moral* (Munich: C. H. Beck).

——(1991). 'Wörter des Jahres 1991', *Sprache und Literatur in Wissenschaft und Unterricht* 22 (68), 107–15.

——(1992). 'Wörter des Jahres 1992', *Sprache und Literatur in Wissenschaft und Unterricht* 23 (70), 116–20.

——(1994). 'Das Stasi-Syndrom', in Heringer *et al.* (1994), 163–76.

——, GUNHILD SAMSON, MICHEL KAUFFMANN, and WOLFGANG BADER (eds.) (1994). *Tendenzen der deutschen Gegenwartssprache* (Tübingen: Niemeyer).

HERMANNS, FRITZ (1992). 'Ein Wort im Wandel: Deutsch—was ist das? Semiotisch-semantische Anmerkungen zu einem Wahlplakat der CDU (1990)', in Burkhardt and Fritzsche (1992), 253–66.

——(1994). 'Deutsche Sprache—deutsche Identität', in Ermert (1994), 187–204.

——(1995). 'Deutsch und Deutschland. Semantik deutscher nationaler Selbstbezeichnungswörter heute', in Jäger (1995), 374–89.

——(1996). '*Deutsche, deutsch* und *Deutschland*. Zur Bedeutung deutscher nationaler Selbstbezeichnungswörter heute', in Reiher and Läzer (1996), 11–31.

HERRMANN-WINTER, RENATE (1977). 'Soziolinguistische Aspekte empirischer Erhebungen zur sprachlichen Varianz', in *Normen in der sprachlichen Kommunikation* (1977), 209–46.

—— (1979). *Studien zur gesprochenen Sprache im Norden der DDR* (Berlin: Akademie-Verlag).

HERTEL, VOLKER, REGINA METZLER, and BRIGITTE UHLIG (eds.) (1996). *Sprache und Kommunikation im Kulturkontext: Beiträge zum Ehrenkolloquium aus Anlaß des 60. Geburtstages von Gotthard Lerchner* (Frankfurt am Main: Lang).

HESS, ANNE-KATHRIN, and HANS RAMGE (1991). 'Der "andere Teil Deutschlands" in Zeitungskommentaren zum "17. Juni"', *Sprache und Literatur in Wissenschaft und Unterricht* (67), 36–47.

HESS-LÜTTICH, ERNEST W. B. (1990). 'Grenzziehungen und Brückenschläge—oder: von der "Sprachspaltung" zur "plurizentrischen Sprachkultur". Ein Rückblick auf die Varietäten des Deutschen', *Rhetorik* (9), 108–22.

—— (ed.) (1992). *Medienkultur—Kulturkonflikt: Massenmedien in der interkulturellen und internationalen Kommunikation* (Opladen: Westdeutscher Verlag).

HEYSE, JOHANN CHRISTOPH AUGUST (1814). *Theoretisch-praktische deutsche Grammatik oder Lehrbuch zum reinen und richtigen Sprechen, Lesen und Schreiben der deutschen Sprache* (Hanover).

HINGST, JÜRGEN (1993). 'Vom Ich zum Wir', in Busch (1993), 45–50.

HOBSBAWM, ERIC (1991). 'Dangerous exit from a stormy world', *New Statesman and Society*, 8 November 1991, 16–17.

HOFFMANN, GREGOR (1997). 'Politische Ritualität als Spiegelbild des Gesellschaftlichen', in Barz and Fix (1997), 349–65.

—— (1998). 'Zur Funktion und Zeichenhaftigkeit des 1. Mai in der DDR', in Fix (1998), 51–100.

—— (2000). '"Arbeit, Brot und Völkerfrieden, das ist unsere Welt!" Rituelle Kommunikation in den Texten zum 1. Mai', in Auer and Hausendorf (2000a), 237–70.

HOFFMANN, MICHAEL (1994). 'Individualisierung als Tendenz? Untersuchungen zum Kommunikationswandel in der DDR', in Sommerfeldt (1994a), 51–69.

—— (1995). 'Filmwerbung zwischen Konventionalität und Originalität. Fortgesetzte Untersuchungen zum Kommunikationswandel in der DDR', *Muttersprache* 1995 (2), 97–118.

HOLLY, WERNER (1992). 'Was kann Kohl, was Krenz nicht konnte? Deutsch–deutsche Unterschiede politischer Dialogrhetorik in zwei Fernsehinterviews', *Rhetorik* 11, 33–50.

—— (1997). 'Language and television', in Stevenson (1997), 341–75.

HOLMES, JANET (2001). *An Introduction to Sociolinguistics*, 2nd edn (London, New York: Longman).

HOPFER, REINHARD (1991). 'Besetzte Plätze und "befreite Begriffe". Die Sprache der Politik der DDR im Herbst 1989', in Liedtke, Wengeler, and Böke (1991), 111–22.

—— (1992a). 'Christa Wolfs Streit mit dem "großen Bruder". Politische Diskurse der DDR im Herbst 1989', in Burkhardt and Fritzsche (1992), 111–34.

—— (1992b). 'Schwierigkeiten der "semantischen Vereinigung". Ein Vergleich deutsch–deutscher Pressetexte', in Hess-Lüttich (1992), 147–65.

—— (1994). 'Vom Konsens zum Dissens. Diskursanalytische Untersuchungen zum Wandel des Sprachgebrauchs der CDU im Herbst 1989', in Busse, Hermanns, and Teubert (1994), 124–42.

—— (1996). 'Wessianisch für Ossis. Vorschläge für eine soziolinguistische deutsch–deutsche Enzyklopädie', in Reiher and Läzer (1996), 94–109.

HÖRSCHELMANN, KATHRIN (2000). ' "Go east, young man . . ."—gendered representations of identity in television dramas about "east Germany" ', in Stevenson and Theobald (2000a), 43–59.

HUDSON, R. A. (1996). *Sociolinguistics* 2nd edn (Cambridge: Cambridge University Press).

HUMBOLDT, WILHELM VON (1963a). *Über die Verschiedenheiten des menschlichen Sprachbaues* (Stuttgart: J. G. Cotta'sche Buchhandlung).

—— (1963b). *Über die Verschiedenheit des menschlichen Sprachbaues und ihren Einfluß auf die Entwicklung des Menschengeschlechts* (Stuttgart: J. G. Cotta'sche Buchhandlung).

IRVINE, JUDITH T., and SUSAN GAL (2000). 'Language ideology and linguistic differentiation', in Kroskrity (2000a), 35–83.

ISING, ERIKA (1994). 'Sprachkultur und Sprachsituation im wiedervereinigten Deutschland', in Bickes and Trabold (1994), 63–87.

ISING, GERHARD (ed.) (1974). *Aktuelle Probleme der sprachlichen Kommunikation* (Berlin: Akademie-Verlag).

J. F. (1846). 'Ein frommer Wunsch in Sachen deutscher Rede', *Jahrbücher der Gegenwart* 1/4, 293–306.

JACHMANN, MAIKA (1994). 'Ost und West im Dialog. Untersuchungen zu Problemen deutsch–deutscher Kommunikation im inszenierten Gespräch Talk-Show', Ph.D. dissertation, Universität Innsbruck.

JACKMAN, GRAHAM (2000). 'Introduction: "Finding a Voice" in the GDR', in Jackman and Roe (2000), 1–17.

—— and IAN F. ROE (eds.) (2000). *Finding a Voice. Problems of Language in East German Society and Culture* (Amsterdam, Atlanta: Rodopi).

JÄGER, LUDWIG (ed.) (1995). *Germanistik: Disziplinäre Identität und kulturelle Leistung* (Weinheim: Beltz Athenäum).

JÄGER, SIEGFRIED (1997). 'Political discourse: the language of right and left in Germany', in Stevenson (1997a), 233–57.

JAHN, FRIEDRICH LUDWIG (1806). *Bereicherung des Hochdeutschen Sprachschatzes versucht im Gebiethe der Sinnverwandtschaft, ein Nachtrag zu Adelung's und eine Nachlese zu Eberhard's Wörterbuch* (Leipzig: Böhme).

JARAUSCH, KONRAD (ed.) (1997). *After Unity. Reconfiguring German Identities* (Providence, Oxford: Berghahn).

JESSEN, RALPH (1997). 'Diktatorische Herrschaft als kommunikative Praxis. Überlegungen zum Zusammenhang von "Bürokratie" und Sprachnormierung in der DDR-Geschichte', in Lüdtke and Becker (1997), 57–75.

JOGSCHIES, RAINER (1993). 'Die vier Wände nach dem Fall der Mauer. Warum die westdeutsche Berichterstattung über die Vereinigung ab Herbst 1989 die Trennung vergrößerte', in Reiher and Läzer (1993), 107–16.

JOHNSON, SALLY (1995). *Gender, Group Identity and Variation in Usage of the Berlin Urban Vernacular* (Frankfurt/Main: Lang).

JOSEPH, JOHN (1987). *Eloquence and Power. The Rise of Language Standards and Standard Languages* (London: Pinter).

KAHLE, EGON et al. (eds.) (1990). *Wirtschaftsbegriffe in Ost und West. 200 ausgewählte betriebswirtschaftliche Begriffe—interpretiert aus marktwirtschaftlicher bzw. planwirtschaftlicher Sicht als Handlungs- und Orientierungshilfe* (Frankfurt: Deutsche Bank AG).

KAPFERER, NORBERT (1992). 'Von der "Macht des Wortes" zur "Sprache der Macht" zur Ohn-Macht der Vernunft. Über die Enteignung der Sprache im real existierenden Sozialismus durch die marxistisch-leninistische Philosophie', in Burkhardt and Fritzsche (1992), 19–42.

KAUKE, WILMA (1997). 'Politische Rituale als Spiegelbild des Gesellschaftlichen. Die Kommunikationskonstellation des Rituals "Jugendweihe" in der DDR und seine Entwicklung nach der Wende', in Barz and Fix (1997), 367–78.

——(1998). 'Ritualbeschreibung am Beispiel der Jugendweihe', in Fix (1998), 101–214.

——(2000). 'Jugendweihe in Ostdeutschland. Ein Ritual im Umbruch', in Auer and Hausendorf (2000a), 271–303.

KELLY-HOLMES, HELEN (2000). 'United consumers? Advertising discourse and constructions of German identity', in Stevenson and Theobald (2000a), 91–108.

KEMPF, W., and IRENA SCHMIDT-REGENER (eds.) (forthcoming). *Krieg, Nationalismus, Rassismus und die Medien* (Münster).

KERN, FRIEDERIKE (2000). *Kulturen der Selbstdarstellung. Ost- und Westdeutsche in Bewerbungsgesprächen* (Wiesbaden: Deutscher Universitäts-Verlag).

KESSLER, CHRISTINE (1997). '"... und fügt sich gut ins Kollektiv ein"—Muster personenbeurteilender Texte in der DDR', in Barz and Fix (1997), 303–14.

KETTEMANN, BERNHARD, RUDOLF DE CILLIA, and ISABEL LANDSIEDLER (eds.) (1998). *Sprache und Politik* (Frankfurt/Main: Lang).

KILIAN, J. (1994). 'Historische Lexikologie und Didaktik. A. Waags Didaktisierung der lexikographischen Bedeutungsgeschichten Pauls', *Zeitschrift für germanistische Linguistik* 22, 31–49.

KINNE, MICHAEL (ed.) (1977). *Texte Ost—Texte West* (Frankfurt/Main: Diesterweg).

——(1990). 'Deutsch 1990 in den Farben der DDR. Sprachlich Markantes aus der Zeit vor und nach der Wende', *Der Sprachdienst* 34 (1), 13–8.

——(1991). 'DDR-Deutsch und Wendesprache', *Der Sprachdienst* 35 (2), 49–54.

——and BIRGIT STRUBE-EDELMANN (1980). *Kleines Wörterbuch des DDR-Wortschatzes* (Düsseldorf: Schwann).

KIRCHHÖFER, D. (1988). 'Für ein dialektisches Verständnis der Erziehung im Unterricht', *Pädagogische Forschung* 5, 81.

KIRKNESS, ALAN (1975). *Zur Sprachreinigung im Deutschen 1789–1871* (Tübingen: Narr).

KLEIN, JOSEF (ed.) (1989). *Politische Semantik* (Opladen: Westdeutscher Verlag).

——and HAJO DIEKMANNSHENKE (eds.) (1996). *Sprachstrategien und Dialogblockaden: linguistische und politikwissenschaftliche Studien zur politischen Kommunikation* (Berlin, New York: de Gruyter).

KLEIN, WOLF PETER, and INGWER PAUL (eds.) (1993). *Sprachliche Aufmerksamkeit. Glossen und Marginalien zur Sprache der Gegenwart* (Heidelberg: Winter).

KLEIN, WOLFGANG, and DIETER WUNDERLICH (eds.) (1971). *Aspekte der Soziolinguistik* (Frankfurt/Main: Athenäum).

Kleines Politisches Wörterbuch (1967). (Berlin: Dietz).

KLEMPERER, VIKTOR (1954). *Zur gegenwärtigen Sprachsituation in Deutschland* (Berlin: Aufbau-Verlag).

KLOSS, HEINZ (1978). *Die Entwicklung neuer germanischer Kultursprachen seit 1800*, 2nd edn (Düsseldorf: Schwann).

KLUGE, FRIEDRICH (1918). 'Vaterland und Muttersprache', in *Wissenschaftliche Beihefte zur Zeitschrift des Allgemeinen Deutschen Sprachvereins*, 5th series, vols. 38–40, 283–90.

KÖHLER, AUGUST (1954). *Vortrag im Deutschen Sprachverein Berlin* (Berlin: Sprachenverlag Leben im Wort).

KOLBE, KARL WILHELM (1804[1], 1818[2]) *Über den Wortreichthum der deutschen und franzö-sischen Sprache* (Berlin: Realschulbuchhandlung).

KOLLER, WERNER (2000). 'Nation und Sprache in der Schweiz', in Gardt (2000*a*), 563–609. *Kommunikation und Sprachvariation* (1981). (Berlin: Akademie-Verlag).

KÖSSLING, RAINER (1996). ' "Republikflucht"—das behördlich nicht genehmigte Verlassen der DDR im Spiegel der Sprache', in Hertel, Metzler, and Uhlig (1996), 239–50.

KRAMER, UNDINE (1996). 'Von Ossi-Nachweisen und Buschzulagen. Nachwendewörter— sprachliche Ausrutscher oder bewußte Etikettierung?', in Reiher and Läzer (1996), 55–69.

—— (1998). ' "Wir und die anderen". Distanzierung durch Sprache', in Reiher and Kramer (1998), 273–98.

KRESS, GUNTHER (1985). *Linguistic Processes in Sociocultural Practice* (Victoria: Deakin University Press).

KRETZENBACHER, HEINZ (1991). 'Das deutsch–deutsche Du', *Deutsch als Fremdsprache*, 181–3.

KREUTZ, HEINZ (1997*a*). 'Aspects of communicative uncertainty in the language of young East Germans during the Wende', *Monash University Linguistics Papers* 1, 11–23.

—— (1997*b*). 'Some observations on hedging phenomena and modifying devices as regional markers in the speech of young east Germans', in Markkanen and Schröder (1997), 208–31.

KRONENBERG, STEPHAN (1993). *Wirtschaftliche Entwicklung und die Sprache der Wirtschaftspolitik in der DDR* (Frankfurt/Main: Lang).

KROSKRITY, PAUL (ed.) (2000*a*). *Régimes of Language: Ideologies, Polities, and Identities* (Santa Fe: School of American Research Press).

—— (2000*b*). 'Regimenting languages: language ideological perspectives', in Kroskrity (2000*a*), 1–34.

KÜHN, INGRID (1993). 'Straßennamen nach der Wende', in *Gesellschaft für deutsche Sprache* (1993), 152–61.

—— (1994). 'Sprachberatung in den neuen Bundesländern—Hilfe bei deutsch–deutschen Sprachproblemen', *Muttersprache* 104/2, 137–42.

—— (1995*a*). 'Aktivierung DDR-spezifischer Archaisierungen', *Muttersprache* (4), 315–23.

—— (1995*b*). 'Alltagssprachliche Textsortenstile', in Stickel (1995), 329–54.

—— (1995*c*). 'Decknamen. Zur Pragmatik von inoffiziellen Personenbenennungen', in Eichler *et al.* (1995), 515–20.

—— (1995*d*). 'Lexik in alltagssprachlichen Textsorten', *Deutschunterricht* 48 (9), 411–17.

—— (1996). 'Von Clara Zetkin zu Dorothea. Straßennamen im Wandel', in Reiher and Läzer (1996), 186–205.

—— (1999). 'Schulnamengebung im politisch-kulturellen Symbolkanon', *Muttersprache* 2, 136–43.

—— (2000). ' "Besonderer Dank gilt der Hausgemeinschaft . . .". Konventioneller Stil und individueller Spielraum in Texten der Alltagssprache', in Reiher and Baumann (2000), 131–52.

—— and KLAUS ALMSTÄDT (1997*a*). 'Deutsch–deutsche Verständigungsprobleme. Erfahrungen aus der Sprachberatung', *Der Deutschunterricht* (1), 86–94.

—— —— (1997*b*). 'Rufen Sie uns an—Sprachberatung zwischen Sprachwacht und Kummertelefon', *Deutsche Sprache* (3), 195–206.

KÜPPER, HEINZ (1987). *Wörterbuch der deutschen Umgangssprache* (Stuttgart: Klett).

LABOV, WILLIAM (1972*a*). *Sociolinguistic Patterns* (Oxford: Blackwell).

—— (1972*b*). 'The study of language in its social context', in Labov (1972*a*), 183–259.

LÄMMERT, KARL, WALTHER KILLY, CARL OTTO CONRADY, and PETER VON POLENZ (1967). *Germanistik—eine deutsche Wissenschaft* (Frankfurt/Main: Suhrkamp).

LANG, EWALD (ed.) (1990). *Wendehals und Stasi-Laus* (Munich: Heyne).

LANGE, BERND-LUTZ, and ULRICH FORCHNER (eds.) (1996). *Bonzenschleuder und Rennpappe. Der Volksmund in der DDR* (Frankfurt/Main: Eichborn).

LATSCH, JOHANNES (1994). *Die Bezeichnungen für Deutschland, seine Teile und die Deutschen. Eine lexikalische Analyse deutschlandpolitischer Leitartikel in bundesdeutschen Tageszeitungen 1950–1991* (Frankfurt/Main: Lang).

LÄZER, RÜDIGER (1993). 'Der gewendete Journalismus im Untergang der DDR. Zum Wandel von Strategien der Kommentierung innenpolitischer Konflikte', in Reiher and Läzer (1993), 87–106.

—— (1996a). ' "Schön, daß es das noch gibt"—Werbetexte für Ostprodukte. Untersuchungen zur Sprache einer ost–west-deutschen Textsorte', in Reiher and Läzer (1996), 206–28.

—— (1996b). ' "Sie könn' das inzwischen wie ein westdeutscher politiker." Metakommunikative Situationsbearbeitung und thematische Steuerung der Argumentation in einer ostdeutschen Elefantenrunde', in Klein and Diekmannshenke (1996), 165–200.

—— (1997). 'Neues von und über Deutsch-Ost und -West. Bemerkungen zu neuen Materialien und Beiträgen in einer andauernden Debatte', *Zeitschrift für Germanistik* 1997 (1), 132–9.

LE PAGE, R., and ANDRÉE TABOURET-KELLER (1985). *Acts of Identity* (Cambridge: Cambridge University Press).

LERCHNER, GOTTHARD (1974). 'Zur Spezifik der Gebrauchsweise der deutschen Sprache in der DDR und ihre gesellschaftliche Determination', *Deutsch als Fremdsprache* 11, 259–65.

—— (1976). 'Nationalsprachliche Varianten', *Forum* 30 (3), 10–11.

—— (ed.) (1992a). *Sprachgebrauch im Wandel. Anmerkungen zur Kommunikationskultur in der DDR vor und nach der Wende* (Frankfurt/Main: Lang).

—— (1992b). 'Broiler, Plast(e) und Datsche machen noch nicht den Unterschied. Fremdheit und Toleranz in einer polyzentrischen deutschen Kommunikationskultur', in Lerchner (1992a), 297–332.

—— (2000). 'Nation und Sprache im Spannungsfeld zwischen Sprachwissenschaft und Politik in der Bundesrepublik und der DDR bis 1989', in Gardt (2000a), 273–302.

LIEBE RESÉNDIZ, JULIA (1992). 'Woran erkennen sich Ost- und Westdeutsche? Eine Spracheinstellungsstudie am Beispiel von Rundfunksendungen', in Welke *et al.* (1992), 127–39.

LIEBSCH, HELMUT (ed.) (1976). *Deutsche Sprache* (Leipzig).

LIEBSCHER, GRIT (2000). 'Arriving at identities: positioning of speakers in German television talkshows', in Stevenson and Theobald (2000a), 189–205.

LIEDTKE, FRANK, MARTIN WENGELER, and KARIN BÖKE (eds.) (1991). *Begriffe besetzen: Strategien des Sprachgebrauchs in der Politik* (Opladen: Westdeutscher Verlag).

LINKLATER, BETH (2000a). 'Narratives of the GDR: what parents tell their children', in Stevenson and Theobald (2000a), 150–66.

LIN-LIU, HWEI-ANN (1993). *Sprachliche Folgen der ideologisch-politischen Spaltung einer Sprachgemeinschaft in Deutschland und China. Ein Vergleich am Beispiel der Sprache in Zeitungen* (Frankfurt/Main: Lang).

LIPPI-GREEN, ROSINA (1997). *English with an Accent. Language, Ideology, and Discrimination in the United States* (London, New York: Routledge).

LÖFFLER, HEINRICH (1998). 'Sprache als Mittel der Identifikation und Distanzierung in der viersprachigen Schweiz', in Reiher and Kramer (1998), 11–38.

LÜDTKE, ALF (1997). ' "... den Menschen vergessen"?—oder: das Maß der Sicherheit: Arbeiterverhalten der 1950er Jahre im Blick von MfS, SED, FDGB und staatlichen Zeitungen', in Lüdtke and Becker (1997), 189–222.

——and PETER BECKER (eds.) (1997). *Akten. Eingaben. Schaufenster. Die DDR und ihre Texte: Erkundungen zu Herrschaft und Alltag* (Berlin: Akademie-Verlag).

LUDWIG, KLAUS-DIETER (1992). 'Zur Sprache der Wende—Lexikologisch-lexikographische Beobachtungen', in Welke *et al.* (1992), 59–70.

——(1996). 'Der "Einheitsduden" oder: Was ist geblieben? DDR-spezifischer Wortschatz im DUDEN von 1991', in Reiher and Läzer (1996), 110–34.

——(1997). 'Wortschatzveränderungen nach 1989 und ihre Widerspiegelung in aktuellen Wörterbüchern des Deutschen', *Der Deutschunterricht* (1), 77–85.

——(2000). 'Von der "Zielsetzung" zur Zielstellung" und zurück. Vorwendewortschatz in Vorwende- und Nachwendewörterbüchern', in Reiher and Baumann (2000), 55–72.

MAAS, UTZ (1984). *'Als der Geist der Gemeinschaft eine Sprache fand': Sprache im Nationalsozialismus* (Opladen: Westdeutscher Verlag).

MAIER, GERHARD (1991). *Die Wende in der DDR* (Bonn: Bundeszentrale für politische Bildung).

MARKKANEN, RAIJA, and HARTMUT SCHRÖDER (eds.) (1997). *Hedging and Discourse. Approaches to the Analysis of a Pragmatic Phenomenon in Academic Texts* (Berlin, New York: de Gruyter).

MAR-MOLINERO, CLARE (2000). *The Politics of Language in the Spanish-Speaking World. From Colonisation to Globalisation* (London, New York: Routledge).

MARQUARDT, EDITHA (1998). 'Feste und Feiern', in Fix (1998), 1–49.

MARR, MIRKO (1998). ' "Mie lache ons hüt buggelich." Imitation und Deritualisierung in der Gegenwelt des Karnevals', in Fix (1998), 215–320.

MARTEN-FINNIS, SUSANNE (1994). *Pressesprache zwischen Stalinismus und Demokratie. Parteijournalismus im 'Neuen Deutschland' 1946–1993* (Tübingen: Niemeyer).

Materialien zur wissenschaftlichen Konferenz 'Zum Sprachgebrauch unter dem Zeichen von Hammer, Zirkel und Ährenkranz' im September 1991 (1992). (Zwickau: Pädagogische Hochschule).

MCNALLY, JOANNE (2000). 'Diverging discourses of east German *Kabarett*: cultural and linguistic "misbehaviour" ', in Stevenson and Theobald (2000*a*), 60–74.

MEINHOF, ULRIKE (2000). 'The new Germany on the screen: conflicting discourses on German television', in Stevenson and Theobald (2000*a*), 23–42.

MERKEL, INA (ed.) (1998). *'Wir sind doch nicht die Mecker-Ecke der Nation.' Briefe an das DDR-Fernsehen* (Cologne, Weimar, Vienna: Böhlau).

——and FELIX MÜHLBERG (1998). 'Eingaben und Öffentlichkeit', in Merkel (1998), 9–32.

MILLS, SARA (1997). *Discourse* (London, New York: Routledge).

MILROY, JAMES, and LESLEY MILROY (1999). *Authority in Language*, 3rd edn (London, New York: Routledge).

MILROY, LESLEY (1980[1], 1987[2]). *Language and Social Networks* (Oxford: Blackwell).

MOSER, HUGO (1962). *Sprachliche Folgen der politischen Teilung Deutschlands* (Düsseldorf: Schwann).

——(ed.) (1964). *Das Aueler Protokoll. Deutsche Sprache im Spannungsfeld zwischen West und Ost* (Düsseldorf: Schwann).

——(1985). 'Die Entwicklung der deutschen Sprache seit 1945', in Besch *et al.* (1985), 1678–707.

MÜHLHÄUSLER, PETER (1996). *Linguistic Ecology. Language Change and Linguistic Imperialism in the Pacific Region* (London, New York: Routledge).

MÜLLER, GERHARD (1992). 'Deutsch 1991. Bemerkungen zur Gegenwartssprache', *Der Sprachdienst* 1992 (1), 1–26.

——(1994). 'Der "Besserwessi" und die "innere Mauer": Anmerkungen zum Sprachgebrauch im vereinigten Deutschland', *Muttersprache* 104/2, 118–36.

NAGUSCHEWSKI, DIRK, and JÜRGEN TRABANT (eds.) (1997). *Was heißt hier 'fremd'? Studien zu Sprache und Fremdheit* (Berlin: Akademie-Verlag).

NAIL, NORBERT (1996). 'Handeln und Sprachhandeln an der Berliner Mauer', *Muttersprache* (4), 302–7.

NEUBRECHT, ALBERT (1994). 'Auswirkungen des politischen Wandels auf die Sprache (aus östlicher Sicht)', *Germanistische Mitteilungen* 39, 3–21.

NEUES FORUM LEIPZIG (ed.) (1989/90) *Jetzt oder nie—Demokratie* (Leipzig: Forum Verlag).

NEULAND, EVA, and MARGOT HEINEMANN (1997). ' "Tussis": hüben und drüben? Vergleichende Beobachtungen zur Entwicklung von Jugendsprachen in Ost und West', *Der Deutschunterricht* (1), 70–6.

NEUMANN, WERNER (1973). 'Ideologische und theoretische Fragen bei den Arbeiten zur marxistisch-leninistischen Sprachtheorie', *Zeitschrift für Phonetik, Sprachwissenschaft und Kommunikationsforschung* 26 (3), 276–83.

NIETHAMMER, LUTZ (1990). 'Das Volk der DDR und ihre Revolution. Versuch einer historischen Wahrnehmung der laufenden Ereignisse', in Schüddekopf (1990), 251–79.

Normen in der sprachlichen Kommunikation (1977). (Berlin: Akademie-Verlag).

OSCHLIES, WOLF (1990). *Wir sind das Volk. Zur Rolle der Sprache bei den Revolutionen in der DDR, der Tschechoslowakei, Rumänien und Bulgarien* (Cologne: Böhlau).

——(1991). 'Zur Software-Erfassung von Broilern in der Datsche des Dispatchers', in *Zum Sprachgebrauch unter dem Zeichen von Hammer, Zickel und Ährenkranz* (1991), 93–108.

OSTOW, ROBIN (1993). 'Restructuring our lives: national unification and German biographies', *The Oral History Review* 21/2, 1–8.

PALM, JÖRG, and STEFAN RICHTER (2000). 'BERATUNG. Im Osten was Neues?', in Reiher and Baumann (2000), 153–68.

PAPE, KORNELIA (1997). 'Schlag-(Wort-)Abtausch im Landesparlament. Analysen zu Debatten über Bildungspolitik', *Deutsche Sprache* 25 (2), 114–22.

——(2000). 'Der aufhaltsame Aufstieg zur direkten Demokratie. Die Verfassungsdiskussion im Landtag von Sachsen-Anhalt', in Reiher and Baumann (2000), 99–114.

PARKES, STUART (1997). *Understanding Contemporary Germany* (London: Routledge).

PÄTZOLD, JÖRG (1992). 'Zwischen Indirektheit und Sprachlosigkeit—der Umgang der Presse in der DDR zwischen dem Stern-Interview Hagers und Oktober '89 mit der Wirklichkeit des real Existierenden', in Welke *et al.* (1992), 93–110.

——and MARGITA PÄTZOLD (1995). 'Gemeinsame Sprache, geteiltes Verstehen. Anmerkungen zur Systematik von Verständnisschwierigkeiten zwischen Deutschen Ost und Deutschen West', in Reiher (1995*b*), 244–62.

PÄTZOLD, MARGITA (1995). 'West beforscht Ost—Anmerkungen zu einigen Analysen und Daten aus meiner ostdeutschen Perspektive', in Czyzewski *et al.* (1995), 402–8.

——(forthcoming). 'Die Kategorie "Vorurteil" als Lernpotential', in Hartung and Shethar (forthcoming).

——and LYDIA MARHOFF (1998). 'Zur sozialen Konstruktion von "Stereotyp" und "Vorurteil"', in Heinemann (1998), 73–96.

PÄTZOLD, MARGITA and JÖRG PÄTZOLD (1998). ' "Sphärengeruch" der Sprache—eigener und fremder', in Reiher and Kramer (1998), 67–128.

PAUL, INGWER (1995). 'Schismogene Tendenzen des Mediendiskurses nach der deutschen Einheit', in Czyzewski *et al.* (1995), 297–327.

—— (1997). 'Sprachreflexivität als Mittel der sozialen Differenzierung', in Barz and Fix (1997), 279–301.

—— (2000*a*). 'Gerahmte Kommunikation. Die Inszenierung ost–westdeutscher Kommuni-kationserfahrungen im Mediendiskurs', in Auer and Hausendorf (2000*a*), 113–50.

—— (2000*b*). 'Verständigung ohne Verstehen. Subjektive Thesen eines Gesprächs-analytikers', in Reiher and Baumann (2000), 182–93.

PEINE, MARGIT, and HELMUT SCHÖNFELD (1981). 'Sprachliche Differenzierung und ihre Bewertung', in *Kommunikation und Sprachvariation* (1981), 214–58.

POHL, INGE (1992). 'Bewegung im ostdeutschen Wortschatz', *Deutsch als Fremdsprache* 29, 173–6.

—— (1994). 'Neologismen des ostdeutschen Wortschatzes im Beschreibungsbereich von Markennamen und Firmennamen', in Sommerfeldt (1994*a*), 99–123.

—— (1997). 'Bedeutung sprachlicher Ausdrücke im Wandel', *Der Deutschunterricht* (1), 50–8.

—— and GERHARD BARTELS (eds.) (1991). *Sprachsystem und sprachliche Tätigkeit: Festschrift zum 65. Geburtstag von Karl-Ernst Sommerfeldt* (Frankfurt am Main: Lang).

POLENZ, PETER VON (1967). 'Sprachpurismus und Nationalsozialismus. Die "Fremdwort-frage" gestern und heute', in Lämmert *et al.* (1967), 111–65.

—— (1987). 'Beitrag zum Podiumsgespräch: Nationale Varianten der deutschen Hochsprache', in Zellweger (1987).

—— (1988). ' "Binnendeutsche" oder plurizentrische Sprachkultur?', *Zeitschrift für germa-nistische Linguistik* 16, 198–218.

—— (1990). 'Nationale Varietäten der deutschen Sprache', *International Journal of the Sociology of Language* 83, 5–38.

—— (1993). 'Die Sprachrevolte in der DDR im Herbst 1989. Ein Forschungsbericht nach drei Jahren vereinter germanistischer Linguistik', *Zeitschrift für germanistische Linguistik* 22, 127–49.

—— (1994). *Deutsche Sprachgeschichte vom Spätmittelalter bis zur Gegenwart*, vol. 2 (Berlin, New York: de Gruyter).

—— (1999). *Deutsche Sprachgeschichte vom Spätmittelalter bis zur Gegenwart*, vol. 3 (Berlin, New York: de Gruyter).

PORSCH, PETER (1992). 'Alltag—Alltagsbewußtsein—Sprache', in Lerchner (1992*a*), 189–202.

PORTELLI, ALESSANDRO (1990). 'Uchronic dreams: working class memory and possible worlds', in Samuel and Thompson (1990), 143–60.

PRINS, GWYN (2001). 'Oral history', in Burke (2001), 120–56.

PULZER, PETER (1995). *German Politics 1945–1995* (Oxford: Oxford University Press).

RADERS, MARGIT (1997). 'Rede-Wendungen in Wende-Reden: Originalität und Inter-textualität in Demosprüchen', *Revista de Filologia Alemana* 5, 275–302.

REICH, JENS (1991). 'Rebhuhnweg überlebt . . . Über den Unsinn von Straßennamen als Sinnbild des politischen Wandels', *Die Zeit*, 1 February 1991, 90.

REIFARTH, GERD THOMAS (2000). 'Can oil unite with water? Braun and Biskupek on German disunity', in Stevenson and Theobald (2000*a*), 75–90.

REIHER, RUTH (1992). ' "Wir sind das Volk." Sprachwissenschaftliche Überlegungen zu den Losungen des Herbstes 1989', in Burkhardt and Fritzsche (1992), 43–58.

—— (1993). 'Das "Zu-sich-selber-Kommen des Menschen". Zum Umgang mit Konflikten in der Kommunikation der DDR', in Reiher and Läzer (1993), 147–60.

—— (ed.) (1995*a*). *Mit sozialistischen und anderen Grüßen. Porträt einer untergegangenen Republik in Alltagstexten* (Berlin: Aufbau-Verlag).

—— (ed.) (1995*b*). *Sprache im Konflikt. Zur Rolle der Sprache in sozialen, politischen und militärischen Auseinandersetzungen* (Berlin, New York: de Gruyter).

—— (1995*c*). 'Deutsch–deutscher Sprachwandel', in Reiher (1995*b*), 232–43.

—— (1996). 'Ein Ossi—ein Wort; ein Wessi—ein Wörterbuch. Zur Bewertung von Sprache und Sprachverhalten der Deutschen Ost und West', in Reiher and Läzer (1996), 32–54.

—— (1997*a*). 'Annäherung und Kontroversen—Sprachentwicklung in Berlin', *Deutsche Sprache* 25 (2), 176–86.

—— (1997*b*). 'Dreiraum- versus Dreizimmerwohnung. Zum Sprachgebrauch der Ostdeutschen', *Der Deutschunterricht* (1), 42–9.

—— (2000). 'Das "Kollektiv" hat sich ins "Team" verabschiedet. Regionale Differenzierungen im ostdeutschen Sprachgebrauch', in Reiher and Baumann (2000), 30–54.

—— and ANTJE BAUMANN (eds.) (2000). *Mit gespaltener Zunge? Die deutsche Sprache nach dem Fall der Mauer* (Berlin: Aufbau).

—— and UNDINE KRAMER (eds.) (1998). *Sprache als Mittel von Identifikation und Distanzierung* (Frankfurt/Main: Lang).

—— and RÜDIGER LÄZER (eds.) (1993). *Wer spricht das wahre Deutsch? Erkundungen zur Sprache im vereinten Deutschland* (Berlin: Aufbau).

——— (eds.) (1996). *Von 'Buschzulage' und 'Ossinachweis'. Ost–West-Deutsch in der Diskussion* (Berlin: Aufbau).

RESÉNDIZ, JULIA LIEBE (1992). 'Woran erkennen sich Ost- und Westdeutsche? Eine Spracheinstellungsstudie am Beispiel von Rundfunksendungen', in Welke *et al.* (1992), 127–39.

RIEMANN, T., *et al.* (eds.) (1969). *Verfassung der Deutschen Demokratischen Republik. Dokumente—Kommentar*, vol. 2 (Berlin).

ROCHE, REINHARD (1991). 'Nach Tische liest man's anders. Texte aus der DDR vor und nach der Novemberrevolution im Blickpunkt der Öffentlichkeit, besonders des (Deutsch)unterrichts', *Muttersprache* 101, 297–307.

RÖDING-LANGE, UTE (1997). *Bezeichnungen für 'Deutschland' in der Zeit der 'Wende'. Dargestellt an ausgewählten westdeutschen Printmedien* (Würzburg: Königshausen & Neumann).

ROE, IAN F. (2000). 'The "Wende" and the overcoming of "Sprachlosigkeit"?', in Jackman and Roe (2000), 55–74.

ROSENKRANZ, HEINZ, and KARL SPANGENBERG (1963). *Sprachsoziologische Studien in Thüringen* (Berlin: Akademie-Verlag).

RÖSLER, IRMTRAUD, and KARL-ERNST SOMMERFELDT (eds.) (1998). *Probleme der Sprache nach der Wende*, 2nd edn (Frankfurt/Main: Lang).

ROTHE, FRANK (2000). 'Der Dinosaurier im Bernstein. Ich, das Überbleibsel aus einer implodierten Galaxis', in Simon, Rothe, and Andrasch (2000), 52–64.

RUNGE, ERIKA (1971). *Reise nach Rostock, DDR* (Frankfurt/Main: Suhrkamp).

RYTLEWSKI, RALF (1992). 'Politische Kultur in der DDR vor und nach der *Wende*', in Burkhardt and Fritzsche (1992), 3–18.

SAMUEL, RAPHAEL, and PAUL THOMPSON (eds.) (1990). *The Myths We Live By* (London: Routledge).

SANDFORD, JOHN (2000). 'The opposition that dare not speak its name', in Jackman and Roe (2000), 19–37.

SANDIG, BARBARA (ed.) (1994). *Europhras 92: Tendenzen der Phraseologieforschung* (Bochum: Universitätsverlag Brockmeyer).

SATZGER, AXEL (1994). 'Deutsch–deutsch: Kommunikation miteinander oder übereinander?', in Bungarten (1994a), 61–8.

SAUER, WOLFGANG WERNER (1988). *Der 'Duden'. Geschichte und Aktualität eines 'Volkswörterbuchs'* (Stuttgart: Metzler).

SCHAAF, S. (1995). 'Zur Redekultur im Landtag von Sachsen-Anhalt', Diplomarbeit, University of Halle.

SCHAEDER, BURKHARD (1981). 'Deutsche Sprache in der BRD und in der DDR. Neuere Arbeiten und Ansichten über das sprachliche Ost–West-Problem', *Muttersprache* 1981 (3–4), 198–205.

——(1994). 'Wir sind ein Wörterbuch—wir sind das Wörterbuch! Duden-Ost + Duden-West = Einheitsduden?', *Zeitschrift für germanistische Linguistik* 22, 58–86.

——(1997). 'Die deutsche Vereinigung im Spiegel der Wörterbücher—oder: Was ist lexiko-graphisch aus der DDR geworden?', in Barz and Fix (1997), 45–73.

SCHAFARSCHIK, WALTER (ed.) (1973). *Herrschaft durch Sprache. Politische Reden* (Stuttgart: Reclam).

SCHÄFFNER, CHRISTINA (1992). 'Sprache des Umbruchs und ihre Übersetzung', in Burkhardt and Fritzsche (1992), 135–54.

——and PETER PORSCH (1993). 'Meeting the challenge on the path to democracy: discursive strategies in government declarations in Germany and the former GDR', *Discourse & Society* 4 (1), 33–55.

——(1998). 'Continuity and change: German discourse after unification', in Chilton, Ilyin, and Mey (1998), 147–72.

SCHARNHORST, JÜRGEN (ed.) (1995). *Sprachsituation und Sprachkultur im internationalen Vergleich* (Frankfurt am Main: Lang).

SCHELLENBERG, WILHELM (1991). 'Zwischeneinschätzungen. Zur Sprachgestaltung von Texten im Spannungsfeld "verordnender"/"vollzugsmeldender" Kommunikation in Institutionen der ehemaligen DDR', in *Zum Sprachgebrauch unter dem Zeichen von Hammer, Zickel und Ährenkranz* (1991), 109–19.

SCHERF, FRITZ-PETER (1991). 'Agrartopolexik im Agrarkollektivismus der DDR', in *Zum Sprachgebrauch unter dem Zeichen von Hammer, Zickel und Ährenkranz* (1991), 120–32.

——(1992). 'Von der TECHNIK bis zur TAIGA—dokumentarisierte Topolexik im Agrarkollektivismus der DDR', in Lerchner (1992a), 167–88.

SCHERZBERG, JOHANNA (1972). 'Zur Struktur des Wortschatzes der Wirtschaftspolitik der DDR', in Schmidt (1972), 187–217.

SCHIEWE, ANDREA, and JÜRGEN SCHIEWE (2000). *Witzkultur in der DDR. Ein Beitrag zur Sprachkritik* (Göttingen: Vandenhoeck & Ruprecht).

SCHIEWE, JÜRGEN (1997). 'Sprachwitz—Sprachspiel—Sprachrealität. Über die Sprache im geteilten und vereinigten Deutschland', *Zeitschrift für germanistische Linguistik* 25 (2), 129–46.

——(1998). *Die Macht der Sprache. Eine Geschichte der Sprachkritik von der Antike bis zur Gegenwart* (Munich: C. H. Beck).

SCHILDT, JOACHIM, and HARTMUT SCHMIDT (eds.) (1986). *Berlinisch: Geschichtliche Einführung in die Sprache einer Stadt* (Berlin: Akademie-Verlag).

SCHIRMER, DIETMAR (1992). 'Auf der Baustelle des gemeinsamen Hauses. Zur Struktur eines politischen Symbols', in Burkhardt and Fritzsche (1992), 211–32.

SCHLIEBEN-LANGE, BRIGITTE (1991). *Soziolinguistik* 3rd edn (Stuttgart: Kohlhammer).

SCHLOBINSKI, PETER (1987). *Stadtsprache Berlin. Eine soziolinguistische Untersuchung* (Berlin, New York: de Gruyter).

SCHLOSSER, HORST DIETER (1990*a*/1999) *Die deutsche Sprache in der DDR zwischen Stalinismus und Demokratie* (Cologne: Verlag Wissenschaft und Politik).

——(1990*b*). 'Das Ende der "Zweisprachigkeit". Sprachliche Aspekte des politischen Zusammenwachsens der Deutschen', in Strunk *et al.* (1990), 26–39.

——(1990*c*). ' "Wir Deutschen"— "Wir in der DDR". Helmut Kohl und Lothar de Maizière zur Unterzeichnung des Staatsvertrags', *Deutschland Archiv* 23 (7), 994–6.

——(1991*a*). 'Deutsche Teilung, deutsche Einheit und die Sprache der Deutschen', *Aus Politik und Zeitgeschichte—Beilage zur Wochenzeitung 'Das Parlament'* 1991 (B17), 13–21.

——(ed.) (1991*b*). *Kommunikationsbedingungen und Alltagssprache in der ehemaligen DDR. Ergebnisse einer interdisziplinären Tagung Frankfurt/Main 30.9.88–1.10.88* (Hamburg: Buske).

——(1991*c*). 'Perspektiven des Zusammenwachsens nach 45 Jahren getrennter Entwicklung', in *Zum Sprachgebrauch unter dem Zeichen von Hammer, Zickel und Ährenkranz* (1991), 133–51.

——(1992*a*). 'Mentale und sprachliche Interferenzen beim Übergang der DDR von der Zentralplanwirtschaft zur Marktwirtschaft', in Welke *et al.* (1992), 43–58.

——(1992*b*). 'Die sprachliche Ost–West-Differenzierung—ein Umweg der deutschen Sprachgeschichte?', in Eifler and Saame (1992), 141–65.

——(1993). 'Die ins Leere befreite Sprache. Wende-Texte zwischen Euphorie und bundes-deutscher Wirklichkeit', *Muttersprache* 103 (3), 219–30.

——(1996). 'Ost und West im Talkshowtest', *Muttersprache* (4), 308–18.

——(1997). 'Fremdheit in einer vertrauten Sprache. Sprachliche Folgen der Teilung Deutschlands', in Naguschewski and Trabant (1997), 197–206.

——(1999): see 1990*a*.

——(2000). 'Von der "niveauvollen Unterhaltung" zur Smalltalk-Kultur. Neue Beobachtungen zu Talkshows in Ost und West', in Reiher and Baumann (2000), 169–81.

SCHMIDER, EKKEHARD (1990). *Werbedeutsch in Ost und West. Die Sprache der Konsumwerbung in beiden Teilen Deutschlands* (Berlin: Arno Spitz).

SCHMIDT, GERHARD (1991). 'Lehrersein in der DDR', in Schlosser (1991*b*), 99–112.

SCHMIDT, HARTMUT (2000). 'Entwicklung und Formen des offiziellen Sprachgebrauchs der ehemaligen DDR', in Besch *et al.* (2000), 2016–37.

SCHMIDT, WILHELM (ed.) (1972). *Sprache und Ideologie. Beiträge zu einer marxistisch-leninistischen Sprachwirkungsforschung* (Halle: Max Niemeyer Verlag).

SCHMIDT-REGENER, IRENA (1998). ' "Von der Akzeptanz des Berlinischen, von Liberali-sierungstendenzen und Berührungsängsten". Spracheinstellungen in der Berliner Sprachgemeinschaft nach 1989', in Reiher and Kramer (1998), 153–86.

——(forthcoming *a*). 'Distanz und Nähe. Soziolinguistische Aspekte deutscher Identität(en) nach 1989', in Kempf and Schmidt-Regener (forthcoming).

——(forthcoming *b*). 'Language attitudes in the Berlin speech community after the fall of the Wall in 1989', *Multilingua*.

SCHMIRBER, GISELA (ed.) (1997). *Sprache im Gespräch: zu Normen, Gebrauch und Wandel der deutschen Sprache* (Munich: Hans-Seidel-Stiftung).

SCHMITT, REINHOLD and KEIM, INKEN (1985). 'Das Problem der subsumtionslogischen Konstitution von Interkulturalität', in Czyzewski *et al.* (1985), 413–29.

SCHMITZ-BERNING, CORNELIA (2000). *Vokabular des Nationalsozialismus* (Berlin, New York: de Gruyter).

SCHÖNFELD, HELMUT (1974*a*). *Gesprochenes Deutsch in der Altmark* (Berlin: Akademie-Verlag).

——(1974*b*). 'Sprachverhalten und Sozialstruktur in einem sozialistischen Dorf in der Altmark', in Ising (1974), 191–283.

——(1977). 'Zur Rolle der sprachlichen Existenzformen in der sprachlichen Kommunikation', in *Normen in der sprachlichen Kommunikation* (1977), 163–208.

——(1983). 'Zur Soziolinguistik in der DDR. Entwicklung, Ergebnisse, Aufgabe', *Zeitschrift für Germanistik* 2, 213–23.

——(1985). 'Varianten, Varietäten und Sprachvariation', *Zeitschrift für Phonetik, Sprachwissenschaft und Kommunikation* 38, 206–24.

——(1986). 'Die berlinische Umgangssprache im 19. und 20. Jahrhundert', in Schildt and Schmidt (1986), 214–98.

——(1989). *Sprache und Sprachvariation in der Stadt. Zu sprachlichen Entwicklungen und zur Sprachvariation in Berlin und anderen Städten im Nordteil der DDR* (= *Linguistische Studien* Reihe *a*, 197) (Berlin: Akademie der Wissenschaften der DDR Zentralinstitut für Sprachwissenschaft).

——(1993). 'Auch sprachlich beigetreten? Sprachliche Entwicklungen im zusammenwachsenden Berlin', in Reiher and Läzer (1993), 187–209.

——(1995). 'Das Berlinische zwischen Kontinuität und Wandel', in Scharnhorst (1995), 207–26.

——(1996*a*). 'Berlinisch in der zusammenwachsenden Stadt Berlin', *Zeitschrift für Germanistik* 1, 144–59.

——(1996*b*). 'Heimatsprache, Proletendeutsch, Ossi-Sprache oder? Bewertung und Akzeptanz des Berlinischen', in Reiher and Läzer (1996), 70–93.

——and JOACHIM DONATH (1978). *Sprache im sozialistischen Industriebetrieb* (Berlin: Akademie-Verlag).

——and PETER SCHLOBINSKI (1997). 'After the Wall: social change and linguistic variation in Berlin', in Stevenson (1997*a*), 119–36.

SCHRABBACK, SUSANNE (2000). 'Ideological practices in east and west German media: reporting the Thuringian miners' hunger strike', in Stevenson and Theobald (2000*a*), 109–30.

SCHREIBER, HERBERT (1994). 'Von PGH "Die Frisur" zu "Coiffeur am Bahnhof"— Bezeichnungen für Geschäfte und Institutionen im Wandel', in Sommerfeldt (1994*a*), 161–9.

SCHRÖDER, MARIANNE (1992). 'Lexikographische Nach-Wende—ein Überarbeitungsbericht', in Lerchner (1992*a*), 263–96.

——(1997*a*). 'Allgemeinwortschatz der DDR-Bürger—zu seiner onomasiologischen Sammlung vor der Wende und zu seinem Gebrauch', in Schröder and Fix (1997), 153–75.

——(1997*b*). 'Falsche Freunde im jüngeren Deutsch', in Barz and Fix (1997), 153–62.

——and ULLA FIX (1997). *Allgemeinwortschatz der DDR-Bürger—nach Sachgruppen geordnet und linguistisch kommentiert* (Heidelberg: Winter).

SCHROETER, SABINA (1994). *Die Sprache der DDR im Spiegel ihrer Literatur. Studien zum DDR-typischen Wortschatz* (Berlin, New York: de Gruyter).

SCHÜDDEKOPF, CHARLES (ed.) (1990). *'Wir sind das Volk!' Flugschriften, Aufrufe und Texte einer deutschen Revolution* (Reinbek: Rowohlt).

SCHÜTTE, WILFRIED (1990). ' "Live aus Leipzig". Talkshows und die DDR-Revolution', *Sprachreport* 1990 (1), 1–3.

SCOLLON, RON, and SUZANNE WONG SCOLLON (1995). *Intercultural Communication* (Oxford: Blackwell).

SEIDEL, UTE (1992). 'Deutschland—einig Wossi-Land? Betrachtungen zu einigen umstrittenen Wörtern', *Deutschunterricht* 45 (3), 149–52.

—— (1993). ' "...denn deine Sprache verrät dich." (Matthäus 26, 73) Nachdenken über unser "besonderes Verhältnis zur Sprache" ', *Deutschunterricht* 46 (3), 134–9.

—— (1998). 'Die neue "öffentliche Schnödigkeit" (Dolf Sternberger). Demütigungen und Beleidigungen im Ost–West-Diskurs', in Rösler and Sommerfeldt (1998), 51–9.

SHETHAR, ALISSA (forthcoming *a*). ' "Die reden janz anders da drüben, die berlinern ständig, wa?" The social meanings of Berlinisch after unification', in Topofsky and Starkman (forthcoming).

—— (forthcoming *b*). 'Sprachideologie und die "Dolmetscher der Träume (Ost)" '.

—— and WOLFDIETRICH HARTUNG (1998). 'Was ist "Ostjammer" wirklich? Diskurs-Ideologie und die Konstruktion deutsch–deutscher Interkulturalität', in Reiher and Kramer (1998), 39–66.

SIEHR, KARL-HEINZ (1993). 'Abwickeln: brisantes Wort—brisanter Diskurs', *Sprache und Literatur in Wissenschaft und Unterricht* (72), 31–47.

—— (1994). 'Abwickeln—auch ein Kommunikationskonflikt. Einige sprachkritische Bemerkungen', in Sommerfeldt (1994*a*), 193–219.

SIMON, JANA, FRANK ROTHE, and WIETE ANDRASCH (eds.) (2000). *Das Buch der Unterschiede. Warum die Einheit keine ist* (Berlin: Aufbau-Verlag).

SMITH, ANTHONY (1991). *National Identity* (Harmondsworth: Penguin).

SOBOTTA, KIRSTEN (2000). ' "Ich lebte auf der anderen Seite der Mauer". Perspektiven in autobiografischen Erzählungen von Frauen über ihr Leben vor und nach der Wende', in Reiher and Baumann (2000), 222–40.

SOMMERFELDT, KARL-ERNST (1992*a*). 'Neue Schulbezeichnungen in Mecklenburg-Vorpommern', *Deutschunterricht* 45 (7–8), 361–2.

—— (1992*b*). 'Straßennamen in Mecklenburg-Vorpommern nach der Wende', *Deutschunterricht* 45 (9), 408–12.

—— (ed.) (1994*a*). *Sprache im Alltag—Beobachtungen zur Sprachkultur* (Frankfurt/Main: Lang).

—— (1994*b*). 'Schulnamen in den neuen Bundesländern nach der Wende', in Sommerfeldt (1994*a*), 221–9.

Sprachliche Kommunikation und Gesellschaft (1976). 2nd edn (Berlin: Akademie Verlag).

STAININGER, OTTO (1995). *WiderWITZIG. Wortwitz und Karikatur um die Wende* (Vienna: Löcker Verlag).

STEINBERG, JONATHAN (1987). 'The historian and the *questione della lingua*', in Burke and Porter (1987), 198–209.

STEVENSON, PATRICK (1993). 'The German language and the construction of national identities', in Flood *et al.* (1993), 333–56.

—— (1995). '*Gegenwartsbewältigung*: coming to terms with the present in Germany', *Multilingua* 14 (1), 39–59.

—— (ed.) (1997*a*). *The German Language and the Real World. Sociolinguistic, Cultural, and Pragmatic Perspectives on Contemporary German*, revised edn (Oxford: Clarendon Press).

STEVENSON, PATRICK (1997*b*). 'The study of real language: observing the observers', in Stevenson (1997*a*), 1–24.

——and JOHN THEOBALD (eds.) (2000*a*). *Relocating Germanness. Discursive Disunity in Unified Germany* (Basingstoke: Macmillan).

————(2000*b*). 'A decade of cultural disunity: diverging discourses and communicative dissonance in 1990s Germany', in Stevenson and Theobald (2000*a*), 1–22.

STEYER, KATHRIN (1997). *Reformulierungen. Sprachliche Relationen zwischen Äußerungen und Texten im öffentlichen Diskurs* (Tübingen: Narr).

STICKEL, GERHARD (ed.) (1995). *Stilfragen* (Berlin, New York: de Gruyter).

——(2000). 'Was West- und Ostdeutsche sprachlich voneinander halten', in Reiher and Baumann (2000), 16–29.

——and NORBERT VOLZ (1999). *Meinungen und Einstellungen zur deutschen Sprache* (Mannheim: Institut für Deutsche Sprache).

STÖREL, THOMAS (1997). 'Im Westen nichts Neues? Zur Kampf-Metaphorik der Arbeitswelt im geteilten und geeinten Deutschland', in Barz and Fix (1997), 93–111.

STÖTZEL, GEORG (1991). 'Entzweiung und Vereinigung. Antworten der Sprache auf die deutsche Frage', *Sprache und Literatur in Wissenschaft und Unterricht* (67), 2–20.

——(1994). 'Der öffentliche Sprachgebrauch in der Bundesrepublik Deutschland seit 1945—Entwicklungen und Auseinandersetzungen', in Heringer *et al.* (1994), 41–80.

——(1995). 'Der Nazi-Komplex', in Stötzel and Wengeler (1995), 355–82.

——and MARTIN WENGELER (eds.) (1995). *Kontroverse Begriffe* (Berlin, New York: de Gruyter).

STRASSNER, ERICH (1985). ' "Ich trage die neue Welt in mir." Argumentationsstrategien angeleitet schreibender Kinder in der DDR', in Debus *et al.* (1985), 243–60.

STREECK, JÜRGEN (1995). 'Ethnomethodologische Indifferenz im Ost–West-Verhältnis', in Czyzewski *et al.* (1995), 430–6.

STRUNK, G., *et al.* (eds.) (1990). *Wiederbegegnungen: Herausforderung an die politische Bildung* (Bonn: Deutscher Volkshochschul-Verband).

SUCKUT, SIEGFRIED (ed.) (1996). *Das Wörterbuch der Staatssicherheit. Definitionen zur 'politisch-operativen Arbeit'* (Berlin: Christoph Links Verlag).

TAJFEL, HENRI, and JOHN C. TURNER (1986). 'The social identity theory of intergroup behaviour', in Worchel and Austin (1986), 7–24.

TANNEN, DEBORAH (1991). *You Just Don't Understand: Women and Men in Conversation* (London: Virago).

TEICHMANN, CHRISTINE (1991). 'Von der "langue de bois" zur "Sprache der Wende" ', *Muttersprache* 101, 252–65.

TEICHMANN-NADIRASCHWILI, CHRISTINE (1993). 'Von der deutschen Zweistaatlichkeit zur Konzeption "Deutschland, einig Vaterland"—Versuch einer linguistischen Beschreibung', in Grewenig (1993), 56–72.

TEIDGE, HELGA (1990). 'Sprachliche Veränderungen bei Wohnungsanzeigen', *Sprachpflege und Sprachkultur* 39 (3), 77–80.

TEUBERT, WOLFGANG (1992). 'Die Deutschen und ihre Identität', in Burkhardt and Fritzsche (1992), 233–52.

——(1993). 'Sprachwandel und das Ende der DDR', in Reiher and Läzer (1993), 28–52.

THEOBALD, JOHN (2000). 'Disgraceland GDR: locating the admirable amongst the abject', in Stevenson and Theobald (2000*a*), 131–49.

THIERSE, WOLFGANG (1993). ' "Sprich, damit ich dich sehe." Beobachtungen zum Verhältnis von Sprache und Politik in der DDR-Vergangenheit', in Born and Stickel (1993), 114–26.

THOMAS, ALEXANDER (1994). 'Kulturelle Divergenzen in der deutsch-deutschen Wirtschafts-kooperation', in Bungarten (1994a), 69–89.

TOPOFSKY, PETER, and RUTH STARKMAN (eds.) (forthcoming). *Unelected Affinities: Interdisciplinary Studies in German Unification* (Bloomington: Indiana University Press).

TOWNSON, MICHAEL (1992). *Mother-Tongue and Fatherland. Language and Politics in German* (Manchester, New York: Manchester University Press).

TREMPELMANN, GISELA (1998). '*Leserinnen/LeserInnen* Ost wie West? Zu Bezeichnungen und Anredeformen für Frauen in den östlichen Bundesländern', *Germanistische Linguistik* (139/140), 33–47.

ULBRICHT, WALTER (1970). 'Schlusswort auf der 13. Tagung des Zentralkomitees der SED', *Neues Deutschland*, 16 June 1970, 4.

USKE, HANS (1986). *Die Sprache der Wende* (Berlin, Bonn: J. H. W. Dietz).

VOGEL, ANJA (forthcoming). '(Ost-)Berliner Identität vs. (Gesamt-)Berliner Identität: eine ethnographische Analyse von Ostberliner Einstellungen gegenüber dem Dialekt im vereinten Berlin', in Hartung and Shethar (forthcoming).

VOLMERT, JOHANNES (1992). 'Auf der Suche nach einer neuen Rhetorik. Ansprachen auf den Massendemonstrationen Anfang November '89', in Burkhardt and Fritzsche (1992), 59–110.

——(1993). ' "Asylantendebatte" in Ost und West. Ein Lehrstück über die Instrumentalisierung politischer Vorurteile', in Reiher and Läzer (1993), 239–71.

WACHTEL, STEFAN (1991). 'Deutsch sprechen. Zu den Sprechkulturen in Ost- und Westdeutschland', *Muttersprache* 101, 157–65.

WAGENER, PETER, and KARL-HEINZ BAUSCH (eds.) (1997). *Tonaufnahmen des gesprochenen Deutsch. Dokumentationen der Bestände von sprachwissenschaftlichen Forschungsprojekten und Archiven* (Tübingen: Niemeyer).

WARDHAUGH, RONALD (1998). *An Introduction to Sociolinguistics*, 3rd edn (Oxford: Blackwell).

WÄTJEN, STEPHANIE (2000). 'Wo liegt eigentlich Eisenhüttenstadt? Die Wandlung von einer Westfrau im Osten zu einer Ostfrau im Westen', in Simon, Rothe, and Andrasch (2000), 45–51.

WEBER, ANDREAS (1989). 'Zweierlei Deutsch im Rundfunk? Eine vergleichende morpho-syntaktische Untersuchung zum deutsch–deutschen Sprachgebrauch', *Muttersprache* (99), 17–26.

WEDEL, MATTHIAS (1990). 'Die Sprache der Stagnation', *Magazin* 2, 5–6.

WELKE, KLAUS (1992). 'Deutsche Sprache BRD/DDR—Reflexion in der Linguistik der DDR', in Welke *et al.* (1992), 1–14.

——, WOLFGANG W. SAUER, and HELMUT GLÜCK (eds.) (1992). *Die deutsche Sprache nach der Wende* (Hildesheim: Olms).

WELLS, CHRISTOPHER (1985). *German: A Linguistic History to 1945* (Oxford: Clarendon Press).

WENGELER, MARTIN (1995). ' "1968" als sprachgeschichtliche Zäsur', in Stötzel and Wengeler (1995), 383–404.

WEYDT, HARALD (1993). '*Zärtl. Sie, m. bet. frl. Figur, die (. . .) eine m.-l. WA bes., sucht . . .* Partnerschaftsanzeigen in Ost und West', in Klein and Paul (1993), 213–19.

WODAK, RUTH, and F. P. KIRSCH (eds.) (1995a). *Totalitäre Sprache—Langue de bois—Language of Dictatorship* (Vienna: Passagen Verlag).

————(1995b). 'Vorwort', in Wodak and Kirsch (1995a), 11–17.

WOLF, BIRGIT (2000). *Sprache in der DDR. Ein Wörterbuch* (Berlin, New York: de Gruyter).

WOLF, CHRISTA (1990). *Reden im Herbst* (Berlin, Weimar: Aufbau).

WOLF, RICARDA (1995). 'Interaktive Fallen auf dem Weg zum vorurteilsfreien Dialog. Ein deutsch-deutscher Versuch', in Czyzewski *et al.* (1995), 203–31.

WOLLE, STEFAN (1998). *Die heile Welt der Diktatur. Alltag und Herrschaft in der DDR 1971–1989* (Berlin: Christoph Links Verlag).

WOOLARD, KATHRYN (1985). 'Language variation and cultural hegemony: toward an integration of sociolinguistic and social theory', *American Ethnologist* 12 (4), 738–48.

——and BAMBI SCHIEFFELIN (1994). 'Language ideology', *Annual Review of Anthropology* 23, 55–82.

WORCHEL, STEPHEN, and WILLIAM G. AUSTIN (eds.) (1986). *Psychology of Intergroup Relations* (Chicago: Nelson-Hall).

Wörter und Wendungen—von der Sprache der Konfrontation zur Sprache der Kooperation (1990). (Berlin: DDR-Komitee für wissenschaftliche Fragen der Sicherung des Friedens und der Abrüstung bei der Akademie der Wissenschaften der DDR).

Das Wörterbuch der Staatssicherheit. Definitionen des MfS zur 'politisch-operativen Arbeit' (1993). (Berlin: Der Bundesbeauftragte für die Unterlagen des Staatssicherheitsdienstes der ehemaligen Deutschen Demokratischen Republik).

WUNDERLICH, DIETER (1971). 'Zum Status der Soziolinguistik', in Klein and Wunderlich (1971), 297–321.

YLÖNEN, SABINE (1992). 'Probleme deutsch–deutscher Kommunikation', *Sprachreport* (2–3), 17–20.

ZELLWEGER, R. (ed.) (1987). *VIII. Internationale Deutschlehrertagung Bern: Ziele und Wege des Unterrichts in Deutsch als Fremdsprache* (Berne: Staatlicher Lehrmittelverlag).

Zum Sprachgebrauch unter dem Zeichen von Hammer, Zickel und Ährenkranz (1991). (Zwickau: Pädagogische Hochschule).

Index

The index covers the Preface, Introduction and Chapters 1–6. English terms are preferred with the wider readership in mind, with German equivalents given only where considered necessary as, for example where the English equivalent is weak. Only authors whose work is extensively discussed are indexed.

inequality *see* social discrimination
inference 68
information model 143, 144, 146, 160
intelligence reports 62
interculturality 235–6
interdiscursivity 108, 110, 200
interpretative prototypes 232
intertextual knowledge 68, 109
interviews 145–6, 161–3, 188, 195, 196
intradiscursivity 108, 110

J

Jammerossi ('whingeing easterner', discourse of)
    208, 210
job interviews 145–7, 161–3
job-seeking advertisements 135–6
Jochmann, Carl Gustav 19
joke culture 208
Jugendweihe (secular confirmation) 75, 76

K

Kabarett 56, 107
Kern, Friederike (Birkner, Karin and) 159
Kluge, Friedrich 19
knowledge, transfer of 142, 146
Kohl, Helmut ix, 53, 95
Köhler, August 32
Kolbe, Karl Wilhelm 22
Krenz, Egon 94, 99, 100, 109

L

Labov, William 176
language advisory services 121, 126
language biographies 188–98
language change
    and continuity 115–85
    process of 4, 137
language choice 180
language cultivation 30
language games 93, 109
language question 15–54, 237
language shift 153
language in use 137
language use 2
    continuity and change in 115–85
langue de bois 55–69, 93

Law on the Unified Socialist Education System
    (GDR) 79
leavers from east Germany 97–8
Leipzig Trade Fair 138
Leipziger Volkszeitung 125
Lerchner, Gotthard 39–40
letter to parents 84–5
letters 84–5, 91, 132–4
lexical developments 115–29
lexical innovation 118–19
lexicography 45, 121, 126
liberated language 110–11
Liebscher, Grit 217–19
linguistic code theory 27
linguistic creativity 109
linguistic crises 5, 15–24
linguistic division thesis (*Sprachspaltung*) 31–4, 37
linguistic nationalism 3, 18
linguistic purism 20
linguistic resistance 180–1
linguistic variables 168
linguistic variation
    attitudes to 172–85
    GDR speech community 92
    and social mobility 152–72
    Soviet model 29
linguistic varieties 39–42, 175, 188
Lippi-Green, Rosina 182–4
literature, national 23

M

magazines 117
Maizière, Lothar de 103
market economy 124, 135, 138, 139
Marxist-Leninist theory 60
mathematics exercises 80
May Day 73–4
media discourse 66–8, 96, 201–4, 214–15
media sources 160
members' resources (MR) 212–13
memory 186–98
Merkel, Angela 165
metacommunicative behaviours 159
metaphors 32, 58, 73
methodology 169
migration 97–8, 155, 169
Milroy, Lesley 153, 169
mixing 148